Heavenly Friends

by

Rosalie Marie Levy

The material used in this book has been drawn from the best sources available.

ST. PAUL EDITIONS

NIHIL OBSTAT:

THOMAS J. RILEY, PH.D.

Censor Librorum

IMPRIMATUR:

+ RICHARD CARDINAL CUSHING

Library of Congress Catalog Card Number: 59-25199

Printed in U.S.A. by the Daughters of St. Paul

The Daughters of St. Paul are an international congregation of religious women serving the Church with the communications media.

"Oh! if thou couldst see the everlasting crowns of the Saints in Heaven, and in how great glory they now triumph, who appeared contemptible heretofore to this world, and as it were even unworthy of life, doubtless thou wouldst immediately cast thyself down to the very earth, and wouldst rather be ambitious to be in subjection to all, than to have precedence over so much as one.

"Neither wouldst thou covet the pleasant days of this life, but wouldst rather be glad to suffer tribulation for God's sake; and esteem it the greatest gain to be reputed as nothing amongst men.

"Oh, if thou didst but relish these things, did they penetrate deep into thy heart, how wouldst thou dare so much as once to complain!

"Ought not all painful labors to be endured for everlasting life?

"It is no small matter to lose or gain the kingdom of God.

"Lift up, therefore, thy face to Heaven; behold I and all My Saints with Me, who in this world have had a great conflict, now rejoice, are comforted now, are now secure, are now at rest; and they shall for all eternity abide with Me in the kingdom of My Father."

Imitation of Christ, Book III, Chapter 47, v. 3, 4.

"We fools esteemed their life madness, and their end without honor. Behold how they are numbered among the children of God, and their lot is among the Saints...."

Wisdom 5:4.

CONTENTS

— A —

— H —

— I —

— J —

— V —

— W —

— Z —

JANUARY

FEAST OF THE CIRCUMCISION

In compliance with the Law arising from the covenant between God and Abraham, when the latter was chosen to be the forebear of the "people" who were to preserve in a corrupt world the knowledge and belief of a Savior for mankind, Jesus was brought by Mary and Joseph to be circumcised on the eighth day after His birth.

According to Jewish custom, on the occasion of the circumcision the child received his name. St. Luke tells us:

"And after eight days were accomplished, that the Child should be circumcised, His name was called Jesus, which was called by the Angel, before He was conceived in the womb". (2:21.)

Regarding this, the great St. Bernard declares:

"Truly it is right that when the Boy was circumcised He should be called Savior (Jesus); because from that moment He already began to work our salvation, pouring out His immaculate Blood for us. If Christians ask why the Lord wished to be circumcised, the answer is, 'For the same reason for which He was born and for which He suffered. None of these were for Himself, but for His elect. Not born in sin, He was circumcised and He died not for His sins; but for those of mankind' ".

✠

MOST HOLY NAME OF JESUS

The Church dedicates the first month of each new year to the Holy Name of Jesus; and she does well, for the great work entrusted to her is the salvation of all flesh; and in this Name "all flesh shall see the salvation of God".

There was a time when Saul hated and persecuted the Name of Jesus. But there came also the time when the converted Saul, the great Apostle St. Paul, loved nothing more tenderly and preached nothing more earnestly and perseveringly than that same Holy Name. Within the range of his fourteen letters he found place for the Name of Jesus two hundred and nineteen times. How many times will he have used that Name on his long and arduous journeys in the manifold dangers and persecutions that beset him, in public addresses and private instructions, and in the many prayers which he sent heavenward both for himself and the faithful brought to Jesus through his ministration? It was St. Paul who advised: "All whatsoever you do in word or in work, all things do ye in the Name of the Lord Jesus Christ". It was St. Paul who gloried in the service of One, to Whom "God has given a Name which is above all names, that in the Name of Jesus every knee should bow, of those that are in Heaven, on earth and under the earth".

Would that we understood the Name of Jesus as the Apostle of the Gentiles understood it! This Name is the most holy and sacred among all names, because, given by God the Father in Heaven, it was borne by God the Son on Earth. "Thou shalt call His Name Jesus for He shall save His people from their sins." It is the Name of Him Who redeemed us, not with the "price of corruptible things as gold or silver", but with His own "precious Blood, as of a lamb unspotted and undefiled".

This Name is a name full of consolation for the poor and the afflicted, as also for all who "suffer persecution for justice' sake". It reminds the poor of One Who in His birth was satisfied with a fodder-box of animals for His cradle, Who in His public life claimed no pillow whereon to cushion His weary Head, and Who in the hour of death chose the hard wood of a cross to stretch out His tired and weak, sacred Body. It reminds the sick and the af-

flicted of One Who sweated dark-red drops of perspiration
in the garden of Gethsemani, Who poured out bright-red,
gushing streams in the courtyard and hall of Pontius Pilate, and Who allowed a last rivulet of Sacred Blood to
color His sacred, opened Side. It reminds the persecuted
of One Whose kindest acts and greatest charities were
misinterpreted; of One Whose sinless life did not protect
Him against lies and names, ranging all the way from
winebibber to blasphemer of the Most High Father.

The Name of Jesus is a powerful name, powerful on
earth and in Heaven; powerful in temporal and spiritual
necessities. Powerful on earth, as we see from the experience of the blind man who, crying out "Jesus, son of David,
have mercy on me", received his sight; powerful in Heav-
en, as we learn from the assurance: "If you ask the Father
anything in My Name. He will give it to you"; powerful in
temporal needs, as appears from the first recorded miracle
of the Apostles, when St. Peter, meeting the lame beggar
in the temple, said: "In the Name of Jesus Christ of Nazareth, arise and walk"; powerful in spiritual needs, for
"in My Name they shall cast out devils".

May the Holy Name of Jesus be our watchword and
shield through the days of the New Year! May it be, to
use the words of St. Bernard, "honey in our mouths!" May
we, obedient to the urging of St. Anselm, another great
Father of the Church, "cherish this sweet, this consoling,
this powerful Name of Jesus; may we have it always in
our hearts and on our lips; and may it be our only food,
our only consolation, our only delight!"

✠

JANUARY 2

ST. FULGENTIUS

Fabius Claudius Gordianus Fulgentius was a descend-
ant of a noble senatorial family in Carthage. At an early
age he was appointed procurator of the Roman province

of Carthage. As this success did not satisfy his spiritual desires, he decided to become a religious. Several years of peaceful life were spent in a monastery founded by a Bishop namd Faustus, who had been exiled by the Vandal king, Henneric.

When Faustus was obliged to flee from renewed persecution, he advised Fulgentius to seek shelter in another monastery not far away. The abbot, Felix, who had been his friend in the world, insisted upon resigning his office to Fulgentius. When, in humility, he declined, it was agreed that he should be a co-Abbot. A raid of Moors made it necessary to move to a safer place.

Fulgentius was ordained Priest by Bishop Faustus; in 508 he was elected Bishop of Ruspa. With fifty-nine other Bishops he was banished by the Arian King Thrasimund to Sardinia. Though the youngest of those exiled, Fulgentius was their spokesman. By books and letters he confounded the Pelagian and Arian heretics, and confirmed the Catholics of Africa and Gaul in their Faith.

Upon the death of Thrasimund the exiled Bishops returned to Africa. After Fulgentius re-established order in his Diocese, he retired to a monastery on the Island of Circe to prepare for death. When complaints were made of his absence, he returned to his labors. Shortly thereafter he fell grievously ill, and distributed all his possessions to the poor. His illness lasted seventy days. He died on January 1, 533, in the 65th year of his life and the 25th of his episcopate.

ST. MACARIUS OF ALEXANDRIA

It is claimed that about the year 335 Macarius gave up his work as a fruiterer to become a hermit in Upper Egypt. Later he took up his abode in the Desert of Nitria, where he was ordained Priest. His life was one of continual conflict with self. He practiced great austerities, and became renowned for his gifts of prophecy and miracle-working. The Arian Patriarch Lucius of Alexandria banished him on account of his steadfast Orthodoxy.

According to Palladius, Macarius died about 395, at an advanced age. It is alleged that he wrote a Rule for Monks and some discourses on spiritual subjects.

✠

JANUARY 3

ST. GENEVIEVE

St. Genevieve, the patroness of Paris, was born at Nanterre, eight miles from Paris, in 422. In 429 St. Germain of Auxerre and St. Lupus of Troyes were sent from Gaul to Britain to combat the heretical teachings of Pelagius. Enroute they stopped at Nanterre. While preaching to the multitude that came out to greet them, St. Germain was attracted by the pious demeanor of a little shepherdess. After the sermon he asked that the child be brought to him. Learning that Genevieve desired to devote herself to God's service, he interviewed her parents and predicted that their child would lead a holy life, and by her example and instruction lead many virgins to consecrate themselves to God. His prophecy was fulfilled. Before his departure the following morning St. Germain saw Genevieve again. After renewing her consecration to Jesus, St. Germain blessed her and gave her a medal engraved with a cross and told her to keep it in remembrance of her dedication.

After the death of her parents, Genevieve went to live with her godmother in Paris, where she led a prayerful life, performing works of charity and corporal austerities. God bestowed upon her the gifts of prophecy and miracles. Some neighbors, jealous of her power, accused the girl of being an impostor and a hypocrite, and treated her visions and prophecies as frauds and deceits. They

even conspired to drown her. When St. Germain sent the
holy child some blessed bread as a token of esteem, the
furor ceased, and she was ever afterwards honored as a
Saint.

In 451 Attila and his Huns were sweeping over Gaul,
and the inhabitants of Paris prepared to flee. Genevieve
encouraged them to hope and trust in God, and urged
them to perform works of penance, stating that if they did
so the city would be spared. They heeded her exhortations;
calm was restored; and Attila's hordes turned towards
Orleans, leaving Paris unharmed.

Several years later the Franks took Paris. During the
siege Genevieve distinguished herself by her acts of charity and self-sacrifice.

After Clovis, who had become the king of the Franks,
was converted by his holy wife St. Clotilda, St. Genevieve
was made his adviser. It was she who conceived the plan
to erect a church in Paris in honor of Saints Peter and
Paul, which was begun by Clovis shortly before he died,
in 511. St. Genevieve died the following year, aged eighty-
nine, and upon completion of the church her body was
interred therein. This fact, and the many miracles performed at her tomb, caused the name of Saint Genevieve
to be given to the church. It was rebuilt several times
during the centuries. The latest restoration was undertaken
shortly before the end of the 18th century. The French
Revolution broke out before these repairs to the ancient
church were completed. In 1791 the church was taken over
by the Revolutionists and given the name of the Pantheon,
to be a burial place for distinguished Frenchmen.

St. Genevieve's relics had been preserved in her
church for centuries. Paris witnessed many striking proofs
of the efficacy of her intercession. In 834 she saved the
city from complete inundation. In 1129 a plague broke
out in Paris, killing 14,000 persons in a short time. The
same day that the shrine of St. Genevieve was carried in
solemn procession through the city only three persons
died and the rest recovered.

✠

JANUARY 4

ST. TITUS

St. Titus, a disciple of St. Paul, was born a Gentile. It seems that he was converted to Christianity by St. Paul, who calls him his son in Christ. Because of his extraordinary virtue, Titus won the particular esteem and affection of St. Paul, who chose him as his secretary and interpreter; calls him his brother and co-partner in his labors; praises exceedingly his solicitude and zeal for the salvation of his brethren (2 Cor. 8:16; 10:4, 18), and in the tenderest manner expresses the comfort and support he found in him (2 Cor. 7:6, 7), insomuch, that, on a certain occasion St. Paul declared that he found no rest in his spirit, because at Troas he had not met Titus.

In the year 51 he accompanied St. Paul to the Council that was held in Jerusalem regarding the Mosaic rites. We learn from the two Epistles of St. Paul to the Corinthians that in the year 56 St. Paul sent Titus from Ephesus to Corinth to rebuke the Corinthians who were scandalizing the Christians and were wavering in their Faith; again, in that same year Titus was sent to procure alms for the poor Christians in Jerusalem. We are told that the Corinthians "received him with fear and trembling". St. Paul meanwhile was anxiously awaiting the result, and while at Troas he wrote, "I had no rest in my spirit, because I found not Titus, my brother". It was when he reached Macedonia that Titus brought the good news of his mission—the sorrow, the zeal, and the generosity of the Christians. St. Paul, full of joy, sent his faithful messenger back to the Corinthians with a letter of comfort.

After St. Paul's first imprisonment, on his return from Rome to the East, he stopped at the island of Crete to preach the Faith of Jesus Christ. Since other churches required his presence, St. Paul ordained his beloved disciple

Titus Bishop of that island, to complete the work he had so successfully begun.

In the year 65 we find that St. Paul sent Titus to preach in Dalmatia (2 Tim. 4:10ff). He again returned to Crete to strengthen the Faith of the people. It was here that he finished a laborious and holy life by a happy death at a very advanced age.

✠

JANUARY 5

ST. SIMEON STYLITES

St. Simeon was a native of Cilicia and became a shepherd, like his father. At the age of thirteen he was so moved upon hearing the Beatitudes read in church, especially, "Blessed are they that mourn"; and "Blessed are the clean of heart", that he begged a holy, aged man to explain their meaning and to tell him how the happiness they promised could be obtained.

He was advised that continual prayer, vigils, fasting, weeping, humiliation, and patiently suffering persecutions were the road to true happiness, and that a life of solitude would afford the best opportunities to practice these good works and establish a man in solid virtue. Simeon withdrew a short distance, and prostrating himself on the ground begged God to conduct him along the way which would lead to his happiness and perfection. He then fell asleep and was favored with a vision. He seemed to be digging a pit for the foundation of a house, and that as often as he stopped to take a breath, which was four times, he was commanded each time to dig deeper. Finally he was told that he might stop, as the pit was deep enough for the proposed foundation, on which he would be able to erect a superstructure of whatever kind and height he pleased.

In the neighborhood was a monastery, to which Simeon then directed his steps. After lying prostrate at the gate for several days, without food or drink, he begged to be admitted as a servant. His request was granted. Having spent two years here, he moved to the monastery of Heliodorus. Simeon increased his austerities and mortifications and ate only one meal a week, which was on Sundays. Because of his singularities in these matters, the Abbot dismissed him.

Simeon then repaired to a hermitage at the foot of Mount Thelamissa and fasted for the whole forty days of Lent, neither eating nor drinking. This method of keeping Lent he followed for the remainder of his life. After three years spent in this hermitage, the Saint moved to the top of the same mountain. His solitude soon became interrupted by the multitudes that came to receive his blessing, and many sick recovered their health.

In order to prevent these causes of distraction St. Simeon, in 423, erected a pillar six cubits high, on the top of which he dwelt for four years; then on a pillar twelve cubits high, where he lived three years; on a third, twenty-two cubits high, ten years; and on a fourth, forty cubits high and about three feet in diameter, which the people built for him, he spent the twenty remaining years of his life: hence the name Stylites, meaning "raised on a pillar". Crowds came to hear him preach and to seek advice. Many Persians, Armenians, Iberians and others were converted by his miracles and discourses.

It was on September 2, 459, that this incomparable penitent, in the sixty-ninth year of his life, in an attitude of prayer, surrendered his soul to God.

✠

JANUARY 6

THE EPIPHANY OF OUR LORD

Epiphany, at one time called "Twelfth Night" or "Little Christmas", is the Feast of the Manifestation of the Child Jesus to the Gentiles.

Pope Leo the Great, in an exhortation delivered to the Christians of his day, says:

"Let, therefore, that most holy day on which the Author of our salvation was made manifest, be honored by us; and let us adore the Omnipotent One in Heaven, to Whom, as a Babe in the manger, the Magi gave homage. Moreover, as they of their riches proffered mystical gifts to the Lord, let us from our hearts offer things worthy of God". Here, as in a nutshell, are the sentiments which must move our hearts on the Feast of the Epiphany, January sixth.

The Word made flesh on Christmas day was known to only a few—to Mary and Joseph, to the shepherds, and to their friends who would believe. As yet He was hidden from His enemies and from the world at large. But a star guided the Magi from the East to Jerusalem, and from Jerusalem to Bethlehem. "The heavens proclaimed the glory of God," and then it was that the knowledge of the true God went forth into the whole world. The kingdoms of the East were enlightened by the message brought by the returning Wise Men; Jerusalem, with its inhabitants, is awakened from slumber by the discovery of its Priests that the prophecy regarding the Messiah's birth is fulfilled; and the great Roman Empire takes notice when the news is brought, that for fear of a Child, Herod, appointed by it to rule as king over the lately acquired Judea, orders and carries out a massacre of innocent children. *Epiphany* means a manifestation of or a showing forth of someone or something. We now realize why this word is used in designating a feast which in many a Christian country is simply known as the Feast of the Three Kings.

The Magi were Gentiles, but they had seen the star of the new-born King of the Jews. And they do not hesitate; they are ready to follow the call. Doubts as to the meaning of the star and complaints about the great distance find no place in their minds and hearts. The intellect is subjected to faith. Obstacles may arise; but they will not be turned away from a recognized duty. The star disappears; they will go on. Jerusalem looms large before them, Jerusalem which will ridicule their journey and their quest for a child. Unafraid, they put their question and wait for the answer. Receiving it, they will not tarry longer but are on their way towards the small and despised Bethlehem. They are guided by the star to an humble dwelling, and they find a poor Mother and in her arms an Infant wrapped in swaddling clothes. Have they been deceived? They bend their knees and adore the Child. What an example to all Christians!

We have seen this Child grow up into manhood, have heard the message of Heaven which fell from His lips, have been witnesses of the wondrous works of His hands; we have heard the testimony of the Father proclaiming Him His Son, and seen the Holy Spirit descending upon Him in the form of a dove; we have watched, one by one, the fulfillment in Him of all the prophecies of Old; we have followed Him in persecutions and sufferings, which ended with His death upon the cross; we have been electrified by His resurrection from the dead and gladdened by His ascension into Heaven, where He is seated at the right hand of the Father. We know that He is our Judge as truly as He is our Savior. We can testify to the growth and the permanency of His Church, of which we are members. Shall we allow ourselves to be outdone in faith by the Magi?

"And opening their treasures, they offered Him gifts: gold, frankincense and myrrh." Gold they offered to their King, frankincense to their God, myrrh to their Savior. "So," says Pope St. Gregory, "shall we, too, offer to the Incarnate Lord gold, and confess that He rules everywhere: we shall offer frankincense and proclaim our faith, that He Who in time appeared amongst men is God from all eternity: we shall offer myrrh, and declare that He Who in His divinity could not suffer was mortal in our flesh."

May the gold of the Magi represent our love, whereby we prefer God to all creatures and assist our fellowman for the sake of God; may the frankincense represent our spirit of prayer, in virtue of which our hearts dwell with God and our minds are fixed upon His holy Will; may the myrrh represent our patience, in which we not only accept our daily trials and sufferings but also subject ourselves to self-denials and penances.

☨

JANUARY 7

ST. LUCIAN

St. Lucian, whose parents died when he was quite young, was born at Samosata, in Syria. He became proficient in rhetoric, philosophy, and the study of Holy Scripture. His large estate he distributed amongst the poor. When St. Lucian became a Priest, in addition to the duties of his holy state, and the performance of works of charity, he studied sacred literature. He purged both the Old and New Testaments of errors that had crept in by the inaccuracy of transcribers or the malice of heretics.

St. Lucian suffered nine years' imprisonment for the Faith in Nicomedia. When brought before Diocletian for trial, he gave an excellent apology for the Christian Faith. Being remanded to prison, an order was issued that he should not be given any food, but when almost dead some dainty meats that had been offered to idols were set before him, which he refused to touch.

Upon his second appearance before the tribunal, St. Lucian gave but one answer to all the questions asked— "I am a Christian". And he repeated the same words while on the rack. His glorious life came to a close, while in prison, by starvation, or, according to St. Chrysostom, by the sword, on January 7, 312.

✠

JANUARY 8

ST. APOLLINARIS

Claudius Apollinaris, an illustrious prelate of the 2nd century, was Bishop of Hierapolis, in Phrygia. Little is known of his life; yet, Eusebius, St. Jerome, Theodoret and others praised him highly. His writings were held in great esteem. He wrote against the heretics of his day, but what has rendered St. Apollinaris' name so famous was his noble apology for the Christian religion addressed to the Emperor Marcus Aurelius about the year 172, shortly after the Emperor's miraculous victory over the Quadi through the prayers of the Christians. St. Apollinaris reminded him of the victory obtained through the prayers of the Christians and implored his protection for them.

In gratitude to the Christian soldiers, Marcus Aurelius published an edict acknowledging his indebtedness to them for his delivery "perhaps by the prayers of the Christians"; he feared to say more, realizing the danger of exasperating the pagans. In the edict he forbade, under pain of death, anyone to accuse a Christian on account of his religion, but lacked the courage to abolish the laws already in force against them. Consequently, many Christians suffered martyrdom, and their accusers were also put to death; as was the case of St. Apollinaris. The date of his death is unknown, but the Roman Martyrology mentions him on January 8th.

✠

JANUARY 9

SS. JULIAN AND BASILISSA

Saints Julian and Basilissa, though married, lived by mutual consent in perpetual chastity. In order to aid the

sick and the poor, they turned their house in Egypt into
a hospital. Basilissa cared for the women, and Julian for
the men. At times they harbored a thousand indigent
people.

St. Basilissa died after suffering severe persecutions.
St. Julian survived her many years, receiving the crown
of martyrdom during the reign of Maximin II, in 313.
Many churches and hospitals in the East and West bear
the name of one or the other of these martyrs.

During the time of St. Gregory the Great St. Julian's
skull was brought from the East to France and given to
Queen Brunehault; she gave it to the convent she founded
at Etampes; later, part of it was presented to the
monastery of Morigny, near Etampes, and part to the
church of the Regular Canonesses of Basilissa in Paris.

✠

JANUARY 10

ST. WILLIAM

St. William, who became Archbishop of Bourges, was
of the illustrious family of the Counts of Nevers. From early
youth he learned to despise the world as well as the empti-
ness and folly of its pleasures, and to be fearful of their
dangers. He received his education from Peter the Hermit,
archdeacon of Soissons, who was an uncle on his mother's
side. All his spare time was employed in exercises of piety.

Shortly after ordination to the priesthood, William
was made Canon of Soissons, and afterwards of Paris. Soon
he resolved to lead a life of solitude, and went to live with
the Monks of Grandmont; later, however, he joined the
austere Cistercian Order at Pontigny, and always considered himself the least among his brethren. He was appointed Abbot of Fontaine-Jean, and then Abbot of Chaalis.

Upon the death of Archbishop Henri de Sully of Bourges, William was chosen as his successor, in November 1200. William was overwhelmed with grief, and only because of the command from the Pope and that of the Abbot of Citeaux, his General, did he acquiesce.

St. William led a saintly life in his new position; he redoubled all his austerities, saying it was necessary for him now to do penance for others as well as for himself. By his zeal he converted many of the Albigenses. While preparing himself for a mission to them he was seized with his last illness, and died on January 10, 1209. He was canonized the following year by Pope Honorius III.

✠

JANUARY 11

ST. THEODOSIUS

St. Theodosius was born of pious parents in Cappadocia, in the year 423. He resolved to follow the patriarch Abraham's example and leave his native country and friends. Accordingly, he set out for Jerusalem, but desiring to consult St. Simeon Stylites went out of the way in order to do so. He visited the famous saint on his pillar, who foretold him several circumstances of his life and instructed him how to act.

After satisfying his devotion in visiting the holy places in Jerusalem, St. Theodosius placed himself under the guidance of a holy hermit named Longinus, who entrusted him with the care of the church of Our Lady near Bethlehem. Not wishing to govern there, he soon retired to a cave at the top of a neighboring desert mountain, where he devoted his time to fasting, vigils, prayers and tears. His food was wild herbs and coarse pulse, and for thirty years he never tasted a morsel of bread.

In time, many desired to serve God under his direction, and in consequence St. Theodosius built a large monastery and three infirmaries near Bethlehem. He divided the Monks according to nationality—Armenians, Greeks and Arabs—, and built a church for each group.

The Patriarch of Jerusalem appointed Theodosius Superior General of all the religious men living in community throughout Palestine, whence he was called the Cenobiarch.

Emperor Anastasius used all possible means to bribe Theodosius to support the Eutychian heresy, but he remained firm, stating that he was ready to lay down his life for the teachings of the Church. The Emperor then issued an order for his banishment, which was executed. Anastasius died soon after, and Theodosius was recalled by his Catholic successor, Justin. Theodosius lived eleven years upon his return without relaxation in his former austerities. After patiently suffering a long and painful malady, St. Theodosius died at the age of one hundred and five, in the year 529.

☩

JANUARY 12

ST. AELRED

St. Aelred was born in the north of England of noble parentage, and became master of the household of King David of Scotland. He ardently desired to devote himself entirely to God, but his attachment to friends delayed his taking definite steps for some time. In order to relinquish all his worldly engagements, Aelred, at the age of twenty-four, left Scotland to enter the Cistercian abbey at Rieval, in Yorkshire. With great fervor he entered upon his new way of life. He speaks of divine charity always in raptures. "What is love? my God!" he asks. "If I mistake not, it is

the wonderful delight of the soul, so much the more sweet
as more pure, so much the more overflowing and inebriat-
ing as more ardent. He who loves Thee, possesses Thee;
and he possesses Thee in proportion as he loves, because
Thou art love. This is that abundance with which Thy
beloved are inebriated, melting away from themselves,
that they may pass into Thee, by loving Thee."

Much against his inclination, St. Aelred was made
Abbot of a new monastery of his Order at Revesby, in
1142, it being the most austere monastery in England, and
the following year of Rieval, where there were three hundred Monks. Pious reading and prayer were his main and
practically sole occupations. His ascetical writings, especially "On Spiritual Friendship" and "Mirror of Charity"
are soul stirring.

St. Aelred died in 1166 at the age of fifty-seven, after
having served as Abbot twenty-two years.

☩

JANUARY 13

ST. VERONICA OF MILAN

St. Veronica was born in a small village near Milan.
Her parents were poor, hard working, pious people. Their
straitened circumstances prevented Veronica from receiving any education, so she never learned to read. She worked
hard and prayed much, and God was calling her to the
religious life. Veronica, anxious about her inability to read
and write, was favored one day with a vision of Our Lady,
who told her to cease her worry, for it was enough if she
knew three things: purity of intention; to abhor murmuring
and criticism; and to meditate daily on the Passion of Christ.

After three years' preparation, Veronica was received
as a lay-Sister in the convent of St. Martha at Milan. She
was assigned to beg from door to door for the daily food.

Every moment of her life she endeavored to fulfill faithfully the will of her Superior, for by so doing she knew she
was fulfilling the Will of God.

For three years before her death, in 1497, St. Veronica
suffered a lingering illness. Never did she ask to be exempted from any duty, always saying: "I must work while
I can, while I have time". It was her delight to help and
serve everyone, and to perform the hardest and most humble tasks; her silence was a sign of her recollection and
continual prayer. God favored her with many extraordinary
graces, and through her exhortations to virtue she converted several obdurate sinners. Her sanctity was confirmed by miracles. She died at the time she foretold,
at the age of fifty-two.

✠

JANUARY 14

ST. HILARY OF POITIERS

St. Hilary was born in Poitiers and educated a pagan.
He testified to this fact later in life and gave an account
of the steps by which God conducted him to the knowledge of His saving Faith. He considered by the light of
reason that man, who is created a moral and free agent,
is placed in this world to exercise patience, temperance,
and other virtues which he, though a pagan, understood
must receive from God a recompense after this life. Then
he ardently set about to learn what God is, and after
some research into the nature of the Supreme Being,
quickly realized the absurdity of polytheism, and was
convinced that there can be only one God Who is eternal,
unchangeable, all-powerful, the first cause and author of
all things. Full of these reflections, he obtained a copy of
the Holy Scriptures. He was wonderfully impressed upon
reading the sublime description of God given by Moses—

I AM WHO AM—, and with the idea of His immensity and supreme dominion, as related by the prophets. The reading of the New Testament completed his inquiries, for he did not presume to measure divine mysteries by his shallow understanding. From the first chapter of St. John he learned that the Divine Word, God the Son, is coeternal and consubstantial with the Father.

Being brought to the knowledge of Faith, Hilary received the regenerating waters of Baptism, and to the end of his life he endeavored to bring others to believe in the Most Holy Trinity, and to encourage all to lead a virtuous life. He soon converted his wife and daughter, and later was ordained to the priesthood. About the year 353 he was made Bishop of Poitiers. Arianism was at that time at the height of its power. St. Hilary supported the sound teachings of the Church in several Gaelic Councils despite the fact that an overwhelming majority of the Bishops present were Arians. For this reason St. Hilary was exiled to Phrygia by the Arian Emperor, Constantius.

During the three years and more of his exile he wrote several learned works. The most esteemed was the twelve-volume work, "On the Trinity, against the Arians", in which he proves the consubstantiality of the Father, Son, and Holy Ghost. Among other things he teaches that the Church is One; outside of it all heresies arise. By this the Church is distinguished, that She, standing always alone whilst the heresies battle Her, in the end confounds them; whereas the heresies, rent by perpetual divisions, tear themselves to pieces. Thus they become the instruments of Her triumph.

Upon St. Hilary's return from exile, he attended the Council of Seleucia, in which Arians, semi-Arians and Catholics fought for the mastery. St. Hilary withdrew to Constantinople, and from there exhorted the heretics to return to the Catholic Faith. He travelled through Gaul, Italy

and Illyria, everywhere preaching against the heretical
teachings of Arianism. He died at Poitiers on January 13,
368. In 1851 St. Hilary was declared a Doctor of the Church.

☦

JANUARY 15

ST. PAUL, THE FIRST HERMIT

St. Paul, born of wealthy parents in Egypt about the
year 230, became an orphan when fifteen years old. He
was well educated and loved God from early youth. During the bloody persecution of the Christians by Decius in
250, Paul fled into the Thebian desert, trusting in God
to provide for his needs. The fruit of a palm tree furnished
the hermit with food; its leaves, clothing; whilst a nearby
spring supplied water to quench his thirst. Having tasted
the great consolations in prayer and penance, St. Paul spent
the remaining days of his life (ninety years) in the desert
in communion with God.

Towards the end of his life the great St. Anthony, who
also had served God for many years in the wilderness, visited St. Paul. While they were discoursing together, a raven
dropped a loaf of bread before them. St. Paul said, "Our
good God has sent us a dinner. In this manner have I
received half a loaf every day these sixty years past; now
you are come to see me, Christ has doubled His provision
for His servants". Having partaken of the food and re-
freshed themselves at the spring, they spent the night
in prayer. Early next morning St. Paul told his guest that
his death would occur soon and that he had been sent
to bury him, adding: "Go and fetch the cloak given you
by St. Athanasius, Bishop of Alexandria, in which I desire you to wrap my body". St. Anthony was surprised, and
hastened to bring the cloak. As he was returning he saw
Paul's soul ascend to Heaven. He found his body kneeling
upright with arms outstretched. Having paid his last re-

spects to the holy corpse, he carried it out of the cave
and buried it. On St. Anthony's return to his abode, he
praised God and related to his Monks what he had seen
and done.

St. Paul died in 342 at the age of one hundred and
thirteen, and is usually called the *first hermit,* to distinguish
him from others of the same name.

✠

JANUARY 16

ST. HONORATUS

St. Honoratus' father was a pagan Roman consular,
living in Gaul at the time of the child's birth. In his youth
Honoratus renounced the worship of idols and became
a Christian. He induced his elder brother, Venantius, to
do likewise. Both desired to give up the pleasures of the
world for the love of Jesus, but their pagan father continually opposed their plans. With the intention of living
unknown in some desert place in Greece, the two brothers chose St. Caprais, a holy hermit, for their Director, and
the three sailed from Marseilles. Venantius died soon
afterwards at Methone, and Honoratus, who also became
ill, was obliged to return to Gaul with his spiritual director. He then tried living a hermit's life in the mountains
near Frejus, but finally settled on a small island, now
known as St. Honore, near the coast. Followed by others,
St. Honoratus founded there, about the year 400, the
famous monastery of Lerins. Some of the hermits lived in
community, while the more perfect, as anchorets; all following the Rule of St. Pachomius under the guidance of
St. Honoratus.

Upon the death of the Archbishop of Arles, St. Honoratus was forced to accept the Archbishopric, and was
consecrated in 425. Three years later he died, worn out
from his apostolic labors and the austere life which he led.

✠

JANUARY 17

ST. ANTHONY

St. Anthony, styled the Patriarch of Monks, was born of wealthy Christian parents at Coma, a small village in Upper Egypt, in 251. Before he was twenty years of age his parents died and he found himself the possessor of a large estate and charged with the care of a younger sister. About six months later he heard read in church the words of Christ to the rich young man: "Go sell what thou hast, and give to the poor, and thou shalt have treasure in Heaven: and come, follow Me". (Matt. 19:21.) Anthony considered these words as addressed to himself and gave away all of his possessions. Placing his sister in a convent, he retired into solitude near Coma and begged an aged hermit to teach him the spiritual life. He visited other solitaries and strove to emulate the principal virtue of each, so that he soon became a perfect model of humility, Christian courtesy, charity, prayer, and all the other virtues.

The devil assailed him by various temptations, but he overcame them all by his confidence in God and by the Sign of the Cross.

About the year 305, when Anthony was fifty-five, to satisfy the importunities of others, he left his mountain retreat and founded his first monastery at Fayum, and another shortly after at Pispir. By gathering together a number of hermits into one community, St. Anthony was the first to establish the religious life as it is known today. He became famous throughout Egypt and even beyond its borders, so that people from all walks of life sought his advice.

In 339 St. Anthony saw in a vision, under the figure of "mules kicking down the altar", the havoc which the Arian persecution was to make two years later in Alex-

andria, and clearly foretold it, as St. Athanasius, St. Jerome and St. Chrysostom assure us. St. Anthony aided
St. Athanasius in his fight against the heretical teachings
of Arianism. When ninety years old he preached a sermon
in Alexandria at the invitation of St. Athanasius, in which
he boldly accused the Arians of heresy.

A most sublime gift of heavenly contemplation and
prayer was the fruit of this great saint's holy retirement.
On January 17, 356, at the age of one hundred and five,
St. Anthony died peacefully in the Lord.

☦

JANUARY 18

FEAST OF THE CHAIR OF PETER

The chair honored by Mother Church is the one that
was actually used by St. Peter in the Catacombs of St. Priscilla.

The Chair itself is a perfectly plain oak arm chair,
with legs connected by crossbars to strengthen it. In
course of time, other supports were added to strengthen
it, but it remains in form and substance the Chair occupied by St. Peter when he instructed the early Christians,
the Chair before which they knelt when he administered
to them the Sacrament of Confirmation.

For many years the Chair was exposed to the public
gaze and was specially venerated on the Feast Day; also
each newly elected Pope was solemnly enthroned on it.
But later it was deemed necessary, in order to preserve it,
to enclose it in metal. It is now encased in bronze, and
rests in the apse of St. Peter's Basilica.

Our Savior by choosing Peter to be the head of the
Apostles gave him precedence over the others. "Thou art
Peter, and upon this rock (Peter) I will build My Church."
It is an indisputably established historical fact that St. Pe-

O God, in giving the keys of the kingdom of heaven to Your blessed Apostle Peter, You also bestowed on him the power of binding and of loosing. Grant that, through his intercession, we may be delivered from the bonds of our sins.

ter labored in Rome during the last portion of his life, and that he died in that city. This constitutes the historical foundation of the claim of the Bishops of Rome to the Apostolic Primacy of Peter, and for the veneration of the "Chair of Peter".

✠

JANUARY 19

ST. CANUTE

St. Canute, son of Sweyn III, King of Denmark, and great-nephew of Canute, King of England, was gifted with excellent qualities of mind and body. He was more renowned for his singular piety than for his courage and skill in war. Upon the death of his father, his eldest brother, Harold, was called to the throne. After a reign of only two years Harold died and Canute succeeded to the Danish throne as Canute IV.

Denmark was Christianized about the year 826, but needed a zealous leader to solidify the good work. St. Canute seems to have been chosen by God for that purpose. He commenced his reign by a successful war against the troublesome barbarous enemies of his country, and by planting the Faith in the conquered provinces of his kingdom. Amidst his glorious victories St. Canute humbly prostrated himself at the foot of the Crucifix, laid there his crown, and offered himself and his kingdom to the King of kings.

After enlarging his kingdom and having provided for its safety and peace he married Eltha, daughter of Earl Roberts of Flanders, by whom he had a pious son, Charles, surnamed the Good, who later became Earl of Flanders.

St. Canute now turned his attention to reforming the abuses in his kingdom, enacting severe, but necessary, laws for the strict administration of justice without respect of persons. The clergy were granted numerous privileges and immunities in order to enhance the people's esteem of them; many churches were erected and adorned; and to the church of Roschild, in Zealand, his capital city, St. Canute gave the valuable crown he wore. By his charity and tenderness he did everything possible to relieve the burdens of his people in order to make them happy. He led an austere, holy life.

A rebellion broke out in the kingdom in opposition to the laws he enacted regarding "the tithes". On July 10, 1086, some of the rebels, headed by his brother Olaf, learning that the King had gone to the church of St. Alban to pray, surrounded it. The King, perceiving his danger, confessed his sins at the foot of the altar and received Holy Communion. His guards defended the church doors, but the Saint, as he knelt with outstretched arms before the altar, recommending his soul to God, was wounded with a javelin thrown through a window, and fell a victim to the cause of His Redeemer.

King Canute was considered a martyr, and at the request of King Eric III of Denmark was canonized by the Church in 1101.

✠

JANUARY 20

ST. SEBASTIAN

St. Sebastian was born in Gaul, but his parents were of Milan, Italy, and he was reared as a Christian in that city. In order to assist the confessors and martyrs in their sufferings, he went to Rome about the year 283, and enlisted in the army. He became an officer and a favorite of the Emperor Diocletian.

Marcus and Marcellinus, twin brothers, had been imprisoned for the Faith, and were on the point of yielding to the pleadings of their relatives. Sebastian, seeing this, exhorted them to remain loyal to Christ. God confirmed his words by a miracle, and many were led to embrace the

O Almighty God, look down upon our weakness, and since the weight of our own evil actions oppresses us, may the glorious intercession of Your blessed martyr Sebastian protect us.

Faith, including the Prefect of Rome and his son Tiburtius. Marcus and Marcellinus met their martyrdom by being nailed by the feet to a post, and after twenty-four hours of suffering were shot to death by arrows.

St. Sebastian, having aided many martyrs heavenwards, was himself impeached before the Emperor, who reproached him with ingratitude and delivered him to some archers to be shot to death. His body was covered with arrows, and he was left for dead. A holy widow went to bury him and finding him alive, took him to her home and cared for him until he was restored to health. Sebastian refused to make his escape, and one day accosted the Emperor for his cruelty to the Christians. Greatly astonished at finding Sebastian alive, whom he supposed had been shot to death, he ordered that he be seized and beaten to death, and his body thrown into the *cloaca* (the sewer of Rome).

St. Sebastian thus suffered a double martyrdom.

✠

JANUARY 21

ST. AGNES

St. Agnes was only thirteen years old when she suffered martyrdom for the Faith in Rome, in 303, during the bloody persecution of Diocletian. Agnes, a beautiful and wealthy child, consecrated her virginity to God at an early age. When twelve years old she was called on to prove her love for God and her hatred of sin.

The young noblemen of Rome vied with one another to win her hand in marriage, but finding her resolution unassailable accused her to the Governor of being a Christian. Agnes ignored the alluring promises of the judge, stating repeatedly that she could have no other spouse than Jesus Christ. He then made use of threats, but Agnes remained adamantly courageous, even desiring racks and death. With a cheerful, fearless countenance she surveyed the cruel executioners. She was then dragged before the idols and commanded to offer incense. St. Ambrose testifies that she "could by no means be compelled to move her hand, except to make the Sign of the Cross"

When the Governor saw his efforts ineffectual, he said he would send Agnes to a house of ill repute, but the Saint answered: "You may stain your sword with my blood, but will never be able to profane my body, consecrated to Christ". The Governor was so incensed that he ordered her to be led there immediately. Her Divine Spouse showed by a miracle the value He sets upon virginity. A shameless youth attempted to approach the child, and in an instant a flash as it were of lightning from heaven struck him blind, and he fell trembling to the ground. His terrified companions raised him up and carried him to St. Agnes, who was at a distance singing hymns of praise to Christ, her protector. Through her prayer the youth's sight was restored.

The Governor, greatly exasperated at seeing himself out-witted by one so young, condemned St. Agnes to be beheaded. The executioner tried to get her to relent; instead, she said a short prayer, bowed her neck to adore God, as the executioner with a trembling hand cut off her head at one stroke. The spectators wept at seeing one so young and fearless in the face of death.

St. Agnes' body was buried near the Nomentan Road, a short distance from Rome. During the reign of Constantine the Great a church was erected over the spot, which Pope Honorius repaired in the 7th century.

✠

JANUARY 22

ST. VINCENT

St. Vincent, a native of Spain, was instructed by Bishop Valerius of Saragossa, who ordained him his Deacon and appointed him, though quite young, to preach and to instruct the people.

In the year 303 the Emperors Diocletian and Maximian published their second and third bloody edicts against the Christian clergy; the following year they were enforced against the laity. Dacian, a most bloody persecutor, was the Governor of Spain who put to death eighteen Christians at Saragossa and apprehended Valerius and Vincent before the promulgation of the edicts mentioned. By order of the Governor, Vincent and his Bishop were dragged in chains to Valencia and kept in prison for a long time, suffering extreme hunger and other tortures. Dacian contented himself with banishing Bishop Valerius, but savagely tormented St. Vincent. First, he was stretched on the rack by his hands and feet and drawn by cords and pulleys until his joints were almost torn apart. While hanging in that posture his flesh was unmercifully torn off with iron hooks. Vincent smiled and called the executioners weak and fainthearted, whereupon Dacian urged them to exert greater strength. The martyr was then bound on a bed of red-hot iron and scourged; salt was rubbed into his wounds, and all the while he remained unmoved with his eyes raised to heaven in prayer. The more he suffered the greater seemed to be his interior joy and consolation of soul.

He was then cast into a dungeon, his legs were placed in wooden stocks, and he was deprived of food and visitors. But God sent His angels to comfort him. The jailer seeing the prison filled with light and the Saint walking and praising God was converted at once to the Christian Faith. Upon hearing this Dacian was enraged, but ordered some rest for the prisoner. The faithful were then permitted to visit him. They kissed his wounds; they wiped them; and the cloths saturated with his blood they preserved.

A soft bed was prepared for St. Vincent, and as soon as he was laid on it he expired. Dacian ordered his body to be thrown in a marshy field, but a crow protected it from

wild beasts and birds of prey. It was then tied to a large
stone, placed in a sack, and thrown into the sea. It was
miraculously washed ashore. Whereupon two Christians,
who had received a revelation, sought the body and placed
it in a little chapel outside the walls of Valencia. God honored these relics with many miracles. They are preserved
today in the Augustinian monastery at Lisbon.

✠

JANUARY 23

ST. RAYMUND OF PENAFORT

St. Raymund was born at Penafort, a castle in Catalonia, of a noble Spanish family. He made such rapid
progress in his studies that at the age of twenty he taught
philosophy at Barcelona, instilling into the students solid
piety and devotion. When he was about thirty he went to
Bologna, Italy, to study canon and civil law, and while
preparing for his doctorate continued to teach, as he had
done in Barcelona.

In 1219, Bishop Berengarius of Barcelona, who had
been to Rome, took Raymund to Barcelona with him, to
the regret of the University of Bologna; ordained him to
the priesthood, and made him his Archdeacon and Vicar-
General. In 1222, at the age of forty-seven, St. Raymund
took the religious habit of St. Dominic in Barcelona, and
was most humble, obedient and fervent. From childhood
he had a tender devotion to the Blessed Virgin. After he
became a Dominican, Our Lady of Ransom in a vision
instructed him to co-operate with his penitent, St. Peter
Nolasco, and King James of Aragon in founding the Order
of Our Lady of Ransom for the Redemption of Captives.

He was commissioned by the Cardinal Legate of Pope
Gregory IX to preach the holy war against the Mohammedans. He acquitted himself with such prudence, zeal

and charity that he sowed the seeds for their overthrow in Spain, and aroused the Christians to penance, for they had been enslaved in soul and body by them.

In 1230 St. Raymund was called to Rome by Pope Gregory IX to be his chaplain and confessor, and he sought his advice in all matters. On the order of the Holy Father, St. Raymund gathered together the decrees of all the Popes and Councils since the collection made by Gratian in 1150. This task consumed three years; the five books are commonly called the Decretals.

In 1235 the Pope named St. Raymund to the archbishopric of Tarragona, the capital of Aragon, but the humble religious declined it as well as other offices of dignity. After returning to Barcelona, where he went to regain his health, he was made Third General of his Order.

King James of Aragon asked St. Raymund to accompany him to the island of Majorca, where the Saint used the opportunity to labor for the welfare of the Church. The Saint tried to induce the King to dismiss a person from his palace who was an occasion of sin to him. The King kept promising this would be done, but when he failed to keep his word St. Raymund begged leave to return to his monastery at Barcelona. The King not only forbade him to leave, but threatened to put to death anyone who would convey him from the island.

With confidence in God, St. Raymund walked to the water's edge, spread his cloak upon the sea, tied one end to his staff for a sail, then making the Sign of the Cross fearlessly stepped upon it. In six hours the wind carried his strange vessel to Barcelona. Gathering up his cloak, dry, he put it on and went to his monastery. The King upon hearing of this miracle became a sincere penitent and disciple of the Saint until his death. A chapel was built at the place where St. Raymund landed. After receiving the Last Sacraments he died on January 6, 1275, at the age of one hundred.

✠

ST. TIMOTHY

St. Timothy was born at Lystra in Asia Minor. His father was a pagan, and his mother, Eunice, a Jewess. When St. Paul preached in their city in 51 she, with Lois, his grandmother, and Timothy, embraced Christianity. Later Timothy became the beloved disciple of St. Paul, forsaking his country, his home and his parents to follow the Apostle and to share in his poverty and sufferings. St. Paul soon recognizing the ability of Timothy for an evangelist, ordained him. Henceforth, he became the constant and much-beloved fellow-worker of the Apostle.

St. Timothy accompanied St. Paul on his missionary journeys from Lystra through Asia; at Philippi, Thessalonica and Berea, in 52. St. Paul, obliged to leave Berea on account of the persecution of the Jews, left Timothy behind him to strengthen the new converts there. When St. Paul reached Athens he sent for Timothy, but upon learning that the Christians in Thessalonica were being persecuted for the Faith, he sent Timothy there to comfort and encourage them. Later Timothy went to Corinth to give an account to St. Paul of his success. This occasioned St. Paul to write his first Epistle to the Thessalonians. He then commissioned Timothy and Erastus to go before him through Macedonia to notify the faithful of his intention and to prepare the alms to be sent to the Christians in Jerusalem. Afterwards Timothy was sent to Corinth to correct certain abuses, while St. Paul waited in Asia for him to return; together they went into Macedonia and Achaia. St. Paul left the Apostle at Philippi, but rejoined him at Troas.

When St. Paul returned to Palestine he was imprisoned at Caesarea for two years, from where he went to Rome. Timothy seems to have been with him all or most of this time. He was made the first Bishop of Ephesus, and while there received two Epistles from St. Paul which bear his name; the first was written from Macedonia in 64, while incarcerated there, urging his "dearly beloved son", to come to see him again before death would summon him. In the year 64, after St. Paul had returned to Rome from the East, he left St. Timothy at Ephesus to govern the church, to ordain Priests and Deacons, and consecrate Bishops.

St. Timothy also suffered imprisonment for Christ, and gloriously confessed His name in the presence of many people, but was set at liberty. He is styled a martyr in the ancient martyrologies.

✠

JANUARY 25

THE CONVERSION OF ST. PAUL

Saul of Tarsus was a most zealous Jew, a Pharisee, of the tribe of Benjamin. Full of hatred for the disciples of Jesus, "he went to the High Priest and asked of him letters to Damascus, to the synagogues: that if he found any men and women of this Way, he might bring them bound to Jerusalem".

As he drew near to Damascus, suddenly a light from heaven shone round about him. Falling on the ground, he heard a voice saying to him: "Saul, Saul, why persecutest thou Me?"

Saul asked, "Who art thou, Lord?"

And He replied: "I am Jesus Whom thou persecutest. It is hard for thee to kick against the goad".

Trembling and astonished, Saul said: "Lord, what wilt Thou have me to do?"

"And the Lord said to him: Arise, and go into the city, and there it shall be told thee what thou must do."

The men who had accompanied Saul stood amazed, hearing a voice but seeing no one. When Saul arose from

O God, who by the preaching of blessed Paul, the Apostle, taught the whole world, grant to us, we beseech You, who today celebrate his conversion, to come to You by imitating his example.

the ground his eyes were opened, but he was unable to see. Led by his companions, he was brought to Damascus. For three days he was without sight, and neither ate nor drank.

The Lord in a vision said to Ananias, a disciple in Damascus: "Arise, and go into the street that is called Strait, and seek in the house of Judas, one named Saul of Tarsus. For behold he prayeth". "But Ananias answered: Lord, I have heard by many of this man, how much evil he hath done to Thy saints in Jerusalem. And here he hath authority from the chief priests to bind all that invoke Thy name."

The Lord then said to him: "Go thy way; for this man is to me a vessel of election, to carry my Name before the Gentiles, and kings, and the children of Israel. For I shall show him how great things he must suffer for my Name's sake".

Ananias went, and entering into the house laid his hands upon Saul, saying: "Brother Saul, the Lord Jesus hath sent me, He that appeared to thee in the way as thou camest; that thou mayest receive thy sight, and be filled with the Holy Ghost. And immediately there fell from his eyes as it were scales, and he received his sight; and rising up, he was baptized".

Immediately Saul (his name now changed to Paul) preached Jesus in the synagogues, that He is the Son of God. He confounded the Jews in Damascus, affirming that Jesus is the Christ, i. e., the Savior foretold by the Prophets. (Acts 9: 1-22.) For twelve years Paul labored to bring the Faith to Jew and Gentiles, and finally suffered martyrdom for that Faith.

✠

JANUARY 26

ST. POLYCARP

St. Polycarp was converted to Christianity by St. John the Evangelist, who appointed him Bishop of Smyrna,

which important See he governed for seventy years. As
St. Ignatius of Antioch passed by Smyrna on the road to his
martyrdom, St. Polycarp respectfully kissed his chains.
These two saints were the link between the Apostles and
future generations of Christians in Asia Minor.

About the year 158 St. Polycarp went to Rome to confer with Pope Anicetus concerning the time for observing
Easter.

In the 6th year of the reign of Marcus Aurelius a
violent persecution arose in Smyrna. To the astonishment
of the infidels the Christians gave heroic proofs of their
courage and love of the Savior. Three days before his martyrdom St. Polycarp in a vision saw his pillow on fire, from
which he understood that he should be burnt alive. He had
concealed himself in a neighboring village, but his whereabouts were revealed by a boy who had been threatened
with the rack. When his pursuers found his abode, St. Polycarp said: "God's Will be done". They endeavored to
persuade him to call Caesar 'Lord', but he resolutely answered: "I shall never do what you desire of me". As he
entered the place where the people were assembled he
heard a voice from heaven say: "Polycarp, be courageous,
and act manfully". When the proconsul urged him to
blaspheme Christ, Polycarp replied: "I have served Him
these fourscore and six years, and He never did me any
harm, but much good; how can I blaspheme my King
and my Savior?"

The proconsul after threatening him with wild beasts,
which Polycarp contemned, said: "If you contemn the
beasts, I will cause you to be burnt to ashes". Whereupon
Polycarp answered: "You threaten me with a fire which
burns for a short time and then goes out; but are yourself
ignorant of the judgment to come, and of the fire of everlasting torments which is prepared for the wicked. Why do
you delay?"

The wood and other combustibles were heaped around
him; his hands were tied; and after praying to Jesus for his
executioners and thanking Him for allowing him to drink

of His chalice, the fire was set to the pile. A mighty flame
encircled St. Polycarp's body, which sent forth a most
fragrant odor. Seeing that the fire did not consume his
body, he was pierced through the heart and his dead body
burned. The Christians carried away the relics of the martyr, which they considered more precious than the richest
jewels or gold, and buried them.

St. Polycarp's letter to the Philippians is still in existence, and his tomb is venerated in Smyrna.

✠

JANUARY 27

ST. JOHN CHRYSOSTOM

St. John was born at Antioch in 344. He was surnamed
Chrysostom, which means "Golden Mouthed", because of
his eloquent sermons and the marvelous good they effected.
His Mother instilled into his heart from early youth the
most perfect maxims of piety and contempt of the world.
It is not surprising, therefore, that John retired into the
mountains near Antioch, in 374, to lead the monastic life.
Four years were spent under the direction of an old Syrian
Monk, and two years in a cave as a hermit. The dampness
of the cave ruined his health and obliged him to return to
Antioch, where he was ordained Priest.

In 398, much against his will, he was raised to the See
of Constantinople. Because of his denunciation of vice, he
made numerous enemies and brought down upon himself
the imperial wrath. At a gathering of Bishops, known as the
Synod of the Oak, St. John was deposed and banished in
the year 403. Public opinion was so strongly in his favor
that the Emperor was unable to prevent his triumphal
return. Two months later, however, when he again openly
denounced vice he was driven to the deserts of Taurus in
Armenia, in defiance of Pope Innocent I, who strenuously
espoused the saint's cause.

St. John's enemies seeing the whole Christian world honoring and defending him, resolved to destroy him. They procured an order from the Emperor to have St. John removed to Cucusus, a secluded and rugged place on the east frontier of Armenia. He corresponded with his friends and never gave up the hope of his return. In 407 the order was given to carry him to Pithyus, a place at the extreme boundary of the empire, near the Caucasus. Two officers were commanded to convey him. Exposed to every hardship, St. John became ill, yet was forced to continue on the journey. Perceiving him in a dying condition, they brought him back four miles to the oratory of a Priest. Exchanging his soiled clothes for white garments, St. John received Holy Viaticum and closed his prayer with his usual doxology: "Glory be to God for all things". As he said "Amen", he sweetly gave up his soul to God.

✠

JANUARY 28

ST. CYRIL OF ALEXANDRIA

St. Cyril was born in Alexandria, Egypt, in 376, and became Patriarch of that city in 412.

Nestorius, a Monk and Priest of Antioch, was made Bishop of Constantinople in 428. Not long thereafter he began to teach heresy. He preached that there are two distinct persons in Christ, that of God and that of man, thus denying the Incarnation, or that God was made man. He also said that the Blessed Virgin should not be styled the Mother of God, but of the man who was Christ, Whose humanity was only the temple of divinity, not a nature hypostatically assumed by the divine Person. The people were shocked, and many Priests separated themselves from the heretic's communion. The errors and blasphemies in his public utterances gave great offense. After expostulating in vain, St. Cyril accused Nestorius to Pope Celestine, who examined Nestorius' doctrine in a Council at Rome; condemned it, and pronounced a sentence of excommunication unless he would publicly condemn and retract it within ten days after notification of the sentence, which he entrusted to St. Cyril. Nestorius appeared more obstinate than ever, which occasioned the calling of the third general Council at Ephesus, which opened in 431.

Nestorius, Cyril, and over two hundred Bishops were present. After waiting twelve days in vain for the Syrian Bishops, the Council, with Cyril, then tried Nestorius, condemned him, and deposed him from his See. Six days later the Syrian Bishops and Nestorius arrived, and excommunicated Cyril. Nestorius and Cyril were both arrested and imprisoned. As Cyril was on the point of being banished three Legates from Pope Celestine arrived. They considered what St. Cyril had done, confirmed the condemnation of Nestorius, and declared null and void the sentence pronounced against St. Cyril.

St. Cyril died in 444, and was declared a Doctor of the Church by Pope Leo XIII. The Alexandrians, Copts and Ethiopians give him the title of "Doctor of the World".

ST. PETER NOLASCO

St. Peter Nolasco was born near Castelnaudary, France, in 1182 or 1189, of a noble family. From his youth he was noted for his piety, almsgiving and charity. After giving all his possessions to the poor he made a vow of virginity, and in order to avoid communicating with the Albigenses went to Barcelona.

The Mohammedans at that time controlled a large part of the Iberian peninsula. Many Christians detained there were cruelly persecuted on account of the Faith. Peter consumed all his patrimony in ransoming as many of them as possible.

After much prayer, and moved by a heavenly vision in 1218, he resolved to found a religious Order similar to that established a few years previously by St. John of Matha and St. Felix of Valois for the redemption of Christian slaves. He received the encouragement of St. Raymund of Penafort and James I, King of Aragon, who it seems had been favored with the same inspiration. The new Order, Our Lady of Ransom, was approved by Pope Gregory IX in 1230, and the members were called Mercedarians. They were bound by a special vow to employ all their substance for the redemption of captive Christians, and if necessary to remain in captivity in their stead.

In the beginning Peter Nolasco and his associates were laymen, but Pope Clement V decreed that the Master General of the Order should always be a Priest.

St. Peter died on Christmas Day, 1256, at Barcelona.

☩

ST. FRANCIS OF SALES

Francis was born of noble and pious parents at Sales near Annecy, France, in 1567. He gave up the prospects of a grand career to become a Priest. It is claimed that even in childhood he had the adult heart of the Saints. To brilliant talent he added the most laborious application, and gained the highest honors of his schools. In virtue he excelled still more. His joy was to be with God in prayer; his recreation, to read the lives of the Saints.

In Paris he completed his Rhetoric and Philosophy with the highest distinction, studying also Theology, Scripture and Hebrew. An event which perhaps marked in his life the transition from extraordinary to heroic occurred at Paris when he was seventeen. This was a temptation to despair. He felt as if it were impossible for him to be saved. All his struggles, his prayers, his study of the grounds of hope, were of no help in his hour of trial. His body visibly wasted away; his soul was burdened with deep melancholy. Nevertheless he continued his exercises of piety and virtue, praying continually to God in words of generous resignation: "Ah, Lord! if I am never to see Thee or Thy sweet Mother in the next world, allow me at least to love You here below". This fearful trial lasted six weeks, and ended suddenly whilst he was saying the *Memorare* with great fervor before a statue of the Blessed Virgin, after he had made a vow of chastity and a promise to say the Rosary every day. From this time he redoubled his fervor and gave all his leisure time to prayer.

On December 18, 1593, Francis was ordained Priest.

When the Duke of Savoy decided to restore the Catholic Faith in the Chablais, and the Bishop of Geneva was applied to for zealous missionaries, Francis volunteered his services. He set out on foot with a Bible, a breviary and one companion, his cousin Louis of Sales. Every door and every heart was closed against him. He was insulted and threatened with death. However, after four years of strenuous labor and prayers hardly a hundred heretics remained. It is claimed that he converted 72,000 Calvinists. All the glory of this result must be attributed under God to the virtues, wisdom, preaching, sufferings and perseverance of "the Apostle of the Chablais".

St. Francis became Bishop of Geneva in 1622, and in union with St. Jane Frances of Chantal founded at Annecy the Order of the Visitation, which soon spread over Europe. A considerable part of the last years of his life were spent in preparing the Constitutions of the Order and composing the "Treatise on the Love of God".

After a life spent in good works, St. Francis died on December 28, 1622. Pope Pius IX conferred on him the rare title of Doctor of the Church.

✠

JANUARY 30

ST. BATHILDES

St. Bathildes was a native of England. As a child she was taken to France and sold as a slave, at a very small price, to Erkenwald, the Mayor of the palace under King Clovis II. As she grew older she was so prudent and virtuous that she was placed in charge of the household.

In 649 King Clovis took her for his royal consort, to the pleasure of his princes and the whole kingdom. This elevation produced no change in Queen Bathildes' humility and other virtues. In her new position she was better able to protect the Church, to care for the poor, and to further all religious undertakings. She bore the King three sons, Clotaire III, Childeric II, and Thierry I, who all sucessively wore the crown.

King Clovis died in 655 when the eldest child was only five years old, which left Queen Bathildes regent of the kingdom for eight years. She aided the Bishops in banishing simony from France, forbade Christians to be made slaves, did everything in her power to promote piety, filled France with hospitals, restored the monasteries of St. Martin, St. Denis and St. Medard; founded the great Abbey of Corbie for a seminary, and the royal convent of Chelles on the Marne.

In 665, when Clotaire was of age to govern, Queen Bathildes entered the convent of Chelles. She seemed to completely forget her worldly dignity, was most humble and obedient, and showed great devotion and charity towards the sick. St. Bathildes was afflicted with a long and severe illness, which she bore with admirable resignation and joy until her death, on January 30, 680.

✠

ST. JOHN BOSCO

From early infancy John Bosco was trained by a saintly mother in the love of God and Our Blessed Lady. Born in 1815 at Murialdo di Castelnuovo, near Turin, Italy, he was a shepherd boy until his fifteenth year, when he began his studies for the priesthood. Ordained in 1841, his first appointment was to visit the city-prisons. The young priest was shocked to find among the prisoners large numbers of boys, a great proportion of whom were orphans or neglected street urchins who had been led into evil-doing by much older companions. Don Bosco proposed to change all this and to make them useful citizens and good Christians. This he would accomplish by instructing them in spiritual matters and by teaching them a trade. He loved boys and soon they loved him.

The growth of this heaven-inspired work has been truly phenomenal. The Salesian Congregation which he founded to carry out his intentions numbers today about 15,000 Priests and Brothers, and over 10,000 Sisters of the Congregation, Mary, Help of Chistians. Some 600 oratories, as they are called, for boys, and a larger number for girls, offer proof of his zeal and of God's blessing. Since 1853, in addition to 70 agricultural schools, 900 trade schools have come into being. A first boarding school was established in 1863. At present there are more than 400 elementary schools, about 200 high schools, and 26 colleges. While much of this work has been inaugurated since Don Bosco's death, in 1888, all was carried out in accordance with his plans.

Beginnings were not easy, since many people readily complained about the noises made by the boys. This resulted in frequent changes of locations. However, Don Bosco finally secured a dilapidated shed at Valdocco, which

O God, You raised a father and teacher of youth in blessed John, Your Confessor, and willed that through him, with the help of the Virgin Mary, new religious families should flourish in Your Church. Grant, we beseech You, that enkindled by the same fire of charity, we may be able to seek souls and serve You alone.

was repaired so that he could conduct classes for his charges. A couple of rooms were set aside for his personal use and for that of his mother, who had now come from Becchi to assist him. The boys were allowed to make as much noise as they liked, with no one to object.

Don Bosco's work soon merited an unheard of reputation. When he asked the warden of the local reformatory to be allowed to take its young prisoners out for a picnic, permission was granted. Three hundred of the boys accompanied Don Bosco into the country; in the evening he led every single one back quietly to the reformatory.

The extraordinary activity of Don Bosco was based on a spirit of profound and lively faith. His hours of prayer were the time for "refilling the reservoir" with supernatural strength. The hours of work were the "time of overflow". Although his labor was upon earth, his spirit ever remained fixed in heaven!

He died in Turin in 1888. All the inhabitants of the Italian city attended his funeral. On Easter Sunday, 1934, at the closing of the Holy Year of the 19th Centennary of the Death and Resurrection of Our Lord Jesus Christ, Don Bosco was canonized by Pope Pius XI.

FEBRUARY

ST. BRIDGET OF IRELAND

In 436 a little daughter was born to an Irish lord, named Duptace, at Fochard in Ulster, and called Bridget in baptism. From her infancy Bridget showed signs of the sanctity to which God's grace was leading her. She was beloved by everyone on account of her amiability and her peaceable, obedient disposition; while a love for the poor seemed to have been born with her. In addition to these virtues she possessed a singular beauty. Her father decided to make a noble marriage for his daughter, but what was his disappointment to find that she was indifferent to all, however desirable as to riches or station or virtues!

When Bridget discovered that her beauty was the cause of so many flattering attentions, she asked God to take this beauty from her and thus put an end to the solicitations of her suitors and of her father. Her prayer was granted; and the loss of an eye, either by disease or an accident, so changed her face that those who had admired her turned away in disgust or in pity; while her father was happy to find her disposed to lead a religious life.

It was Bishop St. Mel, an early disciple of St. Patrick, who gave Bridget the veil. She founded the monastery of Kildaire, the first Religious House of women in Ireland. Many wonderful miracles were wrought by her. The Sign of the Cross seemed to be the one means by which her wonders were wrought. Marvelous was her influence for good over the nascent Church of her country.

Having lived to her eighty-seventh year, St. Bridget had a warning of her death, which took place at her first monastery, Kildaire, on February 1, 523. Her body was buried there. When the Danes invaded and burned Kildaire, St. Bridget's relics were carried to Down-Patrick, where the body of St. Patrick reposed. In 1186 Bishop Mal-

achy found them and they were solemnly transferred to the
Cathedral in his city. During the reign of Henry VIII, the
Cathedral was destroyed and the relics were cast to the
wind. The head of St. Bridget had been given to a church
in Neustadt, Austria, and thus escaped the profanation.

St. Bridget is considered the Second Patron Saint of
Ireland, and has always been held in singular reverence in
that country.

✠

FEBRUARY 2

PRESENTATION OF THE LORD

The aged Simeon, who had been assured by the Holy
Spirit "that he should not see death, before he had seen
the Christ of the Lord", prophesied: "Thy own soul a sword
shall pierce."—and Mary departed from the temple in Jerusalem a "Mother of Sorrows".

She had suffered, it is true, in sympathy with the sufferings of her Divine Son at His nativity; yet, we may well
believe that on that occasion her sorrow was greatly tempered by the emotions of happiness and gratitude. But,
from now on, she is to dread the future, and in anticipation
taste the dregs of that chalice which she will empty beneath
the cross on Golgotha's Hill, when her Son bows His head
in death.

We know that suffering is a punishment resulting from
sin. Mary, however, was the very temple of innocence.
"Thou art all fair, O my love, and there is not a spot in
thee." (Cant. 4: 7.) "Hail, full of grace!" (St. Luke 1: 28.)
Why, then, will she know, more than all other creatures,
the bitterness of affliction? Principally, for two reasons.
She had been chosen from among all men for the high
privilege of closest union with Him Who was the "Man of

Sorrows"; Who, though God and sinless, took upon Himself the appearance of sin in order that He might wash away in His Blood the flood of mankind's iniquities. Naturally, or, shall we say, necessarily His pangs would involve pangs on the part of His Mother. Can a child be afflicted and its mother remain indifferent? Again, for her there had been prepared in Heaven a reward immeasurably surpassing those of all the angels and saints, and she would purchase, in so far as a human being may purchase, this recompense by trials unequalled, except in the sufferings of the Savior. Through thirty-three years she will carry in her mind and thoughts the sword which, in opening the Sacred Side of Jesus, pierced and rent her loving soul.

This Feast, celebrated by the Church on the second day of February, the fortieth after Christmas, brings to Catholics the above thought. It is a thought which must move the heart of every child of Mary—a thought which must call forth sentiments of sympathy and love. But, should it stop there? Will the Feast, with its consecration of Mary to sufferings, teach nothing useful to members of the Church?

Sufferings are unwelcome to human nature; a statement which requires no proof. On the other hand, if proof were required, Holy Scripture proclaims (and experience agrees) that sufferings are most profitable to the souls of men. In life there are various kinds and degrees of suffering. All do, or, at least, should lead the Christian to the ultimate goal of man's existence. Man may suffer the loss of the possessions to which his heart clung; he is taught that earthly goods are unstable, and is urged to direct his efforts towards the inheritance which, alone, is permanent. He may suffer the loss of friends, he may be wounded deeply by their insincerity, their infidelity, their worthlessness; and driven (it should not be that way) to seek comfort in the friendship of Him Who cannot change and Who will not disappoint. There are bodily ills of every description that may pay an unwelcome visit to man, and there are spiritual trials under which it is most difficult to bear up with courage and resignation; yet, all these lay bare the native poverty of man and lead him to place trust with God.

Sufferings are profitable, whatever their form and whatever the source whence they spring. With Mary departing from the temple, with Mary, Mother of Sorrows, Christians will accept the trials which God sends.

✠

FEBRUARY 3

ST. BLASE

St. Blase in the early years of his life studied philosophy; later he became a physician, and in the practice of his profession witnessed so many of the miseries of life and the futility of worldly pleasures that he resolved to spend his remaining days in God's service. Thus he became a physician of souls.

Upon the death of the Bishop of Sebaste, in Armenia, St. Blase was appointed to succeed him. Many miracles were wrought in answer to his prayers.

When Emperor Licinius ordered Agricolaus, Governor of Cappadocia and Lesser Armenia, to persecute the Christians, St. Blase was seized; on his way to prison he met a distracted mother whose only child was dying of a throat disease. She threw herself at the feet of the Saint and implored his intercession. He was so touched at her grief that he offered up his prayers. The child was cured, and since that time he has been invoked in a particular manner, and often effectively, by those suffering from throat ailments.

The following extract from a sermon on St. Blase's day by a Bavarian priest makes timely reading:

"Worse and more frequent than the disease of the throat is the sin of the throat. In the mouth and in the throat there are the tongue, the palate, the windpipe, the voice and language. The throat is the vehicle for eating, drinking, speaking, laughing and singing. Now, who among you has no need of St. Blase's blessing? The throat is a great evil-doer and a sinner against the holy Commandments of God. It is a drunkard like a heathen; it squanders in feasting the bread of wife and children and ruins house and home; it is the murderer of good names, a calumniator mocking God and the saints. It causes drunkenness and all that follows; it laughs to scorn; it makes a sport of virtue and praises vice; it indulges in unbecoming jokes; it lies in speech, in business, in affirmations; it murmurs against the Almighty; it enkindles war in the household and amongst the members of the family; it brings about deadly lawsuits and enmities; it dishonors Friday, the day of the suffering Savior, by frivolously eating meat; in the circle of bad companions it uses bad language and sings songs that dishonor the Christian. This and more the throat does. In truth it is necessary that on St. Blase's day it be scolded and rebuked, and then, blessed and made holy.

"Before you come to lay your throats between the crossed candles you should recognize your sins of the throat and resolve to get rid of them. Your fellowmen and God, the Omniscient, know them. The merciful God, after the prayer of St. Blase's blessing has been offered, will stretch forth His hand. St. Blase, the friend of God, will speak a good word for you in Heaven and is encouraging you with his good example on earth. It depends only on you that you make an effort in self-denial."

☩

FEBRUARY 4

ST. JANE OF VALOIS

St. Jane, daughter of King Louis XI and Charlotte of Savoy, was born in 1464. The King had hoped for a son to succeed him, and was doubly disappointed at Jane's birth because of her deformed body and low stature. Consequently, when the child was five years of age she was banished from the palace. Patiently she suffered the humiliations heaped upon her. At that early age Jane offered her heart to God and longed to honor the Blessed Virgin in some special way.

At the age of twelve, in 1476, notwithstanding her bodily defects, her father married her against her desire to Louis, Duke of Orleans. In 1498 Louis ascended the throne as Louis XII, and shortly thereafter, by false representations, accomplished a separation from his queen. The Queen, who had been a true and loyal wife for twenty-two years, acquiesced in the sentence, exclaiming: "God be praised Who has allowed this, that I may serve Him better than I have heretofore done".

The King, pleased at her submission, gave her the duchy of Berry, Pontoise and other townships. Retiring to Bourges, St. Jane led a life of mortification and prayer, devoting her great revenues to works of charity. In 1500, under the direction of her spiritual adviser, a holy Franciscan Friar, St. Jane founded the Order of Nuns of the Annunciation of the Blessed Virgin.

St. Jane built and endowed the first convent of the Order in 1502. She died in the odor of sanctity in 1505. The Hugenots burned her remains at Bourges in 1562. She was canonized by Pope Clement XII in 1738.

✠

FEBRUARY 5

ST. AGATHA

It was in the year 251 under the persecution of Decius that St. Agatha received the crown of martyrdom at Catania, Sicily. Born of a rich, illustrious family, Agatha consecrated her heart to God from early youth, and she died for love of chastity.

Quintianus, who then governed Sicily, had heard of Agatha's beauty and wealth and took advantage of the laws against the Christians to summon her from Palermo to Catania in order to gratify his sinful desires. Agatha wept and prayed for courage and strength during her journey. When she appeared before Quintianus he ordered her to be placed for a whole month in the hands of a most wicked woman. Agatha's trust in God was not in vain, for He preserved her from all the assaults and stratagems against her purity. Quintianus upon learning of the child's constancy, at the end of that period ordered her to be brought before him. The judge, offended by Agatha's firm answers, commanded that she be whipped and led to prison. Joyously she entered it, recommending her future to God. The following day she was brought again before the tribunal. Because of her firm determination not to commit sin, Quintianus then ordered her to be stretched on the rack. Seeing the holy virgin suffering all cheerfully, he commanded that her breasts be cut off. She was again imprisoned, where she was to be deprived of medication and food. But God Himself was to be her physician. St. Peter in a vision comforted Agatha and healed her wounds. Four days later Quintianus, unmoved by the miraculous cure, caused Agatha to be rolled naked over live coals mixed with broken potsherds. Carried back to prison St. Agatha prayed: "Lord, my Creator, You have protected me from the cradle. You have taken from me the love of the world and given me patience to suffer; receive now my soul". After which words she peacefully surrendered her soul to God.

During eruptions of Mount Etna the veil of St. Agatha was carried in procession and the city of Catania was frequently saved from destruction. Through her intercession the island of Malta, of which she is the patroness, was preserved from the Turks, who invaded it in 1551.

✠

ST. DOROTHY

St. Dorothy, a young and beautiful girl in the city of Caesarea, in Asia Minor, suffered most cruel torments during the persecution of Diocletian because she refused to marry a pagan or to sacrifice to the idols. She converted her two sisters who out of fear had been sent to weaken her in Christianity. The result was just the opposite; Dorothy converted them; both of whom later suffered martyrdom. In consequence of which Dorothy was tortured and condemned to be beheaded. Her body is venerated in the church which bears her name, beyond the Tiber, in Rome.

✠

ST. ROMUALD

St. Romuald was born about the year 956 at Ravenna, of the ducal family called the Onesti. At the age of twenty he witnessed his father, Sergius, fight a duel with a relative to settle a dispute. Romuald was threatened with disinheritance if he refused to be present. Sergius slew his adversary, and Romuald was struck with such horror at his father's crime that he felt obliged to do forty days' penance in the Benedictine monastery at Classe, near Ravenna. So profoundly impressed was he by the good example he witnessed, that he asked to be admitted as a penitent in the Order. His request was granted, and after spending seven fervent, austere years in the monastery he went to live as a hermit near Venice.

Peter Orseolo I, Doge of Venice, soon joined him and together they led a most austere life. Many others sought

Grant, we beseech You, O Lord, that Your blessed Virgin and Martyr, St. Dorothy, who was ever pleasing to You by the merit of her chastity and her confession of Your power, may obtain for us Your pardon. Through Christ our Lord.

permission to follow their way of life, and Romuald was made their Superior. The devil sought in every way to tempt him. Finally Romuald cried out: "Sweetest Jesus, dearest Jesus, why hast Thou forsaken me? Hast Thou entirely delivered me over to my enemies?" At the use of that holy Name the wicked spirits took flight. Such an excess of divine sweetness and compunction filled the breast of Romuald that he shed tears of joy.

He founded many monasteries, the best known being that at Camaldoli, near Arezzo in Tuscany, thirty miles east of Florence. Here, the monastery was surrounded with a number of separate cells for the solitaires who lived under his Rule. For a stricter solitude St. Romuald added the life of a recluse, which he followed for several years. He died on June 19, in his monastery in the valley of Castro. Five years after his death, about 1030, his body was found incorrupt; as again in 1466. February 7th is the anniversary of the translation of his body to Fabriano in 1481. God has honored his relics with many miracles.

☩

ST. JOHN OF MATHA

St. John was born at Faucon, near Provence, France, on June 24, 1169, of pious and noble parents. By vow, his mother dedicated him to God as an infant.

From early youth John was most charitable to the poor, sharing with them his expense money. Every Friday he visited them in the hospital, and did everything possible to relieve their sufferings and to comfort them.

His studies were completed successfully in Paris, where he was ordained to the priesthood. On the day he said his first Mass he was inspired by God to devote himself to ransoming Christian slaves from the Mohammedans. He placed himself under the direction of St. Felix Valois, a holy hermit in the Diocese of Meaux. Convinced that his desire was from God, St. Felix encouraged St. John to carry it into execution. After spending some time in prayer and fasting they went to Rome, in 1197, to consult Pope Innocent III. His Holiness received them graciously, and after deliberating about the matter consented to their erecting a new Religious Order, to be called the Holy Trinity (or Trinitarians) for the Ransoming of Captives, and declared St. John the first Superior.

St. John's work was blessed by God, as many slaves were liberated. On his second return voyage from Tunis, in 1210, with one hundred and twenty slaves he had ransomed, the infidels, enraged at St. John's zeal and success, removed the helm from the vessel and tore the sails, so that all on board might perish at sea. St. John implored God to be their pilot, and hung up his companions' cloaks as sails. With a crucifix in his hands, John knelt on the deck and prayed for a safe voyage. The wind arose and carried the vessel safely to Ostia, the port of Rome, three hundred leagues from Tunis. Two years later, in 1213, St. John died in Rome at the age of sixty-one.

✠

ST. APOLLONIA
AND THE MARTYRS OF ALEXANDRIA

During the reign of Decius many Alexandrians in Egypt met martyrdom for their Christian Faith at the hands of the heathens. Among these was the aged virgin Apollonia. They struck her on the jaws until all her teeth came out; then they made a great fire and threatened to throw her into it if she refused to blaspheme God. Begging a moment's delay, she, under the inspiration of the Holy Spirit, "of her own accord leaped into the flames".

Metras, an old man, had his eyes pierced with reeds, and then was stoned to death. A woman, by the name of Quinta, was the next victim. She was led to a heathen temple and ordered to worship. After cursing the false god again and again, she was stoned to death. The homes of all the Christians were then sacked and plundered. They rejoiced at being able to suffer for Christ's sake.

A civil war among the pagan citizenry put an end to the fury for a while, but the edict of Decius, in 250, renewed the persecution, which filled the city with dread and terror. There were some who lacked the courage to remain steadfast; but many suffered willingly for their faith in Jesus.

✠

ST. SCHOLASTICA

St. Scholastica was the sister of St. Benedict. St. Gregory testifies that she consecrated herself to God from early youth. After her brother moved to Monte Cassino she chose a site five miles lower down on the mountain for a convent for the Sisters under her guidance. Once a year she visited St. Benedict in his monastery. They spent their time together praising God and conferring on spiritual matters.

On the occasion of St. Benedict's last visit to his sister, she urged him to remain until the following day. Unwilling to transgress his Rule, St. Benedict told her he could not pass a night away from his monastery. Realizing that he was resolved to leave, Scholastica begged God to intervene in her behalf. Scarcely had she ended her prayer when a violent storm arose, which prevented St. Benedict and his companions from leaving. He complained to his sister, saying: "God forgive you, sister. What have you done?" She replied: "I asked you a favor and you refused it; I asked it of Almighty God and He has granted it to me". St. Benedict was therefore obliged to comply with her request. They conversed on holy subjects; especially on the happiness of the blessed, to which both ardently aspired, and which Scholastica was soon to enjoy. Three days later as St. Benedict was alone in contemplation on Monte Cassino, as he raised his eyes heavenwards he saw the soul of his sister ascending thither in the shape of a dove.

Filled with joy at her happy passage, St. Benedict informed his brethren of her death and sent some of them to bring her remains to his monastery, which he laid in the tomb that he had prepared for himself.

St. Scholastica died about the year 543.

✠

FEBRUARY 11

OUR LADY OF LOURDES

It was on February 11, 1858, that the first of the eighteen apparitions of the Blessed Virgin Mary to Bernadette Soubirous took place at Lourdes, a small town in the South of France, situated amidst the Pyrenees mountains on the banks of the river Gave. At some distance to the West, and along the bank of this stream, is a wall of high rocks called Massabielle. Hollowed out of rocks by nature, and facing the river is a Grotto about twelve feet in depth and of considerable height. Just on the arch of this Grotto, to the right hand, is a natural niche not very deep. This niche, now marked by a statue of Our Lady, was the scene of the celebrated apparitions.

The Beautiful Lady was dressed in white with a light blue girdle; a white veil covered her head and fell over her shoulders to the ground; her feet seemed to rest on the rose-tree in the Grotto, and their only covering was two large golden roses. Her hands were joined before her breast, and on her right arm hung a Rosary—the beads of

which seemed like drops of milk, whilst the chain and cross
shone like gold. She carried the Rosary in all the eighteen
apparitions. In the earlier ones she was seen to pass the
beads one by one through her fingers, as though designating the means by which she would have praise and petition
offered to God.

On March 25th, the Feast of the Annunciation, when
Bernadette asked the Beautiful Lady her name, she replied:
"I am the Immaculate Conception", and vanished.

An imposing grand Basilica, known as the Church of
the Rosary, now stands on top of the rock above the Grotto
where the apparitions took place. It replaced the one
erected in 1871. Countless spiritual and bodily miracles
have occurred at this wonderful Grotto.

Our Lady of Lourdes' interecession is sought by the
sick and infirm throughout the world.

✠

FEBRUARY 12

ST. BENEDICT OF ANIAN

St. Benedict, born about the year 750, was the son of
Aigulf, Governor of Languedoc. He enjoyed great honors
and possessions while serving as cupbearer to King Pepin
and his son Charlemagne. He soon realized the vanity of
perishable goods, and at the age of twenty resolved to seek
the kingdom of God. He continued in his Court position
three years longer, leading a mortified life. In 774, narrowly
escaping death by drowning in an effort to save his brother,
Benedict made a vow to leave the world. Encouraged by a
holy hermit, he became a Monk in the Benedictine abbey of
St. Seine, near Dijon. God rewarded his austere, prayerful,
monastic life by bestowing upon him great compunction of
spirit, the gift of tears, and a high degree of infused knowledge of spiritual things.

After being made procurator he was most solicitous of the needs of his brethren, of guests, and of the poor. Upon the death of the Abbot in 780, Benedict declined to accept the vacancy and returned to his own country, Languedoc, where he built himself a small hermitage on the brook Anian, upon his own estate. Here he lived for some years in extreme poverty, praying continually to God to teach him to do His Will. His sanctity attracted other solitaires to place themselves under his direction, and in a short time he governed three hundred Religious. He also supervised all the monasteries of Provence, Languedoc and Gascony.

St. Benedict employed his pen to refute the heresy of Bishop Felix of Urgel, and he became the spiritual spokesman for the entire kingdom. The Emperor ordered him to undertake to restore monastic discipline in French and German abbeys. With the assistance of the Emperor, St. Benedict founded the abbey of Cornelimunster, near Aix-la-Chapelle, as a model abbey, and he was the chief instrument in drawing up the code of Rules of St. Benedict, his great namesake, whereby harmony with the Rules of the chief monastic founders was accomplished.

At a meeting of all the Abbots of the empire at Aix-la-Chapelle in 813, at which St. Benedict of Anian was present, it was ordered that all Monks of the West should adopt his Rule. He has therefore been called "the second founder of the Benedictines". This great restorer of the monastic life in the West died in 821, being then about seventy-one years of age.

☩

FEBRUARY 13

ST. CATHERINE OF RICCI

Alexandrina, of the ancient Ricci family, was born at Florence in 1522. At her religious profession as a Third Order Dominican, in 1535 in the monastery at Prato, she took the name Catherine. When still quite young she was chosen to be Novice Mistress, then sub-Prioress and at the age of twenty-five she was appointed perpetual Prioress.

The reputation of her extraordinary sanctity caused many dignitaries of the Church to visit her. Her special devotion was to meditate daily on the Passion of Christ, and Jesus permitted her to miraculously participate in His sufferings every week from Thursday noon to 3 p. m. on Friday.

It is related that St. Catherine conversed with St. Philip Neri in Rome without having left her convent at Prato. Three future Popes—Marcellus II, Clement VIII, and Leo XI—were among the thousands who sought her prayers.

After a long illness St. Catherine passed from this mortal life to everlasting bliss on February 2, 1589, at the age of sixty-seven. She was canonized by Pope Benedict XIV in 1746.

✠

FEBRUARY 14

ST. VALENTINE

In the early martyrologies there are three different St. Valentines mentioned under date of February 14. One was a holy Priest of Rome who was martyred under the Emperor Aurelian in 270; another was Bishop of Interamna (modern Terni), who also suffered in the scond half of the 3rd century, and was buried on the Flaminian Way. Of the third St. Valentine, who suffered in Africa with a number of companions, nothing further is known.

The popular customs of celebrating St. Valentines Day no doubt had their origin in a conventional belief generally accepted in England and France during the Middle Ages, that on February 14, that is, half way through the second month of the year, the birds begin to pair. For this reason the day was considered as specially consecrated to lovers

and as a favorable time for writing love letters and sending lover's gifts. French and English literature of the 14th
and 15th centuries contain allusions to the practice.

✠

FEBRUARY 15

STS. FAUSTINUS AND JOVITA

Faustinus and Jovita were brothers, of noble parentage. During the persecution of the Christians in Lombardy
under the Emperor Hadrian, while the Bishop was being
concealed Faustinus and Jovita fearlessly preached the
Christian Faith. Their unbounded zeal excited the fury
of the heathens, which obtained for them the palm of
martyrdom at Brescia. Neither threats nor torments were
able to shake their constancy after being arrested by
Julian, a heathen lord. When the Emperor passed through
Brescia and learned of their loyalty to Christ, he commanded that the two brothers be beheaded.

Thus they suffered martyrdom about the year 121.
The city of Brescia honors them as its chief Patrons,
possesses their relics, whilst a very ancient church in that
city bears their names.

✠

FEBRUARY 16

ST. JULIANA

St. Juliana was a native of Cumae in Campania, and
suffered martyrdom for the Faith during the Diocletian
persecution. Early in the 13th century her remains were
translated to Naples. Her Acts describe the conflicts which
she is said to have had with the devil. She is represented
in pictures with a winged devil whom she leads by a chain.

✠

FEBRUARY 17

ST. FLAVIAN

St. Flavian was Bishop of Constantinople. The date of his birth is unknown, but his death occurred in Lydia in August, 449. He was elected Patriarch of Constantinople in 447, and his short episcopate was one of conflict and persecution from the beginning. The Emperor's favorite, Chrysaphius, endeavored to extort a large sum of money from Flavian on the occasion of his consecration. By rejecting the demand, Flavian aroused the enmity of the most powerful man in the empire.

In 448, at a Council of Bishops convened at Constantinople by Flavian, he condemned the rising heresy of Eutyches, a Monk, who obstinately denied that in Jesus were two perfect natures. Finally Flavian pronounced the sentence of degredation and excommunication. Pope Leo I approved Flavian's decision.

A long-standing rivalry between Alexandria and Constantinople now became a factor in the dissensions of the condemned heresy. For Dioscurus, Bishop of Alexandria, was willing to join forces with Eutyches; and, without Papal jurisdiction they sent forth a call for an Ecumenical Council to be held under the presidency of Dioscurus, and at Ephesus. In consequence, Dioscurus and the heretics controlled the simulated Council. Flavian and the six Bishops who had assisted in the previous synod were allowed no voice. They were declared to be on trial. Despite the protest of Hilary, the Papal legate (later Pope), Flavian was condemned and deposed. In the violent scenes which followed, Flavian died in his place of exile three days later.

Pope Leo I repeatedly vindicated St. Flavian, but his letter of vindication and commendation did not reach the saint before he died.

✠

ST. BERNADETTE

Bernadette Soubirous was the eldest child of her poor parents, Francois Soubirous and Louise Casterot, of Lourdes, France. Her father had been a miller, but straitened circumstances necessitated his earning bread for his family as a day laborer.

Bernadette, who was a small, delicate child—a martyr to asthma all her life—had been placed while very young as a nurse in a neighboring village. When older, she had charge of a flock of sheep. Early in 1858, at the age of fourteen, she returned to her father's house. She had had no schooling and had not yet made her First Communion, but she had already impressed others with her love of prayer, her innocence, and her hatred of sin.

On Thursday, February 11, 1858, she was sent by her mother, together with her younger sister and a companion, to gather for their fire pieces of wood that had floated down the Gave and had drifted upon the shore just under the Grotto of Massabielle. The two other girls had crossed the little stream, and Bernadette was removing her stockings to follow them when she heard a sound as of a rushing wind. Looking up to the Grotto she noticed that while the leaves of other trees were motionless, the wild rose-tree in the niche was being gently shaken. Instantly, around the niche, an oval ring of brilliant light appeared, and within the niche she saw a Lady of unspeakable beauty, dressed in white with a light blue girdle. She smiled, as if to encourage the child, made a large sign of the cross upon herself with the cross of the Rosary she held, and began to pass the beads through her fingers. Bernadette fell on her knees, took out her Rosary and made a big sign of the cross as the Lady had done, and said her beads.

Our Lady appeared on seventeen other occasions and entered into conversation with Bernadette. On February 18th she said: "I promise to make you happy, if not in this world, at least in the next. Pray for poor sinners" (Feb. 21st). "Penance! Penance!" (Feb. 24th.) "Go and tell the Priests that a chapel should be built here" (Feb. 27th). "I am the Immaculate Conception" (March 25th).

Bernadette suffered much from the opposition of her family, the civil authorities and even the clergy, who refused to believe her regarding the apparitions until the month of October. The Bishop of Tarbes appointed a Commission of ecclesiastics and medical men of long experience to inquire into the reality and nature of the apparitions and miracles that had occurred at Lourdes. Their labors lasted nearly three years. Before the report of the Commission was approved by the Bishop, the fame of Lourdes had spread through Christendom, and the place of pilgrimage was firmly established.

Bernadette made her First Communion before the last apparition, on June 3, Feast of Corpus Christi, and she commenced to go to school, and continued to do so for some years. In 1860 the Sisters of Charity, who had charge of the Hospice at Lourdes, offered her a place in their convent, where she performed light duties. In July, 1866, Bernadette left for Nevers to commence her novitiate at the motherhouse of the Sisters of Nevers. There she remained until her death. "Every day", she said, "I go in spirit to the dear Grotto, and make my pilgrimage there."

Before entering the convent she had had the consolation of witnessing the installation of the statue of the Blessed Virgin and the blessing of the crypt. On September 22, 1878, she made her perpetual vows, and in December of that year she had to appear before the representatives of the Bishops of Tarbes and Nevers, and renew the depositions she had made twenty years before regarding the apparitions at the Grotto.

She was frequently humiliated and at times persecuted by her superiors, but she suffered all courageously and

even sought to be despised. She always defended the truth
of the apparitions. The asthma, her life-long cross, recurred
with frequent crises; a large tumor formed on her knee, and
caries was wasting her bones.

It was on April 16, 1878, Wednesday in Easter week,
that Bernadette's long martyrdom came to an end as she
prayed: "Holy Mary, Mother of God, pray for me, poor
sinner, poor sinner". She was canonized by Pope Pius XI
on December 8, 1933. From the hallowed little Grotto in

Southern France, faith and devotion to St. Bernadette have come into the hearts of Catholics everywhere in the world.

✠

FEBRUARY 19

ST. BARBATUS

St. Barbatus was born in the beginning of the 7th century during the Pontificate of St. Gregory the Great, in the vicinity of Benevento, Italy. He was given a Christian education, and made extraordinary progress in all virtues. As soon as the Canons of the Church permitted it, Barbatus was ordained to the priesthood. After some time he was made pastor of St. Basil's church in Morcona, near Benevento. The parishioners objected to his efforts to reform their lives and to awaken them to repentance. They treated him as a disturber of the peace and violently persecuted him. Seeing their malice conquered by his patience and humility, they had recourse to slanders. So successful was their hatred, Barbatus was obliged to return to Benevento, where he was received with joy by those who were acquainted with his innocence and sanctity.

In 545 Totila, the Goth, laid the city of Benevento in ruins. Then for several ages it was ruled by the Lombards, who were chiefly Arians, among whom were many idolaters. When St. Barbatus commenced his ministry in that city, he found that the Christian converts from Arianism had retained many idolatrous superstitions. He preached zealously against these abuses, without results. Joining his exhortations with fervent prayer and rigorous fasting, he finally aroused their attention by foretelling the calamities that would befall their city from the army of Emperor Constans, which soon thereafter landed in Italy and laid siege to Benevento. Ildebrand, Bishop of Benevento, died during the siege. After peace was restored, St. Barbatus was consecrated Bishop on March 10, 653. He continued the good work he had commenced and succeeded in destroying every trace of superstition in the entire country.

In 680 St. Barbatus assisted at a Council held by Pope Agatho in Rome; the following year at the 6th general Council held in Constantinople, at which the Monothelites were condemned. St. Barbatus died soon thereafter, on February 29, 682, at about the age of seventy years.

☨

FEBRUARY 20

ST. EUCHERIUS

St. Eucherius was born at Orleans, France. Daily his holy mother had offered her child to God, and at his birth dedicated him to His service. Everything possible was done to give the child a good education and to train him to be a virtuous man.

About the year 714 Eucherius entered the Benedictine Abbey of Jumiege, in the Diocese of Rouen, where he spent seven years leading an austere, prayerful life. His uncle was Bishop of Orleans. Upon the death of the latter, in 721, Eucherius was chosen to fill the vacancy.

Charles Martel, who was Mayor of the palace, in order to defray the expenses of his wars and undertakings, often stripped the churches of their revenues, and encouraged others to do likewise. Because Bishop Eucherius opposed his confiscation and distribution of ecclesiastical property, Charles Martel upon his return to Paris in 737, after having defeated the Saracens in Aquitaine and captured Orleans, banished the Bishop to Cologne. His popularity there caused Martel to send him, under guard, to Liege. The Governor was so pleased with his virtue that he made Eucherius the distributer of his large alms, and allowed him to retire to the monastery of St. Trond. Here, all his time was spent in prayer and contemplation until his death on February 20, 743.

FEBRUARY 21

ST. SEVERIANUS

Severianus, Bishop of Scythopolis, resisted with great courage the Eutychian heresies during the reign of Marcian and St. Pulcheria. The Council of Chalcedon condemned these heretical teachings, which had been accepted by many of the Monks of Palestine. Theodosius, an ignorant Eutychian Monk, with a tyrannical temper, under the protection of the Empress Eudoxia, widow of Theodosius the Younger, who lived at Jerusalem, perverted many of the Monks.

After obliging Bishop Juvenal of Jerusalem to withdraw from his See, Theodosius unjustly usurped that important See; raised a cruel persecution, which filled Jerusalem with blood; and then at the head of a band of soldiers carried desolation over the country. Many courageously defended the Faith. No one, however, resisted him with greater zeal and resoluteness than St. Severianus, whose recompense was martyrdom. It was in the latter part of the year 452, or the early part of 453, that the soldiers seized him, dragged him out of the city, and massacred him.

☩

FEBRUARY 22

ST. MARGARET OF CORTONA

This glorious Saint, who was destined by God to draw numberless souls from an evil life to a life of grace, was born in 1247 at Laviano, a hamlet about twelve miles from Cortona, Italy. When seven or eight years old, Margaret's saintly mother died. In time her father remarried, and Margaret was treated harshly by her stepmother. Everyone sympathized with the beautiful girl of sixteen.

About this time a young nobleman from Montepulciano came to reside at the country home of his family,

Hear us, O God, our Savior, so that, while we are gladdened by the memory of blessed Margaret of Cortona, we may learn the affection of a loving devotion. Through Christ our Lord.

not far from Laviano. Hearing of Margaret, he decided to become acquainted with her. Riding to Laviano one day he saw the maiden and was struck by her charming beauty. He continued to visit Laviano, and, shortly, began to lay his net to ensnare her—professing that he loved her. She was invited to the palace at Montepulciano, which she was asked to share with him. Rich dresses and jewels he would give her if she consented to leave the path of virtue. Margaret unhappy with her home life, and desiring to exchange ill-treatment for affection, a poor cottage for a grand house, splendid attire for an humble garb, yielded to the enticements of the young nobleman, and took up abode at his palace.

For a while Margaret, flattered by the attentions she received, felt a joy to which she had been a stranger since her mother's death. However, she was not truly happy; deep down in her heart and soul she realized that her life was one of sin. And though her conscience reproached and stung her, she lacked the courage to break the bonds which had enchained her. God's time, however, was near, when not only His justice would be felt but His mercy, also, shown.

A dispute having arisen over the boundaries of the property of the palace where Margaret was residing, the young nobleman went out to endeavor to settle the disputed claim. He met those who denied his right; a quarrel ensued, and the young man was killed. After several days' absence his faithful dog returned home and led Margaret to the place where her lover had been buried beneath some leaves in the woods. As she gazed upon the corpse before her, the eyes of her soul were opened by God's grace to see that his soul had passed to the judgment seat of God, and what would be her portion unless she repented. She who had fallen to the ground a sinner, arose a penitent.

Margaret returned to the palace a changed woman, and whilst grieving over what she had reason to fear must be the sad state of her lover, she grieved more over her own sins. She determined henceforth to do all in her power to blot them out by prayer and penances. Laying aside the rich robes, she clothed herself in the garb of a penitent, disposed of all the wealth that had been lavished upon her, and then sought a shelter for herself.

Upon reaching Cortona she made a general confession and placed herself under the direction of the Friars Minor. The remainder of her life was devoted to prayer, mortifications, and good works. In order to give herself more completely to God, she retired to a desert place on the hill above Cortona, where she spent the last nine years of her life. As the morning of February 22, 1297, dawned, the soul of Margaret passed into the unveiled presence of God to receive the reward which she had so earnestly striven to gain by her life of penance.

✠

FEBRUARY 23

ST. PETER DAMIAN

St. Peter was born at Ravenna, Italy, in 1007, the youngest of a large family. He was left an orphan when quite young, and his eldest brother, in whose care he was placed, treated him so cruelly that their brother Damian, who was a Priest at Ravenna, had pity on the child and took him to be educated. It has been said that Peter added the name Damian to his own out of gratitude to his brother's kindness.

He made rapid progress in his studies at Ravenna, Faenza, and at the University of Parma, sanctifying his studies by vigils, fasts and prayers. When about twenty-five years old he had already become a renowned teacher at Parma and Ravenna. Displeased with the scandals and distractions of university life, he resolved (about 1035) to leave the world. After a forty days' retreat he took leave of his friends secretly and joined the Monks at Font-Avellano. In 1043 he was made Superior, which office he held until his death in 1072. As his sanctity and wisdom were remarkable, he was engaged on many delicate and difficult missions, including the reform of ecclesiastical communities, which he achieved by his zeal.

St. Peter Damian served as adviser to seven Popes. On November 30, 1057, against his protestations, Pope Stephen IX consecrated him Cardinal-Bishop of Ostia, and also appointed him administrator of the Diocese of Gubbio. He deterred Henry IV, King of Germany, from an unjust divorce of his wife, and labored in defense of Alexander II against the Antipope Benedict X, whom he forced to yield and ask for pardon.

In 1059 Peter was sent as Legate to Milan by Pope Nicholas II, charged with repressing simony. Later he was commissioned to settle discords among various Bishops, and in 1072 to reconcile the inhabitants of Ravenna to the Holy See. On his homeward journey he was seized with fever near Faenza, and after a week's illness at one of the monasteries of his Order, Santa Maria degl'Angeli, now Santa Maria Vecchia, he died as the Monks finished chanting Lauds around his bed.

In 1823 Pope Leo XII pronounced St. Peter Damian a Doctor of the Church, and extended his feast to the whole Church.

✠

FEBRUARY 24

ST. MATTHIAS, APOSTLE

St. Clement of Alexandria assures us that St. Matthias was one of the seventy-two disciples of Jesus. This is also confirmed by Eusebius and St. Jerome. From the Acts of the Apostles we learn that Matthias was a constant follower of the Savior from the time of His baptism by St. John until His Ascension; that during the assembly of the faithful held soon after the Ascension St. Peter declared the necessity of choosing an Apostle to succeed Judas Iscariot. The two chosen as most worthy of the dignity were Joseph, called Barsabas, surnamed the Just because of his extraordinary piety, and Matthias. After praying to God to show which of the two He had chosen, they cast lots, and the lot fell upon Matthias. He was immediately associated with the Eleven, and ranked among the Apostles. (Acts 1:21-26).

✠

FEBRUARY 25

ST. TARASIUS

St. Tarasius was born of a noble family about the middle of the 8th century in Constantinople. His father, George, was a judge, esteemed for his justice, while his mother, Eucratia, was noted for her piety. She brought up her son to practice the most eminent virtues. He was esteemed by all, and was raised to the greatest honors of the empire. After being made Consul, he was appointed First Secretary of State to Emperor Constantine VI and his mother, Empress Irene. In the midst of his courtly life, Tarasius lived like a religious man.

Upon the death of Paul, Patriarch of Constantinople, the third of that name, Tarasius, though a layman, was chosen to succeed him by the unanimous consent of the Court, clergy and people. He accepted on condition that a general Council be convened to end the disputes which divided the Church at that time in regard to holy images. This being agreed to, he was solemnly declared Patriarch and consecrated on Christmas day.

On August 1, 786, the Council was opened at Constantinople, but due to the violent disturbances of the Iconoclasts it adjourned; it met again the following year in the Church of St. Sophia at Nicaea, and its decrees were approved by Pope Adrian. Pursuant to the decrees of the Council, the Patriarch restored holy images throughout the extent of his jurisdiction. He also labored zealously to abolish the practice of simony.

Tarasius persistently refused to marry the Emperor Constantine to Theodota, a maid of honor to his wife, with whom the Emperor had become enamored. He endeavored in every way possible to get the Patriarch to consent to his desire to divorce the Empress Mary in order to marry Theodota, but without success. Because of his refusal to countenance the bigamous marriage, Tarasius was persecuted in many ways during the remainder of the Emperor's reign. St. Tarasius died February 25, 806, after serving as Patriarch twenty-one years and two months.

✠

FEBRUARY 26

ST. PORPHYRY

St. Porphyry, son of a noble, wealthy family of Thessalonica, at the age of twenty-five left his family and friends and went to Egypt, where he consecrated himself to God in one of the renowned religious houses in the Scete desert. After spending five years there in penitential exercises, he went to visit the holy places in Jerusalem. Then he took up his abode in a cave near the Jordan, where he spent five more years performing such severe penance that his health failed and he was obliged to return to Jerusalem to reside. Despite his weakness he visited daily the places that had been sanctified by Our Lord's presence.

Inspired by God, Porphyry sold all his possessions and distributed the money to the poor. In reward for the sacrifice, God miraculously restored his health. In 393, at the age of forty, Porphyry was ordained a Priest by the Bishop of Jerusalem, and entrusted with the care of the relics of the true Cross. He continued to live an austere, penitential life, and in 396, against his wishes, was consecrated Bishop of Gaza. By his zealous labors and the miracles he performed he succeeded in uprooting the pagan practices and converting many of the inhabitants to Christianity.

The heathens seeing their number decrease, began persecuting the Christians. St. Porphyry appealed to the Emperor for protection, and after sending Mark, his disciple, to Constantinople, went himself with John, the Metropolitan, Archbishop of Caesarea. Through the help of St. John Chrysostom they obtained the aid of the Empress, and an Imperial edict enabled the Christians to destroy the pagan temples. Over the site of the most renowned one St. Porphyry erected a Christian church.

Though the holy Bishop lived to see most of the remains of paganism wiped out, he had always much to suffer from those who continued obstinate in their errors. St. Porphyry died February 26, 420, when about sixty years of age.

✠

FEBRUARY 27

ST. GABRIEL
OF OUR LADY OF SORROWS

St. Gabriel was born at Assisi on March 1, 1838. He received the name Francis at Baptism. His father was a talented, pious lawyer, who had been appointed Governor of Umbria when only twenty-two years old, and in 1842 was nominated Grand Assessor of Spoleto; his mother belonged to a most noble family. As she died when Gabriel was only four years old, his father procured a governess and then a tutor for him and the other eight children. In 1849 Francis followed his brothers to the Jesuit College at Spoleto. He assisted at Mass daily. The struggle of some years' standing was going on in his heart, and although not yet courageous enough to embrace it, a decided vocation to the religious life more and more revealed itself.

The first sign came under the form of a grievous sickness, which brought him to death's door. He had recourse to God through Our Lady's intercession, promising that if she obtained his cure he would spend the rest of his life in a religious Order. He recovered rapidly, and enjoyed greater strength and health than before, but his cure led to nothing definite. Then God afflicted him a second time. Thinking that he was about to die, he recalled a picture of the Jesuit Martyr, Andrew Bobola, which had been given to him, and implored God through the merits of His servant to save his life, at the same time renewing his promise to become a Religious. The following morning he awoke cured, and not long after presented himself to the Father Provincial of the Jesuits and asked to be received into the Society. His request was granted, but from day to day Francis deferred the fulfillment of his promise.

It is not known how his vocation shaped itself into the form of the Passionist life, which was abhorrent to his delicate nature. He submitted his difficulty to his director, a Father Tedeschini, S. J., who advised him to wait and pray.

In May, 1855, cholera broke out in Spoleto. In the Cathedral of that city is an ancient picture of the Mother of Jesus, which had been presented to the city by Emperor Frederick Barbarossa. During the epidemic the Catholics had recourse to the Mother of Mercy and solemnly carried the sacred picture to the loggia in front of the Cathedral. From that moment the pestilence ceased. On the Feast of the Assumption a solemn service of thanksgiving was held, in which the picture was carried. Francis was present, and as the procession was drawing near, he raised his eyes, and, from her picture, Mary cast upon him a glance which penetrated his heart, and he heard a distinct interior voice which said to him: "What art thou doing in the world? Hasten to become a Religious!" Francis remained kneeling, his heart filled with interior peace. The victory was won.

After opening his heart to his confessor, Francis made formal application to the Provincial of the Passionists. On September 10, 1856, when only eighteen years old, Francis entered the Passionist monastery and took the name of

Confrater Gabriel of the Sorrowful Virgin. For the first four years of his religious vocation Gabriel enjoyed apparently good health, but during the fifth year he began to feel an ever-increasing weakness, with unmistakable signs of tuberculosis. In spite of all the care bestowed upon him, his illness increased, reducing him to a pitiable state of weakness. On the morning of February 27th, uncovering his breast, Gabriel placed a picture of Our Lady of Sorrows over his heart and, crossing his hands, embraced the picture with such earnestness that no one present remained unmoved. Then raising his eyes to heaven with a look of joyful expectancy, he cried out: "O my Mother, make haste!" Peacefully he rendered his soul to God, at the age of twenty-four, having attained a heroic degree of sanctity by a life of self-denial and charity.

Many miracles occurred at his tomb at Isola, Italy. St. Gabriel was canonized by Pope Benedict XV in 1920.

✠

FEBRUARY 28

STS. ROMANUS AND LUPICINUS

St. Romanus, Abbott of Condat, was born about the year 400. At the age of thirty-five he went to live as a hermit in the lonely region of Condat, and after some time his younger brother, Lupicinus, joined him. Many scholars, among whom was St. Eugendus, placed themselves under the direction of these two holy brothers who founded several monasteries.

Romanus was ordained Priest by St. Hilary of Arles in 444, and with Lupicinus he directed the monasteries at Condat, Lauconne and La Balme until his death.

St. Romanus was buried at La Balme (later Saint-Romain-de Roche), while St. Lupicinus was interred at Lauconne (later Saint Lupicin).

✠

LENT

Lent is a Holy Season—a season different, and intended to be different from other seasons of the year. The Church demands that her children during the forty days of Lent enter into it with the true spirit of these days—days that will be appreciated by all who have an embracing perspective of life and set greater value on their souls than on worldly things.

Lent is a time specially set aside for repentance; is there a Christian who will not repent for offenses against God's laws? Lent is a season of denial of worldly pleasures; is there a man or woman who cannot make the easy sacrifice? Lent is a season of fast and abstinence; and in this matter, may it not be said that many who hitherto excused themselves lightly would find small difficulty, if only they loved their souls at least as much as they cherish their bodies, and in childlike obedience to the Church gave the laws of fast and abstinence a fair trial? Lent is a season of prayer and meditation, of frequent reception of the sacraments and regular attendance at daily Mass and other special devotions held in the parish churches. Will it be questioned that an improvement is possible and desirable?

Those who make good use of the Lenten Season will repair the past, and this done, prepare for the future—a glorious resurrection with and in Christ.

✠

FEBRUARY 29

ST. OSWALD

St. Oswald, of Danish parentage, was reared by his uncle Odo, Archbishop of Canterbury. For some time he was dean of the house of secular Canons at Winchester.

Desirous, however, of leading a stricter life, he entered the Benedictine Monastery of Fleury, where Odo had received the monastic habit. St. Oswald was ordained there, and in 950 returned to England to the Archbishop of York, who was a relative. Oswald took an active part in ecclesiastical affairs in York until St. Dunstan secured his appointment to the See of Worcester.

In 962 Oswald was consecrated by St. Dunstan and became his ardent supporter in his endeavor to purify the Church from abuses. Aided by King Edgar he carried out the Archbishop's policy of replacing the Canons who held monastic possessions.

By the joint action of St. Dunstan and the King, Oswald was made Archbishop of York in 972, and went to Rome to receive the pallium from Pope John XIII. With the sanction of the Pope he retained jurisdiction over the Diocese of Worcester, where he frequently resided in order to promote his monastic reforms. After the death of King Edgar, Oswald's hitherto successful work received a severe setback at the hands of the King of Mercia, who broke up many communities.

St. Oswald died while washing the feet of the poor, as was his daily custom during Lent, and was buried in the Church of St. Mary at Worcester.

MARCH

ST. SWITHBERT

St. Swithbert was one of the twelve missionaries whom St. Egbert encouraged to go from England to Germany, in 690, under the leadership of St. Willibrord.

St. Swithbert labored principally in Friesland (now Holland and North Belgium). Upon a visit to England he was consecrated Bishop by St. Wilfrid, and through his zealous labors made innumerable converts among the pagans.

In his old age, St. Swithbert retired to a monastery which he had built at Kaiserworth on the Rhine. It was here that he died in 713.

✠

ST. SIMPLICIUS

St. Simplicius succeeded Pope St. Hilarius to the See of Peter in 468. All the provinces of the Western empire, outside of Italy, were at that time in the hands of the barbarians, infected for the greatest part with idolatry or Arianism. Rome itself, due to the disorder of the Roman state, fell a prey to foreigners during the eighth year of the reign of Simplicius. His time was spent in comforting and helping the afflicted, and in planting the seeds of Catholicism among the barbarians.

The East was also a cause of great concern to Simplicius; the holy Faith was betrayed on every side; even the Patriarchal Sees of Alexandria and Antioch were occupied by heretics, and nowhere was there a Catholic King.

St. Simplicius strove zealously to maintain the Catholic Faith, upholding the decrees of the Council of Chalcedon, and supported the Eastern Catholics against the Monophysite heretics. In 483, after reigning for fifteen years, eleven months and six days, he went to receive the reward of his labors.

✠

MARCH 3

ST. CUNEGUNDES

St. Cunegundes was the daughter of King Bela IV and niece of St. Elizabeth of Hungary. From her infancy it pleased God to give signs of the eminent sanctity to which she was later to attain. Reluctantly she consented to her marriage with Boleslaus II, Duke of Cracow and Sandomir, who later became King of Poland. Soon after their marriage the pious couple made a vow of chastity, and Cunegundes, amidst the splendor and pomp of the royal household, gave herself up to the practice of the severest austerities. She visited the poor and the sick in the hospitals, and also cared for the lepers with heroic charity.

King Boleslaus died in 1279, and Cunegundes, despite the entreaties of her people that she should take in hand the government of the kingdom, sold all her possessions for the relief of the poor and entered the monastery of the Poor Clares at Sandeck. The remaining years of her life she spent in prayer and penance, edifying her fellow religious by her numerous virtues, especially by her profound humility. She never permitted anyone to refer to the fact that she had once been a Queen and had founded the community at Sandeck.

St. Cunegundes died on July 24, 1292, and in 1695 she was made Patroness of Poland and Lithuania by a decree of the Congregation of Rites, confirmed by Pope Clement XI.

✠

MARCH 4

ST. CASIMIR

St. Casimir, born in 1458, was the third among the thirteen children of Casimir III, King of Poland, and of Elizabeth of Austria, a most virtuous woman, daughter to Emperor Albert II.

Casimir was extremely devout from early childhood and profited by the good example of his learned and holy guardian, John Dugloss, to practice heroic virtue. He consecrated his virginity to God.

At the age of fifteen, when some of the nobles of Hungary begged the King of Poland to allow them to place his son Casimir on the throne, the young Prince refused to employ force to obtain the crown, and spent three months in the practice of penance. The rest of his years were devoted to sanctifying himself: he fasted, wore a hair shirt, slept upon the ground, prayed long hours during the night, and waited at dawn for the church doors to be opened to assist at Mass. He loved to meditate on the Passion of Christ, and had a singular devotion to the Blessed Virgin, which he expressed in a beautiful hymn, a copy of which, by his request, was buried with him.

St. Casimir died of tuberculosis in 1483, after a lingering illness, at the age of twenty-five years and five months. Many miracles were wrought by his intercession, and he was canonized by Pope Leo X. He is the patron saint of Poland and Lithuania, and is proposed to youth as a particular pattern of purity.

When the saint's tomb in the Cathedral of Vienna was opened one hundred and twenty-two years after his death, to transfer the remains to a rich marble vault in the same edifice, his body and the robe of silk with which he had been interred were found whole and incorrupt, emitting a sweet fragrance which filled the church.

☖

ST. JOHN JOSEPH OF THE CROSS

St. John Joseph of the Cross was born on the Island of Ischia, Southern Italy, in 1654. As a youth he led a prayerful, virtuous life. Though of noble birth, he always dressed like the poor, so great was his love of poverty. At the age of sixteen he entered the Franciscan Order, amongst the Friars of the Alcantarine Reform. He was the first Italian to join this Reform, which St. Peter of Alcantara had instituted in Spain.

St. John Joseph led a life of greatest austerity: he slept but three hours each night, fasted constantly, and never drank wine. In 1674 he was sent to found a friary at Afila, in Piedmont, assisting with his own hands in the erection of the building. He was later raised to the priesthood. As Superior, he always insisted upon performing the lowliest tasks in the community. In 1702 he was appointed Vicar Provincial of the Alcantarine Reform in Italy.

He was so zealous for souls that even when ill he would not spare any labor for them. His love for the Blessed Virgin was so great, that he urged his penitents to have great devotion to her.

St. John Joseph was favored with the gift of miracles, and people of all walks of life were brought to him in sickness. He died March 5, 1739, and was canonized by Pope Gregory XVI in 1839.

☖

STS. FELICITAS AND PERPETUA

On March 7, 203, Saints Felicitas and Perpetua, together with three companions, Revocatus, Saturus and Saturninus, suffered martyrdom for the Faith, during the reign of Septimus Severus. For, all subjects of the Roman Empire had been forbidden under severe penalties to become Christians.

Perpetua was a young married lady of noble birth, whose mother was a Christian, and father a pagan. The other four martyrs were slaves, who had received Baptism. They were cast into prison; their trial took place before the Procurator Hilarian. All resolutely confessed their Christian Faith. Perpetua's father and mother did everything possible to induce her to apostatize, but she remained steadfast.

These faithful Christians were then condemned to be torn to pieces by wild beasts. On March 7th the five confessors were led into the amphitheatre. At the demand of the pagan mob they were first scourged. Then after being wounded by the wild animals, they were put to the sword. Their bodies were interred in Carthage, where a magnificent Basilica was later erected over their tomb.

ST. COLETTE

The Church honors St. Colette, who was born in Piccardy, France, in 1380. She tried her vocation in several religious communities before becoming a tertiary of Saint Francis. She revived the Franciscan spirit among the Poor Clares.

Assisted by St. Vincent Ferrer, St. Colette had a share in putting an end to the great Schism of the West.

☩

MARCH 7

ST. THOMAS AQUINAS

The 13th century was a time of extraordinary intellectual activity, which was not without its dangers. In their enthusiasm for learning, students flocked by thousands to the great Universities, which, unhappily, were as often schools of infidelity as of faith. The philosophers owned but one master, Aristotle, a heathen, and as Lacordaire said, " ... unfortunately, Aristotle and the Gospel did not always agree". The great professors, who were the oracles of the day, sometimes tried to make a name for themselves by holding bold theories in matters where original speculation is seldom friendly to the Faith.

It was amidst the confusion of these new opinions that St. Thomas Aquinas was born in the fortress of Rocca-Secca, about the year 1225. It was to the little town of Aquino nearby that he owed his surname Aquinas. His father, the Count, was a nephew of Emperor Frederick Barbarossa; on his mother's side he was descended from the Norman barons who had conquered Sicily two centuries before. The Aquinas family could claim relationship with St. Gregory the Great, and was allied by blood to St. Louis of France and St. Ferdinand of Castile.

The future vocation and sanctity of the little Thomas had been predicted to his mother, the Countess Theodora, by a holy hermit named Bonus. The first words the baby lips were heard to utter were *Ave Maria*. When only five years old his education was begun by the Monks of the celebrated Benedictine Abbey of Monte Cassino, which was only a few miles distant from Rocca-Secca. Thomas made such progress in his studies that his parents sent him, when ten years old under the care of a tutor to the newly-founded University of Naples. Here, his extraordinary talents became more and more manifest, whilst at the same time he made rapid strides in the science of the Saints. He was continually held up as a model to his fellow students in a way most painful to his humility. The rarest gifts of intellect were combined in him with the tenderest piety. His leisure hours were devoted to prayer and good works. It was before the altar in the Dominican church that Thomas poured forth his soul in prayer. At the age of nineteen he was publicly clothed in the white habit of

St. Dominic, but his parents strove in every way possible
to undermine their son's resolution. He was even imprisoned for more than a year in one of the towers of the
Castle, where he had to suffer cold, hunger, and every sort
of privation.

Thomas' constancy was put to a yet more terrible
trial. His two young brothers brought an evil woman into
his chamber; but with a flaming brand snatched from the
hearth the Saint indignantly drove her from his presence.
With the same brand he then traced a cross upon the wall.
Casting himself on his knees before it, he besought God to
grant him the gift of perpetual chastity. As he prayed, he
fell into an ecstasy, during which two angels appeared to
him. Girding him with a miraculous cord, they said: "We
are come from God to invest thee with the girdle of perpetual chastity. The Lord has heard thy prayer; and that
which human frailty can never merit is insured to thee by
the irrevocable gift of God". The girdle was worn by the
Saint until his death, and is still preserved at the Convent
of Chieri in Piedmont. It was only to his confessor,
Brother Reginald, that he revealed this grace shortly before
his death.

Realizing that Thomas would not be overcome by
persecution, his family helped him to escape, like St. Paul,
by letting him down from the tower in a basket to the
Friars, who, by appointment, were waiting below. They
took Thomas to Naples, where he was immediately admitted to profession.

A final attempt was made to shake his constancy. An
appeal was made to the Pope, who summoned Thomas to
Rome. The Saint pleaded his cause so well that His Holiness granted him permission to remain a simple religious,
without further interference with his vocation. The Dominican General then took Brother Thomas to Cologne,
where he became the disciple of St. Albert the Great. Astonished at the genius he displayed, St. Albert put the
learning of his saintly disciple to a public test, and exclaimed before the assembled students: "We call Brother

Thomas 'the dumb ox'; but I tell you he will one day make
his bellowing heard to the uttermost parts of the earth".

In 1245 St. Albert took Brother Thomas as his companion to the General Chapter in Paris. While there he
met a young Franciscan, Bonaventure by name, who was
studying in that city. A bond of closest friendship sprang
up between them. After their three years of study, in 1248
both were raised to the degree of Bachelor of Theology.
In November of that year Thomas returned to Cologne
with St. Albert, where he taught philosophy and theology
for four years. Soon after his return, the Saint was raised
to the priesthood. In 1252 he went to Paris. His success in
teaching there was so great that the vast halls of the Convent of St. James were unable to accommodate the audience
which desired to listen to his wisdom. He took his Doctor's
degree in 1257.

The Church has always venerated his numerous writings as a treasure-house of sacred doctrine. In naming him
the Angelic Doctor, She proclaimed that his science is more
divine than human. His singular devotion to the Blessed
Sacrament shines forth in the Office and Hymns for Corpus Christi, which he composed.

On December 6, 1273, while saying Mass in his convent chapel in Naples he received a revelation that the
end of his labors was near.

Summoned by the Pope to attend the General Council convoked at Lyons for the reunion of the Greek and
Latin Churches, St. Thomas, though ill, accompanied by
Brother Reginald and some other Friars, started on January 28, 1274, for Lyons. On the way his condition grew
worse. Not able to reach a Dominican convent, he was
carried to the Cistercian Abbey of Fossa Nuova. Every
attention was rendered him. His own brethren were in-
consolable at their approaching loss. One of them asked
the Saint what was the best way of living without offending God. He replied: "Be certain that he who walks
in the presence of God and is always ready to give Him
an account of his actions, will never be separated from

Him by sin". These were his last words. Shortly after, he fell into his agony and peacefully expired, March 7, 1274, not yet having completed his 50th year.

St. Thomas was canonized by Pope John XXII at Avignon in 1323. In 1567, St. Pius V conferred on St. Thomas the title of Doctor of the Church; whilst Pope Leo XIII, by a Brief of August 4, 1880, instituted him Patron of all Catholic Universities, Academies, Colleges and Schools.

✠

MARCH 8

ST. JOHN OF GOD

St. John was born in Portugal in 1495. His parents were poor, but devout and charitable. The first years of John's life were spent as a shepherd, in great innocence and purity. In 1522 he enlisted as a soldier and fought in the war against the French; as he did later in Hungary against the Turks. His association with evil companions caused him to lose his fear of offending God and to give up his practices of devotion. At the age of forty, stung with remorse for his past misconduct, he resolved to change his life and do penance for his sins. The greater part of the day and night he devoted to prayer and mortification, lamenting over his ingratitude towards God, and considering in what way he could dedicate himself in the most perfect manner to His service. His compassion for the poor slaves in Africa caused him to go to that country, but on the advice of his confessor John returned to Spain. When he reached Gibraltar his piety suggested that he turn peddler and sell pictures and books of devotion which might exhort his customers to virtue.

At the age of forty-three, in 1538, John settled in Granada, where he opened a shop to carry on the sale of his religious articles. Upon hearing a sermon in that city by the renowned servant of God, John D'Avila, he was so affected that he shed abundant tears and filled the church with his lamentations. After a pilgrimage to one of Our Lady's shrines, he began to sell wood in the market-place to feed some of the poor. Then, in 1540, he hired a house where he could care for the sick-poor. This was the foundation of the Order of Brothers Hospitallers (Brothers of St. John of God) which, by the benediction of Heaven, still exists, principally in the Latin countries. The Archbishop of Granada observed the excellent work for the spiritual and temporal welfare of the poor, and contributed considerable sums to support it. This inspired many other persons to make sacrifices for the needy.

After ten years of hard service in his hospital, St. John fell ill. The saint expired on his knees before the altar on March 8, 1550, at the age of fifty-five. He was glorified by many miracles, and was canonized by Pope Alexander VIII in 1690.

✠

MARCH 9

ST. DOMINIC SAVIO

One of St. Don Bosco's first pupils was Dominic Savio, who was born in Riva, northen Italy, April 2, 1842. From early youth he manifested an unusual seriousness of purpose and intense devotion to the Holy Sacrifice of the Mass and to the Holy Eucharist. When, at the age of seven, he made his First Holy Communion, he formed the motto, "Death, but not sin!"

From St. Don Bosco he learned how the joy of serving God and making Him loved by others can become a powerful means of apostolate. Pope St. Pius X said of him: "A teen-ager such as Dominic, who bravely struggled to preserve undefiled his baptismal innocence to the very last is indeed a saint!" At fifteen, he had become a "giant of the spirit. . . . His was, indeed, the perfection of Christian life—a life drawing its strength from three main sources, namely, Purity, Piety, Zeal!"—Pius XI. And Pope Pius XII declared on the occasion of the solemn canonization on June 12, 1954:

"If in the course of centuries the forces of evil do not cease their attacks against the work of the Divine Redeemer, God does not fail to answer the anguished prayers of His children in danger, raising up souls, rich in the gifts of nature and of grace, who will be a comfort and help to their brethren. When the spirit of revolt and pride causes the consciences of men to grow feeble, God calls to the standard of Christ's Cross heroes of sanctity who radiate the splendors of virginal purity and fraternal charity to serve all the needs of the soul and to maintain in its integrity the fervor of Christian virtues.

"Among the heroes there appears the image of Dominic Savio, the delicate adolescent, weak of body, but with a soul determined upon a pure oblation of itself to the exacting love of Christ."

As he was dying on March 9, 1857, he burst out into an ecstatic exclamation, "Oh, what a beautiful sight I see!"

Dominic Savio is the youngest Confessor in the Church's calendar of saints, and stands out as a hero of school-boy virtue, the shining model of classroom holiness.

✠

MARCH 10

THE FORTY MARTYRS OF SEBASTE

It was about the year 320, under the reign of Emperor Licinius, that these holy martyrs suffered at Sebaste, in Lesser Armenia. Agricola, Governor of the province, brought to the attention of the army the orders of the Emperor for all to sacrifice to the gods. These forty, from different countries, were enrolled in the same troop. They

O God, fountain of heavenly gifts, You showered the angelical youth, Dominic, with the blessings of an innocent life. Grant that, through his merits and his prayers, we, who have not followed him in innocence, may imitate him in penance.

went boldly to the Governor and said they were Christians and that no torments would make them ever abandon their holy religion.

First, the judge endeavored to persuade them; then he threatened them with the most terrifying punishment, but the Governor finding them resolute caused them to be scourged and their sides rent with iron hooks. Then they were chained together and committed to jail. Some days later the Governor re-examined the staunch young soldiers. Finding that they despised the threatened torments he ordered that they be exposed naked on the ice of a frozen lake. A warm bath was prepared on the bank to tempt them to apostatize. Undismayed they ran joyfully to the pond, stripped off their garments, and together they prayed: "Lord, we are forty who are engaged in this combat; grant that we may be forty crowned". The guards ceased not to persuade them to sacrifice, but only one had the misfortune to seek the relief offered, and thereby renounced his Faith. No sooner did he enter the warm water than he expired. His associates were greatly afflicted, but were soon comforted by seeing his place miraculously filled. A sentinel who had been posted to observe if any of the martyrs were inclined to submit had a vision of blessed spirits descending from heaven with thirty-nine crowns for the martyrs. The guard, struck with the celestial vision and the apostate's desertion, was converted by the heroism of the thirty-nine. Casting off his clothes, he took the place left vacant, and was numbered among the forty martyrs who froze to death, one by one.

The following morning the youngest of them was found alive by the officers who came to cast away the dead bodies. Hoping he would still change his resolution, they left him behind. His mother, learning of her son's whereabouts, came to him. She found him quite frozen and not able to move, and encouraged him to persevere. With her own hands she lifted him up and soon thereafter placed his lifeless body in the cart with his companions to be thrown into the flames prepared for the dead bodies.

✠

ST. EULOGIUS OF SPAIN

St. Eulogius, a native of Cordova, Spain, was a loyal Priest in the 9th century when persecution by the Moors was at its height. He distinguished himself by his virtue and learning and was made head of the principal ecclesiastical school in Cordova. He won the affection and respect of all by his humility, mildness and charity, and aided many fervent souls in their desire to serve God. Some indiscreet Christians openly fought against Mohammed and the religion he established. This occasioned a bloody persecution at Cordova in 850, during which St. Eulogius and others were cast into prison. He encouraged the martyrs and wrote his "Exhortation to Martyrdom", addressed to Flora and Mary, virgins, who were beheaded on November 24, 851. They promised to pray for him, and six days after their death Eulogius was set at liberty. The following year a number of others suffered martyrdom, and St. Eulogius encouraged them to be faithful.

In 858, upon the death of the Archbishop of Toledo, St. Eulogius was elected to succeed him. Some obstacle prevented his consecration, and he died for the Faith two months after his election. Leocritia, a virgin of a noble family among the Moors, had been instructed in the Christian religion from early youth by a relative and privately baptized. Her parents upon learning this treated the child badly; and they scourged her daily in an effort to compel her to renounce the Faith. Having made known her condition to St. Eulogius and his sister, stating that she desired to go where she could freely practice her religion, they secretly procured the means whereby she could leave her parents and concealed her for some time with faithful friends. Eventually the matter became known, and all were brought before the cadi. When he threatened to have Eulogius scourged to death, the martyr told him it would do no good for he would never deny his religion. The cadi then ordered that he be taken to the palace and presented before the King's council. Boldly and publicly St. Eulogius announced the truths of the Gospel to them. To prevent their hearing him the council condemned him to be beheaded. As he was being led to execution a guard gave him a blow on the face for having spoken against Mohammed; turning the other cheek, he patiently received a second blow.

Cheerfully Eulogius received the stroke of death outside the city gates on March 11, 859. Four days later St. Leocritia was beheaded. Her body was thrown into the Guadalquivir river, but the Christians recovered it.

✠

MARCH 12

ST. GREGORY I (the Great)

St. Gregory, one of the greatest Popes to fill the Chair of Peter, was a Roman of noble birth. By steady application of God-given powers he gained for himself the reputation of being second to none in the chief branches of learning in his day.

Upon the death of his father Gordianus, a wealthy patrician, Gregory distributed his inheritance among the poor and converted the mansion on the Caelian Hill into a monastery. For several years Gregory lived as an ideal Monk; looked upon by all as a man of deepest spirituality, as one well advanced in the interior life.

Pope Benedict I died in 579 and was succeeded by Pelagius II. This Pontiff compelled Gregory, by obedience, to take upon himself the sacred order of Deacon and the dignity of Cardinal, employing him as secretary. The period was one of acute crisis, as the Lombards were advancing towards Rome. The only chance of safety seemed to be in obtaining help from Emperor Tiberius at Constantinople. In the spring of 579 Pope Pelagius dispatched a special embassy to Tiberius, and sent Gregory as his permanent ambassador to the Court of Constantinople; where he remained for seven years.

In 585 or 586 Gregory was recalled to Rome. With great joy he returned to St. Andrews, of which he became Abbot soon thereafter. At the death of Pope Pelagius in 590, Gregory, after vainly trying by flight to avoid the dignity, was elected Pope. The fourteen years of his Pontificate, despite ill health, were an outstanding model of ecclesiastical rule. He reformed Church discipline; healed schisms; saved Italy by converting the Arian Lombards, who were laying waste the country; aided in the conversion of the Spanish and French Arian Goths; was a champion and protector of the Jews, and sent St. Augustine with his forty monks as the first missionaries to the Anglo-Saxons, thereby earning for himself the title of Apostle of England.

His Letters, Homilies, Biblical Explanations and Ascetical Works comprise several volumes.

The last years of St. Gregory's life were filled with acutest sufferings, yet he would not allow his zeal for the Church to become dim. At last, on March 12, 604, came the long-desired and long-prayed for summons to Heaven. The Church venerates him as one of her four great Doctors of the West, and gave him the title of Gregory the Great.

☦

MARCH 13

ST. EUPHRASIA

St. Euphrasia was born of devout, noble parents. Less than a year after her birth her father died. In order to avoid suitors the young widow took Euphrasia to Egypt, where she owned a large estate. They made their abode near a monastery of holy Nuns, and frequently visited them.

At the age of seven Euphrasia begged her mother's permission to serve God in this monastery. The holy mother wept with joy. Soon afterwards she presented the child to the Abbess, who placed a crucifix in her hands. The young virgin kissed it, and said: "By vow I consecrate myself to Christ". Euphrasia's mother then led her before an image of the Savior; raising her hands towards heaven, she prayed: "Lord Jesus Christ, receive this child under Your special protection. You alone she loves and seeks; to You she recommends herself". Turning to her daughter, she said: "May God, Who laid the foundations of the mountains, strengthen you always in His holy fear". Then leaving her in the care of the Abbess, she left the monastery, weeping.

Upon the death of the child's mother not long afterwards, the Emperor Theodosius sent for the holy virgin to come to Court, stating that he had promised her in marriage to a young senator. Euphrasia wrote him refusing the offer, stating that she had consecrated herself to Christ, and requested that her estates be sold and divided among the poor, the orphans and the Church, and that all her slaves be given their freedom. The Emperor promptly executed her desires shortly before he died in 395.

St. Euphrasia's humility, meekness and charity were an inspiration to all the Sisters. Her openness with her Superior and perfect obedience in performing difficult tasks assigned enabled her to overcome temptations of the devil. She was favored with miracles before and after her death, which occurred in 410, when she was thirty years old.

✠

MARCH 14

ST. MAUD

St. Maud (or Matilda), the daughter of Theodoric, a powerful Saxon Count, was placed by her parents when quite young in the monastery of Erfurt, of which her grandmother Maud was the Abbess. She became a model of all virtues, and remained there until her parents gave her in marriage to Henry, son of Otho, Duke of Saxony, in 913. In

916, upon the death of his father, Henry became Duke of Saxony, and in 919 he was chosen King of Germany. He was a holy and victorious king, and very kind to his subjects. Maud nourished the precious seeds of devotion and humility in her heart by assiduous prayer, and gained domestic victories over her spiritual enemies. She took delight in visiting and comforting the sick and afflicted, and in aiding prisoners to obtain their liberty. Her husband, edified by her good example, helped her in all her pious undertakings. After twenty-three years of married life, God called the King to Himself in 936.

Queen Maud had three sons: Otho, who was crowned King of Germany in 937, and Emperor, at Rome, in 962; Henry, Duke of Bavaria, and St. Bruno, Archbishop of Cologne. In the contest between her two elder sons for the crown, which was elective, she favored Henry, who was the younger, a fault which she expiated by severe afflictions and penance.

The two oldest sons conspired to strip their mother of her dowry, on the unjust pretense that she had squandered the revenues of the state on the poor. After a long, cruel persecution they repented of their injustice, were reconciled to their mother, and restored to her all they had taken. She now showed more liberality towards the poor than before; founded many churches, and five monasteries, the principal of which were at Polden and Quedlinburg. In this latter place she had buried her husband, and her body also rests there. She died on March 14, 968, after receiving the Last Sacraments, and was venerated as a saint immediately after her death.

✠

ST. ZACHARY

St. Zachary was born at San Severino, in Calabria, of a Greek family, and succeeded Pope Gregory III to the Chair of Peter on December 5, 741. He was a man of gentle and conciliatory character, most charitable towards clergy and people. He loved the people of Rome to such a degree that he risked his life for them during the rebellion of the Dukes of Spoleto and Benevento against King Luitprand. The King, out of respect for the sanctity and dignity of the Pope, restored all the territory which belonged to the Church of Rome, and sent back all captives without ransom.

Pope Zachary successfully negotiated peace between the Lombards and the Greek empire; approved the assumption of the Frankish crown by Pepin, and encouraged the holding of the Synod of Cloveshove, which was held in 747 for the reform of church discipline in England in accordance with the advice given by the Pope in imitation of the Roman Church.

Zachary restored many of the churches of Rome, to which he made costly gifts. He also restored the Lateran Palace; established several large domains as the settled landed possessions of the Roman Church; translated to the Church of St. George in Velabro the head of the martyr St. George, which was found during the repairs to the Lateran Palace; carried on theological studies, and translated the Dialogues of St. Gregory the Great into Greek, which were largely distributed in the East.

Pope Zachary proved himself to be an excellent, capable, zealous, charitable successor of St. Peter. He died in March 752, and was buried in St. Peter's.

✠

MARCH 16

STS. ABRAHAM AND MARY

St. Abraham was a rich nobleman of Mesopotamia. To please his parents he entered into matrimony, but desirous of leading a life of virginity, left home immediately after the marriage ceremony (no doubt having obtained the consent of his bride), and took up his abode in a cell near the city of Edessa. After searching for seventeen days, his friends found him. Convinced that he was determined to live the life of a recluse, they left him to commune with God. He walled up his cell-door, leaving only a small window through which he received food.

Upon the death of his parents, St. Abraham distributed their fortune among the poor. As many persons sought his advice and consolation, the Bishop of Edessa ordained him Priest and sent him to preach to the idolatrous inhabitants in the vicinity of Edessa. He was insulted, beaten and exiled three times, but on each occasion returned with greater zeal. For three years he prayed for the persecutors, and had the happiness of baptizing everyone of them.

More convinced than ever of the power of prayer, St. Abraham, after providing for their spiritual needs, returned to his cell, where for nearly fifty years he sang God's praises and implored His mercy for all mankind.

Upon the death of his brother, who left an only daughter, Mary, St. Abraham placed her in a cell near his own in order to be able to train her in the ways of perfection. After twenty years of innocence she began to lead a life of sin and fled in despair to a distant city, where she endeavored to still the voice of conscience. For two years Abraham and his friend St. Ephrem prayed earnestly for her; then, disguised, he went in search of the "lost sheep" and had the happiness of bringing her back to the desert, where she practiced severe penance the remainder of her life. St. Abraham preceded his niece in death by five years, about the year 360.

☨

MARCH 17

ST. PATRICK

St. Patrick was a Gallo-Roman, born in 387. The place of his birth is uncertain. His mother, Conchessa, was closely related to St. Martin, Bishop of Tours, whose disciple Patrick afterwards became. The Saint tells us that his father, Calphurnius, was a Roman officer. It seems a fairly

established fact that Conchessa had been in her youth, as
her son was later, carried into slavery; and that it was from
this state that Calphurnius, won by her beauty and virtue,
rescued her to make her his wife. So it was by one who had
been a slave, and the son of a slave, that the Gospel was
preached to a people who were for many centuries to know
the sorrows of servitude, and amid those sorrows to prepare for better days.

A miracle is said to have signalized the child's baptism.
The blind and aged priest was unable to find water for the
sacrament. Illuminated as to the future sanctity of the
child, he signed with the infant's hand a cross upon the
ground. Immediately a spring of water gushed forth, in
which the baby was baptized, and the priest's blind eyes
were washed and sight restored. The child was, it seems,
christened Succat. The name Patricius, or Patrick, was the
gift of Pope Celestine when the Saint had reached the age
of forty-five, and was commissioned by the Pope to preach
the Gospel in Ireland.

Patrick was sixteen years of age when he was carried
into captivity and sold to Milcho, the chief of North Dal-
raida. During his servitude he spent his waking hours in
prayer, as also a great part of the night. God, Who never
suffers Himself to be outdone in generosity, rewarded the
generous prayer and penance of Patrick by sending His
angel, Victor, down to the lonely shepherd on Mount
Slemish, to give him the strength and comfort that he could
no longer draw from priest or sacrament; and to show him
in vision the future glories of Erin.

For six years Patrick suffered and prayed; at last his
day of freedom arrived. A voice from Heaven told him to
go to France, that beloved country which he so longed to
see: "Behold, the ship is ready". St. Martin was then Bishop
of Tours. He had been consecrated Bishop the year before
Patrick's birth, and welcomed his kinsman to his monastic
home at Marmoutier, by the Loire. But Marmoutier was
soon bereft of its saintly founder, and St. Germanus, Bishop
of Auxerre, became Patrick's guide, teacher and friend.

St. Germanus was sent by the Pope to Britain to attack in one of its strongholds the heresy of Pelagius, and invited Patrick to assist him. It is probable that, owing to his work in Britain, Patrick was sent to Rome to Pope Celestine. St. Germanus recommended him as "a strong husbandman, well fitted for cultivating the harvest of the Lord". Patrick received from the Pope the commission to preach the Word of God in Erin. He was consecrated Bishop, and in 432, after many years' absence, he returned to Ireland. His fame as a wonder-worker soon spread. A burning, apostolic zeal converted numberless souls to the one, true Church of Christ. He taught them about the Blessed Trinity by showing them how the shamrock has three leaves yet is one plant.

For sixty years St. Patrick labored among the Irish, and reached the extraordinary age of 105 years. The Faith of the Irish has been so strong that they have carried the love of Jesus and Mary all over the world. And even today the eyes and hearts of the Irish race are still fondly turned to St. Patrick.

✠

MARCH 18

ST. CYRIL OF JERUSALEM

St. Cyril was born about the year 315 at or near Jerusalem, and was ordained Priest, in 345, by Bishop Maximus of that city, who appointed him to instruct and prepare candidates for Baptism. He filled this charge for several years, succeeding Maximus as Patriarch of Jerusalem in 350, and held this position until his death in 386.

At the beginning of his episcopate on May 7th, about 9 a. m., a cross brighter than the noon-day sun was seen in the air, reaching from Mt. Calvary to Mt. Olivet. It was visible for several hours to the inhabitants, who were struck with reverential fear. St. Cyril reported the incident to the Emperor, and the faithful considered it an omen of victory over the Arian heretics.

During the episcopacy of St. Cyril, Julian, the apostate, a most crafty, dangerous instrument of the devil, sought in every dishonorable way to undermine the Christian Faith. Having failed in his efforts, he finally attempted to falsify the words of Our Savior by rebuilding the Temple at Jerusalem. The Jews were enthusiastic and contributed generously to the cause; every capable Jewish person bearing a share in the labor. St. Cyril beheld all these mighty preparations without the least concern, placing all his trust in the infallible truth of the scriptural prophecies (Dan. 9:27; Matt. 24:2).

According to St. Chrysostom, Sozomen and Theodoret, when the attempt was made to rebuild the Temple, repeated earthquakes and "horrible balls of fire that came out of the earth near the foundations", rendered the place from time to time inaccessible to the scorched and frightened workmen. After many futile attempts the work was abandoned in despair. Before long, Emperor Valens died in a war against the Persians, and the Church had peace.

St. Cyril spent seventeen years of his patriarchate in exile and suffering. In 381 he assisted at the General Council of Constantinople, in which he again condemned the heresies of the semi-Arians and Macedonians. In 386 he passed to a glorious immortality, at the age of seventy. He was declared a Doctor of the Church by Pope Leo XIII.

✠

MARCH 19

ST. JOSEPH

The Church of God glories in her galaxy of holy men and women. In the lives of many of these, there are found recorded stupendous wonders and miracles, which, whilst they elicit admiration, do not strongly move to imitation the rank and file of Christians. The reason is obvious, when it is remembered that ordinary mankind works out its salvation with ordinary graces.

O Lord, may we be helped by the merits of the Spouse of Your most holy Mother, so that we may be granted, through his intercession, what we are unable to obtain for ourselves.

In the life of St. Joseph, to whose veneration the month of March is dedicated, we discover neither miracles nor other extraordinary happenings. Along a common and very simple path the Foster Father of Jesus reached the heights of sanctity—that path the one of faithful, daily fulfillment of duties. Consequently, he is the model for all men, pointing out in his life the sure road to Heaven. "He that doth the Will of My Father Who is in Heaven, he shall enter into the kingdom of Heaven." (St. Matt. 7:21.)

Practically speaking, all men have but one vocation; namely, to serve God and save their souls. However, as various roads lead into our towns and villages, so do many avenues lead into the glorious and eternal City of God. There are many stations in life, all of which come from God and return to God. A conscientious fulfillment of the duties of the particular station in life is all that is required for reaching the goal; and this St. Joseph did in a pre-eminent manner.

As head of the Holy Family, as spouse of the Blessed Virgin Mary, as protector of the Son of God, St. Joseph performed willingly and uncomplainingly the duties as they arose. As an Israelite living under the promulgations of Moses or as a subject of the Romans who, in his days, ruled the land, an order was looked upon as the voice of God and faithfully obeyed. As a workman, the universal lot of man since Adam's sin, labor was accepted with cheerful resignation.

Thus the years of the man, whom God was able to call a "Just Man", passed rapidly and meritoriously. Thus he prepared for himself a death in the arms of Jesus and Mary and a reward not eclipsed by that, with one single exception, of any of God's creatures. And when the allotted time was ended, the God Whom he loved with his whole heart, called him from work to rest, from serving to ruling, from suffering to glory.

The Catholic Church, to use the words of Pope Pius IX, teaches that St. Joseph has been designated by God as "the master of His goods and of His household". St. Joseph is the patron of the Universal Church. In 1955 Pope Pius XII added the title, "Patron of Workmen" for St. Joseph, the feast to be celebrated on May 1. St. Joseph is also the patron of the dying. Everyone should "go to Joseph" in their difficulties, as the Church advises and urges! All men can learn from St. Joseph how perfectly God may be served by a faithful performance of daily duties!

✠

MARCH 20

ST. CUTHBERT

Cuthbert was a shepherd lad who lived in the 7th century in the valley of Lauderdale, England. Nothing is known of his Christian parents, but the child was pious and faithful in the discharge of his duties.

One night he sat wrapped in his sheep-skin under the open sky watching the flocks dozing in their pasture. Occasionally his eyes were raised to the dark clouds that hid the stars from his sight. Suddenly the heavy clouds parted and Cuthbert saw a multitude of floating figures; all of them shining as only the Angels of Heaven are seen to shine by mortals; and this multitude were all descending towards the earth. But, wonderful to behold! no sooner had one touched the earth than all ascended towards Heaven, carrying with them a soul which they had come to bear to its eternal reward. A supreme happiness lifted Cuthbert's mind and heart and senses towards God, and towards that Heaven from which he had seen the angels descending and then returning with their beautiful prize.

The following day a messenger came from the abbey at Melrose to the little hamlet of Lauderdale, saying: "Last night Aiden, the holy man, was called to his rest in God!" When Cuthbert heard this, he exclaimed: "Then it was the soul of the holy man Aiden which I saw last night carried to Heaven by the angels!"

Now Aiden was the Bishop of Lindisfarne, and the missionary and father of the surrounding country. While everybody was bewailing his death, Cuthbert could only remember the glory of his entrance into Heaven. There now burned in the heart of the shepherd-boy a desire to live in such a manner as to die like the holy man Aiden. Across the hills stood the Benedictine abbey at Melrose.

When Cuthbert was just fifteen, as he was passing the abbey one day, he stopped and asked the Abbott Eata to receive him as the "least of the brothers". Father Boisil, the Master of Novices, now a canonized saint, acceded to his request. When Eata was made Abbot of Ripon, he took Cuthbert with him to the monastery founded by King Alcfrid in the southwestern part of Northumbria. Here his duty was to welcome strangers—a post requiring great wisdom and virtue. His zeal knew no bounds.

When Eata returned to beautiful Melrose, he took Cuthbert along. Shortly after their return Boisil, the Master of Novices, died during the pestilence which swept over Northumbria. Cuthbert was appointed to succeed him. Much of his time was spent in attending the sick, instructing the ignorant, and seeking out the unrepenting sinner in the villages nearby.

Cuthbert was called again from his beloved Melrose. Eata was made Abbot and Bishop of Lindisfarne, and he could not go without Cuthbert. Although not thirty years old, Cuthbert was regarded by his Superiors as the one best fitted to fulfill the duties of the Prior of Lindisfarne, and he was inspired to walk more faithfully than ever in the path of prayer which St. Aiden loved.

After twelve years of missionary labor, his soul thirsted for the solitude of the Fathers of the Desert. He asked permission to retire to a small island near Lindisfarne, called Farne, inhabited only by the sea-birds of that region. Permission was at length granted. Many came in their boats to his island of Farne for spiritual help or for consolation. One day the King of Northumbria, with his principal lords, and nearly the whole community of Lindisfarne arrived. The King and his followers knelt for Cuthbert's blessing, and then he begged Cuthbert to accept the bishopric.

For two years Cuthbert labored as Bishop. After a long, painful illness, he received the Last Sacraments; then raised his eyes and his arms to Heaven in a transport of love. He breathed out his soul joyfully to God on the night of March 20, 687. He was only fifty years old, and thirty-five of these years had been lived under the habit of a Benedictine.

✠

MARCH 21

ST. BENEDICT

St. Benedict, the Patriarch of Western Monks, was born in 480 at Nursia in the Sabine mountains, half way between Rome and Ancona. As his father, Anicius Eupropius, was a wealthy, influential patrician, Benedict and his twin sister Scholastica enjoyed the comforts of a well-appointed home under the tender care of their holy mother Abundantia.

Education in Nursia seemed out of the question, so Benedict's father decided to send him to Rome, where he could receive a training suitable to his position. For this purpose he selected a trustworthy servant, Cyrilla, to accompany and take charge of the boy. Rome was at that time a hotbed of vice. Whether Benedict was horrified at the heinousness of sin in that city, or whether he received a direct call from God to give up the world and to seek Him alone, the young Benedict resolved to leave Rome. Cyrilla accompanied him, trudging forty miles until they reached Enfide at the base of the Sabine mountains. After living there for some months, during which Benedict felt free to kneel hour after hour in the village church, his soul absorbed in communing with God, he yearned to be away from everyone, alone with God. He was then fourteen years of age.

Without confiding to Cyrilla, he hurried into the wilds of the mountains to escape notice. Upon reaching the ravine that connects the present Subiaco with Genezzano, on either side of which rugged, bold rocks jutted up in sheer precipices, there came towards him a man in the garb of a monk. At first Benedict was startled, but the saintly manner of the stranger gained his confidence, and after a few words Benedict opened his heart and fully disclosed his designs and aspirations. The holy Romanus felt that this was not a chance meeting, but that God had sent him as a guide to a chosen soul. He procured for Benedict the habit of a monk, and offered to show him a secret cave that would suit his purpose. It was on the right side of the ravine, overlooking a giddy precipice of several hundred feet. The cave was inaccessible from above, so Romanus arranged to provide the youth with food, to be let down in a basket by a rope, to which a bell was attached to warn of its approach.

Benedict was now alone with God. He saw no one, spoke to no one. Without book, or master, or guide, he trusted entirely in God, Who taught him the higher paths of the spiritual life. For ten or fifteen years Benedict dwelt in this cave.

After three years God made known to a Priest, four miles from the cave, of the hunger of His servant Benedict. The Priest brought him food on Easter Sunday, and soon afterwards some peasants climbing up the mountain came upon Benedict in his cave. He helped them spirtually. The fame of the sanctity of the young anchorite soon spread far and wide.

The days of complete solitude had passed, for the sanctity of St. Benedict attracted many earnest men, who desired to join in his heavenly life and to live near him. He soon founded twelve monasteries in the vicinity of Subiaco.

In 529, under a special guidance of God, St. Benedict left Subiaco and its twelve surrounding monasteries to travel a considerable distance to Monte Cassino, where

May the intercession of the blessed abbot Benedict commend us to You, O Lord, so that we may obtain, through his patronage, what we cannot obtain by our own merits.

on the site of an ancient temple of Apollo he erected a
monastery, which was to become the glorious monastic
center of the West. Here, at Monte Cassino, he wrote his
holy Rule, a marvel of wisdom and knowledge of human
nature.

Besides monasteries for men, St. Benedict established
several convents, where holy women followed his Rule.
Over one of them he placed his sister, St. Scholastica. These
men and women were called Benedictines.

Early in 543, St. Benedict announced to his Brethren
the day of his death, March 21st. On that very day, two
of his monks at a distance, separated from each other, had
the same vision. They saw a beautiful path, strewn with
rich garments, decorated with brilliant lamps, leading from
the Saint's cell to Heaven. As they gazed at the sight an
angel said to them: "This is the path by which the beloved
of the Lord, Benedict, ascended up to Heaven".

✠

MARCH 22

ST. CATHERINE OF SWEDEN

St. Catherine was the fourth child of Prince Ulf Gud-
marsson and St. Bridget. From early youth Catherine loved
God intensely; at the age of seven she was placed in the
care of the holy Abbess of the convent of Riseberg to be
educated. She was a very beautiful girl, and when only
fourteen years old her father gave her in marriage to Eggart
von Kurnen, a virtuous young nobleman. St. Catherine persuaded him to join her in a vow of chastity. The happy
couple spent much of their time in prayer, mortification
and works of charity.

In spite of her deep love for her husband, Catherine
accompanied her mother to Rome, where the latter went
in 1349. Soon after her arrival in that city, Catherine received news of the death of her husband in Sweden. She

now lived constantly with her mother, aided St. Bridget in her fruitful labors, and zealously imitated her mother's ascetic life, refusing all offers of marriage.

In 1372 Catherine, together with her brother, accompanied her mother on a pilgrimage to the Holy Land. Upon their return to Rome St. Bridget died. In 1374, in obedience to St. Bridget's wish, Catherine brought back her mother's body to Sweden for burial at the convent of Wadstena, which her mother had founded. Catherine now became the head of the convent. It was the motherhouse of the Brigittine Order, also called the Order of St. Savior. The following year Catherine went again to Rome to promote the canonization of St. Bridget and to procure a new Papal confirmation of the Order. She stayed five years in Italy and then returned to Sweden, bearing a special letter of commendation from the Pope. Not long after her arrival she was taken ill, and died on March 24, 1381.

✠

MARCH 23

ST. VICTORIAN AND OTHERS

St. Victorian had been Proconsul in Africa, and his fellow-sufferers were wealthy merchants of Carthage. Like their humble brethren, they fell victims to the violent fury of the Arian Vandals in 484, during the reign of King Huneric.

After the King had published his cruel edicts, he sent a message to Victorian, promising if he would conform to his religion he would bestow upon him great wealth and the highest honors. Victorian, who was fully aware of the vanity of the pomps of the world, sent this reply: "Tell the King that I trust in Christ. His Majesty may condemn me to torments, but I shall never consent to renounce the Catholic Church, in which I have been baptized. Even if there were no life after this, I would never be ungrateful and perfidious to God, Who has granted me the happiness of knowing Him, and bestowed on me His most precious graces".

The tyrant, furious at Victorian's answer, ordered that he and his companions be put to the torture. These holy Martyrs joyously suffered the pains inflicted upon them, bravely confessing Christ to be the Son of God.

✠

MARCH 24

ST. GABRIEL, ARCHANGEL

St. Gabriel is one of the three Angels honored by the Church with a special feast day. He is mentioned twice in the Book of Daniel (8:16; 9:21), and is called the "Strength of God".

It was the Angel Gabriel who was sent to the priest Zachary, as he stood in the Temple at Jerusalem "on the right side of the altar of incense", to announce that his aged wife Elizabeth would give birth to a son who would be the Precursor of the Savior. As Zachary was incredulous the Angel said to him: "I am Gabriel, who stand before God; and am sent to speak to thee, and to bring thee these good tidings. And behold thou shalt be dumb, and shalt not be able to speak until the day wherein these things shall come to pass, because thou hast not believed my words, which shall be fulfilled in their time". (Luke 1:11-20.)

St. Gabriel's chief mission to mankind, however, was his appearance to the Blessed Virgin Mary at Nazareth, to inform her that she had been chosen by God to be the Mother of the Messias. (Luke 1:26.)

St. Gabriel is called the "Strength of God", either because this title was his right, as herald of the power of God; or because it was his duty to comfort the Virgin, who was naturally timid, simple and bashful, lest she should be affrighted at the novelty of the miracle. This he certainly did by saying: "Fear not, Mary, for thou hast found grace with God". Thus was Gabriel fitly chosen for this work; yea, because he was entrusted with so great a mission, rightly was so great a name assigned to him.

✠

MARCH 25

ANNUNCIATION OF THE BLESSED VIRGIN MARY

St. Luke, the Evangelist, tells us that it was in the sixth month after the conception of St. John the Baptist by Elizabeth, that the Angel Gabriel was sent from God to the Virgin Mary, at Nazareth, a small town in Galilee. Mary was of the House of David and was espoused to Joseph of the same royal family; she had not yet entered the household of her spouse, but was still living in her mother's home when the Angel appeared to her, and said: "Hail, full of grace, the Lord is with thee".

Since Mary did not know the Angel or the reason for his coming, she was troubled, and did not speak. Therefore the Angel continued: "Fear not Mary, for thou hast found grace with God. Behold thou shalt conceive in thy womb, and shalt bring forth a Son; and thou shalt call His Name Jesus. He shall be great, and shall be called the Son of the Most High; and the Lord God shall give unto Him the throne of David His father; and He shall reign in the House of Jacob forever. And of His kingdom there shall be no end". (Luke 1:26-38.)

St. Augustine says that the Virgin understood there was question of the coming Redeemer, but as she had vowed her virginity to God, why should she be chosen amongst women for this great dignity? Filled with fear and astonishment, Mary asked: "How shall this be done, because I know not man?"

In order to remove Mary's anxiety and to assure her
that her virginity would be spared, the Angel answered:
"The Holy Ghost shall come upon thee and the power of
the Most High shall overshadow thee. And therefore also
the Holy which shall be born of thee shall be called the
Son of God". And to convince her of the truth of his word
he made known to her the conception of St. John, saying:
"And behold, thy cousin Elizabeth; she also has conceived
a son in her old age, and this is the sixth month with her
that is called barren: because no word shall be impossible
with God". Mary, in all humility, then replied: "Behold
the handmaid of the Lord, be it done to me according to
thy word".

The Annunciation, therefore, is the beginning of Jesus
in His human nature. "And the Word was made flesh and
dwelt among us".

☧

MARCH 26

ST. LUDGER

St. Ludger was born of noble parentage in Frisia,
about 743. At the child's request he was educated at the
school which St. Gregory had founded at Utrecht, and
made great progress. Desirous of further education, Ludger
went to England, where he spent four and one-half years.
While there he contracted a friendship with Alcuin, which
lasted throughout life.

After Ludger was ordained to the priesthood at
Cologne, in 777, he was engaged for several years in
preaching the word of God in Eastern Friesland, where
he converted a great many pagans and lapsed Catholics,
founded several monasteries, and built many churches.
When the pagan Saxons ravaged the country Ludger was
obliged to leave Friesland. He went to Rome to consult
Pope Adrian II to ascertain God's Will. The next three and
one-half years he spent at Monte Cassino following the
Benedictine Rule, without taking the religious vows.

In 787, after Charlemagne overcame the Saxons and conquered Friesland, Ludger returned to East Friesland and converted not only the Saxons to the Faith but also the province of Westphalia. In 793 Charlemagne desired to make Ludger Bishop of Trier, but he refused the honor, stating that he would be willing to evangelize the Saxons. His offer was gladly accepted, and northwestern Saxony was added to Ludger's missionary field.

Archbishop Hildebald of Cologne in 802, against Ludger's strenuous resistance, consecrated him Bishop of Mimigardeford, which city later changed its name to that of Munster. He founded there the great monastery of Regular Canons to serve his cathedral; built a chapel in honor of the Blessed Virgin Mary on the left of the Aa, and churches in a number of towns.

St. Ludger was favored with the gifts of miracles and prophecy. He foretold the invasions of the Normans from Denmark and Norway and the ravages they would make in the French empire; also, the date of his death. Though seriously ill he continued to perform his pastoral duties to the very last day of his life. He died on Passion Sunday, March 26, 809, and was interred in Werden, where his relics have rested for over eleven centuries.

☩

MARCH 27

ST. JOHN DAMASCENE

St. John Damascene was born at Damascus about 676. He received his education under the tutorship of Coasmas, a Sicilian Monk. Upon the death of his father, John was made chief councillor of Damascus. During his incumbency the Church in the East began to be perturbed by the Iconoclast heresy. In 726, the Byzantine Emperor, Leo the Isaurian, despite the protests of Germanus, Patriarch of Constantinople, issued his first edict against

the veneration of images. John Damascene immediately
entered the ranks against him, defending the ancient practice of the Christians.

In 730 the Isaurian issued a second edict, which not
only forbade veneration of the images, but even prohibited
their exhibition in public places. St. John replied with
greater vigor than before. In a third letter he warned the
Emperor to beware of his unlawful action. His anger
aroused, and being unable to reach St. John with physical
force, he sought to destroy him by forging his signature to
a letter offering to betray into the hands of the Isaurian
the city of Damascus. This letter he sent to the caliph.
Notwithstanding St. John's sincere declaration of innocence,
the caliph ordered that St. John's right hand be severed at
the wrist. The sentence was executed, but through the intervention of the Blessed Virgin the amputated hand was
miraculously restored.

The caliph, now convinced of John's innocence, desired
to reinstate him as his councillor, but John had heard a call
to a higher life. He entered the monastery of St. Sabas,
eighteen miles southeast of Jerusalem, and in due time was
ordained to the priesthood. He was the last of the Greek
Fathers. Pope Leo XIII enrolled him among the Doctors
of the Church.

☧

MARCH 28

ST. JOHN CAPISTRAN

St. John was born at Capistran, Italy, on June 24, 1385.
He owed his education to his mother, since his father died
when he was quite young. John studied law at Perugia,
where he achieved great success. In 1412 he was appointed
Governor of Perugia by the King of Naples, who then held
that city of the Holy See.

War broke out in 1416 between Perugia and the Malatesta. John was sent as ambassador to propose peace to the
Malatesta, who cast him into prison. During his imprison-

ment he began to think seriously about the salvation of his soul. Due to a dream he had, in which he saw St. Francis, who warned him to become a Franciscan, John decided eventually to become a Franciscan Friar.

Before the war broke out he had married a wealthy lady of Perugia, but as the marriage was not consummated he obtained a dispensation to enter religion, which he did on October 4, 1416. After taking his vows he came under the influence of St. Bernardine of Siena, who taught him theology. St. John accompanied St. Bernardine on his preaching tours in order to study his methods. After his ordination to the priesthood he labored ceaselessly for the salvation of souls until his death. He traversed the whole of Italy, preaching to the multitude in the public squares. Like St. Bernardine of Siena he propagated devotion to the Holy Name of Jesus; both were accused of heresy on account of this devotion. He also assisted St. Bernardine in the reform of the Franciscan Order.

Upon a visit to France St. John met St. Colette, the reformer of the Second Order Franciscans, or Poor Clares, with whose efforts he fully sympathized. He was frequently employed on embassies by the Holy See.

St. John was chosen by God to deliver Europe from Islam, which threatened to invade it in the 15th century. Mohammed II had taken Constantinople and was marching on Belgrade. Pope Callixtus III decreed a Crusade, and St. John preached it in Pannonia and other provinces. Supported by the noble Hungarian, John Hunyades, he enrolled 70,000 Christians, who had no other arms but forks and flails. St. John, whose "strength was the Lord", led the left wing of the Christian army against the Turks, and "obtained by their bravery the victory after severe fighting", thus assuring the triumph of the Cross over the Crescent. That very evening 120,000 Turks lay dead or had fled, and Mohammed, wounded, renounced his undertaking against Christian Europe.

St. John died on October 23, 1456, and was canonized in 1724.

✠

MARCH 29

STS. JONAS, BARACHISIUS, AND THEIR COMPANIONS

King Sapor II of Persia, during the 18th year of his reign, excited a bloody persecution against the Christians and destroyed their churches and monasteries. When Jonas and Barachisius, two brothers of Beth-Asa, heard that a number of Christians had been sentenced to death at Huba-ham they went to that city to encourage and help them. When nine of them had received the crown of martyrdom, Jonas and Barachisius were arrested for having exhorted them to persevere in their Christian Faith.

After bravely enduring unspeakable torments, Jonas and Barachisius also laid down their lives for Christ's sake about the year 327.

✠

MARCH 30

ST. JOHN CLIMACUS

St. John was born in Palestine about the year 525. By his extraordinary progress in the arts and sciences when quite young, he was called the Scholastic. At the age of sixteen he renounced all worldly advantages and dedicated himself to God in the religious state. He retired to Mt. Sinai to contemplate on heavenly things, under the direction of Martyrius, a holy Anchorite. Four years later he made his religious profession, having prepared himself by fervent prayer and fasting for the solemn consecration.

In 560, upon the death of Martyrius, having then spent nineteen years in that place in penance and holy contemplation, St. John withdrew into a deeper solitude near the foot of Mt. Sinai. His cell was five miles from the church, where he and all the other Anchorites and Monks of the desert went every Saturday and Sunday to recite the Holy Office and to celebrate the Divine Mysteries.

St. John studied the lives of the Saints, and assiduously read the Holy Scriptures and the writings of the Fathers. He became one of the most learned Doctors of the Church, reaching an unusual height of contemplation. The fame of his holiness drew many to seek his advice. God bestowed on him an extraordinary grace of healing the spiritual disorders of souls.

In the year 600, at the age of seventy-five, forty years of which had been spent in his hermitage, St. John was chosen Abbot of Mt. Sinai and Superior General of all the monks and hermits in that country. Soon after he was raised to this dignity the people of Palestine and Arabia sought his intercession with God during the time of drought and famine. His prayer was immediately recompensed with abundant rains. Pope St. Gregory the Great also recommended himself to his prayers and sent him furniture and money for his hospital, which was used for pilgrims near Mt. Sinai.

A brother Abbot induced St. John to write the rules by which he had guided his life. This book, called *The Climax,* or *Ladder of Perfection,* is a classic in ascetical literature, because of its sublime sentiments and perfect description of all Christian virtues.

Having governed the Monks of Mt. Sinai for four years, St. John resigned the position a little before his death, which occurred in his hermitage on March 30, 605, when he was eighty years old.

☩

MARCH 31

ST. BENJAMIN

St. Benjamin was a Deacon of the Church in Persia in the 5th century. The Christians in that country had enjoyed peace for twelve years, when Abdas, a Christian

Bishop, in 420, indiscreetly ordered the destruction of the Pyraeum, or Temple of Fire, the great divinity of the Persians. King Isdegerdes, who had formerly put a stop to the cruel persecution of the Christians in his kingdom, now demolished all the Christian churches, put to death Abdas, and raised a general persecution against the Christians.

Isdegerdes died in 421, but his son and successor, Varanes, carried on the persecution with greater fury and horror. Among those who suffered martyrdom for the Faith was St. Benjamin. He was beaten and imprisoned. A year later the Emperor obtained his release from the dungeon on condition that he should never speak to any of the courtiers about religion. Benjamin declared, however, that as a minister of the Gospel he would miss no opportunity of preaching the word of God. When the King was informed that St. Benjamin was still preaching the Christian Faith in his kingdom, he ordered that he be apprehended. After undergoing unspeakable tortures St. Benjamin died in the year 424.

APRIL

ST. HUGH OF GRENOBLE

St. Hugh was born near Valence, in Dauphine, in 1053, and chose to serve God in the ecclesiastical state. His father, Odilo, held an honorable position in the army. When nearly fifty years old, on the advice of his son, Hugh, he became a Carthusian Monk, and died in the great Chartreuse monastery when one hundred years of age. Under the direction of Hugh, his mother served God in her own home by prayer, fasting and charitable works. St. Hugh assisted both of his parents in their dying moments.

He accepted a canonry in the Cathedral of Valence. His holiness, gentleness and affability won for him the affection of all who knew him. In 1080 he was appointed Bishop of Grenoble, and took steps immediately to correct the abuses which had crept in. By his rigorous fasts, vigils, and prayers he drew down God's mercy on his flock, and in a short time great improvement was noted in the Diocese.

After two years he resigned his bishopric, and put on the habit of St. Benedict in the austere monastery of Casa-Dei, in Auvergne. For a year he lived a perfect model of all virtues, when Pope Gregory VII commanded him, in virtue of holy obedience, to resume his pastoral charge at Grenoble.

In 1084 St. Hugh gave to St. Bruno and his six companions the land of La Grande, a desert in his Diocese, called the Chartreuse, where they could live in solitude. It was here that St. Bruno founded his famous Order.

St. Hugh implored Pope Innocent II for permission to resign his bishopric in order to die in solitude, but without success. After a lingering illness God called him to Himself on April 1, 1132. Miracles attested the sanctity of his death. He was canonized by Pope Innocent II in 1134.

✠

APRIL 2

ST. FRANCIS OF PAULA

St. Francis was born in 1416 at Paula, in Calabria, Italy, of remarkably holy parents. Though very poor, they were industrious and happy in their humble condition. From early youth Francis showed signs of extraordinary sanctity. At the age of thirteen, warned by a vision of a Franciscan Friar, he entered the Franciscan Order so as to fulfill a vow made by his parents. He gave great edification by his love of prayer, mortification, profound humility, and prompt obedience.

After the end of a year Francis went with his parents on a pilgrimage to Assisi, Rome, Subiaco, and other places. Upon their return to Paula, Francis selected a retired spot on his father's estate, where he lived in solitude; later he chose a more secluded site in a cave on the sea coast, where he remained alone for about six years, leading a life of prayer and mortification.

Two companions joined him in 1435, which caused Francis to build three cells and a chapel to accommodate them. It was in this way that the Order of Minims (the least of all religious) was begun. His disciples having gradually increased, about 1454 the Archbishop of Cosenza gave Francis permission to erect a large monastery and church. Great enthusiasm and devotion on the part of the people were shown towards Francis. Their spiritual life was enkindled into flame by the many miracles which the Saint wrought in answer to their prayers.

St. Francis had an extraordinary gift of prophecy and the discernment of consciences. The last three years of his life were spent in solitude, preparing for death. Pope Leo X canonized him in 1519. In 1562 the Huguenots broke open his tomb and found his body incorrupt. They dragged it forth and burned it, but some of the bones were preserved by the Faithful and enshrined in various churches of his Order.

✠

APRIL 3

ST. RICHARD

St. Richard was born in 1197 at Wiche, near Worcester, England. When quite young, he and his elder brother were left orphans. Richard gave up his studies in order to manage his brother's impoverished farms. He succeeded so well that his brother desired to make over the estate to him. Richard refused not only the estate, but the opportunity of a brilliant marriage, since he desired to give himself to God's service. He resumed his studies which he had begun at Oxford, then in Paris. Returning to England he won his Master of Arts at Oxford, and then went to Bologna, Italy, to study canon law.

St. Edmund, Archbishop of Canterbury, appointed him his Chancellor, and he accompanied the Archbishop when he was banished to France. After his death, Richard retired to a convent of Dominican Friars in Orleans, France, where he was ordained Priest.

When Bishop Nevil of Chichester, England, was dying, King Henry III recommended an unworthy court favorite to the See. The Archbishop declared him unqualified and the presentation void. He preferred Richard of Wiche to that dignity. Richard was consecrated in 1245, but the King refused to recognize the election and seized the revenues of the See. Richard suffered many hardships and persecutions for two years, repaying with favors those who persecuted him. He pleaded his cause before Pope Innocent IV against the King's deputies, and obtained a confirmation of his election.

St. Richard performed his episcopal duties with fervor and charity towards his flock, and thoroughly reformed his See. After two years his revenues were restored. He preached the word of God with that unction and fruitfulness which only an eminent spirit of prayer could

produce. Penitent sinners he received with great tenderness
and charity, but when the rights of the Church were
questioned he remained obdurate, fearing no consequences.

While preaching a holy war against the Saracens, at
the Pope's command, St. Richard fell ill. He foretold his
death, dying in a hospital at Dover on April 3, 1253, at the
age of fifty-six. His body was conveyed to Chichester for
internment in the Cathedral before the altar he had erected.
Miraculous cures occurred at his tomb. The Saint was
solemnly canonized by Pope Urban IV in 1262.

☦

APRIL 4

ST. BENEDICT THE MOOR

St. Benedict's ancestors were brought in chains from
Africa to Sicily. His parents, Christopher and Diana Manas-
seri, were Negro slaves on a farm in San Filadelfo when
Benedict was born in 1526. His youth was spent quietly
on the farm, assisting his parents with their farm work.
The villagers soon recognized the child's goodness and
sincere piety.

When eighteen years old, Benedict was given his freedom. From his meagre wages he helped the sick and needy
as far as it was possible, and they considered his charity
further proof of his holiness. This led them to call him
Il Santo Moro, the Holy Negro. Some jealous people, however, ridiculed his piety and insulted him with remarks
about his race, color and parentage.

Jerome Lanza, a nobleman, had renounced his wealth
and honor to live a hermit's life in the surrounding hills.
Other men had followed his example to lead a life of solitude, prayer and penance in imitation of St. Francis of
Assisi. One day as Jerome passed by he heard some insult-
ing remarks aimed at Benedict. Stopping, he prophetically
said: "You are making fun of this poor Negro now, but

let me tell you that in a few years his name will be famous".
Soon Jerome invited Benedict to join him and the other
hermits. Willingly the humble Negro gave to the poor the
little he had and with great joy joined the group of hermits.
They were not long in recognizing Benedict's many virtues
and his extraordinary holiness. Upon the death of Jerome
Lanza, they unanimously chose Benedict to succeed him
as their leader. Their choice was a wise one, as their reputation for sanctity spread throughout Sicily.

In 1562, when Pope Pius IV advised the hermits to
join one of the older Orders of the Church, Benedict chose
to enter the Order of Friars Minor as a lay-Brother. The
first few years as a Franciscan he spent in solitude in the
nearby Friary of St. Anne. After three years his superiors
called him to St. Mary's, near Palermo, to cook for the
community, and he became a model of virtue. His love of
prayer, his fervent devotion to Jesus in the Blessed Sacrament and to the Blessed Virgin, his humility and meekness,
made a deep impression upon all. He also performed several miracles. As soon as the people of Palermo heard of
the wonderful life of Brother Benedict they began to seek
his help and consolation. He comforted all who were in
trouble, and without pride or vanity went to care for the
poor, to visit the sick and those in prison.

In 1578 the Friars of St. Mary chose this lowly Brother,
who was unable to read or write, to be the Superior of their
Friary. Humbly he accepted the office, in obedience to the
Will of God. Three years later, after an edifying tenure of
office, they desired him to continue as Superior, but Benedict insisted that he should be the Assistant Superior. His
wish was complied with, and he was entrusted with teaching all who came to the Friary to become Franciscans.
Although unable to read, he was able to explain the Holy
Scriptures and the teachings of the Church with beauty
and clarity, thus enabling his proteges to learn that true
holiness does not emanate from great learning or wealth
or station in life, but from union with God through love of
Him and all His creatures. After having faithfully fulfilled

these duties for some years, Benedict asked permission to return to the place he had filled in the kitchen. His request was granted, but he was not to enjoy the peace and quiet of his earlier days.

Benedict's fame had spread, and the Friary was besieged by men of all walks of life seeking his help—even the Archbishop of Palermo, the Viceroy of Sicily, and some theologians. He received all, and sent them away in peace of soul.

Benedict fell seriously ill and foretold the day of his death—April 4, 1589. In 1592, when his tomb was opened, his body was found to be incorrupt, exhaling a sweet perfume. Such crowds flocked to his tomb that his body was transferred, in 1611, to a beautiful shrine in a little chapel provided by King Phillip III of Spain.

Devotion to *Il Santo Moro* has spread to many parts of the Old and New World. In 1807, Pope Pius VII canonized the Holy Negro, St. Benedict the Moor.

✠

APRIL 5

ST. VINCENT FERRER

A most wonderful Christian hero of the 14th century was St. Vincent Ferrer, born at Valencia, Spain, in 1350. His obedience, sweetness of temper, and unusual diligence in early years were considered by all as signs of his future holiness. Whenever he heard anything in praise of the glorious Virgin Mother of God, his soul so overflowed with joy that he could not restrain his tears. And when he read about, or heard a sermon on the Passion of Christ, he would also weep abundantly.

Vincent was not only remarkable for goodness and early piety, but he also excelled in learning, as he was gifted with rare talents. He was never known to dispute or contend with anyone, and strove to conceal, rather than to display, his abilities. These good qualities made him a general favorite with all who knew him.

When Vincent was eighteen he decided to enter the Order of St. Dominic, in Valencia, to the happiness of his parents. He was clothed in the religious habit February 5, 1374, and was professed the following year. For three years he taught the students, and then was sent to complete his studies at Barcelona and Lerida. When only twenty-four, he wrote a book on philosophy, and at twenty-eight received the degree of Doctor or Master in Theology.

It was at Barcelona that the first instance is recorded of that gift of prophecy, for which afterwards he became so remarkable.

For six years he lectured on theological subjects and preached the Word of God to the people. Many came from neighboring towns and villages to hear the words of wisdom that fell from his lips.

During the 14th century two terrible scourges inflicted most serious evil on the Church. The first was the awful pestilence called the Black Death, which devastated the whole of Europe in the middle of the 14th century, killing one-third of the population of the world, including large numbers of the clergy and religious. In order to fill the decimated ranks, men were in many places accepted quickly and without due caution, and thus often without a true vocation. Laxities and irregularities were the natural consequence. St. Vincent not only instructed and converted the laity, but worked a striking reform among the clergy and religious orders where he found it needful.

The second evil under which the Church then groaned was even more serious—the Great Schism. The evils arising from this scandal were many and grievous. St. Vincent was one of those raised up by God's good Providence to bring the schism to an end and to remedy its effects. His labors to promote unity, and the agony of mind he endured in seeing the seamless garment of Christ rent by the schism, affected his health and endangered his life.

He fell gravely ill at Avignon and as he was eagerly welcoming death, a wonderful event occurred. His humble cell was suddenly filled with heavenly light, and he saw Jesus Christ Himself shining like the sun, surrounded by a multitude of angels, while near Our Lord were His two glorious servants, St. Dominic and St. Francis. The gracious Master, after filling Vincent's soul with joy by many loving words, manifested His desires regarding him:

"I have chosen you as the herald of the Gospel, and My Will is that you should go through all Gaul and Spain, preaching the Gospel. . . . My Will is that you should boldly reprove the sins of men, and bid them prepare for the great judgment. Though wicked men will oppose you, fear nothing. I will be with you".

This miraculous apostolate lasted twenty-one years. Besides the labors in Gaul and Spain, he preached throughout Europe. Tens of thousands of persons were converted: Jews, Mohammedans, infidels, heretics. Though speaking only his native Spanish, he was understood in all tongues. Astounding miracles confirmed his words.

His effect on the Jews was especially miraculous. So clear were his arguments from the Old Testament, and so persuasive were his words, that God was pleased through him to convert 25,000 Jews in different parts of Spain; their synagogues were changed into churches.

St. Vincent died in Brittany on April 5, 1419. He was canonized by Pope Callistus III on the Feast of SS. Peter and Paul, June 29, 1455.

✠

APRIL 6

ST. CELESTINE

St. Celestine was born in Rome, and held a distinguished place among the clergy of that city. Upon the death of Pope Boniface, he was chosen to succeed him in September, 422.

Three great events stand out in the Pontificate of St. Celestine: he supported the campaign of St. Germanus of Auxerre against Pelagius; he sent Palladius to preach the Faith to the Scots in North-Britain and in Ireland shortly before St. Patrick's mission there; and he dispatched three Legates from Rome to the general Council at Ephesus with instructions to unite with St. Cyril in condemning the heretical teaching of Nestorius.

This holy Pope received the crown of everlasting glory on August 1, 432, after reigning almost ten years.

✠

APRIL 7

ST. HEGESIPPUS

St. Hegesippus, a primitive Father, was by birth a Jew. He spent twenty years in Rome, from the Pontificate of Anicetus to that of Eleutherius, in 177. He personally visited the principal churches of the East and West, and in 133 wrote a History of the Church, in five volumes, from the Passion of Christ down to his own time, in which he gave proofs of his Faith, showed the Apostolical tradition, traced the succession of Popes from St. Peter to his own day, and testified that no episcopal See or particular church had fallen into the heretical teachings of some men, but had preserved inviolably the truths delivered by Christ to the Apostles. His work was praised by Eusebius and St. Jerome.

✠

APRIL 8

ST. PERPETUUS

St. Perpetuus was the 8th Bishop of Tours, governing that See from 461 to 491. He strove zealously to lead souls to a virtuous life. He had a great veneration for the saints, adorned their shrines, and enriched their churches. His senatorial family possessed very large estates, and he consecrated the revenues from them to the service of the church and the relief of the poor.

The numerous miracles at the tomb of St. Martin in his Diocese attracted so many people that the church built by St. Bricius became too small to accommodate the multitude. St. Perpetuus directed its enlargement, and upon its completion solemnly dedicated the new church. On July 4, 473, he had St. Martin's body translated to it.

✠

APRIL 9

ST. MARY OF EGYPT

When only twelve years old, Mary left her father's home in Egypt without permission and went to Alexandria. There she fell into sin, and remained in that state for seventeen years. In her 29th year she joined several persons and embarked for the Holy Land to celebrate the Feast of the Exaltation of the Holy Cross of our Savior in Jerusalem. On the Feast Day she mingled with the crowd going to church to venerate the Holy Cross. Some secret force, as she related later, prevented her from entering the church. After this occurred three or four times, Mary began to consider what might be the cause. Thinking it was due to her sinful life, she wept bitterly. Looking up she perceived a picture of Our Lady, and begged her help, by her incomparable purity, and promised that if she were able to enter the church to behold the sacred wood of her redemption she would consecrate herself to God by a life of penance, taking the Blessed Mother as her surety.

After this ardent prayer, Mary felt interior consolation, and upon attempting again to enter the church she was able to do so with ease. She venerated the precious wood of the Cross, and considering the incomprehensible mercy of

God and His willingness to receive repentant sinners, she kissed the floor, shedding copious tears. Arising, she went and knelt before the picture of the Mother of God, implored her intercession, and begged that she be her guide. She seemed to hear these words: "If thou goest beyond the Jordan thou shalt there find rest and comfort". Weeping, and looking at the image of the holy Queen of the world, Mary implored that she never abandon her.

Hastily she left the church taking the road which led to the Jordan. That night she reached the church of St. John the Baptist on the banks of the river. Later, she related: "There I paid my devotions to God and received the precious Body of our Savior Jesus Christ". The following morning, after sleeping on the ground all night, she recommended herself to the Blessed Virgin Mary and crossed the Jordan.

Mary of Egypt lived a life of solitude and penance in the desert for forty-seven years, when a holy Monk, named Zosimus, met her there one day, and it was to him that she confided the events of her life. At her request he brought her the Sacred Body of Christ on Holy Thursday. She asked him to return the following year, but this time he found her corpse upon the ground, with an inscription declaring her name, Mary, and the time of her death. Zosimus, miraculously assisted by a lion, dug a grave and buried her. Some authors are of the opinion that the penitent's death occurred in the year 421.

✠

APRIL 10

ST. BADEMUS

Bademus, a wealthy Persian, desirous of devoting himself to the service of God, founded a monastery near Beth-Lapat in his country and governed it with great sanctity. Entire nights were spent in prayer, and sometimes bread and water were his only fare for several days. He trained his Religious in the way of perfection with kindness, prudence and charity. In this wonderful retreat Bademus enjoyed peace of soul and profound happiness.

To test his virtue, God permitted Bademus and his seven Monks to be arrested during the 36th year of the persecution of King Shapur II. Bound with chains, they lay for four months in a prison. Daily they were called out to receive a certain number of stripes. Patiently and joyfully they suffered all for Christ.

During his incarceration, a Christian lord of the Persian court who refused to adore the sun, was likewise cast into prison. Soon his constancy failed and he promised to conform. Endeavoring to ascertain whether he was sincere, the King ordered Bademus to be brought into the prison of Nersan, which was a chamber in his palace, and informed Nersan that if he would kill Bademus his own liberty would be restored. The wicked man agreed. Given a sword, he advanced to plunge it into the Abbot's breast. Nersan stopped, unable for some time to lift his arm. Undaunted, the servant of Christ, with his eyes fixed on him, said: "Unhappy Nersan, to what a pitch of impiety do you carry your apostacy. With joy I run to meet death; but could wish to fall by some other hand than yours: why must you be my executioner?"

Lacking the courage and steadfastness of St. Bademus, with a trembling hand he aimed at the sides of the Martyr, but his strokes were forceless and unsteady. So numerous were the Martyr's wounds that the witnesses were amazed at his invincible patience. Finally, on April 10, 376, with four strokes of the sword, the Martyr's head was severed from his body. Nersan soon after fell into public disgrace and was put to death by the sword.

The infidels reproachfully cast the body of St. Bademus out of the city, but the Christians secretly carried it away and buried it. Upon the death of King Shapur, four years later, the disciples of St. Bademus were released from their chains.

✠

APRIL 11

ST. LEO THE GREAT

St. Leo, surnamed the Great, descended from a noble Tuscan family but was born at Rome. He became Archdeacon of the Church of Rome under Popes Celestine I and Sixtus III. When Sixtus III died, the Roman clergy chose Leo as his successor to the Papal throne, and he was raised to St. Peter's throne on Sunday, September 29, 440. His signal victories over the heretics—Manicheans, Arians, Apollinarists, Nestorians, Pelagians, Eutychians, Novatians and Donatists—prove his zeal for the purity of the Faith.

While the Eastern empire was assailed by heretical teachings, the Western was laid waste by the attacks of barbarians. Attila, the Hun, enriched with the plunder of many nations, marched against Rome. Pope Leo, at the request of the Roman citizenry, went to meet Attila, "the scourge of God", saving the Holy City and averting the destruction of the surrounding country. It was near Ravenna that they met, and contrary to the expectations of everyone, Attila received the Pope with great honor, and through his suggestion concluded a treaty of peace with the empire on the condition of an annual tribute.

Baronius, a writer of the 8th century, states that Attila saw two venerable personages, supposed to be the Apostles St. Peter and St. Paul, standing by the Pope as he spoke. Two years later Rome fell a prey to the Vandals. The Holy Father prevailed upon the Arian Vandal king to restrain his troops from slaughter and burning and to be satisfied with plundering the city, thus saving it from destruction.

Because of his humility, mildness and charity, Pope Leo was reverenced and loved not only by emperors and princes, but by all ranks of people, even infidels and barbarians.

His dogmatic letter to Flavian, Patriarch of Constantinople, in which he defined the Catholic belief on the twofold nature and one person in Christ, was acclaimed as the teaching of the Church at the Council of Chalcedon in 451.

This great Pope filled the Holy See twenty-one years, one month and thirteen days, dying on November 10, 461. He shares the title of "the Great", with only two other Popes—Gregory I and Nicholas I. In 1754, St. Leo was declared a Doctor of the Church.

✠

APRIL 12

ST. JULIUS I

St. Julius I, a Roman, was chosen to succeed Pope Marcus on February 6, 337, and ruled the Church for fifteen years. He received the appeal of St. Athanasius, whom he defended against the accusations of the heretical Arian Bishops of the East. The Arians then demanded a Council, which Pope Julius assembled in Rome in 341. Instead of appearing, the Arians held a pretended Council at Antioch that same year, in which they presumed to appoint as Bishop of Alexandria an impious Arian, Gregory; detained the Pope's Legates beyond the time indicated for their appearance, and then wrote to His Holiness alleging that it was impossible for them to be present on account of the Persian war, and mentioning other impediments.

The Pope readily recognized the pretences and, in a Council at Rome, examined the cause of Athanasius, declared him innocent of the charges made against him by the Arians, and confirmed him in his See. To the Oriental Eusebian Bishops, who had demanded a Council and then refused to attend it, Pope Julius dispatched a letter by Count Gabian. Tillemont called it one of the "finest monuments of ecclesiastical antiquity". The Pope's extraordinary genius, solid judgment, apostolic vigor and resolution, were tempered with great charity and meekness.

Seven synods were held under his episcopate; the third, fourth and seventh decreeing that any Bishop deposed by a synod in his province, has a right to appeal to the Bishop of Rome.

St. Julius died on April 12, 352.

✠

APRIL 13

ST. HERMENEGILD

St. Hermenegild, a son of Leovigild, the Arian King of the Visigoths, was brought up an Arian at the court of Seville. Hermenegild married, in 576, Ingundis, daughter of King Sigebert of France, who was a devout Catholic. Through her holy example and the instructions he received from St. Leander of Seville he embraced the Catholic Faith. When Leovigild learned of his son's conversion, he summoned him back to Toledo; Hermenegild did not obey the command. In a rage Leovigild divested him of the title of King, threatened to deprive him of his possessions, his princess, and even his life, unless he renounced the Catholic Faith. Hermenegild refused. Considering himself a sovereign Prince, he resolved to defend himself, and was supported by the Catholics of Spain. They were not strong enough, however, to defend him against the Arians.

In 584, after a two-years' fruitless struggle, Hermenegild was falsely promised pardon if he would surrender and ask forgiveness. Believing his father sincere, he went and cast himself at his feet. Leovigild embraced him, renewing his promises with many caresses. He then stripped him of his royal raiment, bound him with chains, and had him conducted to the tower of Seville. With torture and bribes he now strove to shake his son's Faith. Hermenegild wrote his father that he considered the crown as nothing, and would rather lose the sceptre and his life than deny the truth of God.

St. Gregory the Great relates that Leovigild sent an Arian bishop to Hermenegild in his prison, on Easter Eve, 585, with a promise that he would forgive him all provided he would consent to receive Holy Communion from the hands of this bishop. Hermenegild firmly refused. Upon receiving word of his son's steadfastness, the King dispatched some soldiers to kill him. He was beheaded on Easter Day, and was later venerated as a martyr.

Through the martyrdom of Hermenegild, his brother, King Reccared, and the entire kingdom of the Visigoths in Spain were converted to the Catholic Faith.

✠

APRIL 14

ST. JUSTIN

St. Justin was born near Sichem, now Pablus, in Palestine, about the year 100. His father, a heathen, brought him up in the errors and superstitions of paganism. Justin spent his youth in reading the poets, orators, historians and scientists. In search of God, he conferred with the philosophers of his day without making any progress. One day he met an old man by the seashore who convinced him that Platonic views regarding God would not bring him happiness; that there were certain holy men who loved God long before the existence of these reputed philosophers, who were called prophets, whose books, still extant, contain many solid instructions about the first cause and end of all things; that their miracles and predictions had procured them such credit that they established truth by authority and not by disputes and elaborate demonstrations of human reason, of which few men are capable; that they inculcated the belief of one only God, the Father and author of all things, and of His Son, Jesus Christ, Whom He had sent into the world. Then he concluded his discourse with this advice: "As for thyself, above all things, pray that the gates of life may be opened unto thee: for these

are not things to be discerned unless God and Christ grant
to a man the knowledge of them". He then departed and
Justin never saw him again, but his conversation made a
deep impression on the young philosopher's soul, and had
enkindled an ardent affection for the true philosophers,
the prophets. Upon further inquiry into the credibility
of the Christian religion, Justin embraced it about the
year 130.

Zealous for the Faith, he traveled to Greece, Egypt
and Italy, and brought many to believe in Christ. In his
"Apologies" and his "Dialogue" he gives many personal
details about his studies and his conversion. In his second
"Apology" Justin says: "I, too, expect to be persecuted and
to be crucified by some of those whom I have named,
or by Crescens, that friend of noise and of ostentation".

It was at Rome, about the year 167, that St. Justin
sealed his testimony with his blood. Surrounded by his
disciples, the prefect said to him: "Do you imagine that by
dying you will enter Heaven and there be rewarded?" The
Saint replied: "I do not only imagine it; I know it".

When St. Justin and the other Christians with him refused to sacrifice to the gods, the prefect ordered them
to be scourged and then beheaded, as the law directed.

St. Justin is one of the most ancient Fathers of the
Church, who has left us many valuable works. He was a
voluminous, learned writer; a witness to the truth, a witness for Christ unto death.

☩

APRIL 15

ST. PATERNUS

St. Paternus was born at Poitiers, about the year 482.
His father, with the consent of his wife, spent the last
years of his life in solitude in Ireland.

Paternus, who had led a holy life, followed his father's
example and embraced the monastic state in the Abbey

of Marnes. Desirous of attaining greater perfection, he went to Wales, and there founded a monastery called Llanpatern-vaur. He had the happiness of visiting his father in Ireland. Paternus was called back to his monastery of Marnes and soon after, with St. Scubilion, a fellow-Monk, and the permission of the Bishop, he embraced a hermit's life in the forest of Seicy, in the Diocese of Constances. He converted many idolaters to the Faith in that vicinity and as far as Bayeux.

At an advanced age St. Paternus was consecrated Bishop of Avranches by Germanus, Bishop of Rouen. After governing his Diocese for thirteen years he withdrew to a solitude in France, and died about the year 550.

✠

APRIL 16

THE EIGHTEEN MARTYRS
OF SARAGOSSA

During the persecution of Diocletian, St. Optatus and seventeen other holy men received the crown of martyrdom on the same day, under the cruel Governor Dacian. Prudentius relates that two others, Caius and Crementius, died of their torments after a second conflict.

The same author also describes the triumph of St. Encratis, or Engratia, virgin. A native of Portugal, her father had promised her in marriage. In order to preserve her virginity and to serve her heavenly Spouse without hindrance, she fled to Saragossa during the persecution under Dacian. When she reproached him for his barbarities, he ordered that she be tormented in a most inhuman manner. Her sides were torn with iron hooks, one of her breasts was cut off, and part of her liver was pulled out. Still alive, she was sent back to prison, where she died from her wounds.

Relics of all these martyrs were found at Saragossa in 1389.

✠

ST. ANICETUS

St. Anicetus, a Syrian by descent, succeeded Pope Pius I, and reigned from the end of the year 157 till about 168. It was during his Pontificate that St. Polycarp of Smyrna visited Rome to confer with him regarding the date for observing Easter. The matter was discussed, but no decision was reached. The Pope, however, permitted the aged saint to celebrate this Feast on the day he had been accustomed to in the Church of Smyrna, that is, on the 14th day of the first moon after the vernal equinox.

St. Anicetus suffered so much for the Faith, that although he did not shed his blood he is considered a martyr.

✠

ST. APOLLONIUS

Commodus VI, son of Marcus Aurelius, succeeded his father in 180. Though a vicious man, out of regard to his Empress, Marcia, who admired the Christian Faith, he acted favorably towards the Christians. During this period of calm many persons of high rank enlisted under the banner of the Cross. Among these was Apollonius, a Roman senator, well versed in philosophy and Holy Scripture. Severus, one of his slaves, accused him of being a Christian before Perennis, prefect of the Praetorium. The prefect immediately condemned the slave to have his legs broken and to be put to death, in accordance with an edict of Marcus Aurelius, who, without repealing former laws against convicted Christians, ordered that their accusers should be put to death.

After the slave was executed, St. Apollonius was ordered to renounce his religion. This he refused to do.

Perennis then commanded him to give an account of his Faith to the Senate. His eloquent defense of the Christian Faith before that body, and his refusal to renounce his religion, resulted in a decree of the Senate that he be beheaded.

It was about the year 186 that St. Apollonius was martyred for the Faith.

☩

APRIL 19

ST. ELPHEGE

St. Elphege was born in 954, of a noble Saxon family. He became a Monk, and after some years as an anchorite became Abbot of the monastery he founded at Bath. In 984 he was made Bishop of Winchester. In 1006, on becoming Archbishop of Canterbury, he went to Rome for the Pallium. The following year the Danes sacked and burned Canterbury, and held Elphege as a prisoner, for whom they expected a large ransom.

He refused to permit his church to assume such expense for him. Consequently he was kept in prison at Greenwich for seven months. On April 19, 1012, his captors, drunk with wine, and enraged because ransom was refused, stoned and finally put Elphege to death by a sword-stroke. His body, after resting eleven years in St. Paul's (London), was translated by King Canute to Canterbury.

☩

APRIL 20

ST. AGNES OF MONTEPULCIANO

St. Agnes was born near Montepulciano in Tuscany, about 1268. At an early age she entered the Dominican convent of Proceno, of which she later became the Prioress. Upon the request of the citizens of Montepulciano, St. Agnes founded the famous convent of Dominican Nuns in that city, which she governed until her death. God bestowed upon her many supernatural graces, and she died in the odor of sanctity in 1317, in her forty-ninth year. She was canonized four hundred years later.

✠

APRIL 21

ST. ANSELM

St. Anselm was born at Aosta, northern Italy, about 1033. Very early in life he manifested a marked predilection for the monastic state, so much so that when he learned that his father destined him for a military and courtly career, he prayed for an illness which might preserve him therefrom. His prayer was heard; yet it was some time before he obtained his desire to become a religious. After entering the monastery at Bec in Normandy, not many years passed before he was appointed its Prior and subsequently was elected Abbot. He was made Archbishop of Canterbury during the Lent of 1093, in spite of his protestations.

Now began the struggle of Anselm's life. King William II, who had named Anselm to the vacant see of Canterbury when dangerously ill and at which time he had promised to undo all the wrongs he had committed against the Church, with health restored he relapsed into his former sins, plundered the Church lands and scorned the Archbishop's rebukes, forbidding him to go to Rome to receive the Pallium. To settle these difficulties a Council was called at Rockingham, in Northamptonshire. The Archbishop addressed his suffragans and explained that the first business was to discuss the obedience due to Pope and King respectively. The Bishops, frightened, would not stand by him, but the barons sided with the Saint, for they respected his courage and saw that his cause was their own. Rather than yield to the King, the Archbishop went into exile. At last the King was obliged to submit to the holy, aged Archbishop.

St. Anselm is known as the father of scholastic theology, and is famous for his devotion to Our Lady, whose Feast of the Immaculate Conception he was the first to establish in the West.

It was on Wednesday in Holy Week, April 21, 1109, in the 16th year of his bishopric, and the 76th year of his life, that St. Anselm breathed his soul into the hands of his Creator.

✠

APRIL 22

STS. SOTER AND CAIUS

In 173 St. Soter succeeded St. Anicetus in the Apostolic See. He comforted his flock by the unction of his discourses, and assisted the poor with generous alms, especially all who suffered for the Faith. He also gave financial aid to distant churches, especially to that of Corinth. St. Soter strongly opposed the heresy of Montanus, and was martyred ten years later under Marcus Aurelius.

St. Caius, whose relics are kept in the sanctuary of St. Sylvester at Rome, governed the Church a century later, and was put to death in 296.

✠

APRIL 23

ST. GEORGE

Although little is known of the life and deeds of St. George, in the Eastern Church he was honored as "The Great Martyr" from the dawn of the fourth century. Born

*O God, You gladden us through the merits and the intercession of bless-
ed George, Your Martyr. Mercifully grant us to attain the gifts of Your
grace, which we ask through him.*

in Cappadocia, Eastern Asia Minor, St. George in early youth followed the life of a soldier under Diocletian. However, when the emperor cruelly persecuted the Christians, St. George publicly rebuked him and resigned his commission as tribune. His glorious martyrdom, after various excruciating torments, ended with beheading.

Soon churches were dedicated in his honor, and his feast day was observed as a holyday of obligation. As the years passed he emerged amongst the people as the patron of the whole Christian East.

It was not long before devotion to St. George spread to the West. The fourth century saw a church erected in his honor in Rome. This church, frequently restored, is the church of St. George in Velabro. There followed churches in France, Italy and Spain, and towns and provinces were dedicated to St. George as their Patron Saint. Even Orders of Knighthood in his honor were founded in Italy, Spain, Bavaria and Russia. Medals were struck in honor of the Saint bearing an equestrian figure of St. George slaying the dragon, with the inscription, "St. George, Patron of horsemen".

In the days of the Crusades, when King Richard the First of England led his soldiers forth to battle the Saracens and to regain the Holy Land, he selected as patron, St. George, the soldier Saint. It is related that when the infidel forces were pressing hard the Christians in battle and Richard the "Lion-hearted" seemed powerless to win the day, St. George, mounted on a white horse, appeared and led the Christians to victory. Similarly, at the siege of Antioch St. George appeared to Godfrey of Bouillon. These apparitions impressed military men, and especially the English knights, who selected as best patron for England for future ages the soldier martyr, St. George. He became the national patron of England, and was declared protector of the Kingdom of England by Pope Bendict XIV.

✠

ST. FIDELIS OF SIGMARINGEN

Mary Rey (St. Fidelis) was born at Sigmaringen, Germany, in 1577. He was educated at the University of Fribourg, Switzerland, and led an austere, prayerful life. For some time he practiced law at Colmar, in Alsace, and came to be known as "counsellor and advocate of the poor". Becoming disgusted with the profession which was an occasion of sin to so many, he decided to enter the Capuchin Order. In 1612 he was ordained Priest, and said his first Mass in their monastery at Fribourg. He was given the name of Fidelis, or Faithful, as his religious name. He sought the most abject and painful employments even when Superior.

The newly founded Congregation de Propaganda Fide commissioned Father Fidelis to go to Switzerland and preach against the heretical teachings of Calvin. Incensed at the wonderful effects of his zealous efforts, the Calvinists aroused the peasants against him by claiming that he was a political agent of the Emperor of Austria.

On April 24, 1622, Father Fidelis made his confession, said Mass at Gruch, and after preaching with more than ordinary zeal, it is claimed he suddenly stood silent with his eyes fixed on Heaven, in an ecstasy, for some time. He foretold his death to several persons.

From Gruch he went to Sevis, where he exhorted the Catholics to remain constant in the Faith. A Calvinist attempted to shoot him while he was preaching in the church there. On his return trip to Gruch, Fidelis was waylaid by twenty Calvinist soldiers, headed by a minister. They called him a false prophet and urged him to embrace Calvinism. But he answered: "I am sent to you to confute, not to embrace your heresy. The Catholic religion is the Faith of all ages. I fear not death". Hearing this, they

stabbed Father Fidelis to death. Many miracles were performed through the Martyr's intecession. He was canonized
by Pope Benedict XIV in 1746.

✠

ST. MARK

St. Mark was by birth a Jew. He was converted to
Christianity by the Apostles after the Resurrection of
Christ, according to Eusebius, St. Austin, Theodoret and
St. Bede. He accompanied St. Paul and Barnabas on their
first missionary journey; afterwards he went to Rome and
acted as interpreter for St. Peter. Origen and St. Jerome
claim he is the same Mark whom St. Peter calls his son.
(1 Peter 5:13.) Papias and St. Clement claim that St. Mark
wrote all that he had learned from St. Peter.

St. Peter sent St. Mark into Egypt and appointed him
Bishop of Alexandria in the 7th year of Nero, and
the 60th of Christ. For twelve years he preached the
Gospel in Lybia, and in Egypt, where he founded the
great Church of Alexandria and made many converts
among the Jews. This success stirred up the heathens
against the Apostle. After ordaining Anianus Bishop, he
returned to Pentapolis, where he preached for two years.
He then decided to return to Alexandria, where he found
an increase in the number of Christians. After encouraging
the faithful, he went to Rome.

The heathens in Alexandria called him a magician on
account of his miracles, and resolved to put him to death.
For a long time God concealed St. Mark from them.
However, on April 24, 68 A.D., some of them found him
as he was offering up the Holy Sacrifice of the Mass. They
seized him, tied his feet with cords, and the whole day long
dragged him about the streets, crying, "the ox must be led
to Bucoles", a rocky place near the sea. The ground was
stained with his blood and strewn with pieces of his flesh.

At night he was cast into prison, in which God comforted him by two visions. The following day, April 25, the infidels repeated their torture until he expired.

The Christians gathered up St. Mark's mangled body and buried it at Bucoles. In the 9th century it was translated to Venice. The Saint is represented in art with a lion at his feet and a scroll in his hand, on which is inscribed the words: *Peace be to thee, O Mark, My Evangelist.*

✠

APRIL 26

OUR LADY OF GOOD COUNSEL

Records dating from the reign of Pope Paul II (1464-1471) reveal that the picture of Our Lady, at first called "La Madonna del Paradiso" and now known as "Madonna del Buon Consiglio", appeared in the old Augustinian church of Santa Maria at Genazzano, about twenty-five miles southeast of Rome, on St. Mark's Day, April 25, 1467.

The venerated picture, about the size of a visiting card, was observed to hang suspended in the air without the slightest apparent support. Immediately devotion to Our Lady in Santa Maria sprang up; groups and pilgrims began to visit the church, while miracles in ever-increasing numbers were wrought at the shrine, as they still continue to be.

The following July, Pope Paul appointed two Bishops to investigate the alleged wonder-working image. In 1630 Pope Urban VIII went to Genazzano on a pilgrimage, as did Pius IX in 1864. Pope Innocent XI had the picture crowned with gold on November 17, 1682.

Pope Benedict XIV approved the Pious Union of Our Lady of Good Counsel on July 2, 1753, and was himself enrolled therein as its first member. Pope Pius IX and Leo XIII were also members. On April 22, 1903, Pope Leo XIII authorized the insertion of the invocation "Mater Boni Consilii" to follow that of "Mater Admirabilis" in the

Litany of Loreto. Ten years previously the same Pontiff
had sanctioned the use of the White Scapular of Our Lady
of Good Counsel for the faithful. There are many churches
and institutions in the United States named in honor of
Our Lady of Good Counsel.

☩

APRIL 27

ST. PETER CANISIUS

St. Peter Canisius was born in Holland on May 8, 1521.
He was one of the first companions of St. Ignatius, and
became a great theologian and preacher. He played a
prominent part in combatting Protestantism in Germany
and at the Council of Trent. He died at Fribourg, Switzerland, December 21, 1597. He was canonized by Pope
Pius XI on May 21, 1925, who at the same time declared
him a Doctor of the Universal Church.

ST. ZITA

Zita was the daughter of very poor, pious Italian parents, agricultural laborers who lived at Bozzanello, three
miles from Lucca. Each morning the family went to early
Mass.

Zita's life passed quietly and happily until she was
twelve years old. Always obedient, loving and good, she
was the joy of her mother's heart. Increasing poverty compelled the parents to try to find their child a situation as
a servant. The father accompanied Zita to Lucca, and there
found for her a position with the Fatinelli family, who
lived in a palace near the church of Frediano. It was here
that little Zita began the life of a servant, and where she
remained for nearly fifty years in spite of the many sufferings she had to endure.

At first all the disagreeable duties were assigned her. She was poorly fed and received very low wages; yet she never complained. Before anyone else arose she could be seen daily at the five o'clock Mass, as had been her practice from early youth. A special devotion to Jesus in His Passion enabled her to bear patiently and cheerfully the ill-temper of her employers; their harsh treatment and unreasonable orders; the quarrelsome and unkind fellow-servants; overwork and fatigue, all of which were her lot. Prayer and Holy Communion, and the constant realization of the Presence of God sustained the Saint in her trials.

Finally Mr. Fatinelli, seeing the success which attended Zita's undertakings, gave her charge of his children and of the household. She scrupulously fulfilled the trust. Her patience gradually conquered the jealousy of her fellow-servants, while her prayers and toil eventually sanctified the whole house. God performed many miracles for His holy, humble servant during her lifetime.

On one of the great Feasts of the Church she had gone to Mass as usual, and after Communion became so absorbed in prayer that she forgot the time until the sun was high in the heavens. She rushed home, it being the morning when it was her duty to bake the bread. Upon arrival, she opened the flour chest, and there, to her amazement, found all the loaves kneaded and ready to be put into the oven. She questioned everyone in the house in vain, and when it came to the ears of her mistress, she gravely said: "It is clear that the Angels have done this for Zita, and that this delicious bread was kneaded by no human hands".

On Saturdays it was Zita's great delight to go to the little church and convent of St. Angelo, about six miles from Lucca, across the river Serchio. One Saturday, detained longer than usual by household duties, she still set out, though evening was coming on. A man on horseback, who knew her, and who was going to the same place, stopped and said: "Do not think of going on to St. Angelo tonight. Darkness will soon be here and you will lose your way, and perhaps perish in crossing the river". But Zita, thanking him, continued on the way, simply saying: "Our Lord will take me there safely". The horseman galloped on. Upon arriving at the church, to his amazement he saw Zita kneeling at the gate in prayer. "How did you get here before me?" he exclaimed. Looking up, smiling, she replied: "As it pleased God, so it has happened".

Zita had a great devotion to St. Mary Magdalen and longed to visit a famous church between Lucca and Pisa that was dedicated to the Saint. At that time there was war between the people of those towns and no one ventured near this church for fear of being robbed or murdered; but this did not deter Zita. Having an evening to spare, she started off, carrying a candle to burn at the Saint's shrine. It was a good ten miles' walk, and when she reached the church it was nightfall and the doors were locked. Overcome with fatigue she sat on the church steps and fell asleep. Meanwhile a violent wind and rain storm arose, but still she slept and her candle continued to burn. Awakening early in the morning, she was surprised to find the church doors open, and that, though the water covered the steps and road, she herself was quite dry. The parish Priest arrived at five o'clock as usual to say Mass and was astonished to find the doors open and Zita praying by the altar. No one but himself had the key, so it was evident that no human hand had opened them.

Zita lived an ordinary life in the eyes of the world, but a supernatural one in sight of the angels, until she was sixty years old. Not a trace of anxiety could be seen on her face as she lay dying. With a smile wreathing her lips and with hands clasped, whilst her eyes looked upward, she passed away on April 27, 1278.

As soon as she had expired a brilliant light was seen above the house, and all the people who saw it ran to the Casa Fatinelli, crying: "The Saint is dead!" Many miraculous cures took place at the time of Zita's funeral. Within forty years of her death all Italy looked upon her as a Saint.

Her tomb was opened in 1446, 1581, 1652 and 1811, and on each occasion the body was found in perfect preservation.

St. Zita was beatified by Pope Innocent XI in 1696, and canonized by Pope Benedict XIV.

✠

APRIL 28

ST. PETER CHANEL

On September 24, 1836, Peter Chanel was one of the first of a group of seminarians, under the leadership of Father Jean Claude Marie Colin, to be professed in the religious institute which was founded in Lyons, France, in 1816, known as the "Priests of the Society of Mary". They are popularly called the Marist Fathers, and are dedicated to the Mother of God to do missionary work.

Peter's parents were poor, humble, devout Catholics. From early youth he desired to consecrate his life to the service of God and the salvation of souls. When the new Order of Priests of the Society of Mary was proposed, he was one of the first interested. For their special mission, Pope Gregory XVI assigned them the difficult, virgin missionary field of the Oceanic Islands. Peter Chanel was the first Christian missionary to land on that far-away isle of Futuna in the South Pacific.

Only three short years of extreme hardships and zealous labor were allotted to Father Chanel on Futuna. The savage tribes of the islands, many of them cannibals, had no apparent interest in the white man's Faith, but they liked Father Chanel personally. They called him "the kind man from afar". Suddenly, truth and charity prevailed. It was on the eve of Peter Chanel's martydom, and the cause of it. A chief's son had asked to be baptized, and it seemed as if the whole tribe would prepare for Baptism and renounce their pagan way of life and their worship of idols.

The chieftain, however, refused to risk this radical change among his people, and ordered the massacre of the few Christians and the death of Peter Chanel.

At daybreak on April 28, 1841, the aborigines of the island of Futuna, bore down upon Peter Chanel at the door of his hut, beat him with war clubs and shattered his bones. As they were about to split open his skull, he cried out, using the language of his assassins—*Malie fuai,* "It is good for me that you are doing this". Thus did Peter Chanel, at the age of thirty-seven, join the red-robed company of martyrs.

Within a short time the number of baptisms was incredible, not only on Futuna, but on Wallis, Tonga and all the other islands. Futuna, itself, has the extraordinary reputation of an all-Catholic population.

St. Peter Chanel was canonized by His Holiness, Pope Pius XII, in 1954.

☩

APRIL 29

ST. PETER OF VERONA

St. Peter of Verona, though his parents were adherents of the Manichean heresy, in early youth was sent to a Catholic school, which resulted that eventually he became one of the most famous among the great list of Dominican Saints. Soon after his ordination he was designated by Pope Gregory IX, and ordered by his superiors, to combat the Manichean errors. Up and down the peninsula he traveled, so that it may be truthfully stated that he evangelized the whole of Italy. Countless souls eagerly listened to his message, and numerous conversions resulted. A special denunciation was reserved for those who, professing the Faith in words, denied the same in their actions.

A certain Carino, joined by other Manichean conspirators. determined to kill the Saint. While on a journey from Como to Milan in 1252, he was waylaid by those bent on silencing him by death. Severely wounded, St. Peter rose to his knees and with his own blood wrote on the ground the words "Credo Deum"—"I believe in God". The enraged conspirators then pierced the heart of the Saint.

Miracles through his intercession were numerous both before and after his death. He was canonized March 25, 1253.

✠

APRIL 30

ST. CATHERINE OF SIENA

It was in 1347 that St. Catherine was born at Siena, a town in Italy not far from Florence. Catherine, and a twin sister who died in infancy, were the youngest of twenty-five children of Giacomo and Lapa Benincasa. The father was a dyer by trade, and noted for his piety.

Little Catherine at a very early age gave signs of future holiness. When but five years old her love of the "Hail Mary" was so great that she would kneel and repeat it on each step of the staircase, as she went up and came down. In her sixth year Our Lord favored her with a wonderful and beautiful vision. One day as she was returning home from a visit to her eldest married sister with her brother Stephen, who was a year or two older than herself, she suddenly saw above the church of St. Dominic a magnificent throne, on which was seated our Divine Savior, clad in pontifical robes, wearing a tiara. With Him were St. Peter and St. Paul, and St. John the Evangelist. Catherine was wrapt in ecstasy with the splendor before her. As she gazed lovingly on her beloved Redeemer, He made the Sign of the Cross over her and smiled with a look replete with love.

From that moment Catherine was no longer a child; ardent love of God became the only motive of her actions. She had a burning desire to imitate the penances, prayers, and practices of virtue of the Saints. Seeking out lonely places, she scourged herself and watched and prayed. She longed for a closer union with her Savior, and when seven years old made a vow of virginity.

The next five years were spent quietly at home. Catherine's mother resolved that the child should be married, and endeavored to obtain a good husband for her. But Catherine had given her heart to Jesus and remained firm in her purpose not to wed any mortal man. All the efforts of her family to hinder her prayerful life served, by the mercy of God, but to increase its fervor. No longer permitted to be alone, Catherine, guided by the Holy Spirit, made a cell of her heart, where she could retire at all times, whether alone or in the company of others, to enjoy the presence of her Beloved, Whom she always found awaiting her within its enclosure.

In her sixteenth year Catherine received the habit of the Third Order of St. Dominic, continuing to live as an anchorite in her father's home. Almighty God favored her with many supernatural graces. On one occasion when meditating on the words, "Create in me a new heart", she beheld her Divine Spouse approach and touch her left side with His hand. She immediately experienced such a shock of pain and love in it as to cause her to swoon with happiness. It seemed to her that her Spouse had taken her heart from her breast. Amazed, she saw Him reappear with a luminous heart in His hand, and she sank trembling and fainting.

As her Divine Spouse approached, these tender words reached her ear: "My daughter, I have thy heart and I give thee Mine, that thou mayest forever live in Me".

From that day Catherine had not only a wound in her side, which crowds came to contemplate respectfully after her death, but in her heart so active a fire, that all material fire seemed cold in comparison with it.

When Catherine asked Jesus why His side had been pierced, He answered:

"It was to reveal to men the secret of My Heart, and make them understand that My love is far greater than the

Grant, we beseech You, O almighty God, that celebrating the memory of blessed Catherine, Your Virgin, we may be gladdened by her annual feast and profit by the example of her great virtue.

exterior manifestations I have given of it. My sufferings have had an end, but My love has none".

Catherine's wonderful life of prayer and penance was crowned by God with the gift of the Stigmata. The gift of prophecy was also bestowed upon her, as well as a marvellous insight into the state of souls.

St. Catherine was indefatigable in her service of the poor. In 1374, when Siena was visited by the plague, Catherine was the angel of the sick and dying, and several wonderful cures were the outcome of her prayers and labors.

At that time Italy was weighted and oppressed with internal struggles, strifes and fierce warfare. There were two claimants for the throne of St. Peter. From her obscure home St. Catherine was summoned to defend the Church's cause, and she was instrumental in bringing about the return of Pope Gregory XI from Avignon to Rome in 1377.

After countless proofs of her virtues, and famous for the gift of prophecy and for many miracles, at about the age of thirty-three St. Catherine passed to her Spouse at Rome on April 30, 1380. She was canonized in 1461 by Pope Pius II, and has been proclaimed a Patron of the Holy City. Her body rests in the Minerva church in Rome. Her "Dialogue" and other writings are a treasure-house of mystic counsel.

In 1970, Pope Paul VI proclaimed Catherine of Siena a Doctor of the Church.

MAY

ST. JOSEPH THE WORKER

On May 1, 1955, during a public audience granted to the Catholic Association of Italian Workers, whose members gathered that day in St. Peter's Square to celebrate the tenth anniversary of their society and to pledge anew their fealty to the Social Science program of the Church, His Holiness, Pope Pius XII instituted the liturgical Feast of St. Joseph the Worker, and assigned this feast-day to the first day of May.

The Pope assured his audience and the "working people of the entire world" that "you have at your side a Shepherd, a Defender and a Father".

It was Joseph, a carpenter, whom God in His Providence chose to be the head of the Holy Family and the foster-father of the Child Jesus, and he is most powerful in his intercession with the Heart of the Savior.

From the office and position to which St. Joseph was chosen by Heaven we readily conclude that he was a man of great virtue and profound holiness. No other mere man was to hold a higher office. He would be "the Watchful Defender of Christ" and "the Chaste Guardian of Mary", the Virgin of virgins. As regards the Saints of the Old Law, St. Joseph definitely surpassed them all in holiness. In him the holiness of all his ancestors, who in the designs of God were to co-operate in the accomplishment of the Incarnation, reached its culmination and perfection. Like Abraham, Joseph was a man of faith and obedience; like Isaac, a man of prayer and vision; like Jacob, a man of patience and self-sacrifice; like Joseph of Egypt, a man of purity; like David, a man according to God's own heart.

Therefore, "Ite ad Joseph"; workers and non-workers, "Go to Joseph".

✠

MAY 2

ST. ATHANASIUS

St. Athanasius was a native of Alexandria, Egypt, being born about the year 296. His parents, virtuous Christians, secured for him the best education possible. He has been styled the "Father of Orthodoxy", "Pillar of the Church", and "Champion of Christ's Divinity". God chose him to defend His Church against the Arian heresy. While only a Deacon, St. Alexander, his Bishop, took him to the Council of Nicea in 325, and there he distinguished himself by his extraordinary zeal and learning. Five months later, as St. Alexander lay dying, he recommended to his clergy and people St. Athanasius for his successor.

For forty-six years, as Patriarch of Alexandria, St. Athanasius employed all his power and authority to bring the Arians back to the unity of the Church. Although exiled five times from his See, he succeeded during those periods to guide his flock by his enlightening treatises on Catholic dogmas. His undaunted courage and unparalleled greatness of soul under the most violent persecutions, surely merited for him a crown equal to that of the glorious martyrs.

In the year 373, St. Athanasius surrendered his soul to his God, Whom he had served so long and faithfully. The Church honors him as one of her greatest Doctors.

✠

MAY 3

ST. ALEXANDER I

St. Alexander succeeded St. Evaristus as Pope in 109, and ruled the Church for almost ten years. He died in 119. His name occurs in several Martyrologies, and he is also styled a martyr by St. Gregory the Great.

FINDING OF THE HOLY CROSS

About the year 326, St. Helena, mother of Emperor Constantine the Great, went on a pilgrimage to Palestine. Upon her arrival at Jerusalem she had a great desire to find the Cross on which Jesus had died for the sins of men. The Christians knew not where it lay, as the heathens out of hatred for them had concealed the spot where Our Savior was buried by covering it with stones and rubbish and erecting on it a temple to Venus. And over the place where He rose from the dead, they had erected a statue of Jupiter.

St. Helena inquired of every one whom she thought likely to furnish some information concerning the holy Cross. She was credibly informed that if she could locate the sepulchre, she would also find the instruments of execution, as it was customary among the Jews to bury the instruments of the punishment near the place where the body of a criminal was buried. The holy Empress, therefore, ordered the demolition of the profane buildings and statues, and the removal of all the rubbish. Upon digging to a great depth, the holy sepulchre, and close by it three crosses, the nails which had pierced the Savior's Body, and the title which had been affixed to His Cross, were found. They knew that one of the crosses was that which they were seeking, and that the others belonged to the two malefactors between whom Christ had been crucified.

It was difficult to determine which was the Cross on which Jesus had died. Therefore the holy Bishop Macarius suggested that the Empress have the three crosses brought to a critically ill lady of renown in Jerusalem, not doubting that God would reveal which was the cross sought. This being done, the Bishop prayed and then applied the crosses singly to the patient. Two of the crosses were tried without effect, but the patient immediately recovered by the touch of the third one.

St. Helena was so overjoyed that she built a church on the spot, and placed therein part of the true Cross in a silver shrine for veneration. Afterwards she carried a portion of the holy Cross to the Emperor Constantine, then at Constantinople, who received it with great veneration; another portion she carried to Rome, which was placed in the Church of the Holy Cross of Jerusalem which she had built there, and where it still remains. St. Paulinus relates that though chips were almost daily cut off from the Cross and given to devout persons, yet the sacred wood suffered no diminution. Twenty-five years after the discovery, St. Cyril of Jerusalem affirmed that pieces of the Cross were spread all over the earth, and compared this wonder to the miraculous feeding of five thousand men, as recorded in the Gospel.

☥

MAY 4

ST. MONICA

St. Monica was born at Tagaste in North Africa, in 332, of Christian parents. Although early instructed in the fear of God and her girlhood was one of singular innocence and piety, yet she was given in marriage to Patritius, a pagan of Tagaste. She obeyed and served him as her master, and labored to gain him to God by her affectionate behavior and holy life. One of the happy fruits Monica reaped from her patience was to see him baptized a year before he died.

They had two sons and one daughter, one son being Augustine, who was born in November, 354. When Augustine was seventeen, his father died. As he grew up his mother endeavored continually to instill into him sentiments of piety. While studying at Carthage he was seduced by the Manicheans and drawn into that heresy. Monica grieved bitterly and prayed incessantly for his conversion. In order to avoid his mother's entreaties, Augustine went to Rome. Upon his arrival he fell dangerously ill, and he attributed his recovery to the prayers of his mother.

From Rome he went to Milan in 384, where he taught rhetoric. While in that city St. Ambrose convinced Augustine of the errors of the Manicheans, and he renounced that heresy, but continued to search for the truth. St. Monica followed him to Milan, and upon learning that he was no longer a Manichee, she redoubled her tears and prayers to God for his conversion. Her sorrow was turned into joy when Augustine was baptized with some of his friends at Easter, in 387. They set out together for Africa. At Ostia, where they were to embark, St. Monica fell ill. Conversing with Augustine one day, she said, "Son, there is nothing now to keep me here; I had but one object in life, and that was to see you a Christian and a Catholic. God has done much more, in that I see you now despising all earthly happiness and entirely devoted to His service".

St. Monica suffered much during her last illness. On its ninth day she surrendered her holy soul to God, at the age of fifty-six, in the month of November, 387. Her remains were interred at Ostia, but in 1430, they were translated to Rome and placed in the Church of St. Augustine.

✠

MAY 5

ST. PIUS V

Of the many saints raised up by God to be pillars of His Church amidst the calamities of the 16th century, St. Pius V was pre-eminent. He witnessed the greater part of that eventful century. Born in 1504, in the little town of Bosco, in Lombardy, during the Pontificate of Julius II who commenced the erection of St. Peter's Basilica, he was elected Pope in 1566, and died in 1572.

His family, Ghislieri by name, had been reduced to poverty. The Saint received the name Michael in baptism, a fitting name for one destined to be a brave warrior and an outstanding captain in the cause of God and the Church.

Pius was five years old when Henry VIII ascended the throne; lived through the reigns of Edward VI and Queen Mary of England; became Pope when Elizabeth had been eight years queen, and died during her reign. It was he who signed the Bull of excommunication against Queen Elizabeth.

His boyhood was spent in caring for his father's sheep, and very early he had the desire to devote his life to the service of God. Much time, therefore, was spent in humble prayer that a vocation to the priesthood might be vouchsafed him. His parent's poverty seemed to be an obstacle to the fulfillment of his desire. God, intending the young shepherd to become the Universal Pastor, led two Dominican religious to his home. Charmed with the boy, they offered to educate him gratuitously. With his father's blessing, the future Pontiff joyfully accompanied the visitors. He rapidly progressed in his studies, and made his profession as a Dominican friar in the Convent of Voghera on May 18, 1521.

Luther had just burnt the Papal Bull and declared war against the Church. The young Dominican, as a Priest, as inquisitor, and later as Bishop and Cardinal was famous for his fearless defense of the Church's faith and discipline, and for the spotless purity of his own life.

The coronation of Pius V as Pope, to succeed Pius IV, took place on January 7, 1566, when he was sixty-two years old, and his Pontificate lasted only six years, three months and twenty-three days. In that short period of time he effected a marvelous reformation not only in the Roman Court, but in the Church throughout the world; he insisted on the observance of all the Decrees of the Council of Trent, just terminated, and published its all-embracing Catechism. Pope Pius V revised the Missal and the Breviary. He insisted on a reformation of Ecclesiastical music.

The watchful and discerning eye of the great Pontiff seemed to be everywhere; no evil escaped his notice, nor virtue which he did not praise, nor suffering in which his heart did not sympathize. Above all, he was on fire with holy zeal when he saw the Faith in danger. To his endeavors and prayers to the Blessed Virgin Mary through the recitation of the Rosary is due the great naval victory of Lepanto in October, 1571, by which Christendom was rescued from the menace of the Turkish Empire.

Six months after the glorious victory of Lepanto St. Pius V died on May 1, 1572. He was canonized by Pope Clement XI in 1711. His shrine is in St. Mary Major's in Rome.

✠

MAY 6

ST. JOHN BEFORE THE LATIN GATE

When the two sons of Zebedee, James and John, strangers as yet to the mystery of the Cross and the nature of Christ's Kingdom, had, by their mother Salome, besought Jesus to allot them the two first places in His Kingdom (implied by sitting at His right and left hand), He asked them whether they were disposed to drink of His chalice, or, in other words, to suffer with Him, in which case they should not fail to be considered in proportion to their fidelity. The two disciples answered confidently in the affirmative, assuring their Divine Master that they were ready to undergo anything for His sake. Whereupon Our Lord foretold them that their sincerity would be tested, and that both of them would be partakers of His chalice of suffering, for the honor and confirmation of the Christian Faith.

It may be said, without exaggeration, that St. John, who so tenderly loved his Master, and was so tenderly beloved by Him, drank of His chalice, and experienced a large share of its bitterness, when he assisted at His crucifixion; feeling then in his soul, by grief and compassion, whatever he saw the Savior suffer on the Cross. This was further fulfilled after the descent of the Holy Ghost when he underwent the like imprisonment, scourging, etc., with

the other Apostles, as is recorded in the 5th chapter of the
Acts of the Apostles. But our Redeemer's prediction was
to be accomplished in a more particular manner, and still
more conformable to the letter, which would entitle him
to the merit and crown of martyrdom.

Domitian, the second emperor who raised a persecution against the Church in the year 95, deluged Rome with
the blood of the Christians. St. John was the only surviving
Apostle, who at that time governed all the churches of
Asia. He was apprehended at Ephesus and sent to Rome
in the year 95. The Emperor condemned him to a most
barbarous death, by ordering him to be cast into a caldron
of boiling oil. The holy Apostle was probably first scourged,
as was the Roman custom with regard to criminals before
execution who could not plead the privilege of being
Roman citizens. Tertullian, St. Jerome and Eusebius affirm
that by order of the tyrant, St. John was thrown into a
vessel of boiling oil. But lo! the Saint came out more fresh
and lively than he had entered the caldron.

This glorious triumph of St. John occurred without the
gate of Rome, called Latina, because it led to Latium. A
church, which has always borne this title, was consecrated
at the spot in memory of this miracle.

St. John suffered above the other Saints a martyrdom of
love at the foot of the Cross of his Divine Master. Nevertheless he received also the crown of this second martyrdom,
to which the sacrifice of his will was not wanting, but only
the execution.

☦

MAY 7

ST. STANISLAUS

Stanislaus Sazepanowski was born on July 26, 1030,
at Sezepanow, in the diocese of Cracow, Poland. His parents had prayed for a child for thirty years before God
answered their prayers. In thanksgiving, they offered him
from his birth to God and educated him at Gnesen and

O God, You see how we are oppressed on every side by our own ills. Grant that the glorious intercession of blessed John, Your Apostle and Evangelist, may protect us.

Paris to be a Priest. Upon the death of his parents, Stanislaus received Holy Orders from the Bishop of Cracow, who made him Canon of his Cathedral, and shortly after his preacher and Vicar-General. When the Bishop died, the King, clergy and people appealed to Pope Alexander II that Stanislaus be chosen to fill the See. Not wishing to resist the Will of God, Stanislaus obeyed, and was consecrated Bishop in 1072. He was most charitable to the poor. Annually he made a visitation of his Diocese and no irregularity escaped his notice.

Boleslaus II was then reigning as King of Poland, leading a lustful, cruel life. Bishop Stanislaus openly rebuked him for carrying off the wife of one of his nobles, and threatened excommunication if he continued in his sinful ways. The King, in a violent rage, vowed revenge. His first recourse was to calumnies. Some years previously the Bishop had purchased an estate of a gentleman named Peter and gave it to his church. The nephews of the deceased Peter were inveigled to accuse the Bishop of not having paid for the estate. The cause was pleaded before the King, but the accusers failed to appear. The Bishop promised to bring the dead man to court within three days to testify for him.

Historians say that after three days of fasting and prayer the Bishop ordered the grave of Peter to be opened, raised him to life and brought him into open court, where he declared that Stanislaus had bought and paid for the land. After the trial, he led Peter back to his grave, and he returned to his former state.

For a while the King was reconciled, but ere long he again treated his subjects like a tyrant. The Bishop's many remonstrances were of no avail; the King threatened him with death if he continued to disturb him. Failing to reform his life, Stanislaus excommunicated the King. Defiantly, he went to the chapel where the Bishop was saying Mass on May 8, 1079. The King ordered his guards to kill the Bishop, but on entering the chapel and seeing a light from heaven they refused to execute the order. After this occurred three times, Boleslaus himself rushed in and slew the Saint at the altar with his own hand.

Poland was then placed under an interdict by the Holy See. Boleslaus, detested by his subjects, fled the country and died miserably. St. Stanislaus was immediately recognized as a Saint and a Martyr by the entire Polish nation. He was canonized in 1253.

☩

MAY 8

APPARITION OF ST. MICHAEL THE ARCHANGEL

Before God created man, He created nine orders of heavenly spirits, including Angels and Archangels, as we read in Holy Scripture. Frequently He has used them as messengers to men. Three are especially mentioned, namely, St. Michael, St. Gabriel and St. Raphael.

Today holy Church honors St. Michael as being the leader of the faithful Angels who opposed Lucifer and his associates in their revolt against God (Apoc. 12:7). The devil is the sworn enemy of God's holy Church, while St. Michael has been chosen as its special protector.

About the year 525, under the Pontificate of Gelasius I, St. Michael appeared in Apulia on the summit of Monte Gargano, near the Adriatic. He requested that a sanctuary should be erected in his honor where God should be worshipped, in memory of himself and of all the Angels. This place became celebrated on account of numerous miracles.

☩

MAY 9

ST. GREGORY NAZIANZEN

St. Gregory, because of his profound skill in sacred learning, was surnamed the Theologian. A native of Arianzos in Cappadocia, he was the eldest son of St. Gregory

Nazianzen the Elder, who from childhood worshipped
false gods. Through the prayers of his wife, Nonna, he
obtained the grace of conversion about the time of the
Council of Nice.

For ten years the younger Gregory read law at Athens
and then joined St. Basil in his monastic solitude near the
river Iris in Pontus. He was ordained Priest in 371, and in
372 was consecrated Bishop of Sasima, a small town in
the See of Tyana, Cappadocia. He refused to take possession of his church of Sasima, but instead governed that
of Nazianzum until his father died the following year. As
soon as another Bishop was installed St. Gregory withdrew
to Seleucia, where he remained five years. In 380 he was
prevailed upon to accept the See of Constantinople. Because of his aged appearance, due to the many austerities
he had performed, his poor garb, and extreme poverty,
the proud citizens at first treated him badly. The Arians
pursued him with calumnies, railleries and insults. The
prefects and governors added their persecutions to the
fury of the populace. But God was with him, and the
Angels guarded him. His cheeks were furrowed with the
tears he shed as he daily prostrated himself before God
to implore His light and mercy upon his people.

Christians flocked to his discourses; heretics and pagans were moved to attend because they admired his
learning and eloquence. The sermons soon bore fruit: in a
short time his flock became very numerous. He succeeded
in conquering the obstinacy of the heretics by meekness
and patience.

St. Gregory remained in Constantinople only one
month, after which he resigned and spent the remainder
of his life in retirement near Arianzum until his death in
390. In his letters he gave to others the same advice, of
which his own life was constantly an example. One instance
will suffice: A holy Priest was unjustly persecuted by slander. St. Gregory wrote to him thus in his third letter: "What
evil can happen to us after all this? None, certainly, unless
we by our own fault lose God and virtue. Let all other

things fall out as it shall please God. He is the Master of our life, and knows the reason of everything that befalls us. Let us only fear to do anything unworthy our piety. We have fed the poor, we have served our brethren, we have sung the Psalms with cheerfulness. If we are no longer permitted to continue this, let us employ our devotion some other way. Grace is not barren, and opens different ways to Heaven. Let us live in retirement; let us occupy ourselves in contemplation; let us purify our souls by the light of God. This perhaps will be no less a sacrifice than anything we can do".

St. Gregory as a writer ranks far above most Greek Doctors; in fact, he is surnamed by the Greeks "the Divine". He is venerated in the East and the West as a Doctor of the Church.

✠

MAY 10

ST. ANTONINUS

St. Antoninus, or Little Antony, was born at Florence, Italy, in 1389, the only child of noble parents. From early childhood he was most pious. His only pleasure was to read the lives of Saints, and when not busy at home or at school, he could always be found in St. Michael's church before the crucifix or in Our Lady's chapel. At sixteen years of age he joined the Friars Preachers (Dominicans) at Fiesole, and while still young was chosen Prior of the Convent of the Minerva in Rome. Afterwards he was successively Prior at Naples, Cajeta, Cortona, Siena, Fiesole, and Florence, where he became Archbishop. His preaching produced great fruit; his charity to the poor was outstanding.

During the pestilence in Florence in 1448, the holy Archbishop exposed himself first, and employed his clergy in assisting the stricken inhabitants. Almost all the Friars died on account of the contagion. Famine followed the pestilence. St. Antoninus stripped himself of almost everything in order to help the afflicted.

Florence was shaken by frequent earthquakes and visited by violent storms during the years 1453 to 1456. The saintly Archbishop, after lodging the afflicted, restored the most distressed by rebuilding their homes. Truly he was the "people's prelate" and the "protector of the poor".

His secretary once said to him that Bishops are to be pitied when they are eternally besieged with requests, as he was. The Saint replied: "To enjoy interior peace, we must always reserve in our hearts amidst all affairs, as it were, a secret closet, where we are to keep retired within ourselves, and where no business of the world can ever enter". Pope Pius II has left us, in the second book of his Commentaries, a most edifying history of the eminent virtues of our Saint and the strongest testimonies of his sanctity.

God called St. Antoninus to the reward of his labors on May 2, 1459, in the seventieth year of his life, the thirteenth of his archiepiscopal dignity. On his deathbed he repeated the words which he often expressed during health, "To serve God is to reign". He was buried, according to his desire, in the church of St. Mark in Constantinople, among his religious brethren, and was canonized by Pope Adrian VI in 1523.

✠

MAY 11

STS. PHILIP AND JAMES

After having chosen Peter and Andrew, our Savior said to Philip, "Follow Me". Although he was a married man and had several daughters, recognizing Jesus as the Messiah, Philip forsook all to follow Him. Immediately he desired to have his friend Nathanael share in his happiness, and going to him said: "We have found Him of whom Moses in the Law and the Prophets did write, Jesus of Nazareth". In wonderment, Nathanael asked: "Can any good come out of Nazareth?" Philip answered, "Come and see". He accompanied Philip and became one of the dis-

O God, You gladden us with the annual solemnity of the Apostles Philip and James. Grant that we may be able to imitate the examples of them, in whose merits we rejoice.

ciples of Jesus, following Him for three years, witnessing His many miracles, and listening to His Divine teachings.

Theodoret and Eusebius assure us that after the Descent of the Holy Spirit, when the disciples dispersed into all parts of the world, St. Philip went to preach the Gospel in the two Phrygias, and that when he died he was buried at Hierapolis in Phrygia. His body is said to now rest in Rome, with that of St. James, in the church dedicated to God under their names.

St. James the Less was also one of the Twelve Apostles. He was called the Less to distinguish him from the other Apostle James, who was the son of Zebedee. When the Apostles dispersed among the nations St. James became the first Bishop of Jerusalem, and governed the Church amidst perpetual dangers on account of the fury of the people and their violent persecutions. Many of the Jews esteemed his purity and his mortified, prayerful life, calling him "the Just". He is the author of one of the canonical Epistles. His singular learning in sacred matters was praised by St. Clement of Alexandria and St. Jerome. He was present with St. Peter and St. Paul at the Council of Jerusalem. Later, when St. Paul escaped the malicious designs of the Jews by appealing to Caesar, to whom he had been sent by Festus in the year 60, the people took vengeance on St. James. Accusing him of violating the laws, they carried him up to the pinnacle of the Temple and threw him headlong down to the ground. He was buried near the Temple, where he was martyred in the year 62 A. D.

☦

MAY 12

STS. NEREUS, ACHILLEUS, DOMITILLA AND PANCRATIUS

Saints Nereus and Achilleus were servants in the household of St. Flavia Domitilla. These zealous Christians were banished by the Emperor Domitian to the island of Pontia on the coast of Terracina. During the reign of Trajan, Saints Nereus and Achilles were beheaded at Terracina, while St. Flavia was burned to death for refusing to sacrifice to idols.

St. Pancratius is said to have been beheaded for the Faith at Rome, at the age of fourteen, under the reign of Diocletian, in the year 304.

✠

MAY 13

ST. ROBERT BELLARMINE, S.J.

St. Robert Bellarmine was born at Montepulciano, Italy, October 4, 1542, the third of ten children. After being educated by the Jesuits he joined their Society in 1560. As a young man he taught Greek, Hebrew and theology. While at Louvain he became famous as a controversialist, and never ceased to defend Catholic doctrine against the onslaughts of the Protestants. In 1598 he was made a Cardinal, and in 1602 was raised to the archbishopric of Capua. In 1605 he was recalled to Rome and appointed head of the Vatican Library. He also served as theological adviser to Popes Sixtus V, Innocent IX, Clement VIII, Paulus V and Gregory XV.

St. Robert Bellarmine died October 17, 1621, and was canonized by Pope Pius XI in 1930. The following year he was declared a Doctor of the Church.

✠

MAY 14

ST. GEMMA GALGANI

Gemma Galgani, who died in the twentieth century, was one of those people whom God, from time to time, chooses to appoint as special witnesses of the Sacred Passion of Christ, by reproducing His sufferings in them.

Gemma was born on March 12, 1878, in a small Tuscan village near Lucca, Italy. Her father was a chemist and an extremely good man; her mother, a most holy woman. It was to her early teaching that Gemma owed the beginning of her devotion to Our Lord's Passion. The Galganis had eight children, of whom Gemma was the fourth, but they were not long to have the tender care of their mother, as she was consumptive.

Gemma received the Sacrament of Confirmation at the age of seven. As she followed the Mass devoutly, she seemed to hear a voice within her ask: "Will you give Me your mother?" She answered, "Yes; but take me with her!" "No!" she again heard the voice say. "Give me your mother willingly; you must stay with your father. I shall take her to Heaven!" Gemma felt constrained to answer "Yes", thereby making her first great sacrifice to God. However, her mother lived until September of the following year, but Gemma was sent to an aunt's home for fear of infection some time before her mother's death. When she was told of her loss, the extraordinary way in which she realized it to be the Will of God, proved the realization of her inspired offering at the time of her Confirmation.

The Christmas after her mother's death Gemma, to her great joy, returned to her father's home in Lucca. He sent her to the school of the Sisters of St. Zita, where she remained until she was sixteen. Soon after she went to St. Zita's, at the age of nine, she made her First Communion. She was unable to express what passed in that moment between her soul and Our Lord. Her promise to be "always good" was consistently carried out. She was loved not only by the Sisters, but by all her companions.

Gemma loved solitude and quiet, and was always most reserved in talking about her spiritual states and feelings to everyone except her special "directress". Her girlhood was marked for suffering in various ways—by interior trials, and an illness which caused the doctor to forbid her to

Hear us, O God, our Savior; so that, while we celebrate the memorial of blessed Gemma, Your Virgin, we may learn from her the affection of a loving devotion.

return to school. Accordingly, in 1894 Gemma left St. Zita's and went home to her father. She grew daily in the longing desire to suffer with her crucified Savior.

This desire was soon gratified, for in 1896 a most severe physical suffering was sent to the holy girl—a diseased bone in the foot, which necessitated scraping. Gemma refused an anaesthetic and bore the torture with heroic patience as she kept her eyes fixed on the crucifix. Soon after her recovery from this severe operation, other troubles began for Gemma and her family. Because of his generosity in helping friends, her father lost his business, and his farm possessions were sold to pay his creditors. About the same time he developed cancer in the throat, and he died in 1897, leaving his children penniless. For a while Gemma went to live with a married aunt, but she didn't like the carefree life there, and after an attack of pains in her back returned, joyfully, to the poverty in the Lucca household.

After a long, suffering illness, Gemma made a vow of chastity, and in February, 1899, joined in a novena to St. Margaret Mary. St. Gabriel appeared to her and promised to make the novena with her; this he did each night, praying with her. She sent for her confessor, went to confession, received Holy Communion, and rose from her bed completely cured, to the intense joy of the household.

When Gemma received Jesus in the Blessed Sacrament, He said to her: "My child, many and yet higher graces will follow the one I have granted you this morning. I will be to you as a father, and *she* shall be your mother (and He pointed to a statue of Our Lady of Sorrows greatly loved by Gemma). Henceforth all suffering seemed as nothing to Gemma.

Shortly after her recovery from this illness she attempted to be a Nun, as she had promised to do while sick, but her health proved not strong enough. Whilst making a Holy Hour on Holy Thursday night, 1899, she was overwhelmed with sorrow for her sins and had a vision of Our Lord on the Cross. It was never effaced from her mind.

One day after she had received Holy Communion, Our Lord said to her, "Gemma, I expect you on Calvary, on that Mount towards which you have been led". On the eve of the Feast of the Sacred Heart, in 1899, Gemma received the sacred Stigmata, or marks of Our Lord's five Wounds, which caused her intense suffering. In addition, the devil sometimes attacked her, and even struck her at times. She always sought the help of the Blessed Virgin Mary, her heavenly Mother.

The Giannini family, admiring the virtues of Gemma, and desiring to relieve her poverty, in September, 1899, adopted her as a daughter. Gemma continued to have many trials and sufferings; also ecstasies. Padre Germano, a Passionist, was her director the last few years of her life. The fame of her sanctity soon spread abroad, and many favors were received through her prayers. She died on Holy Saturday, 1903, and was canonized by Pope Pius XII on the Feast of the Ascension, 1940.

✠

MAY 15

ST. JOHN BAPTIST DE LA SALLE

St. John Baptist de la Salle, founder of the Institute of the Christian Schools, was born at Rheims, April 30, 1651. He studied theology at the Sorbonne and was ordained to the Priesthood April 9, 1678.

He was instrumental in opening two free elementary schools for the poor in Rheims. Daily he visited the young teachers to encourage them, as "they were like abandoned sheep without a shepherd", and he "assumed the responsibility of uniting them". In 1683 he resigned his canonry, and the following year distributed his fortune to the poor. He endured many trials and persecutions on the part of certain ecclesiastical authorities.

De la Salle's Institute for the Christian education of youth and the cultivation of faith, piety, mortification and obedience, after many severe trials began to flourish. God had given His blessing to the work of the Christian Brothers, as they are popularly known today.

In 1705 he established the first boarding college in the educational world at Saint-Yon, wherein he inaugurated the system of modern secondary instruction. Later he added a technical school to develop the mechanical skill of the students.

Prior to the 17th century there were no Sunday schools. The Christian Academy, founded by de la Salle for the adult parishioners of Saint Sulpice in 1699, was the first of its kind in the history of education. The program included not only the ordinary branches taught in other Sunday schools, but added geometry, architecture and drawing.

In 1684 he opened a normal school in Rheims where young men were trained in the principles and practices of the new method of teaching. The same year he established for youths who were destined to enter the Brotherhood a Christian academy, or preparatory novitiate, in which they were taught the sciences, literature, and the principles of scientific pedagogy. Consequently, he is recognized as the father of modern pedagogy. He was one of the greatest thinkers and educational reformers of all time.

De la Salle's last years were spent in retirement at Saint-Yon, where he revised the Rule of his Institute before giving it to Brother Barthelemy, the first Superior General.

St. John Baptist de la Salle died on Good Friday morning April 7, 1719, after having blessed the Brothers assembled at his bedside. His final words were: "In all things I adore the Will of God in my regard". He was canonized by Pope Leo XIII on May 24, 1900.

ST. DYMPHNA

St. Dymphna, Patroness of those afflicted with nervous and mental disorders, was born in Ireland in the 6th

century. Her father was a pagan King; her mother a devout Christian. Dymphna was a sweet, charming child,
beautiful like her mother. At an early age she consecrated
her virginity to Jesus, Whom she chose as her Spouse.

The happiness of Dymphna's childhood, however, was
early marred by the death of her good mother. Her father,
grief stricken for a long time, was eventually persuaded
by his counsellors to seek solace in a second marriage. He
commissioned certain of his courtiers to find a lady who
would be as beautiful and good as his first spouse. In vain
did they visit many countries. Upon their return they reported that they were unable to find anyone as charming
and kind as his own lovely daughter, Dymphna.

The King, following their evil suggestion, decided to
marry Dymphna, who was fifteen years old. With persuasive, flattering words he made known to her his intention.
Horrified at the suggestion, she asked for forty days to
consider the matter. Immediately she sought the advice
of Father Gerebran, the saintly Priest who had baptized her
as an infant. He suggested that she leave the country at
once. Accompanied by Father Gerebran, the court jester
and his wife, Dymphna hastily left for the continent. After
a short stay in Belgium, near the present city of Antwerp,
they resumed their journey until they reached the small
village of Gheel.

When the King learned of his daughter's flight he was
intensely angry, and set out immediately with some of his
followers. After some time he learned of Dymphna's place
of refuge. At first he tried to persuade her to return with
him. When Father Gerebran rebuked him for his wicked
intention, the King gave orders that Father Gerebran
should be put to death. With one blow the executioners
struck him on the neck and severed his head from his
body. Thus another glorious martyr entered the Kingdom
of Heaven.

With heroic courage Dymphna rejected all her father's
further attempts to induce her to return. Infuriated, he
drew his dagger and struck off the head of his own child.

The holy virgin's body fell at the feet of her insanely raving father. Another virgin-martyr joined the ranks of the Divine Lover of souls on May 15th, between 620 and 640.

After some time the villagers of Gheel placed the bodies of the two martyrs in a cave, which was the manner of burial in those days. Several years later the residents of Gheel decided to give the bodies a more suitable burial. When the earth was removed from the cave's entrance the workmen were greatly amazed to find two beautiful white tombs, carved from stone as if by angelic hands. Upon opening St. Dymphna's coffin there was found lying on her breast a red tile, with the inscription: "Here lies the holy virgin and martyr, Dymphna". The Saint's remains were then placed in a small church. Later a magnificent church, the Church of St. Dymphna, was erected on the site where the bodies were originally buried. The relics of St. Dymphna now repose there in a beautiful golden reliquary.

Increasing numbers of miracles and cures occurred, so that the fame of St. Dymphna, as Patoness of those afflicted with nervous and mental disorders, spread far and wide. The afflicted who have invoked the name of St. Dymphna praise her highly for help obtained.

✠

MAY 16

ST. SIMON STOCK

St. Simon Stock is the Carmelite to whom the Heavenly Mother gave the brown cloth Scapular, to which through the centuries the Holy See has attached tremendous indulgences to those who wear it.

St. Simon Stock was born at Aylesford in Kent, England, about 1165, and died at Bordeaux, France, in 1265. He entered the Carmelite Order in 1213, and became General of the Order in 1245.

ST. UBALDUS

St. Ubaldus was born of a noble family at Gubbio, Italy. He made great progress in his studies and then entered the Seminary of St. Secundus to complete his education. The Bishop of Gubbio made him Prior of his Cathedral and, in time, brought about several needed reforms.

In 1126, St. Ubaldus was chosen Bishop of Perugia, but he went to Rome and implored Pope Honorius II to excuse him. The request was granted, but two years later when the See became vacant at Gubbio, the Pope directed the clergy to elect St. Ubaldus. His Holiness consecrated Ubaldus Bishop with his own hands in 1129. Ubaldus distinguished himself by his mortified, humble, charitable, zealous reign.

After Emperor Frederick Barbarossa in his cruel wars had taken and plundered Spoleto, he threatened to do the same to Gubbio. Ubaldus, in order to protect his flock, met the Emperor on the road, and during the interview softened the heart of the tyrant to compassion, thus obtaining the safety of his people.

During the last two years of his life, St. Ubaldus suffered a complication of maladies, which he bore with heroic patience. After receiving the rites of the Church, he expired on May 16, 1160. Many miracles were performed at his tomb. He was canonized by Pope Celestine III in 1192.

✠

MAY 17

ST. PASCHAL BAYLON

St. Paschal Baylon was born in 1540, in the little village of Torre-Hermosa, in Aragon, Spain. His virtuous parents were so poor they could not afford to send the boy to school, but while tending the sheep he managed to learn to read from the help given by some of his companions.

He loved solitude and spent much time in meditating on the life of Christ. At the age of twenty-four he entered the austere convent of reformed Franciscans, near the town of Monfort, Spain. At his request he was admitted, in 1564, as a lay-Brother. His love of poverty and humility, and his ardent love and devotion for the Blessed Sacrament animated his whole life. Often he was favored with ecstasies and raptures.

On one occasion, when the General of his Order was in Paris, Paschal was sent to him about some important business of his province. It was a perilous journey, because the Huguenots were armed in the cities through which he had to pass. Undaunted, Paschal traveled in his Habit, without even sandals, and was often pursued by the Huguenots with sticks and stones. He received a wound which caused him to be lame for the remainder of his life. Twice he was taken for a spy, but it was not God's Will that he should receive the palm of martyrdom, and he returned safely to his convent.

St. Paschal died in the odor of sanctity at Villa Reale, near Valencia, on May 17, 1592, at the age of fifty-two. His corpse was exposed for three days, during which time the multitudes from all parts visited the church and witnessed the many miracles by which God attested the sanctity of His servant. St. Paschal was canonized by Pope Alexander VIII in 1690. In 1897 he was declared Patron of all Eucharistic congresses and confraternities.

✠

MAY 18

ST. VENANTIUS

St. Venantius was born in Camerino, Italy. At the age of eighteen he suffered many torments for the Faith and was beheaded during the persecution of Decius, in 250, in his native city. Pope Clement X, when Bishop of Camerino, had a special devotion to this young Martyr.

✠

ST. PETER CELESTINE

St. Peter was born in 1221 of holy, charitable parents, who had twelve sons. After the father's death, recognizing Peter's extraordinary inclination to piety, his mother gave him a literary education. He always considered the salvation of his soul of greatest importance. At the age of twenty he left school and retired to a solitary mountain, where he made himself a small underground cell, in which he spent three years practicing great austerities.

When his whereabouts were discovered, he was persuaded to leave his solitude and become a Priest. He was ordained at Rome, but in 1246 returned into Ambruzzo and lived for five years in a cave on Mount Morroni. Many desired to place themselves under the hermit's direction; overcoming his humility St. Peter admitted the most fervent. When his solitude became too disturbed, he went with some of his disciples to an almost inaccessible cavern on top of Mount Magella. Here they lived in scattered cells. The rule of life that St. Peter gave them formed the foundation of a new Benedictine congregation, called the Celestine Order. In 1274 Pope Gregory X approved this religious Order, and the Founder lived to see thirty-six monasteries and six hundred Monks and Nuns following his Rule.

Upon the death of Pope Nicholas IV, the Papal throne remained vacant two years and three months. The Cardinals assembled at Perugia in 1294 and unanimously chose Peter to fill the vacancy. His resistance was of no avail, and he was consecrated at Aquila, taking the name Celestine. Reigning only four months, the Pontiff held at Naples a consistory of the Cardinals at which the King of Naples and many other persons were present. After reading the solemn act of his abdication on December 13, 1294, St. Celestine took off his pontifical robes and put on his

religious Habit. Then he came down from his throne, knelt
before the assembly to beg pardon for his faults, and requested the Cardinals to choose a worthy successor to
St. Peter. St. Celestine stole away quietly to his Monastery
of the Holy Spirit at Morroni to resume his hermit life.
Pope Boniface, his successor, alarmed at the multitudes
that resorted to Morroni to see St. Celestine because of the
reputation of his great sanctity, implored the King of Naples
to send him to Rome. The Saint endeavored to flee, but the
Governor of Naples, on the order of the King, conducted
him to Pope Boniface at Anagni. Fearing the danger of tu-
mults and of a schism, His Holiness confined St. Celestine
in the citadel of Fumone, nine miles from Anagni, under a
guard of soldiers. Two of his Monks were assigned as his
companions, and the Saint sang the Divine praises continually. He suffered many insults and hardships, yet never
complained.

On Whit-Sunday, 1296, after hearing Mass with extraordinary fervor, he told his guards that he would die before
the end of the week. Immediately he fell ill, and the following Saturday, May 19th, after finishing the last psalm of
Lauds, at the words "Let every spirit praise the Lord",
St. Celestine peacefully expired, at the age of seventy-five.
Many miracles are authentically recorded of him, and he
was canonized by Pope Clement V in 1313.

✠

MAY 20

ST. BERNARDINE OF SIENA

St. Bernardine was born of the noble family of Albi-
zeschi, at Masse, Italy, in 1380. When three years of
age he lost his mother, and his father, who was the chief
magistrate of the town, died before the child was seven
years old. His maternal aunt cared for him for five years
and instilled into his heart a spirit of fervor and piety,
for which she herself was remarkable. Every Saturday he
fasted in honor of the Blessed Virgin. When seven years

old his uncles in Siena placed him in school in that city. After completing the course in philosophy, he studied civil and canon law, and then Sacred Scripture.

At the age of seventeen Bernardine was enrolled in the Confraternity of Our Lady in the hospital of Scala, and for four years served the sick. In 1400 a dreadful pestilence caused havoc in several sections of Italy. When it reached Siena Bernardine persuaded twelve young men to assist him in caring for the sick and the dying. God preserved Bernardine, but upon his return home he fell ill from a fever, which lasted four months. Hardly had he recovered, when he went to attend his blind and bedridden aunt. Upon her death fourteen months later, Bernardine retired to a house near the city; here in solitude he fasted and prayed to ascertain the Will of God in the choice of a state of life. Some time later he entered the Franciscan Order of the Strict Observance at Columbaria, near Siena. He made his profession on September 8, 1404. Because of a defect in his speech, his success as a preacher at first seemed doubtful. After imploring the help of the Virgin Mary, the obstacle was miraculously removed. His first sermon was preached on September 8, 1417, and his career as a preacher ended only when he died. He was considered one of the foremost Italian missionaries of the 15th century. Everywhere he preached devotion to the Holy Name of Jesus. The popularity of this devotion is due in great measure to the burning zeal and eloquence of St. Bernardine.

In 1427 he refused the bishopric of Siena, so as to be able to continue his service to a greater number of souls. In 1431 he likewise refused the bishopric of Ferrara, and in 1435 that of Urbino. Amidst the greatest applause and honors, the most sincere humility was always shown in St. Bernardine's words and actions, and he ever strove to conceal the talents with which God had enriched him. Nevertheless, God was pleased to honor His servant before men. He miraculously cured many lepers and other sick people, and it is claimed that he raised four dead persons to life.

St. Bernardine was appointed Vicar-General of his Order in 1438, and was responsible for reviving discipline among the Franciscans. After five years he obtained a discharge from his office, and then continued his preaching career until he was stricken with fever, from which he died on May 20, 1444. When the news of his death spread abroad there was universal regret. "The star of Italy", it was said, "had set; the Saint was dead." Many miracles occurred at his tomb. St. Bernardine's remains are kept in a crystal shrine, enclosed in one of silver, in the Franciscan church at Aquila. He was canonized by Pope Nicholas V in 1453.

☩

MAY 21

ST. HOSPITIUS

St. Hospitius became a recluse in the ruins of an old tower between Villafrance and Branlieu, not far from Nice, which is still called after him, Cap-Saint-Hospice. He lived only on bread and dates, wore an iron chain, and practiced other penances. He was honored with the gifts of prophecy and miracles. According to the Roman Martyrology, St. Hospitius died on May 21, 681.

☩

MAY 22

ST. RITA

St. Rita of Cascia, "the advocate of the hopeless", was born May 22, 1381, at Rocca Porrena, a town about two miles from Cascia. Her parents, Antonio and Amata Mancina, were called the "Peacemakers of Christ" for their successful efforts in reconciling enemies and settling disputes.

St. Rita was baptized in the Church of Santa Maria in Cascia four days after her birth. When she was brought

O God, You deigned to bestow upon St. Rita so great a grace as that of loving her enemies, and to bear in her heart and on her brow the signs of Your love and of Your passion. Grant us, we beseech You, that through her merits and intercession, to be able to forgive our enemies and to contemplate the pains of Your passion, so as to obtain the reward promised to the meek and to those who mourn.

home and laid in her cradle, a swarm of bees surrounded her, of a kind entirely unknown in the country, who not only flew around her and over her, but went in and out of the mouth of the sleeping child without injuring her.

Rita's childhood was one of happiness to her parents. To satisfy her desire of a life of union with God by prayer, her parents fitted up a little room in their home as an oratory, where she spent all her spare moments. At the age of twelve, however, she desired to consecrate herself to God in the religious state. Pious though her parents were, their tearful pleadings to postpone her noble purpose prevailed on Rita, and they gave her in marriage, at the age of eighteen, to an impulsive, irascible young man, who was well fitted to try the patience and virtue of the holy girl. Two sons were born to them, each inheriting their father's quarrelsome temperament. Rita continued her accustomed devotions, and her sanctity and prayers finally won her husband's heart so that he willingly consented that she continue her acts of devotion.

Eighteen years had elapsed since her marriage, when her husband was murdered by an old enemy; both of her sons died shortly after. Rita's former desire to consecrate herself to God again took possession of her. Three times she sought admittance among the Augustinian Nuns in Cascia, but her request was refused each time, and she returned to her home in Rocca Porrena. God Himself, however, supported her cause. One night as Rita was praying earnestly in her humble home she heard herself called by name, while someone knocked at the door. In a miraculous way she was conducted to the monastic enclosure, no entrance having been opened. Astonished at the miracle, the Nuns received Rita, and soon enrolled her among their number.

St. Rita's hidden, simple life in religion was distinguished by obedience and charity; she performed many extreme penances. After hearing a sermon on the Passion of Christ she returned to her cell; kneeling before her crucifix, she implored: "Let me, my Jesus share in Thy suffering, at least of one of Thy thorns". Her prayer was answered. Suddenly one of the thorns detached and fastened itself in her forehead so deeply that she could not remove it. The wound became worse, and gangrene set in. Because of the foul odor emanating from the wound, she was denied the companionship of the other Sisters, and this for fifteen years.

Miraculous power was soon recognized in Rita. When Pope Nicholas IV proclaimed a jubilee at Rome, Rita desired to attend. Permission was granted on condition that her wound would be healed. This came about only for the duration of the trip. Upon her return to the monastery the wound from the thorn reappeared, and remained until her death.

As St. Rita was dying, she requested a relative to bring her a rose from her old home at Rocca Porrena. Although it was not the season for roses, the relative went and found a rose in full bloom. For this reason roses are blessed in the Saint's honor.

After St. Rita's death, in 1457, her face became beautifully radiant, while the odor from her wound was as fragrant as that of the roses she loved so much. The sweet odor spread through the convent and into the church, where it has continued ever since. Her body has remained incorrupt to this day; the face is beautiful and well preserved.

When St. Rita died the lowly cell was aglow with heavenly light, while the great bell of the monastery rang of itself. A relative with a paralyzed arm, upon touching the sacred remains, was cured. A carpenter, who had known the Saint, offered to make the coffin. Immediately he recovered the use of his long stiffened hands.

As one of the solemn acts of his Jubilee, Pope Leo XIII canonized St. Rita on the Feast of the Ascension, May 24, 1900.

✠

MAY 23

ST. JULIA

St. Julia was a noble virgin of Carthage. When that city was taken by Genseric, in 439, Julia was sold for a slave to a pagan merchant of Syria. Patiently and cheerfully she performed the most mortifying employments assigned her. All her spare time was spent in praying or reading books of piety.

On one occasion her master took her with him on his journey to Gaul. Upon reaching the northern part of Corsica he cast anchor and went ashore to join the pagans in their idolatrous observance of a festival. Julia remained some distance away, as she refused to be defiled by the supersticious ceremonies which she abhorred. The Governor of the island, a bigoted pagan, asked the merchant who the woman was who dared to insult the gods. He informed him that she was a Christian and that although he had been unable to make her renounce her religion, because of her diligence and faithfulness he could not dispense with her service. Whereupon, the Governor offered the merchant four of his best female slaves in exchange for her. He replied: "No; all you are worth will not purchase her; for I would freely lose the most valuable thing in the world, rather than be deprived of her".

When the merchant was drunk and asleep, the Governor endeavored to compel Julia to sacrifice to his gods by offering to procure her liberty if she would comply. She resolutely refused, stating that she had as much freedom as she desired since she was permitted to serve Jesus Christ. In a transport of rage the Governor ordered St. Julia to be struck on the face, the hair of her head to be torn off, and, finally, that she be hanged on a cross until she expired.

In 763 Desiderius, King of Lombardy, removed her relics to Brescia from La Gorgona, where they had previously been taken by some Monks on that island.

✠

MAY 24

OUR LADY, HELP OF CHRISTIANS

When Napoleon left Elba and returned to Paris, Murat was preparing to march through the Papal States from Naples. On March 22, 1815, Pope Pius VII fled to Savona, and there crowned the image of Our Lady of Mercy on May 10, 1815. After the Congress of Vienna and the battle of Waterloo he returned to Rome, July 7, 1815. On September 15, 1815, in order to give thanks to God and Our Lady **he instituted, for the Papal States, the Feast of Our Lady, Help of Christians.**

Since 1868, when St. John Bosco founded the Salesian Congregation, which is dedicated to Our Lady, Help of Christians, this Feast in honor of Our Lady has attained great fame.

✠

MAY 25

ST. GREGORY VII

Gregory VII, one of the greatest of the Roman Pontiffs and one of the most remarkable men of all times, before he became Pope, was known as Hildebrand. Born in Tuscany in 1020, he was sent to Rome to be educated under his uncle who was Abbot of St. Mary's monastery on the Aventine Hill. Later he embraced the Benedictine Rule at the famous monastery of Cluny in France.

Three great evils—simony, concubinage, and the custom of receiving investiture from lay hands—were then afflicting the Church. He never ceased to obliterate these corruptions.

Hildebrand was called back to Rome, and for some years filled many responsible positions. He served as

archdeacon under five Popes. St. Leo IX esteemed him
highly, ordained him sub-deacon, and appointed him Abbot
of St. Paul's Outside-the-Walls, which lay almost in ruins
because the major part of its revenues had been usurped
by powerful laymen. Hildebrand succeeded in recovering
its lands, and restored the monastery to its ancient splendor.

Pope Victor II sent Hildebrand as Legate to France
to stop the practice of simony in the collation of ecclesiastical benefices. He was also closely associated with the
three succeeding Popes: Stephen II, Nicholas II and Alexander II. Upon the latter's death, in 1073, Hildebrand was
compelled to fill the vacancy. He immediately called upon
the clergy throughout the world to lay down their lives
rather than betray the laws of God to the will of princes.
Rome was in rebellion due to the ambition of the Cenci.
Pope Gregory excommunicated them. As a consequence
they laid hands on him during the Christmas midnight
Mass, wounded him, and cast him into prison. The following day the people rescued him.

His next conflict was with Henry IV, Emperor of
Germany, who openly relapsed into simony, and pretended
to depose the Pope. Gregory excommunicated him. The
people turned against Henry, and he finally sought absolu-
tion of Gregory at Canossa. Unfortunately, he did not
persevere; he set up an antipope, and besieged Gregory
in the castle of St. Angelo. The aged Pontiff was obliged
to flee.

We are assured that no Pontiff since the time of the
Apostles undertook more labors for the Church or fought
more courageously for her independence. While he was
saying Mass, a dove was seen to come down on him; the
Holy Spirit and thereby bearing witness to the supernatural
views that guided him in the government of the Church.
When he was forced to leave Rome, because the people
became incensed by the excesses of his Norman allies, he
withdrew to Monte Cassino, and later to the castle of
Salerno, where he died the following year on May 25, 1085.
His last words were: "I have loved justice and hated

iniquity, therefore I die in exile". He was buried in the church of St. Matthew at Salerno, and was canonized by Pope Benedict XIII in 1728.

✠

MAY 26

ST. PHILIP NERI

A most popular and likeable saint in the annals of the Church is St. Philip Neri, who was known in his boyhood days as "Pippo Buono" (good little Phil). He was born in Florence, Italy, in 1515.

At the age of eighteen he was sent to a childless, wealthy relative in the expectation that he would become his heir. The Holy Spirit was tugging at his heart, telling him he was made for higher things. Soon he left for Rome, without money and without plans. He lived in a bare, unfurnished room. Long hours were spent in prayer, after which a "street-corner" apostolate was inaugurated. From the very beginning this apostolate consisted in engaging all sorts of people in conversation. A customary greeting was: "Well, brothers, when shall we begin to do good?"; a greeting which under the Providence of God was to bear fruit in so far that many did "begin to do good"— caring for the sick, aiding the poor and enlightening the uninstructed.

Directed by his confessor, Philip studied for the priesthood, and was ordained May 23, 1551. Upon ordination, the flame in his soul was lashed into an all-consuming fire. Granting himself no respite, he labored unceasingly for the salvation of souls; and so successfully that he earned the title "Apostle of Rome".

A small group of Priests was soon gathered, who desired to assist in this spiritual apostolate; thus was born the Congregation of the Oratory, which was approved in 1575.

St. Philip enjoyed many mystical experiences. God enriched him with gifts of prophecy, of insight into souls, and other supernatural powers.

He died May 26, 1595, and was beatified six years later. Canonization followed in 1623.

✠

MAY 27

ST. BEDE

A prodigy of learning, a burning light of the Church, the illustrious ornament of the Anglo-Saxon Church, and the first English historian, such was St. Bede who was born about the year 673. He became a Benedictine Monk, and wrote many historical and biographical works, including beautiful lives of Anglo-Saxon Saints, commentaries on portions or books of Sacred Scripture, homilies and sermons, as well as essays on astronomy, geography, music and poetry.

Up to the hour of his death, on Ascension Day, 735, the Saint was engaged in translating the Gospel of St. John from the Greek. One of the contemporaries of St. Bede tells us that "He spent that day joyfully", and in the evening his attendant said, "Dear master, there is yet one sentence unwritten". To which he replied, "Write it quickly". His attendant obeyed promptly, saying, "Now it is written". The Saint answered: "Good! thou hast said the truth—*consummatum est;* take my head into thy hands, for it is very pleasant to me to sit facing my old praying-place, and there to call upon my Father". While singing, "Glory be to the Father, and to the Son and to the Holy Spirit", just as he said "Holy Spirit", his holy soul went forth to meet his Triune God.

✠

ST. AUGUSTINE OF CANTERBURY

St. Augustine shares with St. Gregory the Great the title of Apostle of the English people. In 596 thirty-nine monks, under their Abbot Augustine, from St. Andrew's monastery in Rome, were commissioned by Pope Gregory the Great to evangelize the Anglo-Saxons in England.

It was on the Isle of Thanet, at or near Ebbsfleet, that they landed, and King Ethelbert welcomed them.

One day the King sent for the monks, whom he determined to interview in the open, the better to resist, as he thought, any magic arts. Augustine and his fellow-laborers came in procession, chanting their litanies, bearing a silver cross and a painted picture of Jesus Christ. The King bade them to be seated, and listened attentively while they preached the Word of Life. Aided by God's grace, the King received Baptism, to the great joy of St. Augustine, on June 1st, the eve of Pentecost. Many others followed his example and were received into the One, True Fold of Christ.

Learning of the wonderful success of St. Augustine, Pope Gregory appointed him a Bishop in 601, and soon thereafter as the Metropolitan of the Anglo-Saxons, with authority to found twelve suffragan Sees. St. Augustine chose Dovernum, now Canterbury, for his Metropolitan See.

After several years of evangelical labor among the Anglo-Saxons, St. Augustine died at Canterbury in 605.

✠

ST. MARY MAGDALEN OF PAZZI

At her baptism this saint was named Caterina. From early youth she loved prayer and penance, showed great charity for the poor, possessed an apostolic spirit of teaching religious truths, and a charm and sweetness of nature that made her a general favorite. Above all her spiritual characteristics was her intense attraction towards the Blessed Sacrament.

When ten years old she made her First Holy Communion, and soon thereafter vowed her virginity to God. At fourteen she was sent to school at the convent of Cavalaresse. As she led such a mortified and fervent life the Sisters prophesied that she would become a great Saint.

In December, 1582, she entered the Carmelite convent of Santa Maria degl'Angeli. She chose this convent because the Rule permitted the daily reception of the Holy Eucharist. In 1583, upon her investiture, she took the name of Maria Maddalena (Mary Magdalen); and on May 29, 1584, being then so ill that they feared she would not recover, she was professed. From the time she received the religious Habit until her death the Saint's life was one series of raptures and ecstasies.

For five years (1585-1590) God permitted her to be tried by terrible inward desolation and temptations, and by external diabolic attacks. Her courageous severity and deep humility enabled her to overcome them and made her virtues shine more brilliantly in the eyes of her community.

St. Mary Magdalen's life in no way interfered with her usefulness in the convent. She served as Novice Mistress for six years, and in 1604 was made Superior. She was renowned for a miraculous gift of reading her subjects' hearts, and performed many miracles, not only for her own community but for outsiders.

Her life of suffering for the love of God and the salvation of mankind closed after an illness of nearly three years of indescribable painfulness, borne with heroic joy to the end. Innumerable miracles followed the Saint's death. She was canonized by Pope Clement IX on April 28, 1669.

꙳

MAY 30

ST. JOAN OF ARC

During the reign of Edward III, England waged against France a war which lasted a hundred years. Consequently, France had been a prey to misfortune during that long period of time. When France was at its darkest hour, when all seemed lost, God raised up Joan of Arc to revive the hopes of the discouraged soldiery.

Jeannette or, as she was afterwards called, Jeanne d'Arc, was born on February 6, 1412, in the little village of Domremy, about 140 miles southeast of Paris, on the banks of the Meuse and bordering on Lorraine. Her parents were hard-working, faithful, pious Catholics. Joan had one sister and three brothers. Her days were spent with the usual occupations of a peasant girl. She was well brought up and attended daily Mass.

The tide of war had reached the borders of Lorraine. Joan was forced more than once to fly into the woods with her parents before bands of marauders, who sacked and burnt their home. Her mind was full of the terrible events of the times. Distinguished by her virtues and piety, her soul was ready to do God's Will. When the message came, she heard and saw and obeyed. Here, in her own simple words, is the story of the first coming:

"I was thirteen when I had a Voice from God for my help and guidance. The first time I heard this Voice I was very much frightened; ... The Voice seemed to come to me from lips I should reverence. I believe it was sent me from God. When I heard it for the third time I recognized that it was the Voice of an Angel".

Her first Voice came with a vision of St. Michael, whom she saw before her eyes, surrounded by the Angels of Heaven, and when they went from her she wept. The other Voices were those of St. Catherine and St. Margaret, whose "faces were adorned with beautiful crowns, rich and precious", and whose Voices were "beautiful, sweet and low". In May, 1428, her Voices told Joan to go and find the King of France in order to help him reconquer his kingdom; to take up arms in defense of her country and to lead the French soldiers to victory. She left Vaucoulers on February 23, 1429, for her military adventure, which lasted until May 23, 1430, when she was taken prisoner by the Burgundians at Compiegne. Despite the many difficulties she had to contend with she compelled the English Generals to raise the siege of Orleans, and conducted Charles VII of France in triumph to his Coronation at Rheims on July 17th. By his side stood the Maid who had brought the deliverance of his land and people, and when the ceremony was over she knelt at his feet and hailed him as King.

Joan remained with the army in a hopeless struggle against intrigue and jealousy on the one hand, and the vacillation of King Charles on the other. In vain she endeavored to induce the King to march on Paris. It was while she was covering the retreat of her men at Compiegne, as they were being attacked by the Duke of Burgundy, that she was captured. There was great joy among the Burgundians on that 24th of May, 1430. After being detained at Marguy for three or four days, the "Maid of Orleans" was sent to a castle named Beaulieu, in Vermandois, where she lingered for four months.

On July 14, 1430, Cauchon, Bishop of Beauvais, claimed her prisoner in the name of the King of England since she had been captured in his Diocese. The Duke of Burgundy delivered Joan to him for ten thousand gold francs. She was brought to Rouen for trial. The questions put to her chiefly concerned her Voices and visions, her assumption of man's dress, her Faith, and her willingness to submit to the Church. Time after time she solemnly stated, "As firmly as I believe in the Christian Faith and that God hath redeemed us from the pains of hell that Voice hath come to me from God and by His command". She pleaded to be taken before the Pope, but her judges refused, and, finally, condemned her to the stake for heresy. Two servants conducted Joan to the stake which had already been erected. She was burned alive as a heretic and traitor on May 30, 1431. The spectators wept.

Joan begged Brother Isambard, who stood by her to the end, to bring the cross from the church and hold it before her eyes until she died. An Englishman made a little wooden cross out of two sticks and gave it to her. she took it, pressed her lips devoutly upon it, and put it in her bosom underneath her dress and against her body.

At the request of her mother and brothers, Joan's trial was reviewed twenty-five years later, and she was cleared of the charges which had been brought against her. On May 8, 1869, a petition for the canonization of the "Maid of Orleans" was presented to Pope Pius IX, signed by Bishop Dupanloup of Orleans and twelve other Bishops of France. In 1920, after a lapse of nearly five centuries, the Catholic Church formally canonized Joan of Arc.

☦

MAY 31

QUEENSHIP OF MARY

From the earliest centuries of the Catholic Church, Christians have addressed suppliant prayers and hymns of praise and venerated the Blessed Virgin Mary. The hope they placed in the Mother of the Savior, Jesus Christ, has never failed. They have looked upon her as Queen of Angels, Queen of Patriarchs, Queen of Prophets, Queen of Apostles, Queen of Martyrs, Queen of Confessors, Queen of Virgins. Because of her eminence, she is entitled to the highest honors that can be bestowed upon any creature, for she is the glorious Queen of the Universe.

St. Gregory Nazianzen called her "the Mother of the King of the entire universe", and the "Virgin Mother who brought forth the King of the entire world".

St. Jerome stated that "We should realize that Mary means Lady in the Syrian language", while St. Chrysologus says that "The Hebrew name 'Mary' means 'Dobrina' (Lady) in Latin".

Moreover, Epiphanus, the Bishop of Constantinople, wrote to the Sovereign Pontiff Hormisdas saying that we should pray that the unity of the Church may be preserved "by the grace of the Holy and consubstantial Trinity and by the prayers of Mary, our Lady, the holy and glorious Virgin and Mother of God".

And His Holiness Pope Pius XII, in his Encyclical Letter of October 11, 1954, "On the Royal Dignity of the Blessed Virgin Mary and on the Institution of Her Feast"—the Queenship of Mary—to be celebrated throughout the **entire world every year, reminds us what Pope Pius IX said of Mary:**

"Turning her maternal heart toward us and dealing with the affair of our salvation, she is concerned with the whole human race. Constituted by the Lord, Queen of Heaven and earth, and exalted above all the choirs of Angels and the ranks of the Saints in Heaven, standing at the right hand of her only-begotten Son, Our Lord Jesus Christ, she petitions most powerfully with her maternal prayers, and she obtains what she seeks. And she cannot fail".

Therefore, His Holiness Pius XII concludes that "From the monuments of Christian antiquity, from liturgical prayers, from the Christian people's profound sense of religion, and from the works of art that have been produced, We have collected statements asserting that the Virgin Mother of God possesses royal dignity.... From so many testimonies gathered together there is formed, as it were, a farsounding chorus that praises the high eminence of the royal honor of the Mother of God and of men, to whom all created things are subject and who is 'exalted above the choirs of Angels unto heavenly kingdoms'....

"We commend that on the festival there be renewed the consecration of the human race to the Immaculate Heart of the Blessed Virgin Mary. Upon this there is founded a great hope that there may arise an era of happiness that will rejoice in the triumph of religion and in Christian peace. Therefore let all approach with greater confidence now than before to the throne of mercy and grace of our Queen and Mother to beg help in difficulty, light in darkness and solace in trouble and sorrow; and let them strive to free themselves from the servitude of sin. . . . Whoever, therefore, honors the Lady-ruler of Angels and of men—and let no one think himself exempt from the payment of that tribute of a grateful and loving soul—let him call upon her as most truly Queen and as the Queen who brings the blessings of peace, and that she may show us all, after this exile, Jesus, Who will be our enduring peace and joy."

ST. ANGELA MERICI

St. Angela Merici, foundress of the Ursulines, was born in Lombardy March 21, 1474, at Desenzano. At the age of eleven she was left an orphan, and together with her elder sister went to live with her uncle in the neighboring town of Salo, where they spent a holy life. She always tried to please Jesus, the Spouse of her soul. When her sister met with a sudden death, without being able to receive the Last Sacraments, Angela was greatly distressed. She became a tertiary of St. Francis and increased her prayers and mortifications for the repose of her sister's soul. She implored God to reveal to her the state of her deceased sister, and it is claimed that by a vision she was satisfied that her sister was with the Saints in Heaven.

When Angela was twenty years old her uncle died, and she returned to her paternal home at Desenzano. Realizing the need for better instruction of young girls in the Christian religion, she converted her home into a school, which soon bore abundant fruit. Daily she gathered all the little girls of Desenzano and taught them the elements of Christianity.

It is said that one day while in ecstasy she had a vision in which it was revealed to her that she was to found an association of virgins who would devote their lives to the religious training of young girls. Before long Angela gladly accepted an invitation to establish a similar school at Brescia. "The disorders of society", she claimed, "are caused by those in families; there are few Christian mothers, because the education of young girls is neglected."

In 1524, while on a pilgrimage to the Holy Land, she became suddenly blind on the island of Crete. She continued her journey, however, and upon her return was cured while praying before a crucifix at the same place where she was struck by blindness a few weeks before.

During the jubilee year 1525, she went to Rome to gain the indulgences. Pope Clement VII, having heard of her holiness and success as a religion teacher, invited Angela to remain in Rome, but she, shunning publicity, returned to Brescia.

It was on the 25th of November, 1535, that Angela chose twelve virgins and laid the foundation of the Ursuline Order in a small house near the Church of St. Afra in Brescia. Its object being the Christian education of youth, she placed it under the patronage of St. Ursula, the leader of an army of virgins. After serving five years as Superior of the newly-founded Order, she died in 1540 at Brescia with the name of Jesus on her lips, and was buried in the Church of St. Afra. Pope Pius VII added her name to the calendar of Saints in 1807.

✠

FEAST OF CORPUS CHRISTI

The Feast of Corpus Christi (Body of Christ) is celebrated in the Latin Church on the Thursday following Trinity Sunday (in U.S.A., on the Sunday following Trinity Sunday) to solemnly commemorate the institution of the Holy Eucharist.

Prior to the 13th century the faithful were satisfied with celebrating the institution of this Divine Mystery on

Holy Thursday. The instrument in the hand of Divine Providence was St. Juliana of Mont Cornillon in Belgium. She was born in 1193 at Retinnes near Liege. Being left an orphan when quite young, she was educated by the Augustinian Nuns of her native city. Here, she made her religious profession and later became Superioress. From early youth she had a great veneration for the Blessed Sacrament, and ardently desired a special feast in Its honor. It is claimed that this desire was increased by a vision of the Church under the appearance of the full moon having one dark spot, which signified the absence of such a feast. She made known her ideas to Bishop Robert of Liege and several other members of the Hierarchy, including Pope Urban IV. Bishop Robert was favorably impressed, called a Synod in 1246, and ordered the celebration to be held the following year. He did not live, however, to see his order executed, but the feast was celebrated for the first time by the Canons of St. Martin at Liege.

The recluse Eve, with whom St. Juliana spent some time, and who was also a fervent adorer of the Holy Eucharist, now urged Bishop Robert's successor to request the Pope to extend the celebration to the whole world. Since the heretics of that period had attacked the Real Presence of Jesus Christ in the Holy Eucharist, and innumerable miracles and special revelations had occurred to concentrate the attention of the Christian world on this dogma, Pope Urban IV, always an admirer of such a feast, published the Bull "Transiturus" on September 8, 1264, decreeing the annual celebration of Corpus Christi on the Thursday next after Trinity Sunday, and at the same time granted many Indulgences to the faithful for attendance at Mass and at the Office. The Holy Father requested the Angelic Doctor, St. Thomas Aquinas, to compose the Office, which is one of the most beautiful in the Roman Breviary.

JUNE

FEAST OF THE MOST SACRED
HEART OF JESUS

The month of June is dedicated by the Church to the Sacred Heart of Jesus, Who is love incarnate. This is the truth which the Church would have us meditate upon during the month; this the theme from which the Church hopes that her children will draw lessons to guide their daily lives. She bids us remember the lance-pierced Heart from which flowed torrents of redeeming grace. She asks us to recall Our Lord's plaintive plea, "Behold this Heart which has loved men so much, and which receives in return for the most part nothing but ingratitude, contempt, irreverence and sacrilege. We are urged to draw near this merciful and compassionate Heart and to repose our fears, doubts and anxieties therein. We are encouraged to link our hearts with His in love, and to pray that we may love Him more and more.

In the letter of the Great Apostle St. Paul, we read that "Charity is patient, charity is kind, charity is not provoked to anger, but beareth all things, hopeth all things, endureth all things". The Heart of Jesus is charity, or love, that meets this definition fully, faultlessly. Did ever a heart have cause to grow impatient with men, to be provoked to anger, to make return to creatures with unkindness, applying the measure that they so often use with their Creator, as did the Heart of the Savior? Yet, His Heart bears and endures; It hopes until the end for better things from all men.

This is the Heart of the true Good Shepherd Who, leaving the choirs of the Blessed Spirits in Heaven, was ready for every sacrifice and effort in the quest "to find and save that which was lost".

For over 1900 years now, the Heart of the Divine Shepherd has sent and will continue to send forth from the tabernacles of Catholic churches Its call to straying sheep, beckoning them to good pastures; It pursues and will not tire of pursuing with graces all who have strayed from the path of righteousness.

This is the forgiving Heart of the Father of countless prodigal sons and daughters, that overlooks the fact that they cast Him aside for the lure of the unknown, when the world and its pleasures beckoned and as long as good things were within grasp or to be hoped for, that welcomes them back with a kiss of tenderness and with tears of joy, restoring them to sonship, and that in so doing would have it be known that their return consummates deepest longings and desires.

This is the Heart of a Samaritan pouring oil and wine into the wounds of enemies; of a Judge refusing to condemn trembling souls taken in sin, only asking that sin be abandoned; of a Master arising in defense of Mary Magdalenes and continuing to visit the homes of sinners and publicans; this the Heart of God that tries to recall a Judas who has betrayed, that reclaims a Peter who has denied, that rewards with eternal happiness a thief who repents with dying breath, that pleads in anguish with an angered Heavenly Father: "Father, forgive them, for they know not what they do".

The Heart of Jesus is a burning furnace of love for us. The fire of love for us in His Heart—in Heaven and in our tabernacles—has not been extinguished, nor has it diminished in fervor. Therefore, during the month of the Sacred Heart, may all Catholics prove that their hearts have caught fire from the burning Heart of Jesus and are now glowing with love for the Heart that loves all men.

✠

JUNE 1

ST. PAMPHILUS

Pamphilus belonged to a noble family of Beirut (in Phoenicia), where he received a good education. After selling all of his property he gave the proceeds to the poor; then left his native land for Alexandria and placed himself under Pierius, head of the famous Catechetical School. Eventually he settled in Caesarea where he was ordained to the priesthood, collected his famous library, and established a school for theological study. Much of his time was spent in producing accurate copies of the Holy Scriptures.

Diocletian commenced his bloody persecution in 303. In November, 307, Pamphilus was brought before the Governor. Refusing to sacrifice to the gods, he was cruelly tortured and then cast into prison. During his incarceration he continued to copy and correct manuscripts. He was without further torture until sentenced to be beheaded in February, 309.

✠

JUNE 2

STS. MARCELLINUS, PETER AND ERASMUS

The exorcist Peter was sent to prison during the reign of Emperor Diocletian. While imprisoned he converted his jailer and all his family, and brought them to the Priest Marcellinus, who baptized them. Serenus, the judge, ordered them both to appear before him; they courageously bore witness to Jesus Christ. They were condemned to death, and after cruel torments were beheaded, about the year 303.

St. Erasmus, Bishop, one of the "fourteen auxiliary Saints", lived in the solitudes of Lebanon. He was martyred in Campania under the Emperors Diocletian and Maximian, obtaining the glorious palm of martyrdom in 303. St. Benedict had a great devotion towards St. Erasmus. He is invoked for internal diseases.

✠

JUNE 3

ST. CLOTILDE

St. Clotilde, Queen of France, was a daughter of Chilperic, whose older brother was the tyrannical King of

Burgundy who killed his wife and all his other brothers except one, in order to usurp their kingdoms. Clotilde was reared in her uncle's Court. Though educated among Arians, it was her happiness to be instructed in the Catholic Faith. She married Clovis I, King of the Franks, and by her good example and prayers endeavored to win him to God. Fear of offending his people delayed his conversion. However, after his miraculous victory over the Alemanni, he embraced Christianity, and built many religious institutions at the request of St. Clotilde. Among these was the grand church of Saints Peter and Paul, now called the Church of St. Genevieve.

St. Clotilde suffered greatly on account of the dissensions between her sons. Her most sensible affliction was the murder of the two eldest sons of Clodimir, in 526, by their uncles Childebert and Clotaire. This tragedy aided in weaning her heart from the world.

The remaining years of St. Clotilde's life were spent in performing good works, fasting, penance and exercises of piety. She longed for Eternity, and foretold her death thirty days before it occurred. She departed this life on June 3, 545, and in accordance with her request was buried in the Church of St. Genevieve.

ST. KEVIN

Saint Kevin (or Coemgen) was an Abbot of Glendalough, Ireland, who lived in the 6th century. He was baptized by St. Cronan, and from his 12th year studied under monks. Eventually he embraced the monastic state and founded the famous monastery of Glendalough (the Valley of the Two Lakes), which became the parent of several other monastic foundations. After firmly establishing his community he retired into solitude for four years. At the earnest entreaty of his monks, Kevin returned to Glendalough. His followers were so numerous that Glendalough actually became a city in the desert, and eventually an espiscopal see. It is now incorporated with Dublin.

St. Kevin's house and St. Kevin's bed of rock are still to be seen, and for centuries the Seven Churches of Glendalough have been visited by pilgrims from many countries.

Many legends have grown up around Kevin. When asked whether they were true, his only reply was "God is all-powerful". He died on June 3, 618 at the age of one hundred twenty.

☩

JUNE 4

ST. FRANCIS CARACCIOLA

Francis, of the noble family of Caracciola, co-founder with John Augustine Adorno of the Congregation of the Minor Clerks Regular, was born in Villa Santa Maria, in the Abruzzo (Italy), October 13, 1563. He received in baptism the name of Asconia. From infancy he was remarkable for his gentleness and uprightness. At the age of twenty-two he was cured of leprosy and made a vow to become a Priest. After distributing his goods to the poor, he went to Naples in 1585 to study theology, and was ordained to the priesthood in 1587.

Giovanni Agostina Adorno wrote a letter to *Ascanio* Caracciola begging him to assist him in founding a new religious institute. By mistake the letter was delivered to our saint, who regarded it as evidence of God's Will towards him. In consequence, he assisted in drawing up the Rules for the new Congregation, which was approved by Pope Sixtus V in 1588.

In spite of his refusal, Francis was chosen General on March 9, 1593, in the first house of the Congregation in Naples. He made three visits to Spain to establish the foundations under the protection of Philip II and Philip III. Pope Paul V desired to confer an important bishopric on him, but he steadfastly refused it.

St. Francis died at Agnone on the vigil of Corpus
Christi, June 4, 1608, while negotiating with the Oratorians
to convert their house into a college for his Congregation.
He was canonized by Pope Pius VII May 24, 1807.

✠

JUNE 5

ST. BONIFACE

St. Boniface, the apostle of Germany, was an Anglo-
Saxon, born in Devonshire, England, in 680, and received
the name Winfrid at his Baptism. When only five years old,
some holy Benedictine Monks preaching in that country
came to his father's home. Winfrid was deeply impressed
and longed to be a religious, but his father exerted his authority to change the boy's mind until the child was afflicted
with a serious illness. Seeing in it the hand of God chastis-
ing him for opposing his son's vocation, he left Winfrid free
to pursue his vocation. At thirteen years of age he was sent
to Exminster to be educated, and before he left he received
the religious Habit of the Benedictines, taking the name of
Boniface. He was ordained to the priesthood when thirty
years old, and was so highly thought of by his superiors
that he was entrusted with an important commission to the
Archbishop of Canterbury.

Night and day the holy servant of God bewailed the
misfortune of those people living in idolatry. In 716 he
went into Friesland to preach the Gospel. This missionary
expedition proved a failure. Upon his return to England he
was chosen Abbot of the monastery. In 718 he went to
Rome to ask the Pope's blessing on his proposed new mission, and received his authority to preach to the German
tribes. He began with Bavaria and Thuringia, and his life
was in constant danger. The work was slow, but his courage
never failed. He next visited Friesland, Hesse and Fran-
conia, everywhere striving to enlighten the infidels.

In 723 Pope Gregory II consecrated St. Boniface Bishop, with full jurisdiction over the German tribes. He
continued his spiritual conquests, and founded many
churches and monasteries throughout the country. Obtaining new laborers from England, he stationed them in Hesse
and Thuringia. In 732 the new Pope, Gregory III, constituted St. Boniface Archbishop and Primate of all Germany;
in 738, Papal Legate, and in 747, Archbishop of Mainz.
Several years before his death he founded the Abbey of
Fulda (where his body now rests), as the center of all
German missionary work.

Although advanced in years, St. Boniface appointed a
successor to his monastery and set out to convert a pagan
tribe. One day while waiting to administer Confirmation to
some newly-baptized Christians, a band of enraged infidels
rushed into the tent. His attendants desired to resist them,
but St. Boniface would not permit it, declaring that the day
he had long awaited was come, which would bring him to
the eternal joys of the Lord. Then he encouraged the rest
to meet with cheerfulness and constancy a death which
would be to them the gate of everlasting life.

St. Boniface, at the age of seventy-five, was martyred
on June 5, 755, at Dokkum, with fifty-two of his companions. Innumerable miracles have been wrought by God
through the intercession of St. Boniface.

✠

JUNE 6

ST. NORBERT

St. Norbert was born at Xanten in the Rhineland about
1080, of a princely family. He possessed rare talents, yet
permitted himself to be carried away by worldly pleasures.
He even received the ecclesiastical tonsure with a worldly
spirit, and though he later was ordained subdeacon, failed
to change his spirit or his conduct. His cousin, Emperor

Henry IV, appointed him his almoner, and Norbert sought in vain contentment and peace of mind in his life of dissipation and luxury. God awakened him from his spiritual lethargy by a narrow escape from death.

One day while horseback riding a severe storm broke and a ball of fire, or lightning, fell in front of his horse. Frightened, the horse threw his rider, who lay like one dead for nearly an hour. Coming to, he cried to God, like St. Paul, "Lord, what wilt Thou have me to do?" An interior voice replied: "Turn away from evil, and do good; seek after peace, and pursue it". Upon the spot he became a sincere penitent and resolved to lead a new life.

Norbert left the Court and retired to his canonry to lead a life of silence and retirement. Two years were spent in tears, holy prayer and penance, in preparation for Holy Orders, which he received from the Archbishop of Cologne, when thirty-two years of age. First he exposed the abuses of his own Order, and after having obtained the Pope's permission he preached penance with incredible fruit in France and the Netherlands.

In 1120, in a lonesome valley called Premontre, the Bishop of Laon erected a monastery for St. Norbert, who assembled thirteen brethren from Brabant desirous of serving God under his direction. The number soon increased to forty, and on Christmas day, 1121, these Canon Regulars, as they were called, made their profession. They followed the Rule of St. Augustine, and led an austere life. Later they were known as Norbertines or Premonstratensians. Their fervor renewed the spirit of the clergy, enlivened the faith of the people, and destroyed heresy.

At the Diet of Spire in 1126, St. Norbert was appointed Archbishop of Madgeburg. By his authority, eloquence, and example he reformed both the clergy and laity of his Diocese. Several attempts were made to take his life, but he calmly said: "Can you be surprised that the devil, after having offered violence to our Divine Head, should assault His members?"

St. Bernard and St. Norbert labored strenuously to prevent or remedy the disorders of the schism which occurred after the death of Honorius II.

St. Norbert suffered a four months' illness, and died the death of the just at Madgeburg on June 6, 1134. He was canonized by Gregory XIII in 1582. He is usually depicted in art holding a ciborium, on account of his extraordinary devotion to the Blessed Sacrament.

✠

JUNE 7

ST. ROBERT OF NEWMINSTER

St. Robert studied at the University of Paris, where it is claimed he composed a commentary on the Psalms. After being ordained to the priesthood he served in the parish church at Gargrave. Later he became a Benedictine at Whitby, England, from where, with the Abbot's permission, he joined the Cistercian Reform of Fountains. About 1130 he headed the first group sent out from Fountains and established the Abbey of Newminster at Morpeth in Northumberland.

St. Robert's holiness of life, even more than his words, guided his brethren to perfection. He was favored with the gifts of prophecy and miracles, and was united in spiritual friendship with St. Bernard of Clairvaux, and St. Godric, the holy hermit of Durham. He died in 1159, and his tomb in the church of Newminster became a place of pilgrimage.

✠

JUNE 8

ST. MEDARD

St. Medard was born at Salency, France, about 457. **His father, Nectard, was a French nobleman, while his** mother, Protogia, was a lady of extraordinary piety, descended from an ancient Roman family which had settled in Gaul. Protogia converted her husband from paganism and instilled into Medard a tender compassion for the poor. From an early age it was also his delight to assist the needy, to fast, and to spend considerable time in prayer. When he was old enough his parents sent him abroad to pursue his higher studies. Upon his return they entreated the Bishop to instruct him in Sacred Scripture. At the age of thirty-three Medard was ordained a Priest, and became one of the most illustrious prelates of the Church in France.

In 530 St. Medard was consecrated Bishop by St. Remigius. He continued his austere life and, although seventy-two years of age, redoubled his labors. No opportunity was lost in his efforts to dispel idolatry throughout his Diocese. The inhabitants of Flanders were the most savage and fierce barbarians of all the Gauls and Franks, rendering St. Medard's task difficult and perilous. He inspired them with the meek spirit of Jesus and made them a civilized, Christian nation.

Having completed this great work in Flanders, St. Medard returned to Noyon. Shortly afterwards he fell sick and died, in 545. The entire country lamented the loss of their common father and protector. His body was laid to rest in his own Cathedral, but King Clotaire was so moved by the many miracles wrought at St. Medard's tomb that he translated his remains to Soissons.

☦

JUNE 9

ST. COLUMBA

St. Columba, or Columkille, was born of a noble family at Gartan, County Tyrconnel, Ireland, in 521. Deeply religious from early youth, he was ordained a priest at Clonard. From the day of his arrival there he began to manifest the gift of prophecy. Truly marvelous was his zeal in founding and regulating monastic institutions, with their churches and noble halls of learning. Historians attribute to him as many as one hundred in Ireland, though he left its shores in his forty-second year, while in the prime of manly vigor.

It was in 563 that St. Columba departed for Scotland. Into the vast places he wandered, bearing the glad tidings of salvation; everywhere winning souls and planting the Cross of his crucified Lord. The perils and labors of St. Columba and his companions were great, but their victory was outstanding and complete. Convinced by St. Columba's arguments and his miracles, the tribes submitted and were baptized. The Picts, in gratitude, gave him the island of Iona, where he founded his celebrated monastery, the school of apostolic missionaries and martyrs. The numerous monasteries established by St. Columba, whether in Erin or in Alba, acknowledged his jurisdiction and were subject to him.

In the 30th year of his apostleship and exile, while wrapt in prayer, a celestial light was seen round him. He had a vision of Angels who told him that the day of his death had been deferred four years, in answer to the prayers of his companions. The Saint wept bitterly, crying out, "Woe is me that my sojourning is prolonged!" for he longed to reach his eternal home.

His peaceful death occurred on the 9th of June, 597, in his 76th year, surrounded in choir by his spiritual children. His relics were carried to Down, and laid in the same shrine with the bodies of St. Patrick and St. Brigid, where they remained for centuries. Henry VIII and his followers had no regard for church or shrine or relics, and Lord Deputy Gray, in his campaign of plunder and profanation, robbed the Cathedral of Down; afterwards he gave it to the flames, and demolished the shrine of the Saints.

✠

JUNE 10

ST. MARGARET OF SCOTLAND

St. Margaret was long the faithful wife of King Malcolm Canmore, the third of his name.

Princess Margaret's early life was darkened by many adverse events, but brightened by her piety. Her father Edward, a Saxon prince, and Agatha, her mother, a scion of the royal houses of Germany and Hungary, were disinherited and exiled.

Margaret was eleven or twelve years old when the greatest changes in her life occurred. Her father after a long period of exile was summoned to return to his country, at the time governed by his uncle Edward, known in later years as "the Confessor". Margaret's life in England was not very different from what it had been in Hungary, for the saintly Edward kept an austere court. Each morning at dawn the entire household attended Mass.

High indeed had been the hopes with which Prince Edward and his family had taken up their abode in England. It was not long, however, before Margaret's father died and she was called upon to bear all the difficulties and anxieties of the troubled, stormy periods that followed upon her father's death, and that of her saintly uncle shortly afterwards.

England could no longer be a safe home for them, and Princess Agatha prudently prepared to leave the country. Some historians claim that it was her intention to go to Scotland and place herself under the protection of King Malcolm. Landing on the coast of Scotland, the voyagers had to walk towards Dunfermline. King Malcolm met them on the way and took the party to his own castle, or "Tower" as it was called, and entertained them for many months. The following spring, in the year 1050, Princess

Margaret and King Malcolm were married, and she reigned
Queen of Scotland until her death in 1093. Promptly she
threw herself into the manifold duties incumbent upon a
wife, who was also the consort sovereign of a wild and
turbulent people. Two years later their home and capital
was changed to Edinburgh, Malcolm Canmore being the
first of the Scottish Kings to make the little burgh of
St. Edwin the chief seat of the kingdom.

Amidst her varied duties, Margaret found time to
converse with God, and she won her husband to imitate
her sanctity. He would rise at night to pray with her. She
did not rest until she saw the laws of God and His Church
observed throughout the realm.

St. Margaret spared no pains in the education of her
eight children, and their sanctity can be attributed to the
prudent zeal of their holy mother. Before five each morning
she dressed and fed nine infant orphans; she also distributed food and alms to three hundred of the poor in her
kingdom. She was the most trusted counsellor of her husband, and she labored for the material improvement of her
country.

King Malcolm had often had wars with William the
Conqueror. Queen Margaret was opposed to her husband
going to battle with William Rufus. She was in ill-health
at the time and shortly after her husband left she became
worse. Yet each day she dragged herself to the chapel to
assist at Mass. On November 16, 1093, she had to leave
the chapel and be supported to her own chamber. Her end
was near. The Chaplain, her maids, and her children
were around her couch. She bade them not lament for her
as she would soon reach the Home where she had longed
to be. Then turning to her confessor, she earnestly begged
him to guard and watch over her children and bring them
up in the fear of the Lord. With the words "Deliver me,
O Lord" she breathed her pure soul into the hands of God.

So much loved and honored had she been that
successive generations cried aloud for her canonization.
Many churches were built in her honor; many miracles
were performed at her tomb.

Pope Innocent III placed St. Margaret's name on the calendar of the Church's Saints in 1251.

✠

JUNE 11

ST. BARNABAS

St. Barnabas was of the tribe of Levi, but born in Cyprus and, as Holy Scripture relates, was one of the seventy-two disciples of Jesus. The first mention we find of him is in the Acts of the Apostles (4:36), where it is related that "the multitude of believers had but one heart and one soul; neither did anyone say that aught of the things which he possessed was his own". No one in particular is mentioned on this occasion but Joseph, a rich Levite from Cyprus, who sold his land "and brought the price and laid it at the feet of the Apostles". The Apostles changed his name from Joseph to Barnabas, the son of consolation. It was he who "introduced" St. Paul to the Apostles, and thus to the Church.

Later St. Barnabas accompanied St. Paul during his evangelization of the pagans in Cyprus. The Church in Jerusalem "sent Barnabas as far as Antioch. . . . And Barnabas went to Tarsus to seek Saul; whom, when he had found, he brought to Antioch. And they conversed there in the Church a whole year; and they taught a great multitude, so that at Antioch, the disciples were first named Christians.

"Now there were in the Church which was at Antioch, prophets and doctors, among whom was Barnabas, and Simon who was called Niger, and Lucius of Cyrene, and Manahen, who was the foster brother of Herod the tetrarch, and Saul. And as they were ministering to the Lord, and fasting, the Holy Spirit said to them: Separate me Saul and Barnabas, for the work whereunto I have taken them. Then they, fasting and praying, and imposing their hands upon them, sent them away" (Acts 11:21-26; 13:1-3).

Although Barnabas was not one of the "Twelve", the Church has always honored him as an Apostle. According to tradition, St. Barnabas died for the Faith in Cyprus.

✠

JUNE 12

ST. JOHN OF ST. FACUNDO

St. John was a hermit of the Order of St. Augustine. He was born at Sahagun, or St. Facundo, in the province of Leon, Spain, in 1419, and educated in his home town by the Benedictine Monks. He went to Salamanca and Burgos to complete his education. Upon receiving the ecclesiastical tonsure his father procured him a small benefice. Soon he secured several others, but his conscience reproached him and he resigned all except one small chapel, where he offered up the Holy Sacrifice of the Mass daily, preached frequently, and gave catechetical instruction. He lived a retired, mortified, prayerful life.

Having received his Bishop's consent, St. John studied theology for four years at Salamanca, after which he was stationed in the parish church of St. Sebastian. In 1463 he took the religious Habit among the hermits of St. Augustine in Salamanca, and held the offices of Master of Novices and Prior. His fearless preaching brought about a marvelous change in the social life of the city. Without respect of persons, he reproved those living a sinful life. A certain Duke whom St. John had rebuked sent two assassins to murder him. At the sight of the holy man they were struck with remorse, and falling at his feet begged his pardon. The Duke fell ill, and through the prayers of St. John, whom he had attempted to murder, confessed his sincere repentance and was restored to health.

St. John foretold his death, and passed away on June 11, 1479. He was glorified by many miracles before and after his death, and was canonized by Pope Alexander VIII in 1690.

✠

ST. ANTHONY OF PADUA

St. Anthony was born in Lisbon, Portugal, in 1195, but received his surname on account of his long residence at Padua. His baptismal name was Ferdinand, which he changed for that of Anthony when he entered the Franciscan Order. His parents were noted for their nobility and virtue, and they placed Ferdinand at an early age with the Canons of the Cathedral in Lisbon to be educated. At fifteen he joined the Canons Regular near that city, but two years later requested to be sent to Coimbra, one hundred miles distant. He had lived at Coimbra almost eight years when Don Pedro of Portugal brought from Morocco the relics of five Franciscans who had been recently crowned there with martyrdom. Ferdinand was greatly affected at the sight, and conceived an ardent desire to lay down his life for Christ. Not long after, some Franciscan Friars came to his monastery begging alms for their community. Ferdinand told them of his desire to join their Order, and received their encouragement. When he made known his ambition to his superiors they endeavored to dissuade him, and he suffered much from their ridicule and bitter reproaches.

Finally Ferdinand obtained the consent of his Prior, and in 1221 received the Franciscan Habit, taking the name of Anthony. After some time spent in solitude, prayer and penitential austerities, desiring martyrdom he obtained permission to go to Africa to preach the Gospel to the Moors. Soon after his arrival, however, he became very ill and was obliged to return to Spain to regain his health.

At the age of twenty-seven he was performing humble tasks in the little solitary hermitage of Mount Paul near Bologna, carefully concealing his learning and talents. During an assembly of neighboring Dominicans and Franciscans held at Forli, the Dominicans, as visitors, were requested to address the gathering; all excused themselves saying they were not prepared. Anthony's Guardian then **ordered him to speak and to say whatever the Holy Spirit** would inspire him to say. St. Anthony begged to be excused, but his Superior insisted that he comply. St. Anthony spoke with such eloquence, erudition and unction that everyone present was astonished.

When St. Francis was informed of the discovery of this hidden treasure, he sent St. Anthony to Vercelli to study theology. Then for some years he taught sacred science with great success at Bologna, Toulouse, Montpellier and Padua. At length he forsook the schools, and for nine years was a missionary preacher in France, Italy and Sicily, turning men's hearts to God and performing miracles. St. Anthony has been called "the hammer of heretics" and a "wonder-worker". He is one of the most popular Saints of the Church.

While spending a night with a friend in Padua, his host saw brilliant rays streaming under the door of the Saint's room. Looking through the keyhole he beheld a beautiful Child standing upon a book which lay open upon the table, and clinging with both arms around Anthony's neck. An ineffable sweetness filled his soul. When the Child vanished St. Anthony opened the door and commanded his friend, for the love of Him Whom he had seen, to "tell the vision to no man" as long as he was alive.

On June 13, 1231, after spending ten years in the Franciscan Order, St. Anthony died. When his death became known the children ran about the streets crying, "The Saint is dead!" Innumerable miracles testified his sanctity. In 1232, in compliance with the Paduans' request, Pope Gregory IX caused St. Anthony's name to be added to the calendar of Saints. Thirty-two years later a beautiful church was built for the Franciscans in Padua, and St. Anthony's remains were translated into it. The flesh was all consumed, but the tongue, which had always praised God, was found incorrupt.

In 1946 Pope Pius XII proclaimed St. Anthony a Doctor of the Universal Church.

✠

ST. BASIL THE GREAT

St. Basil, one of the four great Doctors of the East, was born at Caesarea in Asia Minor. His parents, as well as his paternal grandparents, two of his brothers and one sister are all honored as Saints. After attending the schools in Caesarea and Constantinople, St. Basil then studied in Athens, and there met again St. Gregory Nazianzen, whom he had first met in Caesarea; they became staunch friends.

Upon completion of his studies, St. Basil was regarded in Athens as an oracle both in sacred and profane learning. He returned to Caesarea and opened a school of oratory, and was prevailed upon to plead at the bar. Seeing himself applauded by his countrymen, and dreading the honors of the world, he determined to renounce the world. His holy sister Macrina, and his friend Gregory Nazianzen, encouraged him in his resolution.

After visiting some monasteries and hermits in Egypt, Palestine and Syria, St. Basil founded a monastery on the river Iris, in Pontus, and became the father of monastic life in the East. His Rule is followed, even today, by all oriental Monks. Alarmed at the dangers of the Church on account of the Arian heretics, who were supported by the Court, when his Bishop summoned him from his retirement, St. Basil hastened to defend the Church against their heretical teachings. Upon his arrival in Caesarea he opposed the Arians with so much prudence and courage they were obliged to desist from their pretensions with shame and confusion. St. Basil preached to his people daily, morning and evening; throngs came to listen to him, and Cappadocia was saved for the Catholic Faith.

In 370 he was consecrated Archbishop of Caesarea, and lived in the greatest poverty possible, fasted, performed great austerities, and prayed continually. Peace was restored

to the Church in 378 by Emperor Gratian. That same year
St. Basil fell sick and prepared himself for his passage to
eternity. The entire populace was grief-stricken when their
holy Archbishop died on January 1, 379.

☩

JUNE 15

ST. GERMAINE

Germaine Cousin was born in 1579 in Pibrac, a small
village ten miles west of Toulouse, France. She has been
termed "The saint without a history".

From her earliest years Germaine was a frail, sickly
child, and throughout her life was afflicted with scrofula, a
tubercular condition, affecting particularly the glands of the
neck. In addition, her right arm and hand were deformed
and partially paralyzed. In spite of her many afflictions, the
emaciated child possessed a charming, sweet disposition.

Besides bodily sufferings, Germaine endured harsh,
cruel treatment from her stepmother, who had a deep
aversion and hatred for the little girl. Often her face was
swollen and covered with blood from the blows administered by the brutal woman. The child was almost starved
to death, being given only a few crusts of moldy black
bread daily; her bed was a pile of leaves and twigs under
the stairway of the barn, amidst the squalor of the animals.
Abandoned and forlorn, it was here that she spent her
nights, cold, hungry and sick.

It would seem that the stepmother sought by her
inhuman treatment to bring about the child's death. But
God was watching over her.

At break of day, summer and winter, Germaine was
obliged to drive the sheep into the fields to graze and to
watch them until evening. While the sheep were grazing
Germaine had to spin. If the allotted wool was not spun,
she was severely punished.

Even the villagers showed a hostile attitude toward the forlorn child. The children, however, loved to listen to her speak about the goodness and love of God as she shepherded her flock.

With no opportunity to attend school, Germaine never learned to read or write. The catechetical instruction given after the Sunday Mass in the village church, she eagerly drank in as she prepared for her First Holy Communion. Like our Blessed Lady, she "pondered in her heart" all she learned about the Lord Jesus and His Blessed Mother. The long hours of solitude in the fields during the day and in the stable at night were spent by this innocent child in sweet communion with God, and she never complained of her hard life.

The village church was the only place where Germaine was welcome. Each morning she could be seen there kneeling before Our Lady's shrine after assisting at Mass. In order to reach the church it was necessary to cross the Courbet. Ordinarily it was only a small stream, but after a heavy rain it would become a raging torrent. On several occasions when the stream was full, the villagers were amazed to see the rushing waters separate as Germaine approached, and that she was able to cross to the opposite side on dry land as the Israelites had crossed the Red Sea.
It wasn't long before the people of Pibrac began to talk about this and the other wonderful happenings in the life of the unwanted child.

Although ravenous wolves infested the forest near the village, the stepmother sometimes ordered Germaine to take the sheep there. While other villagers' flocks had been dispersed and destroyed by these wild animals, never once did they harm Germaine's sheep. She would strike her distaff into the ground and the sheep would huddle around it and remain there safely while she would go to Mass.

Her biographers also relate that one evening as several of the townspeople passed the stable where Germaine slept, they heard a heavenly melody emanating therefrom. Peering through a crack, they saw the child kneeling in ecstatic prayer, her head crowned wth a radiant light. Attempting to enter, the celestial hymn was renewed, and they fled in awe.

One wintry day, shortly before her death, some of the village folk saw the stepmother pursuing Germaine as she drove the sheep down the road. Screaming loudly, she accused the girl of having concealed in her apron some bread she had stolen from the home of her stepmother. Threatening to strike the child, she demanded that Germaine unfold the apron. When she obeyed, fragrant flowers, not grown in that region, fell to the ground.

The villagers' attitude of contempt now changed to one approaching veneration, but Germaine's life on earth was nearing its end. One night early in the summer of 1601, at the age of twenty-two, she died, as she had lived, alone with God. Her remains were interred in the village church, as was the custom in those days.

In 1644 a relative desired to be buried next to Germaine. When the stones were removed, to the astonishment of the grave-digger there was found the body of a beautiful young girl in a state of perfect preservation. His pick had struck the girl's nose, and the wound was bleeding. Some of the older residents identified the girl as Germaine Cousin. Miracle after miracle occurred. On June 29, 1867, the neglected little waif of Pibrac was enrolled upon the list of Saints by Pope Pius IX. In 1877 the citizens of Toulouse erected a stone monument in Saint Germaine's honor. Annually thousands of pilgrims visit the church of Pibrac, where the sacred body of Saint Germaine is enshrined.

✠

JUNE 16

ST. JOHN FRANCIS REGIS

St. John Francis Regis was born January 31, 1597, at
Font-Couverte, Languedoc, France. At the age of five he
fainted when he heard his mother speak of the terrible
misfortune of being eternally damned. He was a modest,
quiet, studious child, and when the Jesuits opened a college
at Beziers John was one of the first to be enrolled. His
seriousness increased with his years; frequently he retired
to the chapel and could be seen bathed in tears in the
presence of Jesus. In his eighteenth year he was visited with
a serious sickness. Soon after his recovery he made a retreat
to decide on a state of life. Following the advice of his
confessor, he asked admittance into the Society of Jesus.
The Provincial readily received him and he entered his
noviceship with great joy at Toulouse when nineteen
years old.

After his ordination in 1631, he began his apostolic
work at Montpellier and spent himself in preaching to the
unlettered people of Languedoc and Auvergne. He made
many converts among the Huguenots; established an association of women to procure aid for prisoners; and
founded confraternities of the Blessed Sacrament. In his
works of mercy God frequently helped him by miracles.
On one of his missionary journeys in November, 1637,
snow and ice filled the valleys and precipitous crags he had
to cross. Despite the fact that he fell and broke his leg,
with the help of his companion he continued the remaining
six miles of the journey. Instead of seeing a surgeon when
he reached his destination, he insisted on going into the
confessional. After hearing confessions for several hours
the parish Priest learned of his accident. When the leg was
examined it was found to be miraculously cured.

St. John's successes everywhere were wonderful, but,
as in the life of every Saint, God permitted him to be

misunderstood and persecuted. He edified all by his humility and saintly life. While on his way to his last mission assignment he fell ill and took refuge in an abandoned house. Exposed to the piercing winter wind, pleurisy set in. The following morning he crawled to the church and opened the mission. After preaching three times on Christmas day and three times on St. Stephen's day, he went to hear confessions and fainted twice. The physicians found him seriously ill. On December 31, 1640, at the age of forty-three, St. John Francis Regis rendered his pure soul to God. He was canonized by Pope Clement XII in 1737.

✠

JUNE 17

ST. AVITUS

St. Avitus was a native of Orleans, France. He led a monastic life and became Abbot of the monastery at Micy, near Orleans. Desiring to live the life of a recluse, he resigned the abbacy and joined St. Calais on the frontiers of La Perche. Soon others joined them and St. Calais retired into a forest. King Clotaire erected a church and monastery for St. Avitus and his companions, which afterwards became a Benedictine convent for women called St. Avy of Chateau-dun, in the Diocese of Chartres.

St. Avitus died in 530 and was buried with great pomp in Orleans.

✠

JUNE 18

ST. EPHREM

While a mere youth St. Ephrem became a religious in his native city, Nisibis, Syria. Later he retired near Edessa to be a Monk, refusing the dignity of the priesthood. Much of his time was spent in writing commentaries on

Holy Scripture, and composing hymns which inflamed the hearts of the people. So much so, that he has been called **the Harp of the Holy Spirit.**

During the famine of 378, which raged throughout Mesopotamia, St. Ephrem labored unceasingly to aid the suffering. He is honored not only in the East but also in the West. In 1920 Pope Benedict XV declared St. Ephrem a Doctor of the Church.

✠

JUNE 19

ST. JULIANA FALCONIERI

It was in answer to the prayers of her aged parents that Juliana was sent by God to bless their union. The first words the child uttered were Gesu, Maria. At sixteen years of age she consecrated her virginity to God and received from the hands of St. Philip Benizi the religious veil of the "Mantellate", which is the Third Order of the Servites.

Juliana's reputation for prudence and sanctity drew many devout persons to join the Institute. Although she was their spiritual Mother, it was her delight to serve all the Sisters. Often she spent whole days in prayer, practiced great austerities, and frequently received great heavenly favors. She aided the sick and the poor, reconciled enemies, and reclaimed sinners.

St. Juliana in her old age suffered various painful illnesses, which she bore patiently and cheerfully. Because of a stomach ailment which caused constant vomiting, she was deprived of receiving her Divine Spouse in the Sacrament of the Altar. As death was approaching she begged to see and adore once again the Blessed Sacrament. When the Sacred Host was brought into her cell, It suddenly disappeared out of the hands of the Priest. After her death the figure of the Host was found imprinted on the left side of her breast, by which prodigy it was thought Jesus had miraculously satisfied the Saint's desire to receive Holy Communion.

St. Juliana died in her convent in Florence in 1340, at the age of seventy, and miracles have been frequently effected through her intercession. She was canonized by Pope Clement XII.

✠

JUNE 20

ST. SILVERIUS

Silverius, born in Frosinone, Italy, was the son of Pope Hermisdas, who had been married before he entered the ministry. After the death of Pope Agapetus the Holy See was vacant forty-seven days. Silverius, though only a deacon at that time, was chosen to fill the vacancy and was ordained on June 8, 536.

When Justinian became master of Rome the Empress Theodora, a violent and crafty woman, resolved to promote the sect of the Acephali, which rejected the Council of Chalcedon. Anthimus, Patriarch of Constantinople, was suspected of aiding the Acephali, and against the wishes of the Canons the Empress used her influence in having him transferred from the See of Trapezus to that of the Imperial City. Pope Agapetus visited Constantinople in 536 and refused to communicate with Anthimus because of his heretical beliefs concerning the two natures in Christ. Justinian banished the Bishop, and St. Mennas was consecrated Bishop by Pope Agapetus to replace Anthimus.

This caused the Empress great uneasiness, and she never ceased to find a way in which to recall Anthimus. Finally she wrote Pope Silverius demanding that he either acknowledge Anthimus as the lawful Bishop, or go in person to Constantinople to re-examine his cause. The Pope refused, stating that to comply with her request would betray the cause of the Catholic Faith. He thereby incurred the hatred of the Empress, who from that time was determined to have him deposed. She succeeded in inducing Vigilius, archdeacon of the Roman Church who had gone

to Constantinople to attend the late Pope Agapetus, to
condemn the Council of Chalcedon and to permit the three
deposed Eutychian Patriarchs to receive Holy Communion
after she had promised to make him Pope and to give him
seven hundred pieces of gold. Then the Empress commanded General Belisarius to drive Silverius out and to
contrive the election of Vigilius as Pope. Pope Silverius
was accused of high treason and was banished first to
Patara and then to a small island off Naples, where he
died on June 20, 538.

The Bishop of Patara, who was an Oriental Bishop,
defended Silverius by going to the Emperor in Constantinople and threatening him with Divine judgments
for the expulsion of a Bishop, saying "There are many kings
in the world, but there is only one Pope over the Church
of the whole world".

☩

JUNE 21

ST. ALOYSIUS GONZAGA

Aloysius, the eldest son of Ferdinand Gonzaga, Mar-
quis of Castigliona and a gallant soldier, was born on
March 9, 1568. The father's pride was to rear his son to be
a soldier. His mother, on the other hand, was very pious,
and there seems to have been a special grace about the
child from his earliest days.

At the age of seven, a wonderful spiritual light dawned
upon his soul with so clear an understanding of the things
of God, that he later spoke of that time as the period of
his conversion.

When nine years old Aloysius made a vow of perpetual virginity, and by a special grace was ever exempted
from temptations against purity.

It was at Monferrato that Aloysius resolved to become
a religious, and he spent much time in prayer and penance.
On the feast of Our Lady's Assumption, 1583, for which he

had prepared with great fervor, as he was praying after Holy Communion in the chapel of Our Lady in the church of the Jesuits at Madrid, now called St. Isidore, suddenly a distinct voice came to him, bidding him enter the Society of Jesus, and telling him to inform his confessor as soon as possible of what had occurred. His confessor, well aware of his fitness, told him he must first receive his father's approval.

Whilst his mother rejoiced on learning of his determination to become a religious, for three years his father refused his consent. On November 24, 1585, Aloysius entered the Jesuit novitiate, after having obtained his father's permission. Two years later he took his vows. Those who knew best the secrets of his soul found that he had ascended to heights of holiness which are never even dreamed of but by a few.

During his last year of theology a malignant fever broke out in Rome. Thousands were dying of the disease. The Father General of the Society of Jesus summoned Aloysius back to the Eternal City. He often had said that he feared the dignity and responsibility of the priesthood, and would be glad if God would call him while he was still in His grace. His desire was soon to be granted.

Father Acquaviva opened a hospital for the poor suffering, starving people. St. Aloysius volunteered for the work. Not content with begging for alms, he nursed the most loathsome cases. One day on his way to the hospital he found a poor wretch in filthy rags, lying on the ground, stricken by the plague. He raised him up and gently and tenderly carried him to the hospital.

The contagion struck the weary youth, and he was forced to take to his bed. Within a week he received the Last Sacraments, rejoicing that he was going to God. He died a little after midnight between the 20th and 21st of June, 1591, the octave-day of Corpus Christi, at the age of twenty-three, while repeating the holy Name of Jesus.

The Saint's body, glorified by many miracles, lay for some time in a humble tomb in the "Church of the Annunciation" of the Roman College. It now rests in the Gesu in Rome. St. Aloysius was canonized in 1726 by Pope Benedict XIII, who proclaimed him "Patron of Youth".

☩

JUNE 22

ST. JOHN FISHER

St. John Fisher was born at Beverly, Yorkshire, England, in 1459, the eldest son of Robert Fisher, a well-to-do merchant, and of Agnes, his wife. After completing his early studies, he was sent to Michael House, Cambridge; of which University he was eventually appointed Vice-Chancellor.

Lady Margaret Beaufort, Countess of Richmond and mother of the then reigning Henry VII, having heard of Fisher's holiness and learning, appointed him, about 1497, her confessor and almoner, and was influenced by his advice in the most important matters.

A vacancy occurred in the bishopric of Rochester in 1504, and by a Bull dated October 14, 1504, by Pope Julius II, Dr. Fisher was selected to fill it. Rochester was the poorest of all the English Sees; but Fisher continued in this See until his death.

In the same year, 1504, he was appointed Chancellor of Cambridge University. Whilst he was Chancellor, Prince Henry, afterwards Henry VIII, was under his care, and during the earlier part of his reign Henry was proud of the respected position of the Bishop, his former tutor, his friend and teacher, and was greatly influenced by him. However, in April 1509, Henry VII died. Bishop Fisher, one of the best preachers of the day, delivered the sermon at his funeral. Henry VIII ascended the throne on April 22, 1509, and married a few months later, by dispensation granted by Pope Julius II, Catherine of Aragon. The Bishop was appointed her spiritual adviser. Some years later the King, tiring of his wife and infatuated with Anne Boleyn, a maid, pretended worry over his marriage and asked the Holy See for a declaration of nullity, on the ground that the Papal dispensation had been invalid. The effort for a separation from his lawful wife ended in failure. The King then determined to take the law into his own hands.

Wolsey, who was acting as Legate of the Pope, and to whom the King attributed the failure of his application, was disgraced, as well as the entire body of the clergy. Henry was not acting merely out of revenge or avarice; he was plotting to aggregate in his own hands all ecclesiastical power. In his violent temper he demanded that the King "be acknowledged as sole protector and the supreme head of the Church and clergy of England". Many of the clergy were disposed to grant the King's demand, but Bishop Fisher firmly refused. As long as he was at liberty he had been the boldest of the clergy in resisting the changes in matters of religion. At last Henry determined to use violent measures to silence the Bishop. All of his property was seized and he was committed to prison in the Bell Tower in April, 1534, where he was treated most cruelly throughout a year. Though deprived of all his books, St. John Fisher wrote three spiritual works during his incarceration.

When Parliament met in November, 1534, a special Act was passed accusing him, and a few others, for the very offense for which he had already suffered the penalties for seven months; his See and bishopric of Rochester was to be void and vacant as though he were actually dead, on the second of January following. Moreover, an Act was passed ratifying what had been done by the King's Commissioners. It was also enacted at the same session that "the King, our sovereign lord, his heirs and successors, kings of this realm, shall be taken, accepted, and reputed the only supreme head on earth of the Church of England, called Anglicana Ecclesia, and shall have and enjoy annexed and united to the imperial crown of this realm, as well the title and style thereof, as all honors, dignities, immunities, profits and commodities to the said dignity of supreme head of the said Church belonging and appertaining". And it was made high treason for any person to express by "writing or words that the King our sovereign lord should be heretic, schismatic, tyrant, infidel, etc."

It was under this statute that Bishop Fisher and Sir Thomas More were tried, condemned, and executed.

It was on the morning of June 22, 1535, that St. John Fisher's head, with one stroke of an axe, was severed from his body. While on the scaffold he prayed for the King and for the people, and died with the *Te Deum* on his lips. The following day his head, being first parboiled, was fixed upon a pole and set up upon London Bridge, where it remained two weeks and was then thrown into the river to make room for the head of Sir Thomas More.

Thus ended a noble and saintly life; thus perished one of England's greatest sons, a victim to a tyrant's lust and ambition, a martyr who gave glorious witness to the sanctity of the marriage bond and to the supremacy of Christ's Vicar on earth! St. John Fisher was canonized by Pope Pius XI in 1935.

☩

JUNE 23

ST. ETHELDREDA

St. Etheldreda was the third daughter of the holy king Annas of the East Angles, and was a sister to Saints Sexburga, Ethelburga and Withburga. To please her friends Etheldreda married Prince Tonbercht, but they lived together in perpetual chastity. Three years later he died, leaving Etheldreda as a dowry the isle of Ely. Here she retired into solitude, spending five years in close communion with God. Egfrid, powerful king of Northumberland, hearing of Etheldreda's virtues, extorted her consent to marry him. For twelve years they lived happily together, as if she were his sister, and her time was spent in exercises of devotion and charity.

Seeking the advice of St. Wilfrid, Etheldreda was advised to leave her husband, and she received the religious veil from St. Wilfrid's hands. She entered the monastery of Coldingham under the Abbess St. Ebba, but in 672 returned to the isle of Ely and founded a double monastery upon her own estate. She lived a holy life, and after a lingering illness breathed forth her pure soul wth deep sentiments of compunction on June 23, 679.

According to her request, St. Etheldreda was buried in a wooden coffin, but when her sister Sexburga succeeded her in the government of the monastery, she had her body taken up, placed in a stone coffin and translated into the church. Upon this occasion the body was found incorrupt, and the physician who had made an incision in the swelling in her neck a short time before she died, was surprised to see the wound perfectly healed. St. Bede testified that numerous miracles were wrought by the application of St. Etheldreda's relics and the linen cloths that were taken from her coffin.

✠

JUNE 24

NATIVITY OF ST. JOHN THE BAPTIST

St. John the Baptist, son of the holy Priest Zachary and St. Elizabeth, was chosen by God to be the herald of the world's Redeemer, the voice to announce to men the Eternal Word and to prepare souls for His coming.

After the Incarnation of the Son of God, when His Virgin Mother visited her cousin Elizabeth, the babe John in his mother's womb leaped with joy in the presence of the Savior and was sanctified. At an early age St. John was **inspired by the Holy Spirit to retire into the desert, and** remained there "until the day of his manifestation to Israel". He was clothed in a garment of rough camel's hair, girt about with a leather girdle, and his only food was "locusts and wild honey".

Men of all walks of life flocked from "Jerusalem and all Judea, and all the country about the Jordan" to listen to

O God, You rendered this day venerable for us by the birth of blessed John the Baptist. Grant to Your people the grace of spiritual joys, and direct the minds of all the faithful on the way of eternal salvation.

him. The simple folk considered him a prophet (Matt. 11:9).
The gist of his teaching was "Do penance: for the kingdom
of heaven is at hand" (Matt. 3:2).

To confirm the good dispositions of his listeners, John
baptized them in the Jordan. Lest the people might think
that he was the Christ (Luke 3:15) he insisted that he was
only the forerunner of the Messiah, stating "I indeed baptize you with water; but there shall come One mightier
than I, the latchet of Whose shoes I am not worthy to loose:
He shall baptize you with the Holy Spirit and with fire...."
(Luke 3:16.)

The Precursor had been preaching and baptizing for
some time when Jesus came from Galilee to the Jordan, to
be baptized by him. Afterwards John continued his ministry
in the valley of the Jordan. Priests and Levites were sent
by the Jews to ask "Who art thou?" John confessed "I am
the voice of one crying in the wilderness, make straight
the way of the Lord, as said the prophet Isaias". (John
1:19-23.)

"The next day John saw Jesus coming to him and he
saith: Behold the Lamb of God, behold Him Who taketh
away the sin of the world. This is He of Whom I said:
After me there cometh a man, Who is preferred before me:
because He was before me . . . and I gave testimony, that
this is the Son of God." (John 1:29-34.)

Because John rebuked Herod for his evil deeds, especially his public adultery, Herod imprisoned the Baptist.
The ire of Herodias never abated; she watched for her
chance. It came during a birthday feast which Herod gave
to the "princes, and tribunes, and chief men of Galilee".
Pleased with the dancing of Herodias' daughter, Salome,
he promised the damsel anything she desired. She consulted
her mother, and at her suggestion said, "I will forthwith
thou give me in a dish, the head of John the Baptist". The
king was struck sad, but "because of his oath, and because
of them that were at table, he would not displease her:
but sending an executioner, he commanded that his head

should be brought in a dish: and he gave it to the damsel, and the damsel gave it to her mother". (Mark 6:21-28.)

Thus was done to death the greatest "amongst them that are born of women".

✠

JUNE 25

ST. WILLIAM

St. William, the founder of the religious Congregation of Monte-Vergine, was left an orphan in infancy. Reared piously by some friends, at the age of fifteen he desired to lead a penitential life and left his native country, Piedmont, to make a pilgrimage to St. James' shrine in Galicia. Afterwards he chose a desert mountain in the kingdom of Naples, where he lived in perpetual contemplation and practiced most rigorous penitential austerities.

Upon being discovered and his contemplation interrupted, St. William moved to Monte-Vergine, between Nola and Benevento. Two Priests in the vicinity learning of his whereabouts and of his austere practices obliged him to permit some fervent men to live with him and imitate his austere life. Thus, in 1119, was laid the foundation of the religious Congregation of Monte-Vergine. St. William died June 25, 1142.

✠

JUNE 26

STS. JOHN AND PAUL

Saints John and Paul were officers in the army under Julian the Apostate. They were martyred for the Faith about the year 362, under Apromanus, who was prefect of Rome and a bitter enemy of the Christians. The circumstances of their martyrdom are unknown. However, under the Basilica of Saints Giovanni and Paolo in Rome the original tombs of John and Paul were rediscovered. They are covered with paintings of which the martyrs are the subject.

☩

JUNE 27

ST. LADISLAUS

Ladislaus I, son of King Bela of Hungary, was born in 1041. Much against his will he was compelled by the people to ascend the throne in 1080. The good laws and discipline which St. Stephen had established had been obliterated by the confusion of the times, but St. Ladislaus soon restored them.

He led a most austere, frugal and abstemious life, but was most generous to the Church and the poor. He had no time for vain pleasures or idle amusements, because he was fully occupied in performing the duties of his station and religious exercises, always having in view the Divine Will and God's greater honor.

St. Ladislaus vigorously defended his country and the Church. He not only drove the Huns out of his kingdom, but vanquished the Poles, Russians and Tartars, and added Dalmatia and Croatia to his realm. As general-in-chief, he was preparing to command the great expedition of the Christians against the Saracens to recover the Holy Land, when God summoned him to Himself on July 30, 1095. He was canonized by Pope Celestine III.

☩

JUNE 28

ST. IRENAEUS

St. Irenaeus was born in Asia Minor of Christian parents about the year 120. Historians claim he was a pupil of St. Polycarp, the disciple of St. John the Evangelist.

During the persecution of Marcus Aurelius, Irenaeus was a Priest of the Church of Lyons, in France. The clergy of that city, many of whom were suffering imprisonment for the Faith, sent him to Rome with a letter to Pope Eleutherius regarding Montanism, a heresy which declared some grave sins after Baptism are not remissible.

Irenaeus succeeded St. Pothinus as the second Bishop of Lyons, in 177. He divided his activities between the duties of his pastorate and writing against the various outgrowths of the heresy known as Gnosticism, which was violently spreading in Gaul and elsewhere. He also wrote in Greek many works, which have secured for him an exceptional place in Christian literature.

The exact date of death of St. Irenaeus is unknown; it must have occurred at the end of the second, or the beginning of the third, century. He is said to have suffered martyrdom for the Faith in the persecutions of Emperor Severus in the year 202. His name is derived from the Greek word meaning peace, and this was one of his characteristics. He was a man of peace, who made peace among men, and between God and men.

☦

JUNE 29

STS. PETER AND PAUL

From the year 258 the memory of St. Peter and St. Paul was celebrated on June 29 in Via Appia ad Catacumbas (near San Sebastiano fuori le mura), because it was on this date that the remains of the Apostles were translated there. Later their remains were restored to their former resting place: St. Peter's to the Vatican Basilica and St. Paul's to the church on the Via Ostiensis. In the place *Ad Catacumbas* a church was also built as early as the 4th century in honor of these two Apostles.

The church was consecrated June 29, to the martrydom of the Apostles Peter and Paul.

✠

FIRST MARTYRS OF THE CHURCH OF ROME

This memorial is in honor of the nameless followers of Christ brutally killed by the mad Emperor Nero as scapegoats for the fire in Rome. The pagan historian Tacitus and St. Clement of Rome tell of a night of horror (August 15, 64) when in the imperial parks Christians were put into animal skins and hunted, were brutally attacked, were made living torches to light the road for Nero's chariot. From 64 to 314 "Christian" was synonymous with "execution victim."

O God, who taught the multitude of the Gentiles by the preaching of blessed Paul the Apostle; grant, we beseech You, that we, who celebrate his feast, may also experience his patronage with You.

JULY

MOST PRECIOUS BLOOD
OF THE REDEEMER

It is well-known to pious Catholics that the month of July is dedicated to the Most Precious Blood of the Redeemer. This solemnization was ordered by Pope Pius IX, in those dark ages when he was in flight at Gaeta. It is also understood that supreme homage is given to the Sacred Blood. As we adore the Sacred Heart, because it is the Heart of Jesus, Who is God, so we adore the Most Precious Blood.

The Blood of Jesus is the fountain of salvation. Each drop that flowed from the wounds of the Savior is a pledge of man's eternal salvation. All races of the earth have been ransomed, and all individuals, who will allow the saving power of the Sacred Blood to be applied to their soul, are heirs of Heaven. St. John Chrysostom calls the Precious Blood "the savior of souls"; St. Thomas Aquinas, "the key to Heaven's treasures"; St. Ambrose, "pure gold of ineffable worth"; St. Mary Magdalene de Pazzi, "a magnet of souls and pledge of eternal life". The sins of mankind, in their number, in their offense to the Supreme Being, in the effects on transgressors, are mammoth-like; yet, the Precious Blood of Jesus is not frightened by numbers, it has in Itself the power to appease an angered God and to heal wounded creatures.

The Precious Blood is a cleansing bath. Unlike all other blood, which stains, the Blood of Jesus washes clean and white. According to the words of St. John, in the Apocalypse, the Angels wonder, and the question is asked: "These that are clothed in white robes, who are they?" and the Lord answers: "These are they that have washed their robes, and have made them white in the Blood of the Lamb". For no other reason did the Precious Blood

flow but to regain for the souls of men the beautiful dress
of innocence, and, once regained, to preserve it throughout life and into eternity.

The Blood of the Savior is a well of consolation for
troubled hearts. Can anyone, confidingly, look at the Sacred
Blood trickling down from the Cross without taking courage to carry on, in spite of the difficulties which are the
common lot of all? One glance at the Cross must be able to
drive away fear. And, another, must be able to instill trust
in Him Who did not rest until the last drop, mingling with
water, oozed out of an opened Heart. He, Who was willing
to do so much for men, must be willing to overlook and
forget the frailties which they deeply regret; He must be
willing to come to their assistance when harassed, to defend
them when tempted, to comfort them when afflicted. The
Blood of Jesus must be for Christians what the north-star
is to mariners.

Would that men on earth honored the Precious Blood in
the manner in which they who are in Heaven give honor and
praise and thanksgiving! They understand that It merited all
graces for them. They proclaim that It purchased the glory
which they enjoy. Without It, they would have remained
slaves of Satan and outcasts from the eternal mansions of
God. Let us profess that we owe to the Sacred Blood of
Jesus all that we have in this life, and that to It we shall
owe all that we shall enjoy in a better and eternal life!

"Glory be to the Blood of Jesus, now and forever, and
throughout all ages!"

✠

JULY 2

VISITATION OF THE
BLESSED VIRGIN MARY

The Visitation commemorates the visit which the
Blessed Virgin Mary made to her cousin, St. Elizabeth,
when told by the Archangel Gabriel that her cousin, in her
advanced age, was to have a child.

Elizabeth lived six miles distant from Jerusalem in the little village now called Ain-Karem. As Mary saluted Elizabeth, the mother of St. John the Baptist, she was greeted with the words: "Blessed art thou among women, and blessed is the fruit of thy womb". To which Mary responded: "My soul doth magnify the Lord: and my spirit hath rejoiced in God my Savior. Because He hath regarded the humility of His handmaid; for behold from henceforth all generations shall call me blessed. Because He that is mighty hath done great things to me; and holy is His name. And His mercy is from generation unto generation, to them that fear Him. He hath showed might in His arm: He hath scattered the proud in the conceit of their heart. He hath put down the mighty from their seat, and hath exalted the humble. He hath filled the hungry with good things; and the rich He hath sent away empty. He hath received Israel His servant, being mindful of His mercy: As He spoke to our fathers, to Abraham and to his seed forever". (Luke 1: 36-55.)

In 1389, Pope Urban VI instituted the Feast of the Visitation in order to procure the end of the Great Schism.

✠

JULY 3

ST. LEO II

St. Leo, a native of Sicily, was elected Pope a few days after the death of St. Agatho (January 10, 681), but was not consecrated until nineteen months later (August 17, 682). He died on June 28, 683. The most important act accomplished by him during his short Pontificate was his confirmation of the acts of the Sixth Ecumenical Council (680-681). This Council had been held in Constantinople against the Monothelites, and had been presided over by the Legates of Pope Agatho.

St. Leo is called by his contemporary biographer both learned and just.

✠

ST. BERTHA

St. Bertha, daughter of Count Rigobert and Ursana, was related to an English king. At the age of twenty she married Siegfrid. After his death she became a nun in the monastery she had built in northern France. Two of her five daughters, Gertrude and Deotila, followed her example. Because St. Bertha refused to give Gertrude in marriage to Roger, or Rotgar, out of revenge he endeavored to slander her with King Thierri III. The King, convinced of Bertha's innocence, treated her kindly and protected her.

After Bertha's return to her monastery, she was instrumental in erecting three churches,—one in honor of St. Omer, another in honor of St. Vaast, and the third in honor of St. Martin of Tours. Having established a regular observance in her community, St. Bertha named St. Deotila Abbess, whilst she spent the remainder of her life as a recluse, communing with God. St. Bertha died about the year 725.

✠

ST. ANTHONY MARY ZACCARIA

St. Anthony Mary Zaccaria was born at Cremona, Lombardy, in 1502. From early youth he was remarkable for his ability, piety and zeal. He became a doctor of medicine; but in 1528 was ordained a Priest. He labored unceasingly to restore Church discipline, and with that end in view founded the religious Order known as the Barnabites, under the patronage of St. Paul the Apostle.

God favored St. Anthony with many supernatural gifts and graces. He died at Cremona, July 5, 1539, and was canonized by Pope Leo XIII.

✠

JULY 6

ST. THOMAS MORE

Thomas More, born in London in 1480, was the son of Sir John More, one of the Judges of the King's Bench. He was sent to one of the best schools then existing in London, St. Anthony's, in Threadneedle Street. At the age of fourteen he became a page in the household of Cardinal Morton, Archbishop of Canterbury. Two years later, on the advice of the Cardinal, More was sent to Oxford, where he remained two years. He was not eighteen years old and began the study of law at the Inn of Court of London. Strongly disposed to embrace a religious life, the famous Dean Colt, his director, advised that to be a layman and a married man was best for him.

More was twice married, first, at the age of 23 or 24 to the daughter of an Essex gentleman, Colt of New Hall. This first union brought him happiness unalloyed, but it was not of long duration. His wife bore him three daughters and a son, and died about six years after their marriage. Two or three years later, he married a widow, seven years his senior, to govern his house and bring up his children. She was an attentive and thrifty housewife and was kind to the children, but she was hard, narrow and worldly, and never comprehended More's character, which was considerably above and beyond her. Consequently, she became an adversary instead of a consolation to him in his last great trial.

At the age of 24, More became a member of the House of Commons and distinguished himself by his opposition to the exactions of King Henry VII. In 1509, when More was twenty-nine, Henry VII died, and his son Henry VIII, then a youth of eighteen, succeeded.

More won high favor with Henry VIII and the King's great minister, Cardinal Wolsey. Both appreciated his talent and qualities. He was made successively, and without

his own seeking, a knight, a Privy Councillor, Treasurer of
the Exchequer, and Chancellor of the Duchy of Lancaster.
And when Wolsey was deprived of the Great Seals and was
banished to his diocese of York, Sir Thomas More replaced
him in 1520, when he was 49 years of age. More was the
first layman who, for a considerable period, had been raised
to that dignity. He held the Seals for about two years and
a half.

The King having lived for nearly twenty years with
his excellent and virtuous wife, Catherine of Aragon, fell in
love with Anne Boleyn. He sought an annulment of his
marriage from the Pope, Clement VII. It was Wolsey's
failure in this matter that caused his downfall. The King
repeatedly tried to get More to back him, but More firmly
refused to do so.

When the King offered More the chancellorship, he
accepted it only on condition that he would not be asked
to take any part in the matter of a divorce. And when it
became apparent that the decision of the Holy See would
be adverse to the wishes of the King, More had to choose
between his conscience as a Catholic and the honors and
rewards of this world. He supplicated Henry to relieve him
from his office of Chancellor. The King, with reluctance,
accepted his resignation in 1532. More was then 52 years
of age.

He was not to live unmolested in his retirement. First,
Henry VIII summoned him to be present at his public marriage with Anne Boleyn. More refused, and earned the
implacable hatred of both. Henry had now determined to
sever himself wholly from the jurisdiction of the Pope, and
to declare himself sole head of the Church of England. This
was, of course, complete and absolute schism, a total separation from the body of the Catholic Church.

The oath of supremacy was tendered to the clergy,
who freely took it, but as yet it had not been tendered to
any layman. It was resolved to begin with Sir Thomas
More, in the expectation that if he did not resist no other
would. He refused. A second effort was made to have him

sign. Again he refused. There followed his incarceration in
the Tower of London, his condemnation to death, and beheading at Tyburn on July 5, 1535. Four hundred years
later, in 1935, he was numbered among the canonized
Saints.

✠

JULY 7

SS. CYRIL AND METHODIUS

Saints Cyril and Methodius, brothers, were born in
Thessalonica of a senatorial family. Renouncing secular
honors they became Priests, and were consecrated Bishops
by Pope Adrian II.

When the Khazars (a people living between the Dar-
danelles and the Aegean sea) sent to Constantinople for a
Christian teacher, St. Cyril was chosen, and his brother
accompanied him. Their next mission was to Moravia, as
the people there desired someone to instruct them and
conduct Divine service in the Slavonic tongue. St. Cyril
invented an alphabet which enabled them to translate the
Gospels and liturgical books into Slavonic, which aided
immensely in the conversion of the Slavic people to Christianity.

St. Cyril died in Rome on February 4, 869; and St. Methodius, worn out from his strenuous labors, died on April 6,
885.

✠

JULY 8

ST. ELIZABETH OF PORTUGAL

St. Elizabeth, daughter of Peter II, King of Aragon,
was born in 1271. At the age of twelve she was given in
marriage to Denis, King of Portugal, by whom she had two
children: Alfonso and Constance. Elizabeth was very pious;

she assisted at daily Mass, and spent considerable time in spiritual reading. She practiced severe austerities, performed heroic acts of charity, and proved to be a saintly wife.

In time, the king's jealousy, flowing from his own unfaithfulness, caused Elizabeth great suffering, but she showed no bitterness and endeavored in every way to reclaim him. In all her trials Elizabeth committed herself to the sweet disposal of Divine Providence, realizing that God, her merciful Father, would protect her.

When Alfonso took up arms against his father, Queen Elizabeth was called upon to make peace between them. On the pretext that she had aroused Alfonso to fight his father, the Queen was exiled to Alemquer. When the King saw that she was innocent he gave her Torres Vedras to govern, which task she ably fulfilled. On two other occasions Elizabeth reconciled Alfonso with his father, and also settled a disagreement which arose between Denis and Ferdinand of Castile, his son-in-law.

A jealous page of the Queen, who envied a pious faithful page, made a slanderous remark affecting Elizabeth. The King, determined to kill the youth, told a lime-burner to cast into his kiln a page whom he would send on a certain day on an errand to inquire "Whether he had fulfilled the King's commands?" On the day fixed, the page was sent. As he was in the habit of assisting at daily Mass, on passing a church he stopped in and remained for two Masses. The King, impatient to learn whether his orders had been executed, sent the informer to inquire. As he was the first to reach the kiln, he was cast into the furnace and was consumed. Soon afterwards the first page arrived; having inquired whether the King's commands had been executed, he brought back word to the King that they had been. The delay saved the innocent youth, and the King upon learning the particulars adored the Divine Providence.

Through the prayers of Elizabeth and those of others, together with the patience and love which she showed in bringing up his illegitimate children, she won for the King the grace to rise from the depths to which he had fallen and to become a devoted husband and a truly Christian King. After his death in 1325, Elizabeth wished to become a Poor Clare Nun, but upon the entreaties of her people, out of charity she remained in the world and took the Habit of a tertiary with the Poor Clares of Coimbra. The remainder of her life was spent in charitable works. She fell ill at Estremoz, where she had gone to reconcile her son and grandson, and after receiving the Last Sacraments died peacefully at the age of sixty-five, in the year 1336. She was canonized by Pope Urban VIII in 1625.

☩

JULY 9

ST. MARIA GORETTI

St. Maria Goretti, the child martyr of purity, was born in Corinaldo, Italy, on October 16, 1890. Her parents were very poor share-croppers who lived in the Pontine Marshes. The good Catholic mother taught her daughter to love God whole-heartedly and to hate sin above all things. Rather to die than to commit sin became her simple rule of life. Everyone loved Maria. She grew to be a beautiful girl; she had bright chestnut hair, perfect features, and a radiant smile which reflected a rare modesty of soul.

Maria suffered martyrdom at the hands of a nineteen year old youth who had become infuriated by her constant rebuffs to his unchaste advances. On July 5, 1902, with a poised dagger, he demanded her surrender. The alternative was death. Courageously, promptly, and heroically Maria refused, crying out: "It is a sin. God does not want it". Fourteen times the cruel knife pierced her virginal body. Death came the following day, the feast of the Most Precious Blood. The little Saint implored pardon for her murderer: "I forgive him. . . May God forgive him . . . I want him with God in paradise like the repentant thief".

Maria was interred in the Church of Our Lady of Grace in Nettuno in charge of the Passionist Fathers, who had instructed Maria in life and had promoted her cause after her death. Her shrine has become a place of pilgrimage, and many miracles have been wrought through the power of her intercession. The greatest miracle of all is the conversion of her defiant murderer, who three times before the Sacred Congregation of Rites became her principal witness. With most humiliating self-abasement he said: "It is my duty. I must make reparation and do all in my power for her glorification. I have sinned deeply, but I feel confident of salvation. I have a Saint in Heaven praying for me".

It took the Church only fifteen years to approve the heroic virtue and martyrdom of this young girl, who died rather than offend God. She was beatified by Pope Pius XII on April 27, 1947. Among the immense crowd that thronged St. Peter's Basilica on that memorable occasion were Maria's own mother, brother and two sisters. The Holy Pontiff congratulated Mrs. Goretti for the "incomparable happiness of having seen her daughter elevated to the honors of the altar". He compared Maria with St. Agnes, stating that "the delicate grace of these adolescent girls might make us overlook their courage; yet strength is the virtue of virgins and martyrs".

On June 25, 1950, Pope Pius XII placed Maria Goretti's name on the calendar of the Saints. Her aged mother, paralyzed and in a wheelchair, was present also at the Canonization ceremony.

✠

JULY 10

ST. FELICITAS AND HER SEVEN SONS

St. Felicitas, a holy widow of Rome, was distinguished for her piety and charity. It was during the reign of Marcus Aurelius, about the year 165, that she and her seven sons were arrested and tried by the Prefect Publius for publicly practicing the Christian Faith and encouraging others to renounce the worship of false gods. Taking Felicitas aside, Publius offered her the strongest inducements if she would freely sacrifice to the gods. She refused. In a rage, he said:

"Unhappy woman, is it possible you should think death so desirable as not to permit even your children to live, but force me to destroy them by the most cruel torments?" Felicitas replied: "My children will live eternally with Christ if they are faithful to Him: but must expect eternal death if they sacrifice to idols." Failing in his effort, Publius cited her to appear with her sons in the forum of Mars for trial.

After encouraging her sons to sacrifice their lives cheerfully for Christ, courageously she witnessed their sufferings, which merited them their crowns of martyrdom. Four months later St. Felicitas was beheaded for being a Christian.

☩

JULY 11

ST. PIUS I

St. Pius I reigned as the Vicar of Christ from the year 140 to 154. He condemned the false teachings among the faithful of Rome by the Gnostic heretics Valentinus, Cerdon and Marcion.

St. Pius I died for the Faith under the reign of the Emperor Marcus Aurelius on July 11, and was buried on the Vatican Hill.

☩

JULY 12

ST. JOHN GUALBERT

St. John Gualbert was born at Florence, Italy, in the year 999. One Good Friday, after hearing a sermon on how Christ had pardoned His enemies as He hung dying on the Cross, John was walking towards Florence, followed by his armor bearer. As he reached a narrow pass he found himself face to face with the man who had murdered his brother Hugo. It was considered a duty and was the custom of the nobles of that century to avenge such a death, and John had determined to do so. Thinking that his last hour had come, the man fell to his knees, stretched out his arms in the form of a cross and begged John to spare his life for the sake of the Crucified Savior. Visibly moved, John freely pardoned the murderer, saying:

"I can refuse nothing that is asked of me for the sake of Jesus Christ. I not only give you your life, but also my friendship forever. Pray for me that God may pardon me my sin".

Then they embraced each other and parted.

When John came to the Benedictine monastery, he went into the church and knelt before a Crucifix to ask pardon for his sins. As he raised his eyes he saw the Crucified Savior miraculosuly bow His Head as if granting the pardon John had requested. Shortly afterwards he donned the Benedictine Habit to live a life of prayer and solitude at San Miniato. Desiring stricter solitude, he left there and went with the Camaldolese in the desert of Camaldoli in the Apennine Mountains, but did not remain there long.

At Vallombrosa, midway between Camaldoli and Florence, St. John founded a monastery of strict Benedictine Observance in 1070, which he governed until his death three years later. He had a great love for holy poverty, and was most charitable to the poor. He was endowed with the spirit of prophecy, and through his prayers restored many to health. He was never ordained a Priest, but left about twelve houses of his Order when he died at the age of seventy-four. He was canonized by Pope Celestine III.

✠

JULY 13

ST. EUGENIUS AND COMPANIONS

The Roman Martyrology states the following regarding these Saints:

"In Africa, the holy confessors, Eugenius, Bishop of Carthage, renowned for his faith and his virtues, and all the clergy of that church to the number of five hundred or more (among them being many young boys who ministered as Lectors or Readers), in the persecution under the Arian Hunneric, King of the Vandals, were scourged and starved, and at last (rejoicing always in the Lord) driven into banishment. Conspicuous among them was the Archdeacon Salutaris, and the dignitary next in rank to him, Muritta, who had each twice previously suffered for Christ".

Guntamund, who succeeded Hunneric, recalled St. Eugenius to Carthage to open the Catholic churches, and permitted all the exiled Priests to return. After reigning twelve years, his brother Thrasimund was called to the crown. Under this ruler St. Eugenius was again banished. He died in exile on July 13, 505, in a monastery which he had built and governed near Albi.

☩

JULY 14

ST. BONAVENTURE

St. Bonaventure is one of the glories of the Seraphic Order of St. Francis. He was the friend and companion of St. Thomas Aquinas, and ranks with him among the six chief Doctors of the Catholic Church: Saints Ambrose and Augustine, Jerome and Gregory, Thomas Aquinas and Bonaventure. He was born in 1221 at Bagnorea, not far from Viterbo, Italy, of pious parents. At his Baptism he was called John, after his father, but this name was later exchanged for that of Bonaventure on account of the following remarkable occurrence.

At the age of four he fell dangerously ill. His holy mother, Ritella, made a vow that if the child were restored to health she would give him to God. She then took him to St. Francis and pleaded with him to pray for the recovery of her dear son. Moved with pity, St. Francis knelt down in prayer; then rising, he blessed the child, and the little one was instantly cured; nor did he ever after suffer from any sickness until his last illness. St. Francis, beholding the marvelous manifestation of the Divine goodness, and foreseeing the child's future career, exclaimed: "O buona ventura!" that is, "O good luck!" Hence the name of Bonaventure, by which the Saint was called from that time.

Ritella's first care was to inspire her son from his tenderest years with sentiments of true piety and devotion. He made rapid progress in his studies. Upon reaching the age of seventeen, he learned from his mother that she had made a vow to consecrate him to the service of God. Moved by gratitude to St. Francis, Bonaventure entered the Franciscan Order. In 1241 or 1242 he went to Paris to pursue his theological studies. Among the prominent professors at the University was the celebrated Franciscan theologian, Alexander of Hales. Bonaventure was one of the most conspicuous among the numerous disciples of this great master.

It was at the University of Paris that Bonaventure became acquainted with St. Thomas Aquinas, who was five years younger than himself. The holy friendship which sprang up between them lasted through life.

Soon after his ordination Bonaventure began to give lectures to the Friars Minor; and on the death of John of Rochelle, who had succeeded Alexander of Hales, he was appointed to fill the chair left vacant at the University. As he was only twenty-three years old, and the age of twenty-five was required for this office, an exception was made in Bonaventure's case. Students thronged to hear him, and the lustre of his teaching was reflected on the whole Franciscan Order.

In 1257, at the suggestion of Pope Alexander IV, St. Bonaventure was chosen General of his Order. He soon restored the peace which had been disturbed by internal dissensions. In 1273 Pope Gregory X consecrated St. Bonaventure Cardinal and Bishop of Albano. One of his reasons for raising the Saint to the dignity of a Cardinal, was his desire to see him direct with greater authority the labors of the General Council which had been convoked at Lyons, and was to begin on May 1, 1274. The chief objects for which the Council had been convoked were: the union of

the Greeks with the Catholic Church, the defense of
the Holy Land, and the improvement of ecclesiastical
discipline.

On June 29th St. Bonaventure saw the union with the
Greeks completed, and assisted at the solemn *Te Deum*
which was sung in thanksgiving. The following day he fell
ill. His condition would not allow him to receive Holy
Viaticum. Deeply grieved, but resigned, he asked that the
Blessed Sacrament be brought to his room. And, lo! the
Sacred Host left the hand of the Priest and placed Itself
on the Saint's heart, filling him with ineffable sweetness.
It was in this transport of heavenly joy that Bonaventure
breathed his last on the night of July 14, 1274. The Pope
and all the prelates of the Church assisted at his funeral
on Sunday, the 15th.

St. Bonaventure was canonized by Sixtus IV in 1482. A
century later he was declared a Doctor of the Church. Several miracles wrought by the Saint's intercession are recorded
in the Acts of his canonization. During the plague in Lyons,
in 1628, the clergy and people carried St. Bonaventure's
relics in procession, and immediately the plague ceased.

St. Bonaventure wrote Commentaries on Holy Scripture, many ascetical and mystical treatises, and a beautiful,
touching Biography of St. Francis of Assisi, the Founder
of his Order.

✠

JULY 15

ST. HENRY II

Henry II was born in 972, and was educated by
St. Wolfgang, Bishop of Ratisbon, at the abbey of Hildesheim. Henry succeeded his father as Duke of Bavaria in
995. Soon thereafter he married Kunegunda, daughter of
the Count of Luxemburg, with whom he lived in virginity.

On June 16, 1007, St. Henry was consecrated Emperor
of Germany in the Cathedral of Mainz. His desire upon ascending the throne was to reign for the greater glory of God.

In order to protect his subjects, he sometimes engaged in wars, in all of which he met with success. By his prudence, courage and clemency, he stifled several rebellions in Germany and Italy. He annexed Poland, Bohemia, Moravia and Burgundy to his kingdom, and won Pannonia and Hungary to the Church. He respected the rights and possessions of the Church, and helped the Bishops in their work of reform.

After securing the Faith in Germany, Henry marched into Italy and overcame Ardovinus, a Lombard lord who had caused himself to be crowned King of Milan. The second time he revolted, the Emperor marched again into Italy, defeated him in battle and deprived him of his territories, but did not take away his life. Later Ardovinus became a Monk.

St. Henry marched in triumph to Rome, and was crowned Emperor of the Holy Roman Empire in St. Peter's Basilica by Pope Benedict VIII in 1014. His travels through his kingdom had as their objects only to promote piety, to enrich the churches, to relieve the poor, and to prevent unjust usurpations and oppressions. His health failed some years before his death, which occurred at the castle of Grona, near Halberstadt, on July 15, 1024. His body was interred in the cathedral he had built at Bamberg. Fifteen years later St. Kunegunda was also buried there. St. Henry was canonized in 1152 by Pope Eugenius III.

☩

JULY 16

OUR LADY OF MOUNT CARMEL

On the summit of Mount Carmel in Palestine, stands an imposing monastery, the Mother-house of the Carmelite Order, founded in 1156. Mount Carmel was visited by the prophets Elias and Eliseus.

According to Carmelite tradition, the Blessed Virgin Mary appeared to St. Simon Stock, sixth General of the Carmelite Order, in 1251, holding a scapular in her hand. As she gave it to him, she said: "This shall be the privilege for you and for all Carmelites, that anyone dying in this habit shall be saved". She also directed him to found a Confraternity, the members of which should consecrate themselves to her service and wear this scapular.

Therefore, the Feast of Our Lady of Mount Carmel commemorates the favors granted by Our Lady on Mount Carmel. In 1726, the Feast was extended to the Universal Church by Pope Benedict XIII.

✠

JULY 17

ST. ALEXIS

St. Alexis was the only son of a wealthy Roman Senator of the 4th century, and in compliance with the will of his parents he married a rich, virtuous lady. On the very day of the nuptials, by a special inspiration from God, he left Rome and fled to Edessa, where he spent seventeen years as a mendicant near the entrance of the church of Our Lady.

When he was discovered to be a stranger of distinction, he returned to his father's house, where he was received as a poor pilgrim. He lived there, unknown, until his death, bearing the contumely and ill treatment of the servants with heroic patience and silence. Upon his death, from a letter written in his own hand, it was learned whom they had sheltered.

God bore witness to St. Alexis' sanctity by many miracles. His remains are interred in the ancient church of St. Boniface in Rome.

✠

JULY 18

ST. CAMILLUS OF LELLIS

Camillus was born in 1550 at Bacchianicio, Italy, a town of the diocese of Chieti, of the noble family of the Lelli. His mother died when he was quite young. At the age of nineteen, together with his father, Camillus entered military service and served in the army until 1574. He had contracted a violent passion for cards and gambling, and sometimes lost even the necessaries of life.

After some years of a worldly life, Camillus endeavored to enter the Capuchin Order and the Grey Friars. A running sore in one of his legs, which was considered incurable, made it impossible for him to make his religious profession. Therefore he went to Rome, where he served the incurable sick for four years in St. James Hospital with great fervor. Grieved to see the sloth of the hired servants in attending the sick, Camillus was inspired, in 1582, to found a Congregation known as the Ministers of the Sick, who should be desirous to devote themselves to nurse the sick out of fervent charity, and to procure for them all spiritual help possible. St. Camillus was encouraged by St. Philip Neri to become a Priest, and two years later he was ordained.

In 1586, Pope Sixtus V confirmed his Congregation, which spread from Rome to Milan, Genoa, Florence, Bologna, Messina, Palermo, Ferrara, and other places. St. Camillus persevered in caring for the sick and dying until his death in 1614, at the age of sixty-four. He was canonized by Pope Benedict XIV in 1746, and was declared a Patron Saint of the infirm by Pope Leo XIII.

✠

JULY 19

ST. VINCENT DE PAUL

It was on the Tuesday in Easter-week, April 24, 1576, that Vincent, son of poor parents in Pouii, southern France, first saw the light of day. He grew up amidst the hard life of those around him. When still a child his duty was to guard the few sheep his father possessed.

Vincent loved the poor; gave them the few sous at his disposal, and even his clothes. He was not only kind but prayerful. When twelve years of age, his father placed him at school with the Franciscans in Dax, near by. The boy studied so diligently that in four years' time he became tutor to the children of a prominent lawyer. Shortly thereafter he entered the University of Saragossa, Spain, but did not remain long there on account of the disputes on "grace".

Vincent returned to France and resumed his studies with distinction at Toulouse. In 1600 he was ordained Priest. Soon thereafter he was captured by three Turkish pirates and carried into Barbary and sold into slavery. Finally, he converted his renegade master, and escaped with him to France, where his apostolic work brought innumerable souls back to God. Appointed Chaplain-general of the galleys of France, he was able through his tender charity to bring hope into the prisons where despair had hitherto reigned. At night he went through the streets of Paris seeking the children who were left there to die.

Rarely has one man undertaken as much as St. Vincent did; rarely has anyone accomplished as much. He was not only the savior of the poor, but also of the rich, for he taught them to perform works of mercy.

The Societies of Charity of pious ladies which he had founded in so many parts of France to nurse the sick-poor grew and prospered under the devoted direction of a widow, Madame Le Gras. But it soon became evident that something more stable and more firmly constituted was needed to carry on the work. In 1634, under the guidance of Madame Le Gras these charitable ladies were formed into a religious community, known as the Sisters of Charity of St. Vincent de Paul, under the spiritual direction of his own Congregation of the Mission, or Lazarists.

The sanctification of the clergy by retreats before ordination has become the peculiar work of the Lazarists.

St. Vincent is perhaps best known as the friend and protector of the multitude of helpless abandoned infants in the streets of Paris.

The Society of St. Vincent, the Lazarists, and the Sisters of Charity, still comfort the afflicted with the charity of St. Vincent de Paul.

After receiving the Last Sacraments, while seated on a chair, for he was too weak to be moved to his bed, St. Vincent died in the house of St. Lazare on September 27, 1660. The French Revolutionists sacked the house and shrine of the Saint, but respected his remains. St. Lazare is at present a prison. A new shrine is now in the beautiful chapel of the Lazarists in the Rue de Sevres at Paris.

✠

JULY 20

ST. JEROME EMILIANI

St. Jerome was born of noble parents in Venice. In early youth he served in the army of his country, and then was appointed governor of a fortress in the Treviso mountains. Taken prisoner, he was cast into a dungeon and loaded with chains. After imploring the aid of the Blessed Virgin, St. Jerome was miraculously set free. He returned to Venice and gave himself up wholly to prayer and to works of charity. His compassion for abandoned orphans moved him to rent a house where he could care for them. At his own expense he clothed, fed and instructed them in the Christian truths. Later he founded orphanages in Brescia, Bergamo, and other places. At Somasco, near Bergamo, he founded a Congregation called the Somaschi.

St. Jerome died at Somasco on February 8, 1537, of a contagious disease he contracted while visiting the sick. His Congregation was approved by Pope Pius V, and he **was canonized by Pope Clement XIII.**

✠

JULY 21

ST. PRAXEDES

St. Praxedes, daughter of Pudens, a Roman Senator, and sister to St. Pudentiana, lived in the 2nd century during the reign of Pope Pius I and Emperor Antoninus Pius. She was a fervent Christian, and employed her wealth in relieving the poor. By the comfort and help she afforded the martyrs she hoped to make herself partaker of their crowns. This was not to be her lot. But when she could no longer endure the great slaughter of the Christians she prayed God that, if it were expedient for her to die, He would take her away from these great evils.

On July 21st she was called to Heaven to receive the reward of her charity. She was buried in the tomb of her father and sister on the Salarian way. An ancient, notable church in Rome perpetuates St. Praxedes' memory, and bears testimony to the esteem of sanctity in which she was held by the early Christians.

✠

JULY 22

ST. MARY MAGDALEN

All four of the Evangelists mention Mary Magdalen, who at one time was "possessed by seven devils". The 7th chapter of St. Luke tells us that she was at one time a sinner. However, the same Evangelist states that "when she knew that Jesus sat at meat in" the house of Simon, a rich Pharisee, she "brought an alabaster box of ointment; and standing behind at His feet, she began to wash His feet with tears, and wiped them with the hairs of her head, and kissed His feet, and anointed them with the ointment" (7:38). Jesus forgave her her sins, saying: "Thy faith hath

O Lord, grant that we may be helped by the intercession of blessed Mary Magdalene, in answer to whose prayers You raised from the tomb her brother Lazarus four days after death.

saved thee; go in peace". Afterwards she followed Him and His twelve Apostles as He traveled through the cities and towns preaching and evangelizing the kingdom of God. (Luke 7, 50.)

St. Luke (chap. 10) also relates that when Jesus "entered into a certain town ... Martha received Him into her house", that she had a sister called Mary, who sat at the Lord's feet listening to His word, and that when Martha complained because Mary was not helping her serve, the Lord said, "Martha, Martha, thou art careful and art troubled about many things. But one thing is necessary. Mary hath chosen the best part, which shall not be taken away from her". And St. John (chap. 11) records that Jesus visited the home of Martha and Mary in Bethania to raise their brother Lazarus from the dead, and again visited their home six days before the pasch.

Mary Magdalen was one of the few faithful women who stood by the Cross of Jesus during His crucifixion and death (Mark 15, 16; John 19, 20). And it was to her that the Risen Savior first appeared (after His Mother) on the day of His Resurrection.

According to the Liturgy of the Catholic Church, St. Mary Magdalen is the same person as Mary the sinner, Mary of Bethany, the sister of Lazarus and Martha, the Magdalen at the foot of the Cross and at the Tomb, and the first witness of the Resurrection of Jesus.

☧

JULY 23

ST. APOLLINARIS

St. Apollinaris, the first Bishop of Ravenna, was crowned with martyrdom during the reign of Vespasian in the year 79. It is claimed that Apollinaris came from Antioch with St. Peter, who appointed him Bishop of Ravenna. He endured great torments for Christ; was banished three times from Ravenna, and while in exile preached the Gospel in Asia Minor, on the banks of the Danube and in Thrace.

St. Peter Damian states that Apollinaris sacrificed himself as a living victim for the true Faith by the sufferings he endured for twenty-nine years.

✠

JULY 24

ST. CHRISTINA

St. Christina suffered many torments and a cruel death for the Faith in the persecution of Diocletian at Tyro, a city which stood formerly on an island in Lake Bolsena in Italy, but which long ago disappeared under the waters of the lake. It is claimed that she destroyed her father's idols of gold and silver, and gave the pieces to the poor. For this reason he had her scourged with rods and then cast into a dungeon. Christina's faith remained unshaken during all the torments she endured. Her relics are preserved at Palermo, Sicily.

✠

JULY 25

ST. JAMES

St. James, brother of St. John the Evangelist, son of Zebedee and Salome, was called the Great to distinguish him from the other Apostle of the same name who was Bishop of Jerusalem, and surnamed the Less, perhaps because he was smaller in stature or because he was the younger.

St. James was by birth a Galilean, and by profession a fisherman with his father and brother John. One day as they were repairing their nets, Jesus passed by. He invited James and John to follow Him, and they immediately left their father and their nets to do so.

St. James was present when Jesus raised Jairus' daughter from the dead, at the Transfiguration on Mt. Tabor with Peter and John, and, again, in the Garden of Gethsemani during the Agony of the Savior. After preaching the Gospel in Judea and Samaria, St. James set out for Spain, where he converted many.

From the Acts of the Apostles (12:2), we know that he was the first of the Twelve to give his life for his Master, being beheaded by King Herod Agrippa in the year 43. Upon his death his body was miraculously transplanted from Jerusalem to Spain, where he has always been venerated as the Apostle of that country. His shrine at Saragossa is one of the most famous places of pilgrimage in the Christian world.

✠

JULY 26

ST. ANNE

Holy St. Anne had the inestimable privilege of being chosen by God from eternity to be the mother of the Mother of the Savior of mankind. According to tradition St. Anne and her spouse, St. Joachim lived in Nazareth. They were of the tribe of Juda and of the royal House of David, and are venerated by the Church as the parents of the Blessed Virgin Mary. Both have been honored as Saints from early times.

God bestowed upon St. Anne wonderful gifts and graces, and she longingly and devoutly prayed for the advent of the Redeemer.

When we contemplate Mary's Immaculate Heart, we have some faint idea of the sanctity and holiness of her mother, good St. Anne. Innumerable churches and chapels in every century have been erected in her honor. During the past three centuries miracles have occurred at her shrine at Beaupré, Canada.

The relics of St. Anne are said to have been brought from Palestine to Constantinople in the 8th century and were still kept there in the church of St. Sophia in 1333. The head of St. Anne was venerated in Mayence, Germany, up to 1510, when it was stolen and brought to Duren in the Rhineland.

St. Anne is Patroness of Brittany; of the province of Quebec, Canada; Patroness of women in labor, and of miners.

✠

JULY 27

ST. PANTALEON

St. Pantaleon was a well-known Christian physician in the 4th century. He was instructed in the Faith of Jesus Christ by the Priest Hermolaus, and was baptized. He soon persuaded his father Eustorgius to become a Christian. Later he openly preached the Faith of the Savior in Nicomedia, and encouraged all to embrace His teaching.

During the reign of the Emperor Diocletian, St. Pantaleon was mangled on the rack and tortured by having red-hot plates applied to his body. He bore the violence of these tortures calmly and bravely. It was between the years 303 and 305 A.D. that he was finally beheaded and obtained the crown of martyrdom. He is considered with St. Luke the Patron Saint of medical men.

✠

JULY 28

ST. VICTOR I

St. Victor, a native of Africa, succeeded St. Eleutherius as Pope, in the year 189. Vigorously he opposed the heresies of that time, and excommunicated those who taught the blasphemous error that Christ was only a man, not God. He ruled the Church for ten years zealously and energetically, maintaining the purity of the Faith with unity. He confirmed the decree of Pope Pius I, which ordered the Feast of Easter to be celebrated on a Sunday. In order that this rite might be afterwards brought into practice, Councils were held in many places; and finally at the First Council of Nice it was decreed that the Feast of Easter should be always kept on the Sunday following the 14th day of the first moon after the vernal equinox.

St. Victor died in 201. He is styled as a martyr by some writers in the 5th century. In some Martyrologies he is called only Confessor, though his dignity and zeal exposed him to continual persecutions, for which alone he might deserve the title of Martyr.

✠

JULY 29

ST. MARTHA

St. John tells us in his Gospel that St. Martha was the sister of Mary and Lazarus. It was she who received Jesus into her house and complained because Mary sat at the feet of the Savior, communing with Him, instead of helping with the household duties. In reply, Jesus said: "Martha, Martha, thou art careful and art troubled about many things: But one thing is necessary. Mary hath chosen the best part, which shall not be taken away from her". (Luke 10: 41, 42.)

On the occasion when Lazarus was ill, the sisters sent Him word, "Lord, he whom Thou lovest is sick". After the Ascension of Jesus, Martha and Mary and Lazarus were put aboard a ship without sails or oars by the enemies of Christianity. Divine Providence guided the ship to the eastern shore of France, where Lazarus became the Bishop of Marseilles, Mary Magdalen a hermit, and Martha the foundress of a group of pious women who performed charitable works.

✠

JULY 30

ST. GERMAIN OF AUXERRE

St. Germain was born at Auxerre in the 4th century of a noble family in Gaul. He studied Civil Law in Rome, and was made Governor of his native Province by the Emperor Honorius. His life prior to the year 418 was far from edifying. By the grace of God he reformed, and not long after he was ordained to the Priesthood he became Bishop of Auxerre. For thirty years he governed that diocese, winning many souls to the Church.

As the Pelagian heresy was devastating England, the reigning Pontiff chose St. Germain to save the British people from being ensnared by those heretical teachings. Together with St. Lupus of Troyes he preached in the highways and byways throughout Britain. Courageously he met the heretics face to face, and completely overcame them with the Catholic Faith. He attributed his success to the intercession of St. Alban, to whom St. Germain offered public thanks at his shrine. He also led the British people to their famous Alleluia victory over the Saxons. St. Germain later visited England with St. Severus.

While on an errand of mercy to the Court of Emperor Valentinian III, St. Germain died at Ravenna, Italy, on July 31, 448. In accordance with his dying request, his remains were interred at Auxerre, but they were lost during the French Revolution.

✠

JULY 31

ST. IGNATIUS LOYOLA

Inigo or Ignatius Loyola, born in the year 1491, was a son of the illustrious, ancient family of Loyola in Spain. In his youth he served as a page to King Ferdinand of

Spain. Soon tiring of the soft court life he sought escape
in the life of a soldier. The Duke of Najera, a relative,
accepted him into his service, and Ignatius, brave and
universally popular, quickly won fame in the conquests of
Najera.

In the summer of 1521, a small group of Spanish soldiers were defending the unfinished citadel of Pamplona
(formerly Pampeluna) against an invading army. Ignatius
fell, wounded. An army surgeon unskillfully set the broken
leg, and in consequence the wounded soldier underwent
several operations, which, in the end, left him lame.

During a long convalescence, it was the Will of God
that Ignatius, having little else to read and amuse himself
with, should have placed into his hands a Life of Jesus,
and a volume of the Lives of the Saints. In consequence,
one certain night, strongly moved by longings for higher
things, Ignatius arose from his bed, and kneeling before a
picture of our Lady, dedicated himself in an ardent prayer
to his Blessed Mother. Soon thereafter he retired to the
great sanctuary of our Lady which nestles under the crags
and peaks of Montserrat. On the way he had bound himself
by a vow of chastity in honor of Mary.

After scaling the precipitous mountain Ignatius began
his new way of life with a general confession made to a
Benedictine monk, a saintly Frenchman. Laying aside his
fine clothes he spent the night in prayer before the statue
of our Lady within the old church. And at dawn at Mary's
shrine he hung up his rapier and dagger before receiving
Holy Communion. Later he descended the rough moun-
tainside and sought shelter in the hospice of St. Lucy in
Manresa. There he would live a life of poverty and prayer
among the poor of Jesus Christ.

In the cave of Manresa God communicated to him
choicest gifts, and revealed that system of Christian perfection which is known as the *Spiritual Exercises*. A spiritual fire had been enkindled in his heart for the salvation
of all souls. However, his plan for the evangelization of
the Holy Land failed; and he now realized, at the age of

thirty-three, in 1524, that more education was necessary, and he began to study Latin. Gradually the plans of God were made known to His servant. He clearly saw that a new Order was needed, and he commenced to gather in companions. Realizing that he should not confine his work to Spain alone, he went to Paris in 1528 to complete his studies. At the college of St. Barbara Ignatius met Francis Xavier, James Lainez, Peter Favre, Simon Rodriguez, as also others, who later joined with him when he founded the Society (Company) of Jesus to fight for the greater honor and glory of God.

On Christmas night, 1538, in the subterranean chapel of the Basilica of St. Mary Major, in Rome, where the relic of the holy crib of Bethlehem is kept, St. Ignatius said his first Mass. For eighteen years he labored unceasingly for the salvation of souls. In 1556, at the age of sixty-five, he expired with the word, "Jesus, Jesus", on his lips. He was canonized in 1622 by Gregory XV, and his relics lie in a sumptuous chapel within the Church of the Gesu, which was built in place of Santa Maria della Strada, in Rome.

AUGUST

ST. PETER-IN-CHAINS

In the year 44 A.D. Herod Agrippa, then king of the Jews, in order to win the affection and applause of his people, put to death the Apostle James. Seeing this pleased the Jews, he cast St. Peter into prison and placed a guard of soldiers to prevent his escape.

The night before Herod intended to present St. Peter before the people, "Peter was sleeping between two soldiers, bound with two chains: and the keepers before the door kept the prison". During the night an angel of the Lord stood by Peter, and a bright light filled the prison chamber. The angel struck Peter on the side, raised him up, and said: "Arise quickly. And the chains fell off from his hands". Then the angel told him: "Gird thyself; and put on thy sandals. And he did so". And the angel said to him: "Cast thy garment about thee, and follow me". Peter obeyed. Passing through the first and second ward, they came to the iron gate that led to the city, which of itself opened to them. Going out, they passed on through one street, and immediately the angel departed. (Acts 12:1-10).

During the reign of the younger Theodosius, when his wife Eudocia went to Jerusalem to fulfill a vow, she was there honored with many gifts. Notable above all the rest was the gift which she received of an iron chain adorned with gold and precious stones, which they affirmed to be the very one whereby the Apostle Peter had been bound by Herod. Eudocia piously venerated this chain, and thereafter sent it to Rome to her daughter Eudoxia, who carried it to the Supreme Pontiff. He then showed her another chain, by which the same Apostle had been bound when Nero was Emperor. When the Pontiff placed the Roman chain together with that which Eudoxia had brought from Jerusalem, it happened that they fitted together in such a manner that they seemed no longer two chains, but a single one, made by the same workman. On account of this miracle, the holy chains began to be held in such great honor, that a church was erected in the 4th century with the title of Eudoxia on the Esquiline hill, in which they were deposited. It was **dedicated under the name of St. Peter ad Vincula.**

✠

AUGUST 2

ST. ALPHONSUS MARY De LIGUORI

St. Alfonso, called in English St. Alphonsus, the eldest of the seven children of Don Joseph and Donna Anna, was born near Naples on September 27, 1696. Four of the children were sons, of whom three became Priests. Of the three daughters, two entered religion. This indicates the piety of the family.

The spiritual training of Alphonsus was entrusted to Father Pagani, a holy Priest of the Oratory of St. Philip Neri, who directed Alphonsus for thirty years.

At the age of sixteen, the talented, conscientious boy took his degrees in both Civil and Canon Law. Many clients of distinction presented themselves to the young lawyer. Among them was a person who had a lawsuit of great pecuniary importance against another princely family. Alphonsus studied the cause with great care and promised himself success. But God, Who intended His servant for another state of life, permitted Alphonsus to overlook one point which caused him to lose the case. This made Alphonsus realize how unstable and uncertain is earthly success, and he retired from the court, determined to labor only for the glory of God.

On October 23, 1723, with permission of Cardinal Pignatelli, Archbishop of Naples, Alphonsus took the clerical habit and began his ecclesiastical studies. Divine Providence had decreed that our Saint should not only be a learned man, but also a great missionary preacher. He was ordained Priest on December 2, 1726.

In order to further his missionary work, St. Alphonsus founded the missionary Congregation of the Most Holy Redeemer (Redemptorists). At the age of sixty-five he became Bishop of St. Agatha, and his untiring zeal, charity and patience are a model for Bishops. One week after assuming his new office, he started a course of spiritual exercises in his cathedral for his people, and once a year thereafter a mission or retreat was given in every part of his diocese.

In 1766, St. Alphonsus established at St. Agatha the Redemptoristine Nuns. This convent has ever since been a source of benediction to the town.

St. Alphonsus made a vow never to lose time. At the age of forty-nine he wrote his first book, and in his 83rd year had published about sixty theological and ascetical volumes, when his director forbade him to write more.

The last seven years of the Saint were a continual purification of his spirit through suffering and detachment from everything he loved, however holy it might be. Intense mental as well as bodily sufferings became his portion night and day. One of his favorite ejaculations was: "All my hope is in Jesus, and after Jesus, in my loving Mother Mary".

As the Angelus bell rang at noon on July 18, 1787, St. Alphonsus resigned his holy soul into the hands of the Redeemer, Whom he had so fondly loved, so zealously preached, and Whom, co-operating with His grace, he had so glorified during his long life of ninety years and ten months.

Many miracles followed immediately after the death of the Saint, by which God testified to the glory of His servant. He was canonized by Pope Gregory XVI on May 26, 1839, and on March 23, 1871, Pope Pius IX, after consulting the Congregation of Sacred Rites, declared him to be a Doctor of the Universal Church.

✠

AUGUST 3

FINDING OF THE RELICS
OF ST. STEPHEN

In 415 a priest named Lucian miraculously found the
relics of St. Stephen. In a revelation he learned that the
sacred body was in Kapher-Gamala, some distance to the
north of Jerusalem. The relics were exhumed and carried to
the church of Mount Sion. In 460 they were translated to the
basilica erected by the Empress Eudocia, outside the Damascus Gate, on the spot, according to tradition, where
St. Stephen was stoned to death. In the early part of this
century the site of the Eudocian basilica was identified and
a new edifice was erected on the old foundations by the
Dominican Fathers.

✠

AUGUST 4

ST. DOMINIC

It was at Calaroga, a Spanish town near the Pyrenees,
that St. Dominic was born in 1170, of the Guzman family.
Before birth, the mother of St. Dominic dreamt that she
had given life to a dog bearing a lighted torch which was
setting the world on fire, and during his baptism, the noble
lady who held him saw on his forehead a star of light.

When Dominic was ordained Priest at the age of
twenty-four his parents were dead. At the request of the
Bishop, Dominic soon afterwards joined the Chapter of
Reformed Canons of Osma, his native diocese. Although
youngest in age, he was named Superior. He accompanied
his Bishop to France, and was greatly saddened when he
witnessed the ravages of the Albigensian heresy. Hence-

forth Dominic's life was devoted to the conversion of heretics and the defense of the Faith. From the record of his life St. Dominic was a man of conspicuous and eminent talent, and was probably one of the greatest orators that ever lived.

The Albigenses were amazed and angered by the learned discourses of St. Dominic. At Fanjeaux occurred a celebrated prodigy. A public thesis written by Dominic was cast into the fire. The document written in opposition by the Albigenses was cast into the flames and consumed, whilst Dominic's was thrown out of the fire three times unscathed. This miracle was spread abroad and converted many. This miraculous episode is sculptured in the marble of the Saint's tomb at Bologna.

Dominic remained for two years faithfully serving his Bishop at Montpellier, in southern France. Here the immoral Albigensian heresy had reached its height and was causing tremendous havoc. Dominic continued to preach against it for eight years after the return of the Bishop to Osma; working many miracles and converting countless souls.

It is declared that St. Dominic "was admonished by the Blessed Virgin to preach the Rosary to the people as a singular remedy against heresy and sin". Popes Leo X, St. Pius V, Gregory XIII, Sixtus V, Clement XI, Innocent XIII, Benedict XIII, and Pius IX, have, with a singular consent and in a most formal manner, attributed the Rosary to St. Dominic.

When in his 46th year, and with six companions, he began the great Order of Preaching Friars, this Order with that of the Friars Minor, founded by his contemporary friend St. Francis of Assisi, was the chief means God employed to renew Christian fervor during the Middle Ages. In addition, St. Dominic founded his Second Order for nuns for the education of Catholic girls, and his Third Order, or Tertiaries, for persons of both sexes living in the world.

O God, you deigned to enlighten Your Church with the merits and the teaching of Blessed Dominic, Your Confessor. Grant that through his intercession, she may never be deprived of temporal aid and may always advance in spiritual growth.

Among the miracles which bear witness to St. Dominic's sanctity are the raising of three persons from the dead.

St. Dominic died in Bologna on August 6, 1221, when fifty-one years of age.

✠

AUGUST 5

OUR LADY OF THE SNOW

This Feast is celebrated to commemorate the dedication of the church of Santa Maria Maggiore (St. Mary Major) on the Esquiline hill in Rome. The church was originally erected by Pope Liberius (352-366), and was called after him "Basilica Liberii". It was restored by Pope Sixtus III (432-440) and dedicated to Our Lady.

According to legend, during the Pontificate of Liberius, the Roman patrician John and his wife, who were without heirs, made a vow to donate their possessions to Our Lady. They implored her to make known to them in what manner they were to dispose of their property in her honor. During the night of August 5th snow fell on the summit of the Esquiline hill and, in obedience to a vision which they had the same night, they built a basilica in honor of Our Lady on the spot which was covered by snow.

Originally the feast was celebrated only at Santa Maria Maggiore; in the 14th century it was extended to all of the churches of Rome, and finally it was made a universal Feast by Pope Pius V.

✠

AUGUST 6

TRANSFIGURATION OF CHRIST

The Feast of the Transfiguration of Christ is celebrated to commemorate the manifestation of the Divine glory as recorded in the 17th chapter of St. Matthew. Jesus brought

Peter, James and John up on a high mountain and was there transfigured before them. The face of the Savior shone "as the sun, and His garments became white as snow", and "there appeared to them Moses and Elias talking with Him". Peter said to Jesus: "Lord it is good for us to be here. If Thou wilt, let us make here three tabernacles, one for Thee, and one for Moses, and one for Elias".

As he was speaking a bright cloud overshadowed them, and a voice out of the cloud said: "This is My beloved Son, in Whom I am well pleased: hear ye Him". The disciples "fell on their faces and were very much afraid". Jesus came and touched them, and said: "Arise, and fear not". Looking up they "saw no one, but only Jesus".

☩

AUGUST 7

ST. CAJETAN OF THIENNA

St. Cajetan was born at Vicenza, in Lombardy, in 1480, of noble, pious parents. His mother recommended him from his birth to the patronage of the Blessed Virgin, and from his earliest years he was regarded as "the Saint". As he grew older he was known as "the hunter of souls".

Cajetan took his degree of Doctor in Civil and Canon Law at Padua. After embracing the ecclesiastical state he founded a chapel at Rampazzo for the benefit of those who lived a great distance from the parish church. Then he went to Rome hoping to lead an obscure life, but was compelled by Pope Julius II to accept the office of protonotary Apostolic in his Court. Upon the death of the Pope, Cajetan returned to Vicenza, joined the Confraternity of St. Jerome, and devoted himself to nursing the sick and the poor.

In obedience to his confessor, Cajetan then went to Venice to reside in the new hospital of that city, where he pursued his former manner of life.

It was a common saying in Rome, Vicenza, and Venice, that Cajetan was "a seraph at the altar and an apostle in the pulpit".

Upon the advice of the same spiritual director, Cajetan left Venice and returned to Rome. In conjunction with John Peter Caraffa, afterward Pope under the name of Paul IV, and several others, Cajetan instituted the Theatines, or Regular Clerks, to serve as models for the clergy. Caraffa, who was Bishop of Chieti at the time, was chosen head of the new religious Order, which became one of the most prominent during the revival of Christian piety in the 16th century. St. Cajetan, who succeeded Caraffa as General of the Theatines, in order to counteract the evils of Calvinism, introduced the Forty Hours Adoration of the Blessed Sacrament.

When Rome was sacked by the Germans, St. Cajetan was cruelly scourged to extort from him riches which he did not possess. Being discharged in a weakened condition, St. Cajetan and his companions left for Venice, where they were kindly received. Later he governed the house of his Order in Naples, where he was able to check the advances of Lutheranism. The last four years of his life were spent in that city. He died of grief because of the discords of the inhabitants, suffering in his last moments a kind of mystical crucifixion. He was canonized by Pope Clement X in 1671.

✠

AUGUST 8

CYRIACUS, LARGUS, SMARAGDUS AND OTHERS

It was during the persecution of the Emperors Diocletian and Maximian Herculeus, in 303, that St. Cyriacus, a holy deacon of Rome, under Popes Marcellinus and Marcellus, together with Largus, Smaragdus and twenty other Christians were tortured and then put to death for the Faith.

Cyriacus and his companions were imprisoned for a long time. He performed many miracles; freed the daughter of Diocletian from a demon; delivered the daughter of the King of Persia from an evil spirit; baptized the King and four hundred and thirty others, and then returned to Rome. There he was seized by command of Emperor Maximian, bound in chains and dragged before the chariot. Four days later he was taken out of prison, had boiling pitch poured over him and then was exposed on a scaffold. Finally he was put to death by the axe with Largus, Smaragdus and twenty others in the gardens of Sallust on the Salarian way.

Their bodies were interred by a Priest named John on that same road on March 16th; on August 8th Pope Marcellus and the noble lady Lucina wrapped them in linen shrouds and embalmed them with precious spices, and then translated them to her estate on the Ostian way, on the seventh milestone from the city.

☩

AUGUST 9

JOHN BAPTIST MARY VIANNEY

The Curé of Ars, as John Mary Vianney is generally known, was born in 1785, at Dardilly, a village not far from Lyons, France. His parents were respectable, pious farmers. John often said that he owed all his holiest impressions to his deeply religious mother. Even while very young, prayer was his delight. When his mother saw his extraordinary devotion, her one idea was that he should some day become a Priest. But she had to endure many trials before this hope could be realized. The French Revolution closed their parish church and exiled or murdered their Priests.

John was then eight years of age, and was given charge of the cows and sheep on his father's farm. Each morning he led them out to browse in the fields near his home. This was the school in which Our Lord trained the boy for the interior life, like another St. Vincent de Paul.

On account of the troubled state of the times, John did not make his First Communion until he was eleven years old. From that moment he increased daily in fervor, piety and obedience. In the midst of his hard work he never lost the habit of interior prayer, nor his sense of the continual presence of God. Later, he often said: "When I was alone in the fields ploughing or sowing I would pray aloud, but when others were with me I used to pray in my heart. O those were happy days! I often used to say to myself, as I struck my hoe or spade into the ground: 'So must I cultivate my soul, to pluck up the evil weeds and to prepare it for the good seed of the good God'".

After the French Revolution and the Napoleonic wars had ended, John was ordained Priest. This, however, was not accomplished without a long and hard struggle, for in spite of his humility, sweetness and piety which had won the esteem of all, he was sadly deficient in the learning usually required for candidates for the priesthood. Cardinal Fesch, upon learning from all John's superiors that he was a model of piety, exclaimed: "That is enough. I will receive him—Divine grace will do the rest". He was accordingly ordained sub-deacon at Lyons by the Bishop of Grenoble, deacon the following July, and six months later, on August 9, 1815, when twenty-nine years of age, was ordained Priest at the same place.

For two years he served as curate at Ecully. He refused to accept the pastorate upon the death of the venerable pastor. Three months later he was appointed Curé of Ars, an obscure village in Central France. All the remaining days of his life were spent here devoted to converting sinners and guiding countless souls to God. The greater part of each day found him engaged in the confessional. The fame of his sanctity drew multitudes from all parts of France to seek his help and spiritual advice.

The holy Curé died August 4, 1859, in his seventy-third year. More than three hundred Priests and representatives of all the Religious Orders came to pay their last tribute of reverence to the departed Saint. He was illus-

trious in many miracles, and Pope Saint Pius X added him
to the number of the Blessed; whilst Pius XI, in the holy
year of 1925, canonized him.

✠

AUGUST 10

ST. LAWRENCE

St. Lawrence was the first of the seven Deacons of
the Roman Church. He assisted the Pope when celebrating
Mass, distributed the Holy Eucharist to the faithful, administered the Church's possessions, and dispensed the
revenues among the poor.

St. Lawrence was one of the victims of the persecution of the Emperor Valerian in 258, like Pope Sixtus II
and many other members of the Roman clergy. In August,
258, the Emperor issued an edict commanding that all
Bishops, Priests and Deacons should be put to death immediately. This command was promptly carried out. Pope
Sixtus II was arrested in one of the catacombs and executed
at once. Two other Deacons, Felicissimus and Agapitus,
were put to death the same day. Four days later, on August 10th, St. Lawrence also suffered a martyr's death.
He was laid on an iron bed in the shape of a gridiron,
under which were placed half-lighted coals, so as to prolong his tortures and make his death more painful.

Pope Damasus built a basilica in Rome, which he
dedicated to St. Lawrence. It is now known as that of
San Lorenzo in Damaso.

✠

AUGUST 11

ST. TIBURTIUS

St. Tiburtius was a Roman deacon, son of the Prefect of Rome. He was condemned to death by fire in 286 A.D., but armed with the Sign of the Cross he survived the flames unharmed. He was then led forth and decapitated. His remains were found in the Catacomb of St. Callixtus in Rome.

ST. SUSANNA AND ST. PHILOMENA

St. Susanna is said to have been the niece of Pope St. Caius. She possessed not only beauty but learning, and was so highly regarded that the Emperor Diocletian desired her to marry his son-in-law, Maximian. Preferring to remain a virgin, Susanna refused to accept the offer. Wholeheartedly and with such sincere conviction did she praise the Faith that two of the officers, whom the emperor had sent to ascertain the cause of her refusal, were converted to Christianity. Exasperated, Diocletian ordered Susanna to be beheaded in her home. Her martyrdom occurred about the year 295.

Saints Tiburtius and Susanna loved Jesus so intensely that they willingly sacrificed their lives for the Faith He had bestowed upon them. Earthly comforts and pleasures meant nothing to these holy souls when compared with the heavenly reward promised by the Savior to those who believe in, and follow, Him.

St. Philomena was also a virgin and martyr. Pope Saint Pius X and Saint John Mary Vianney, of recent memory, both held St. Philomena in the highest esteem. She was also numbered among the faithful Christians who suffered martyrdom in Rome during the reign of the Emperor Diocletian.

One is apt to think of the saints and martyrs as people who lived in the years of long ago. But saints are not of any one period of time or of any one place. Christ is their WAY and their LIFE. There are many saints today who live in Christ and in whom Christ lives; they desire the salvation of all men: some are aiding the poor, others the sick, the suffering and the dying; still others are laboring to spread the Kingdom of Christ by their teaching and good example in homelands or in foreign lands.

Countless Christians are undergoing persecution for their Faith in many parts of the world today, and are accepting hardship, misunderstanding, persecution and suffering for the love of Christ; numberless others have suffered martyrdom for being loyal Christians. Some will be canonized by the Church, others will not be, because they are not in public life but nevertheless are saints in the sight of God, and the name of each one is inscribed in golden letters in the Calendar of the Saints in Heaven.

✠

AUGUST 12

ST. CLARE

St. Clare was born of noble parents in 1196, in the city of Assisi, overlooking the plain of Umbria. Her mother was a woman of great holiness. Before Clare's birth she made a pilgrimage to the Holy Land, a long and arduous journey in those days. On her return, just before her daughter's birth, as she was praying before the crucifix in the monastery at Assisi for the safe delivery of her child, she heard a voice saying to her: "Have no fear, woman; you will bear your child safely, and she will be a torch to give a clear light to the world". So when the child was born soon after, she called her Clare, for in Latin the word *clara* means shining or bright.

Clare never left Assisi. She was carefully taught and cared for by her mother. The child's greatest joy was to give alms to the beggars. In the Lent of 1212, when Clare was fifteen years old, St. Francis began to preach at Assisi, and Clare was one of the many who flocked to hear him. Every word he uttered found an echo in her heart, and she wished to follow him. For three years, however, Francis kept Clare in suspense. It had not yet entered into his plan to provide for women in his apostolic work.

It is said that to try the strength of Clare's purpose St. Francis bade her put on coarse clothes and beg her bread through the streets of Assisi, and she did so, unrecognized in her disguise. He did not allow her to change her way of life in her own home, but bade her keep her heart poor and lowly under the rich clothes her parents provided for her. The only Rule under which a woman could place herself in the 12th century was the Benedictine. But God works in His own way in each heart, and He demanded such an act of faith in this wonderful strong soul as seems to us even now superhuman in its divine imitation of the "folly of the Cross".

So after three years of hesitations, anxieties and difficulties, on the eve of Palm Sunday, Clare went to St. Francis and begged him to receive her into his Order. Seeing her great determination, he bade her come to the church of St. Mary of the Angels the following night to make her vows to him and his Brothers. At the appointed time Clare made her vows, and, putting on the Franciscan dress and the rough cord round her waist, she was received into the Franciscan Order. Temporarily she stayed at the Benedictine convent of San Paolo at Bastia.

Her father and relatives were furious, but Clare remained adamant in her determination. A few days later she moved to the convent of St. Angelo Michele, about a mile from the city, and her sister Agnes joined her. Unable to settle down under the Benedictine Rule, St. Francis soon made over to them the church and convent of San Damiano, which still exist on the outskirts of Assisi.

For forty years Clare was enclosed in her convent at San Damiano, where she practised the greatest austerity. She was filled to overflowing with God's grace, and lived in unceasing communion with Him in prayer and contemplation. Her miracles were all worked in direct answer to prayer. Bishops and Cardinals visited Clare in her poor convent. She was joined by several women of her own family.

After the death of St. Francis, in 1226, Clare was thrown on her own resources. In 1253, after many cruel illnesses and great mental suffering, Clare lay on her deathbed. For seventeen days she endured her agony, but no word of complaint ever passed her lips. It was on August 11, 1253, that she died, and as the chronicles say, "she had, for the poor life of poverty and bitterness, the blessed kingdom of Paradise".

With great ceremony the Requiem Mass was sung in the presence of Pope Innocent IV and the Cardinals. At the wish of the people of Assisi, St. Clare's body was placed in the church of San Giorgio, where it has rested ever since. Pope Alexander IV inscribed her name in the catalogue of the Saints on August 12, 1255.

✠

AUGUST 13

ST. JOHN BERCHMANS

St. John Berchmans was born at Diest in Brabant, on March 13, 1599. When John was but seven years old, M. Emmerick, the parish Priest remarked with pleasure that the Lord would work wonders in the soul of the child.

John's mother was stricken with a long and serious illness when he was nine years old, and he spent several hours daily by her bedside, consoling her with his affectionate, though serious words.

He was naturally kind, gentle and affectionate; was endowed with a keen intellect and a retentive memory. What distinguished him most, however, from his companions was his piety. When hardly seven years old he was accustomed to rise early and serve two or three Masses with the greatest fervor. He attended religious instructions

and listened to Sunday sermons with the deepest recollection; made pilgrimages to the sanctuary of Montaigu,
a few miles from his home, reciting the rosary as he went,
or absorbed in meditation.

When he entered the Jesuit college at Mechlin he
was enrolled in the Sodality of the Blessed Virgin and
resolved to recite her Office daily. Towards the end of his
rhetoric course, he felt a distinct call to the Society of
Jesus. He overcame the opposition of his family, and was
received into the novitiate at Mechlin on September 24,
1616. Two years later he was sent to Antwerp to study
philosophy. After a few weeks, he journeyed by foot to
Rome to continue the same study. He arrived at the Roman
College on December 31, 1618.

Early in August, 1621, he was selected by the Prefect
of Studies to take part in a philosophical disputation at
the Greek College which was under the charge of the
Dominicans. Upon returning to his college he was seized
with a violent fever, from which he died on August 13th,
at the age of twenty-two years and five months.

He was accustomed to say, "If I do not become a
Saint when I am young, I shall never become one". He
always conformed his will to that of his Superiors and
to the Rules. "My penance", he would say, "is to live the
common life. . . . I will pay the greatest attention to the
least inspiration of God." He was most faithful in the
performance of all his duties. When he died, many people
came to see him and to invoke his intercession. He was
canonized by Pope Leo XIII in 1888.

✠

ST. EUSEBIUS

About the end of the 3rd century, during the reign of
Diocletian and Maximian, Eusebius, a Roman patrician and
holy Priest, suffered martyrdom for the Faith in Palestine.

A church on the Esquiline hill in Rome is dedicated to him. It is said to have been built on the site of his house, and is mentioned in the Acts of a Council which was held in Rome under Pope Symmacus in 498.

☩

AUGUST 15

THE ASSUMPTION OF MARY

"Precious in the sight of the Lord is the death of His Saints", says the word of God. How precious, then, the death of Mary, the Mother of Christ and the Queen of all Saints. On the 15th of August, which is a holyday of obligation binding all Catholics to assist at the holy sacrifice of the Mass, we commemorate Mary's most precious death and her glorious Assumption into Heaven. On November 1, 1950, His Holiness, Pope Pius XII, proclaimed the dogma of Mary's Assumption.

Conceived without original sin, born in sanctifying grace and preserving the same all the days of her life upon earth, without the slightest tarnish of venial sin or imperfection, Mary verified the words of the holy writer: "Thou art all fair, O my love, and there is not a spot in thee" (Cant. 4:7). Virtues were added to virtues and increased in depth and splendor with her years. There was no standstill in her spiritual life. She outranked all the Saints of the Old Testament, who were imperfect types of her, and all of the New Testament, who have modeled themselves according to her example. Her death could not be otherwise than precious.

Death is accompanied by suffering and fear. It is natural for man to fear death. The belief that he who fears death must have a burdened conscience is not quite correct. Surely, one conscious of mortal sin has not the consolation of hope which fortifies the just person. Death is punishment, and logically, as a punishment, is something to be feared. If death were not an evil in one way or the other, where would its punishment be? The thought of Our Savior in the Garden of Gethsemani will remind us that He, Who had taken upon Himself our human nature, feared death and the suffering which preceded it. He took upon Himself all the punishments of men's sins, both original and actual, and He feared. In the case of Mary, however, who was not the Victim for sin, and whose soul had not been tainted, not even by the sin of Adam, we believe that her death was without suffering and without fear—a most precious death.

We also commemorate Mary's most glorious Assumption into Heaven. Her divine Son raised her above every creature in Heaven and on earth. She has been crowned the Queen of the Angels and Saints, in glory and in power of intercession surpassing all. She is loved and honored as a tender mother and a mighty advocate with God by the faithful on earth.

✠

AUGUST 16

ST. JOACHIM

The Church honors St. Joachim, husband of St. Anne and father of the Blessed Virgin Mary. He was of the tribe of Juda and of the House of David. Holy, indeed, must have been his life to have been chosen by God to be the father of the Mother of the Savior of Mankind.

St. John Damascene's discourse on the birth of the Virgin Mary contains these words:

"O blessed couple, Joachim and Anne! To you is every creature indebted. For through you, every creature has offered to the Creator this gift, the noblest of gifts, namely, that chaste mother who alone was worthy of the Creator. Rejoice Joachim, for from thy daughter a Son is born to us; and His name is called the Angel of great counsel, that is, of the salvation of the whole world. . . .

"O blessed couple, Joachim and Anne! And indeed you are known to be pure by the fruit of your bodies, as Christ said in a certain place: By their fruits you shall know them. You ordered your lives by rule, as was pleasing to God and worthy of her who was sprung from you. For the chaste and holy exercise of your office, you brought forth the treasure of virginity."

ST. ROCH

St. Roch, an eminent servant of God, was born at Montpellier, France, in the 14th century. He served the plague stricken in Italy while on a pilgrimage of devotion to Rome. He bore incredible pains patiently and joyfully, and God was pleased to restore him to health. He then returned to France and practiced austere penances. The last years of St. Roch's life were spent at Montpellier, where it is claimed he died in 1327. Many cities have been speedily delivered from the plague by imploring his intercession. This was especially the case in Constance during the General Council which was held there in 1414.

St. Roch's body was translated from Montpellier to Venice in 1485, where it is honored in a beautiful church; certain portions of his relics, however, are shown at Rome, Arles and other places.

✠

AUGUST 17

ST. HYACINTH

St. Hyacinth, son of the noble family Konski, was born at the castle of Lanka in Silesia, Poland, in 1185. He studied at Cracow, Prague and Bologna. At Bologna he merited the title of Doctor of Law and Divinity.

While on a trip to Rome with his uncle, Ivo Konski, Bishop of Cracow, Hyacinth met St. Dominic and was one of the first to receive at his hands at Santa Sabina, Rome, in 1220, the Habit of the newly established Order of Friars

Preachers. After making his religious profession he was appointed superior of the little group of missionaries sent to Poland. Enroute he established a monastery of his Order at Friesach in Carinthia, a province of South Austria. The missionaries were favorably received in Poland, and their preaching produced splendid fruits.

St. Hyacinth founded communities in Cracow and various other places. After preaching in Prussia, Pomerania, Lithuania, Denmark, Norway and Sweden, he returned to Cracow, where he died a saintly death on August 15, 1257. God glorified His servant by numberless miracles. St. Hyacinth was canonized by Pope Clement VIII, in 1594.

☩

AUGUST 18

ST. HELENA

St. Helena was born about the year 250, the only daughter of Coel, a British king, who resided at Colchester and lived on friendly terms with the conquering Romans. Helena married Constantius Chlorus, a pagan, who was descended from Emperor Claudius II, and from Vespasian. This marriage was a very happy one for twenty years; their only child, Constantine, born at York, soon gave promise of his future greatness.

When the edicts against the Christians were ordered to be carried out in Britain, Constantius had to publish the decree, but he retained the pagans and Christians employed in his household, convinced of the loyalty of the latter.

In 293 there were two Emperors, Diocletian and Maximian Herculeus, and they resolved to associate with themselves two Caesars to assist in their wars and in the government of distant countries. Maximian chose Constantius on condition he would divorce his wife and marry Theodora, the widow of Maximian's son. The position was too tempting, and Helena soon found herself in the bitter and most undeserved position of a repudiated wife.

Upon Constantius' death on July 25, 306, his son
Constantine was immediately saluted Emperor by the
army. No longer a repudiated wife, St. Helena now held the
proud position of mother of an Emperor. Her devoted son,
as if to make up to her for past slights and sufferings,
showered upon her honors and dignities.

After the conversion of her son, the Empress Helena,
then over sixty years of age, also became a Christian. She
assisted the Emperor in many charitable works.

In 326, the 21st year of Constantine's reign, St. Helena
was inspired to go to the Holy Land and search for the
Cross of Jesus, that Cross whose appearance in the sky over
the battlefield had converted her son in 312. Underneath
it, in Greek characters, were the words "In hoc signo
vinces"—"Through this sign thou shalt conquer".

The aged Empress spared no pains to find where the
Cross might be buried, and God blessed her efforts. Over
the spot where it was found, St. Helena immediately had
erected the Basilica of the Holy Cross. Upon completion of
this great church, a large piece of the holy Cross was
placed there, in a rich silver shrine, with the utmost solemnity on September 15, 335. This feast, called the
**Triumph of the Cross, is still observed by the Catholic
Church.**

St. Helena spent the remaining days of her life in the
East and in Rome. It was in Rome that she breathed her
last, about the year 328.

St. Helena's name is revered by Catholics everywhere
for the work she accomplished in finding the Cross of
Christendom.

✠

ST. JOHN EUDES

St. John Eudes was born in France in 1601. His father,
Isaac Eudes, had originally been destined for the priesthood, but as his brothers died during the plague in 1587,

Isaac returned to the paternal house to administer the family property. In 1598 he married Martha Corbin, a most virtuous woman. As their happy union was not blessed with children, the pious couple made a pilgrimage in February, 1601, to the well-known sanctuary of Our Lady under the title of Our Lady of Recovery. On November 14 that same year a son was born, to whom they gave the name of John. Five other children were also born to them, all of whom were subsequently married.

From his earliest youth John was a child of prayer, and his mother trained him to practice the solid virtues--obedience, humility, gentleness. In 1615, he was sent to the Jesuit College at Caen, and completed his philosophical studies with distinction in 1621. Before returning home he had decided to embrace the ecclesiastical state. His parents, however, wished him to marry, but being good Christians and realizing that it was God's Will, they withdrew their opposition to his designs. John, therefore, received the tonsure and minor orders in September, 1621, and then returned to Caen to pursue his theological studies.

Because of the corruption of the clergy at that time, John was in doubt about becoming a secular Priest on account of the dangers to which he would be exposed. His director advised him to enter the Congregation of the Oratory in France, which had been founded by de Berulle in 1611, on the lines of St. Philip's Oratory. John hastened to Paris, and was received in the Oratory on March 25, 1623. On December 20, 1625, he was ordained a Priest.

During the plague which devastated Normandy in 1627, Pere Eudes went to the plague-stricken field to console the sick and dying, and to administer to them the Holy Viaticum. So great was the panic that no one would give him shelter. Two months passed and then, the plague abating, he was directed by de Berulle, who had in the meanwhile been made a Cardinal, to repair to the house of the Oratory at Caen. Four quiet years were spent there when the Fathers of that Oratory were attacked by the plague. Eudes nursed his brethren, and all but two recovered. Not long after, he himself fell so ill that his life was despaired of. Through the fervent prayers of the Carmelites and other religious at Caen, he was restored to health and vigor.

The next few years (1632-1643), Pere Eudes devoted himself entirely to missionary work in various parts of France. His success as a preacher was immense, due to the intense earnestness and natural eloquence of a singularly gifted man.

He founded the well-known Religious Congregation called after him, the Eudists, whose chief work is directing Ecclesiastical Seminaries and preparing youth for the priesthood. In 1641 he also founded the Congregation of "Our Lady of Charity of the Refuge", the Congregation from which two centuries later the Congregation of the Good Shepherd was to spring. It was on the Feast of the Immaculate Conception, 1641, that the community of Our Lady of Refuge was definitely established to care for wayward and penitent girls.

St. John Eudes had great devotion to the Sacred Hearts of Jesus and Mary, and was the author of several ascetical works. After receiving the Last Sacraments, the holy old man breathed forth his soul to God on August 19, 1680. He was canonized by Pope Pius XI in 1925.

✠

ST. BERNARD OF CLAIRVAUX

St. Bernard was born at Fontaines, near Dijon, in Burgundy, in the year 1090, the third son of Tescelin and his wife Aleth, both of whom were worthy to be the parents of a Saint. All of their children were offered to God at their birth, and God accepted the offering, for their six sons became Monks at Citeaux and their one daughter a Nun. But Bernard was especially devoted to God's service. The death of his mother at the end of his school life left him desolate, for he was not quite twenty and had not yet found his vocation. Life in the world did not satisfy him, and he could not be deaf to the voice of God that bade him take His yoke upon him. Whilst wavering to obey the call, his mother appeared to him and reminded him that it was not for the vanities of the world that she had brought him up with such tender care.

Harassed with doubts and perplexities, one day he entered a church and prayed for guidance. He heard a voice saying to him in the words of the Apocalypse (22:17), "And he that heareth, let him say: Come"; and when he left the church he had determined to accept the invitation of God. But he did not go alone: first his uncle, then his brothers, and finally several of his friends resolved to follow where he led, until he had gathered around him thirty disciples. For six months they led a community life at Chatillon, and when all difficulties had been removed they set out for Citeaux. Bernard's arrival was the turning point in the history of Citeaux, as the entry of so many postulants ensured the future of the Order.

In 1115, Bernard, although young in years and young in the monastic life, was chosen to found a new monastery. The site selected presented almost hopeless difficulties. It was in the diocese of Langres, on the left bank of the Aube, called the Valley of Bitterness. Later the name was changed, perhaps by Bernard himself, to Clara Vallis (Clairvaux, or the Bright Valley). Bernard with twelve companions (four of whom were his brothers) set out to face the hardships that awaited them—cold, hunger, and the want of everything. Bernard encouraged his companions by precept and example. When their needs became known, relief was given. Later this monastery became known as the celebrated Abbey of Clairvaux, of which St. Bernard remained Abbot for the rest of his life. Clairvaux, in turn, gave birth, even during the lifetime of its founder, to one hundred and sixty other Cistercian houses.

St. Bernard became the most conspicuous person in the 12th century. The effect of his fervent, eloquent preaching in the diocese of William of Champeaux was astonishing and instantaneous. Men of all classes followed him to Clairvaux. He became, and remained until his death, the arbiter of kings, the counsellor of Popes, the champion of the Church. The influence he wielded on the spirituality of the West was enormous. He was commissioned by Pope Eugene III, to preach the Second Crusade in 1146. His preaching kindled the enthusiasm of Christendom and influenced the European politics of his age.

St. Bernard died at Clairvaux on August 20, 1153, and was buried in the Ladye-Chapel of his Abbey. Since its destruction in 1792, his relics have been venerated in the neighboring parish church. St. Bernard was canonized by Pope Alexander III, in 1804, the first of the Cistercians to be so honored; and he was proclaimed a Doctor of the Church by Pope Pius VIII, in 1830.

☩

AUGUST 21

ST. JANE FRANCES DE CHANTAL

St. Jane Frances was born on January 23, 1572, the second child of Benigne Fremyot, President of the Dijon Parliament, who belonged to one of the oldest and most honorable families of Burgundy. His wife died a year and a half after the birth of Jane, when their long-desired son was born. Burgundy at the time was overrun by the Calvinists, and the new heresy prevailed everywhere. Consequently Jane was thoroughly instructed in the Catholic Faith. She was a precocious child, remarkable from her earliest years for her strength of character. She received a very good education and had great compassion for the sick and the poor.

From the time she received her First Holy Communion, Jane felt a strong desire to devote herself in some way to God's service. Because of the troubled religious and political situation in Burgundy, Jane, now fifteen, went with her sister to Poitou, but there she was greeted with sadder sights, as the Hugenots had either ruined or desecrated the churches in Anjou and Touraine.

In 1591, Jane, upon the request of her father, returned to Dijon. He had chosen Christopher de Chantal, second Baron of the name, who was deeply religious and highly educated, to be her husband. The wedding took place the following year. Four children, one boy and three girls, blessed the union. Each was offered to God and dedicated to the Blessed Virgin by their pious mother. In the autumn of 1601, the Baron de Chantal was accidentally shot while out hunting with two friends, and died nine days later.

After recovering from the shock, Jane de Chantal laid aside her expensive clothes and distributed those of her husband to the poor. She prayed that God might give her a holy Director, who would make known more clearly the Divine Will. One day as she rode around her property looking after her servants, she saw at a little distance a person who looked like a Bishop, walking towards her. His countenance was serene and heavenly, and she felt a great inward peace. At the same moment the following suggestion was given to her soul: "This is the guide, well beloved of God and man, in whose hands you will place your conscience. She rode quickly to the spot, but found no one there. At the same hour a similar manifestation was vouchsafed to the Bishop of Geneva, who rapt in ecstatic prayer saw in a vision the face of a young widow and a new religious congregation, of which it seemed that she would be the first Mother, while he himself was to be its guide and instructor.

For a time Madame de Chantal visited her father at Dijon, and on her return to Bourbilly, as she was praying one day in the chapel, she suddenly saw herself surrounded by a great crowd of virgins and widows, and heard a voice saying, "This is the generation that shall be given to thee, my faithful servant, a chaste and chosen generation, and I will that it be holy". She was greatly comforted, but had not the least idea what the vision foretold.

It was in 1604, while visiting her father-in-law, that she met the Bishop of Geneva, who had been invited to preach the Lenten sermons at Dijon. She no sooner beheld Francis de Sales, as he took his place in the pulpit, than she recognized him as the Bishop of her vision. It was not long before she placed herself under his direction. Upon his advice, she provided for the care of her children, renounced all her earthly possessions in their favor, and determined to abandon the world.

It was on Trinity Sunday, 1610, that she laid the foundation of the "Order of the Visitation" at Annecy, France. Postulants soon applied and the community grew. The faith of the Sisters was called forth by the plague which devastated France, Savoy and Italy from 1626 to 1631.

The remainder of St. Jane's life was spent in incessant and arduous labors for the good of the Order. She died on December 13, 1641, as she repeated the Holy Name of Jesus three times. It is said that at the moment of her death St. Vincent de Paul saw her soul ascending to Heaven like a ball of fire. She was canonized by Pope Clement XIII, on July 16, 1767.

✠

AUGUST 22

IMMACULATE HEART OF MARY

In compliance with the request made by the Blessed Virgin Mary in one of her apparitions to the three little children at Fatima, Portugal, in 1917, His Holiness, Pope Pius XII in 1942 consecrated the world to the Immaculate Heart of Mary.

During her sixth and last apparition, in the presence of 70,000 people, when Lucy asked the Beautiful Lady her name, she replied: *I am the Lady of the Rosary.* Then solemnly she gave her last message to the children: *People*

*must amend their lives, ask pardon for their sins, and not
offend Our Lord any more for He is already too much
offended.*

After a vision these children had of Hell, which was
so terrible that Lucy said they would have died of fright
were it not for the fact that the Blessed Virgin Mary was
near and told them that they would go to Heaven, she
then stated: "You have seen Hell where the souls of
poor sinners go. To save them, God wishes to establish
throughout the world devotion to my Immaculate Heart".
Consequently, in 1945, Pope Pius XII established this new
Feast of the Immaculate Heart of Mary and extended it
to the Universal Church.

✠

AUGUST 23

ST. PHILIP BENIZI

St. Philip Benizi, the ornament and great propagator
of the newly founded Order of Servites, was born in
Florence, Italy, on August 15, 1233. Through the virtuous
care of his parents, and assisted by a special grace, Philip
preserved his soul from sin and daily advanced in the fear
of God. He was sent to Paris and then to Padua to study
medicine, where he took the degree of Doctor. Upon his
return to his native city, Philip earnestly begged God to
direct him into the path which would enable him to perfectly fulfill His Divine Will.

In a vision Our Lady bade him enter the Order of
Servites, which was under her special patronage. He was
admitted as a lay-Brother in 1254. When his learning
and talents were discovered his Superiors bade him to
prepare for Holy Orders. He was ordained in 1259, and
became assistant to the General, and in 1267, the Fifth
General of his Order. He made the sanctification of his
religious brethren the primary object of his zeal. He
preached the word of God wherever he went, and pos-

sessed an extraordinary talent in converting sinners and in reconciling those who were in dissension with one another.

Thinking that his life was closing on account of his poor health, he set out to make the visitation of the houses of his Order. It was at Todi, Italy, that he calmly expired on August 22, 1285. To give place to the octave of the Assumption—now the Feast of the Immaculate Heart of Mary—St. Philip Benizi's feast is observed on August 23rd. He was canonized by Pope Clement X in 1671, though the official Bull in the matter was only published by Pope Benedict XIII in 1724.

✠

ST. BARTHOLOMEW

St. Bartholomew was one of the twelve Apostles chosen by the Savior of the world. Many learned theologians have considered him to be the same person as Nathanael, the "Israelite without guile", mentioned in St. John's Gospel (1:29-51).

Born in Cana of Galilee, he was a doctor in the Jewish law, and became a faithful disciple of Jesus; he was one of the witnesses of His miracles and of His glorious Resurrection. He is also mentioned among the other disciples who were gathered together in the Upper Room after the Ascension of Christ praying, and who received the Holy Spirit with the rest.

Tradition tells us that after the Ascension he preached the Gospel in Northwest India and in Asia Minor, and that he suffered martyrdom in Greater Armenia. In this latter place he converted to the Christian Faith the King, Polymius, and his Queen, and likewise twelve cities. This excited great hatred against him on the part of the priests of that nation. They constantly inflamed Astyages, brother of Polymius the King, against the Apostle, to such a degree that he commanded Bartholomew to be flayed alive in a most cruel manner, and to be beheaded; in which martyrdom he gave up his soul to God.

✠

ST. LOUIS IX

King Louis VIII of France reigned only three years when death brought his promising career to a premature close. The eldest of his children, who also bore the name of Louis, was then but a boy of twelve. He was born at the castle of Poissy, on the Seine five miles from Paris, on April 25, 1215. His mother, Blanche, daughter of King Alfonso of Castile, was a wise, prudent and capable mother. She instilled into her son's tender soul the highest esteem for the Church, the strongest sentiments of piety, and a particular love of charity. She frequently said to him when he was still a child: "My son, I love you with all the affection of which a mother is capable; but I would rather see you drop dead at my feet than that you should ever commit one mortal sin". The King later in life remarked to others that the impression which this early lesson made on his mind was never effaced, and that a day never passed in which he did not recall it.

Upon the death of King Louis VIII on November 7, 1226, Blanche, the Queen-mother, was declared Regent for her twelve-year old son Louis. His coronation took place on the first Sunday of Advent, 1226, and he reigned for forty-four years. His sweetness of character, his unalterable evenness of temper, his love of justice, his vigilance in preventing troubles, and, above all, his holy life and tender piety won the hearts of all his subjects.

The Queen Regent chose Margaret, eldest daughter of Count Berenger of Provence, who was related to the

*O almighty and eternal God, Who, on the feast of Your blessed Apostle,
Bartholomew, filled this day with a holy and venerable joy; grant to Your
Church, we beseech You, to love that which he believed and to preach that
which he taught.*

royal house of Aragon, as a suitable consort for her son, when not quite nineteen years old. Louis went to Sens to meet her, and the marriage was celebrated in that city on May 27, 1234. A few days later the young Queen was also crowned there. In her the king found a faithful wife and a companion after his own heart. Both were equally inclined to piety and charity, and the blessing of God descended upon this happy union. Through their son, Philip, the Royal House of France was perpetuated.

In April, 1236, the King, having completed the 21st year of his life, took the reins of the government into his own hand, but he continued to show such deference to his mother that he never undertook anything without consulting her. Never did France enjoy more peace and tranquillity than during the reign of this holy King. Under his royal robe he wore the rough Franciscan habit; and he died, as St. Francis had desired to die, on his way to the Holy Land.

This humble monarch saw in all his servants his brothers in Christ. His charity was not confined to the poor of his own country; the Christians of Palestine and the East were on more than one occasion the objects of his bounty.

In 1239, Baldwin II, Latin Emperor of Constantinople, presented St. Louis the holy Crown of Thorns worn by our Savior, which had been formerly kept in the imperial palace. In 1241, St. Louis received from Constantinople, with other relics, a large piece of the true Cross. To preserve these sacred memorials of Christ's Passion with due reverence, the holy King built the magnificent edifice in Paris known as the Sainte Chapelle, or Holy Chapel. Under his patronage Robert of Sorbonne founded the "College de la Sorbonne", which became the seat of the theological faculty of Paris.

St. Louis, through his personal qualities as well as his saintliness, increased for many centuries the prestige of the French monarchy. Pope Gregory IX and Frederick II, as well as Henry III of England and his barons, chose King Louis as arbiter.

After assuring the external and internal peace of his kingdom, St. Louis turned his eyes to the East. In 1248 he gathered around him the chivalry of France and embarked on the 1st Crusade to rescue from the infidels the land which the Savior had trod. The death of his mother recalled him to France. In 1270 he set forth on a 2nd Crusade to fight the infidels. In August his army landed at Tunis, and though victorious over the enemy nearly half the men succumbed to a malignant fever. St. Louis was one of the victims. He died in sight of Tunis, in 1270. His remains were brought back to Paris by his son Philip, and interred in the Church of St. Denis. Many miracles have been wrought by the intercession of St. Louis. He was canonized by Pope Boniface VIII in 1297.

✠

AUGUST 26

ST. ZEPHYRINUS

St. Zephyrinus, a native of Rome, occupied the See of Peter from 202 to 219. During his Pontificate Emperor Severus raised the fifth most bloody persecution against the Church, which continued until the death of Severus in 211. St. Zephyrinus was the support and comfort of the persecuted Christians during those troublous times. He rejoiced at the triumph of the Martyrs, but his heart was deeply wounded by the fall of apostates and heretics. Eusebius tells us that this holy Pope exerted his zeal so vigorously against the blasphemies of the two heretics, that they treated him in the most insolent manner; but it was to his glory that they called him the principal defender of Christ's Divinity.

St. Zephyrinus was crowned by martrydom under the emperor Antoninus, and was buried on the Appian Way, near the cemetery of Callistus, on the seventh of the Calends of September (August 26).

✠

ST. JOSEPH CALASANCTIUS

St. Joseph Calasanctius was a native of Aragon, Spain. Born in 1556 of noble Christian parents, he was educated at Valencia. From early youth in his zeal for souls he taught Catechism to his companions. After he was ordained a Priest, New Castle, Aragon and Catalonia were edified by his holy life and apostolic works until in a vision he learned he should go to Rome, where he would find the task God wished him to undertake.

Moved at seeing so many of the unlearned poor living a sinful life, in 1617 he founded for their benefit the Congregation of Clerks Regular of the Pious Schools. For twenty years he labored among them, suffering ill-health as well as persecution from among his own subjects, who accused him to the Holy Office. At the age of eighty-six he was led through the streets to prison, and his Congregation, which Pope Gregory XV had permitted to make solemn vows, was reduced by Pope Alexander VII to its original state of simple vows. The privilege of making solemn vows was not restored until after the Saint's death. His life of sacrifice was crowned by a holy death in Rome on August 25, 1648, at the age of ninety-two.

✠

ST. AUGUSTINE OF HIPPO

St. Augustine, the most illustrious Doctor of the Church of Christ, was born on November 13, 354, at Tagaste, Africa. His father, Patricius, a pagan, was baptized a little before his death; his mother was St. Monica.

Augustine had been instructed in the rudiments of Christianity in his early youth but, like the prodigal son, at the age of sixteen had the misfortune to lose his Faith and innocence. He continued to lead his irregular life until he was thirty-two. Through his pride, at the age of twenty he fell into the Manichean heresy while at Carthage.

In his twentieth year he returned home to his mother at Tagaste and opened a school of grammar and rhetoric. His mother never ceased to pray for his conversion. In 375 Augustine went to Carthage, where he had spent four years pursuing his studies, and opened a school of rhetoric, where he taught for eight years. Disgusted at the disorderly behavior of the students, Augustine resolved to go to Rome. It was while there that he severed relationship with the Manicheans, with whom he had spent nine years. His search for truth finally led him to the One, True, Fold of Christ. Two Latin words: Tolle Lege; Tolle Lege: "Take up and read; Take up and read", caused him to peruse the Epistles of St. Paul. Opening the book his eyes fell upon the words, "Not in rioting and drunkenness; not in chambering and impurities; not in contention and envy; but put ye on the Lord Jesus Christ, and make not provision for the flesh in its concupiscences". (Romans 13:13, 14.) He read no further; all the darkness of his previous life was dispelled.

It was in the year 387, the thirty-second of his age, that after listening to sermons by St. Ambrose in Milan he was converted and was baptized. He intended to return to Africa with his mother, but she died unexpectedly while they were at Ostia. St. Augustine therefore spent a year in Rome and returned to Tagaste in 388. After distributing his goods to the poor he founded a monastery on one of his former estates, which was the beginning of the great Augustinian Order.

Early in 391, St. Augustine was ordained Priest by Valerius, and after settling in Hippo was consecrated Bishop in 395. The following year he succeeded Bishop Valerius. On August 28, 430, while the Vandals were besieging his episcopal city, St. Augustine died. For thirty-five years he had been the center of ecclesiastical life in Africa, and the Church's greatest champion against heresy. Among his ninety-six works are his "Confessions" and the twenty books of "The City of God", familiar to many learned people of our own day; refutations of Manichaeism, Donatism, Pelagianism and other heresies of his time; and those that deal with spirituality, philosophy, history, exegesis and morals. More than 400 of his sermons and 217 of his letters are extant today.

St. Augustine was a philosopher and dogmatic theologian, as well as a mystic and a powerful controversalist.

✠

AUGUST 29

BEHEADING OF ST. JOHN THE BAPTIST

For four thousand years man longed and prayed for the advent of the Messiah promised by God to Adam and Eve in the Garden of Eden after they had disobeyed His command. In the Eternal Providence of God the one chosen as the "Forerunner of the Messiah", and to announce His arrival when that time came, was St. John the Baptist.

The Gospel of St. Luke describes the announcement to the High Priest Zacharias that he and his wife Elizabeth, both in their advanced age, were to be blessed with a son "whose nativity shall rejoice many", "who shall be filled with the Holy Ghost even from his mother's womb", "who shall go before Him in the spirit and power of Elias".

The mother of St. John was the cousin of Mary, the Mother of Jesus, who rose up after the announcement of her Divine Motherhood and the motherhood of her aged cousin for the visit which brought forth sanctification of St. John in the womb of his mother and the praise "Blessed art thou among women, and blessed is the fruit of thy womb", to be followed by the glorious "Magnificat" of Mary.

After reaching manhood St. John led an austere, penitential, holy life for many years in the desert. He pointed out Jesus to the people by the Sea of Galilee, and later poured the water of Baptism over Him. It was he who upbraided the tetrarch Herod Antipas for having defied the Divine and human laws and married Herodias, wife of his brother. For this reproof Herod imprisoned St. John. About a year later Herod celebrated his birthday by inviting many of the prominent people of Galilee. On that occasion Salome, the daughter of Herodias by her lawful husband, was present. Salome's dancing so pleased Herod that he swore he would give her anything she desired even though it would be half of his kingdom. Salome sought her mother's advice. Herodias suggested that she ask that the head of St. John the Baptist be brought immediately to her on a dish.

Having made the oath, though an iniquitous one, Herod acquiesced to the girl's demand, and ordered that St. John be beheaded. Thus died the Forerunner of Jesus, about a year before the death of Our Savior.

The Baptist's head, or part of it, is venerated in the Church of St. Sylvester in Rome. Another portion is honored in Amiens, France, having been brought there during the Crusades.

Let no Christian ever forget the encomium which fell from the lips of Jesus regarding His Forerunner:

"Amen I say to you, there hath not risen among them that are born of women a greater than John the Baptist". (Matt. 11:11.)

✠

AUGUST 30

ST. ROSE OF LIMA

It seems that God allowed one of the oracles of heathen Peru to predict the birth and virtues of a child of the Incas, long before Christianity came among them in 1531. The prophecy ran thus: "When a strange (or foreign) race shall conquer Peru, the sun will claim his bride from among the daughters of the Incas, and thus the family of the children of the sun may return whence they came". This tradition has come down through the centuries among the Peruvians, and they believe it to have been fulfilled in St. Rose of Lima.

When Rose was born in 1586, only fifty years after the Spanish conquest, she was noble by right of her Peruvian mother, in whose veins flowed the blood of the Incas, as well as on the father's side, who came from a Spanish family of high descent. The child was baptized Isabel, but their parents soon changed her name to Rose on account of her beauty.

While still a mere child, her parents were astonished to see her refuse little dainties of which children are so fond, and to take in their place the coarsest, least refreshing food on the table. When Rose was five years old, one day as she was playing with her brother, he threw, accidentally, some mud against her hair. She did not show any signs of anger, but as she turned to leave him, he said gravely: "Do not be displeased, my sister; I did not mean to do it. Besides, the ringlets of girls are sometimes cards that draw them to perdition". The words sank deep into her heart. She recalled having been told why her name had been changed. One night, dreaming of this, Rose saw the Blessed Virgin Mary, to whom she told her uneasiness. This heavenly Mother, who is called "A rose among thorns", replied to her: "Your name, dear child, is very pleasing to my Son; henceforth you are to call yourself Rose of Mary".

Her father suddenly lost his fortune. Rose regarded this as an opportunity to practice her favorite virtues, and her fidelity was equaled by her cheerfulness. In vain did her parents put before her the advantages of a good marriage, for she had already chosen her Spouse, and she would serve Him, like St. Catherine of Siena, as a humble daughter of St. Dominic in his Third Order. This permitted

Almighty God, dispenser of all good gifts, You provided blessed Rose with the dew of heavenly grace, and willed her to bloom among the Indians for the splendor of virginity and of patience. Grant to us, Your servants, to follow the fragrance of her sweetness, and to be worthy to become the sweet odor of Christ.

her to live with her family, and to continue to serve them. Every Saturday Rose adorned the Chapel of the Rosary from her garden. She was very skillful with her needle, and delighted in embroidering the vestments and laces used at the altar.

Once when there was no money to buy bread, Rose went to the closet and opened the chest, believing that God would provide for them, and there, indeed, were the loaves she desired, only whiter and of more beautiful shape than she had ever made. Another day when there was no honey, one of the necessaries of life in Peru, Rose went with confidence to the place where it was usually kept, and found sufficient to last them for eight months. Many other instances of favors received might be cited, but space forbids.

It was Rose who encouraged the people of Lima to erect the convent of St. Catherine of Siena in Peru, and pledged her word that the money required would be supplied. When her mother tried to dissuade Rose from persisting in her extravagant notion, Rose replied; "Well, my mother, you will see all that I have said coming true; for you will enter this convent, in it receive the Habit of a religious, make your vows and die in the peace of the Lord". All of which came to pass.

Our Lord was pleased to reveal to Rose the time of her death, which took place on August 24, 1617. A short time before she died she was continually in raptures and ecstasies, notwithstanding the intense suffering she was undergoing. Two hours before she expired, she said to her confessor in confidence: "O father, what great things I could tell you of the pleasures and consolations which God will bestow upon His Saints for all eternity! I go with inconceivable delight to contemplate the adorable Face of God, Whom I have loved all my life". As she said twice, "Jesus be with me!" her ardent soul quitted earth for Heaven. She died in her thirty-first year, and was canonized in 1671.

✠

AUGUST 31

ST. RAYMUND NONNATUS

St. Raymund was born in Catalonia, Spain, in 1204, and at an early age entered the newly-founded Order of Our Lady of Ransom. Ordained in 1222, he spent nine years in North Africa ransoming Christian slaves. He finally gave himself as a hostage to obtain the liberty of one of them since he did not have the full amount of the ransom money demanded by the slave merchant at Tunis.

St. Raymund suffered terrible hardships for eight months before his Order succeeded in freeing him. Upon his return to Europe he was greatly venerated, and was raised to the Cardinalate by Pope Gregory IX.

On August 30, 1240, St. Raymund died a holy death, at the age of thirty-seven, as he was returning to Rome from a mission in Spain. Seized with a violent fever while at Cardona, he prepared himself for death. His relics are enshrined in the chapel of St. Nicholas, near the place where he formerly lived. Many miracles have been wrought through his intercession, and in 1657 his name was inserted by Pope Alexander VII in the Martyrology.

SEPTEMBER

SEPTEMBER 1
ST. GILES

St. Giles has been venerated for many ages in France and England. It is claimed that he was born in Athens, of noble extraction. As he found it impossible to enjoy the obscurity and retirement in his native country because his extraordinary piety and learning had attracted the world to himself, he sailed to Gaul (now France). At first he established himself in the wilderness near the mouth of the Rhone; then near the river Gard, and, finally, in a forest in the diocese of Nimes. He spent many years in solitude contemplating God. His only companion was a deer. The Saint's retreat was found by the King's hunters, who had pursued the animal to its place of refuge.

In time St. Giles consented to receive some disciples. He built a monastery for them in his valley, which he placed under the Rule of St. Benedict. The numerous miracles he wrought increased his reputation for sanctity throughout Gaul, and many churches have been erected in his honor.

St. Giles died in the 8th century.

✠

SEPTEMBER 2
ST. STEPHEN

Geysa, fourth Duke of Hungary, and his wife were converted to the Faith. In a dream she saw the Protomartyr St. Stephen, who assured her that the son she bore would complete the work she and her husband had commenced, and that he would abolish idolatry from the nation. The child was born in 977, and received the name Stephen at Baptism. Upon the death of his father, he succeeded him as King of the Hungarians when quite young, and proved to be an able, zealous ruler. He strove to root out idolatry, and converted many to the Christian religion. He founded many monasteries, churches and Bishoprics in Hungary, and dedicated the country to the Blessed Virgin Mary. He was anointed and crowned King of Hungary in the year 1000. Pope Sylvester II bestowed upon St. Stephen the title of "Apostolic King".

For centuries St. Stephen's excellent code of laws formed the basis of the laws of Hungary.

God sent His servant many severe trials, all of which he bore with Christian fortitude and perfect submission to His holy Will. Perceiving that his last hour was drawing near, he assembled his nobles and recommended the choice of a successor, obedience to the Holy See, and the practice of Christian piety. After receiving the Last Rites of the Church, he expired peacefully on the Feast of the Assumption of Our Lady, August 15, 1038. He was canonized by Pope Benedict IX.

✠

ST. PIUS X

Joseph Sarto, the eldest of ten children, was born of humble parents on June 2, 1835, at Riese in the diocese of Treviso, Italy. He evidenced extraordinary intellectual endowments, high moral character, and solid piety from early youth. After four years of study at the Latin School in Castelfranco, he availed himself of a scholarship to attend the seminary at Padua to study for the priesthood. His superiors were convinced of his sterling qualities of soul and of his solid piety.

Five years were spent at the seminary. During the final year he was appointed Director of Ecclesiastical Chant and of the seminary choir. He was ordained on September 18, 1858, in the Cathedral at Castelfranco.

Father Sarto's first appointment was to the parish church at Tombolo, in charge of the aged, gentle, wise Archpriest Antonio Constantini, who wrote prophetically:

"They have sent me as curate a young Priest, with orders to mould him to the duties of a pastor; in fact, however, the contrary is true. He is so zealous, so full of good sense and other precious gifts that it is I who can learn much from him. Some day or other he will wear the mitre, of that I am sure. After that—who knows?"

On July 14, 1867, after eight years of zealous, hard work at Tombolo, Father Sarto was appointed by Bishop Zinelli to be Archpriest of Salzano, in the diocese of Treviso, where he was "all things to all men". His favorite task was to instruct the children in the tenets of the Catholic Faith. He knew that "By the Catechism the soil is prepared for the seed of God".

Bishop Zinelli made Father Sarto Canon of the Cathedral of Treviso on November 28, 1875, appointed him Chancellor of the diocese, and spiritual director of the Seminary. When Bishop Zinelli died in 1879, Canon Sarto, who had been vicar general for three years, became the vicar capitular until a new Bishop was appointed in 1880.

In a consistory held on November 10, 1884, Pope Leo XIII named Canon Sarto to fill the difficult post of the Episcopal See of Mantua. He was consecrated Bishop on November 16, 1884, and assumed his duties on April 18, 1885. His achievements were manifold and far-reaching. God, again, blessed his labors.

Pope Leo XIII, on June 12, 1893, created Bishop Sarto Cardinal; three days later in a public consistory he was named Patriarch of Venice, which post he held for nearly ten years. His first act was to visit his dear mother at Riesi,

O God, for the protection of the Catholic faith and for the restoration of the universe in Christ, You filled holy Pius, the Supreme Pontiff, with celestial wisdom and apostolic fortitude. Grant that, following his teachings and examples, we may merit the eternal reward.

his boyhood home. Crowds thronged around his carriage as he traversed the road from Castelfranco, where fifty-five years previously he had walked barefoot to school with his shoes over his shoulders and a crust of bread in his pocket.

As at Tombolo, Salzano and Mantua, long hours were spent in teaching the old and young; giving sympathy and help to his flock.

On July 20, 1903, the long, fruitful pontificate of Leo XIII drew to a close. Cardinal Sarto was elected Pope on August 4, 1903; five days later the coronation ceremony took place in St. Peter's.

The pontificate of Pope St. Pius X abounds with an overflowing zeal "to restore all things in Christ". Liturgy—the Missal—the Breviary—Ecclesiastical Chant—Codification of Canon Law—Catholic Social Action—all these made demands upon his pastoral zeal. But he will always be known, primarily, as the Pope of the Holy Eucharist. For he was determined that the faithful should imitate the example of the earliest Christians. In consequence, he urged the reception of frequent and even daily Holy Communion for all in the state of sanctifying grace and of right intention. He insisted that children be allowed to the Spiritual Banquet prepared by Jesus at an earliest age, and declared that they were bound to fulfill the precept of the Easter Communion as soon as they reach the age of discretion.

In a series of more than fourteen pronouncements of the Holy See, nearly all within the year 1907, Pius X laid open, and, in so doing, destroyed the cancerous growth of Modernism which, in his day, with renewed force, threatened to undermine the organic life of the Church.

Pope St. Pius X labored until the very last days of his life. His Will and Testament contained the words: "I was born poor, I have lived poor, and I wish to die poor". He rendered his gentle soul to its Creator on the morning of August 20, 1914, and was canonized by Pope Pius XII, May 29, 1954.

✠

SEPTEMBER 4

ST. ROSALIA

St. Rosalia is venerated not only at Palermo, her native city, but throughout Sicily, of which she is patroness.

Rosalia was the daughter of Sinibald, who was descended from the imperial family of Charlemagne. From her earliest years Rosalia despised worldly honors and lived as a recluse in a cave on Mount Pelegrino, three miles from Palermo, where she died and was buried in 1160, after spending sixteen years in practicing austere penances whilst her soul was constantly united to God in prayer.

St. Rosalia's body was not found until the 17th century, buried in a grotto under the mountain. It is claimed that the Saint saved Sicily from the plague in 1625, and that innumerable cures have occurred since then at her shrine. In 1927 Pope Pius XI raised her feast day to the rank of a holy day of obligation in Palermo. The citizens celebrate it by carrying the Saint's shrine in procession on top of a large carriage filled with musicians, and drawn by forty mules. Prayers and hymns are sung in the Saint's honor, whilst displays of fireworks illuminate the sky overhead. Pope Urban VIII enrolled her in the Roman Martyrology.

✠

SEPTEMBER 5

ST. LAURENCE JUSTINIAN

St. Laurence Justinian, the first Patriarch of Venice, was born in that city in 1380. From early youth he longed to be a Saint, and at the age of nineteen, already blessed with the grace of supernatural prayer, entered the austere Congregation of the Canons Regular of St. George in Alga, near Venice, of which he later became the General, much against his inclination.

The fruit of the excellent spirit of prayer and compunction and the paths of interior virtue with which St. Laurence was endowed, enabled him after being ordained to the priesthood to prudently direct souls.

Pope Eugene IV, aware of the eminent virtue of St. Laurence, obliged him to leave his cloister and to accept the Bishopric of Venice in 1433. In this dignity he laid aside none of the austerities he had practiced in the cloister. He drew heavenly light, invincible courage, and indefatigable vigor from diligence in prayer, which directed and animated his conduct, and which enabled him also to pacify the most violent dissensions amongst the people. He governed a populous diocese in most difficult times, and solved great and intricate affairs with heavenly inspired aids.

An incredible number of people called daily at the holy Bishop's palace for advice, comfort and alms. And whilst the gate swung wide to all, the poor knew that his pantry and his meager funds would relieve their needs.

When the Patriarch of Grado died in 1451, Pope Eugene transferred the patriarchal dignity and office to the See of Venice.

St. Laurence was seventy-four years old when he wrote his last work, entitled, "The Degrees of Perfection". His writings on Mystical Contemplation are most sublime, yet simple. He died peacefully on January 8, 1455, and was canonized by Pope Alexander VIII in 1690.

✠

ST. ELEUTHERIUS

St. Eleutherius lived in the 6th century. He was Abbot of St. Mark's near Spoleto, Italy, and was noted for his humility and holiness. St. Gregory the Great, a contemporary, unable to fast one Easter eve, due to extreme weakness, requested Eleutherius to accompany him to the church of St. Andrew to implore God to grant him sufficient strength that he might be able to fast and to offer the Holy Sacrifice on the Feast of the Resurrection. The holy Abbot's prayers were answered.

St. Eleutherius resigned his Abbacy and died in St. Andrew's monastery in Rome, about the year 585. His body was afterwards translated to Spoleto.

✠

SEPTEMBER 7

ST. CLOUD

St. Cloud, or Clodoaldus, was born in 522, the third son of Clodomir, King of Orleans, France, and grandson of Clovis and St. Clotilde. Not quite three years old when his father was killed, Cloud and his two younger brothers, Theobald and Gunthaire, were cared for by their grandmother Clotilde in Paris. The children's self-seeking uncles, Childebert, King of Paris, and Clotaire, King of Soissons, after dividing the kingdom of Orleans between them, stabbed with their own hands Theobald, who was only eight years old, and Gunthaire, seven.

By a special Providence of God Cloud's life was spared, and in time he renounced the world to devote himself to the service of God in the monastic state. He rejected the many opportunities offered to recover his father's kingdom, preferring to strive for the heavenly realm.

After leading an austere life of prayer and holy contemplation for some time, he removed from his first hermitage and placed himself under the direction of St. Severinus, a holy recluse near Paris. It was from his hands that St. Cloud received the monastic habit. He made great progress in Christian perfection, but desiring to live unknown to the world withdrew secretly into Provence, where he spent several years, during which time he wrought many miracles.

Once his hermitage became known, many sought his spiritual help. Realizing that the remoteness of his solitude availed him nothing, St. Cloud returned to Paris, where he was received with great joy. At the earnest request of the people he was ordained to the priesthood in 551 by Bishop Eusebius of Paris. Later St. Cloud retired to Nogent (now called St. Cloud) on the Seine, where he built a monastery. He bestowed his entire inheritance on churches and in relieving the poor. He was indefatigable in instructing the people of the surrounding country.

St. Cloud died at Nogent about the year 560.

✠

SEPTEMBER 8

NATIVITY OF THE
BLESSED VIRGIN MARY

Out of purest love, God created man and placed him on earth. The happiness of Heaven was to be his, provided he observed the laws of his Creator. However, since our first parents, Adam and Eve, disobeyed God's law, they and their descendants—all mankind—forfeited the right to the heavenly bliss promised them. Pain, suffering and death became the lot of all men. And yet, the Eternal Creator, banishing our first parents out of Paradise, did not send them forth into a vale of tears bereft of all. He left to them the great virtue of hope—hope in a Redeemer, and a new chance to reach God's Kingdom. Foretelling how this should eventuate, God addressed the serpent: "I will put enmities between thee and the woman, and thy seed and her seed; she shall crush thy head" (Gen. 3:15).

It was the unsullied Lily of heavenly purity, the holy Virgin Mary, whom God looked upon with complacency and selected to be the Virgin-Mother of the Savior. By a special dispensation of God, Mary was conceived without the stain of original sin. From the first moment of her

Immaculate Conception God infused into her soul all the gifts of the Holy Spirit; she was "full of grace". No stain of sin ever marred the beauty of her soul.

On the 8th day of the month of Tisri (September), the anniversary day of the dedication of Solomon's Temple, Mary, the Mother of the world's Redeemer was born. What joy and happiness must have filled the souls of her beloved parents, St. Joachim and St. Anne!

According to some ancient writers, Mary was born near Jerusalem, and St. Luke (1:26) relates that at the time of the Annunciation she lived at Nazareth.

Mary exceeded in grace and beauty any human ever born, and she will be forever blessed among women.

✠

SEPTEMBER 9

ST. PETER CLAVER

During the 17th century the city of Cartagena on the northern shore of South America, was the central point in the struggle in which the European nations were engaged for the wealth of the New World. Its splendid harbor made it the market for all the treasures of Mexico, Peru, Potosi, and the West Indies. But it became the scene of the most hideous slave traffic that ever disgraced the name of man, and cried to Heaven for vengeance.

Amidst this avarice, corruption, and cruelty, God raised up a Saint who for forty years was the visible sign of His protecting Providence to hundreds of thousands of the most abject and abandoned of His creatures. It was the holy Peter Claver, "the slave of the slaves forever", as he named himself when he made his religious profession in the Society of Jesus. His life was one of heroic love, of unreserved sacrifice, of supreme mortification.

Peter was born at Verdu, near Barcelona, Spain, in June, 1581. At birth he was consecrated to God by pious parents. To promote as best they could the promise made, they sent their son to Solsona to pursue his studies, where he spent several years under the tutelage of an uncle who was a Canon of the Church. As the years passed the marks of a vocation to the priesthood grew clearer, and Peter was sent to Barcelona, where he would have an opportunity to cultivate the many gifts wherewith God had endowed him.

It was in this city that he learned to know the Society of Jesus, which he entered in August, 1602. He made his vows on August 8, 1604, and wrote at that time:

"I consecrate myself to God till death, looking on myself henceforth as a slave whose whole office lies in being at the service of his Master, and working with all my soul, body and mind to please and satisfy Him in all and by all".

Shortly afterwards he went to the Jesuit Seminary at Gerona, where he was employed in teaching. The following year he was sent to Majorca to pursue the studies in philosophy. Here at the Jesuit college he met St. Alphonsus Rodriguez, a lay brother and porter, advancing towards the close of a life of heroic virtue. The lay brother and porter received from God the glorious task of moulding to its great work the heart of the Apostle of the Negroes.

Peter Claver was ordained Priest in New Granada, Colombia, South America, in March, 1616, and in 1622 was sent to the Jesuit college at Cartagena. Ten or twelve thousand Negro slaves, torn away from their families and their native Africa were transported and unloaded yearly at this port. Covered with wounds and alive with vermin, they received neither pity from the white men who bought them nor a second thought from the slave traders who bartered them for beads and showy trifles.

It was to these poor, deeply afflicted human beings that Peter Claver devoted his life for nearly forty years. He was their apostle, father, physician and friend. He fed them and nursed them with the utmost tenderness in their loathsome diseases. No matter how tired he might be, when news reached him of the arrival of another slave-ship, St. Peter at once went on board to bring comfort for body and soul to his dear slaves.

God so blessed his labor, that he was able to baptize forty thousand of these African Negro slaves.

The Passion of Our Lord was the strongest attraction of St. Peter Claver's soul. He was often absorbed the entire night in contemplation, with a crown of very sharp thorns on his head. He died September 8, 1654.

When the news of the death of the great benefactor of the Negroes reached the inhabitants of the city, they cried, "The Saint is dead. The Saint is dead". Many miraculous cures attested the sanctity of the servant of God. He was canonized by Pope Leo XIII, and given the title of "Apostle of the Negroes".

✠

SEPTEMBER 10

ST. NICHOLAS OF TOLENTINO

St. Nicholas was born at St. Angelo, Italy, about 1245. His parents were poor in this world's goods, but rich in virtue. Advanced in years, they made a pilgrimage to the shrine of St. Nicholas of Bari, and earnestly implored God to send them a son who should faithfully serve Him. Their prayers were answered, and the child received the name of his patron at Baptism.

From his earliest years Nicholas seemed to have been gifted with an extraordinary share of divine grace. He had a tender love for the poor, fasted three days a week, and spent hours in prayer. He joined the hermits of St. Augustine at Tolentino, and was professed during his 18th year. He was assigned to several different houses of his Order, and while at Cingole was ordained Priest by the Bishop of Osimo. The last thirty years of his life were spent at Tolentino, where his zeal for souls produced wonderful fruit.

God favored St. Nicholas with many heavenly gifts and enabled him to cause a number of miraculous cures. After suffering various painful diseases for a long time, St. Nicholas died on September 10, 1306. He was canonized by Pope Eugene IV in 1446, and his tomb at Tolentino is held in veneration.

✠

SEPTEMBER 11

STS. HYACINTH AND PROTUS

It was towards the end of the 3rd century that these two brothers, Hyacinth and Protus, suffered martyrdom for the Faith during the persecution of the Christians by Valerian.

They were chamberlains to the holy virgin Eugenia, with whom they were baptized by Bishop Helenus. They studied sacred literature, and lived for some time in Egypt among the ascetics practicing humility and holiness of life. Later they accompanied Eugenia to Rome, where they were arrested during the reign of Gallienus on account of their profession of the Christian Faith, and were martyred.

In 1592 Pope Clement VIII caused the sacred remains of these Martyrs to be deposited in the church of St. John Baptist, belonging to the Florentines.

✠

SEPTEMBER 12

MOST HOLY NAME OF MARY

The feast of the Holy Name of Mary was instituted by Pope Innocent XI to commemorate the victory of the Christian army, under the command of John Sobieski, King of Poland, over that of the Turks near Vienna on September 12, 1683.

Devout Christians never tire of pronouncing the sweet name of Mary, and of exclaiming as St. Bernard did, "O clement, O loving, O sweet Virgin Mary".

✠

SEPTEMBER 13

ST. EULOGIUS

Eulogius, a Syrian by birth, became one of the most learned and one of the greatest lights of the Church in the century in which he lived. His sincere humility, together with his spirit of holy compunction and prayer, edified all with whom he came in contact.

The Eutychian heresy was at that time divided into various sects. The fury and tyranny of their quarrels had thrown the churches of Syria and Egypt into great confusion, whilst many of the Monks of Syria had become careless in their moral lives and had also adopted many errors against the Faith. In these grave dangers and needs of the Church Eulogius was recalled from his solitude and made Priest of Antioch by the Patriarch St. Anastasius. Eulogius, whilst living at Antioch, united with St. Eutychius, Patriarch of Constantinople, to combat the enemies of the truth.

In 583, upon the death of the Patriarch John of Alexandria, St. Eulogius was raised to that patriarchal dignity, at the earnest desire of Emperor Justinian. Two years later Eulogius was obliged to visit Constantinople regarding Church matters. Whilst there he met St. Gregory the Great, and there arose between them a close friendship. Several letters are extant which he wrote to Eulogius.

Many excellent works were written by St. Eulogius against the Acephali and other sects of the Eutychians; also six books against the Novatians of Alexandria. He died about the year 606.

✠

SEPTEMBER 14

THE TRIUMPH OF THE CROSS

The miraculous appearance of the Cross to Emperor Constantine who, in consequence became a Christian and gave freedom to the Christian Church, and the discovery of the true Cross by his mother, St. Helena, caused a Feast of the Exaltation of the Holy Cross to be celebrated at Jerusalem from the year 335. Later, but as early as the 5th and 6th centuries, it was promulgated as a general Feast among the Greeks and Latins.

ST. CATHARINE OF GENOA

St. Catharine was born at Genoa in 1447. From her earliest years she seemed to be a child of spiritual benedictions. She practiced heroic self-denial, possessed a serious love of prayer, and had great devotion toward the Sacred Passion of Christ. At twelve years of age God favored her with very special graces during the time of prayer. When thirteen years old she earnestly desired to consecrate herself to God in a contemplative Order. But, in obedience to her parents and following the advice of those from whom she sought God's holy Will, Catharine was married by her father to a young nobleman of Genoa. For ten years she suffered grievous afflictions from him; which contributed to her more perfect sanctification. His profligate life caused her to shed continual tears to God for his conversion. Her prayers, patience and good example finally effected this, and he died a penitent in the Third Order of St. Francis.

Now freed from the servitude of the world, Catharine desirous of uniting the active with the contemplative life by ministering to Christ in His sick-poor, determined to devote herself to the service of the sick in the large hospital of the city, of which she acted as Directress for many years, and attended the patients with incredible tenderness. Her charity extended beyond the hospital, even to lepers and other sick persons throughout the city.

The necessity for the spirit of universal mortification and perfect humility to prepare the way for the pure love of God to be infused into the soul, is the principal lesson which she inculcates in her treatises "On Purgatory" and "A Dialogue".

After suffering a long painful illness, St. Catharine expired in great peace and tranquillity on September 14, 1510, at the age of sixty-two. God was pleased to testify to her sanctity by many miracles. Eighteen months after her death, St. Catharine's body was found untouched by corruption. She was canonized by Pope Benedict XIV.

☩

SEPTEMBER 15

FEAST OF THE SEVEN SORROWS OF THE BLESSED VIRGIN MARY

The object of this Feast is the spiritual martyrdom of the Mother of God, and her compassion with the sufferings of her Divine Son.

The seven Founders of the Servite Order in 1239, five years after they established themselves on Monte Senario, standing under the Cross, took up the Sorrows of Mary as the principal devotion of their Order. The Feast observed on the Friday before Palm Sunday did not originate with them, but by a provincial synod at Cologne (1413) to expiate the crimes of the iconoclast Hussites. Prior to the 16th century it was limited to the dioceses of North Germany, Scandinavia and Scotland; afterwards it spread over part of Southern Europe and became popular in France. It was extended to the entire Latin Church by a Decree of Pope Benedict XIII on April 22, 1727.

By order of Napoleon, Pope Pius VII was arrested on July 5, 1808, and detained a prisoner for three years at Savona, and then at Fontainebleau. He was set free on March 17, 1814, the eve of the Feast of Our Lady of Mercy. The Pontiff attributed the victory of the Church, after so much agony and distress, to the Blessed Virgin, and on his triumphal march to Rome visited many of her shrines and crowned her images. The people thronged the streets to catch a glimpse of the venerable Pontiff who had so bravely withstood the threats of Napoleon. He entered Rome May 24, 1814, and was enthusiastically welcomed. In order to commemorate his sufferings and those of the Church during his exile, he extended the Feast of the Seven Sorrows of Mary to the Universal Church on September 18, 1814.

✠

SEPTEMBER 16

ST. CYPRIAN

St. Cyprian was born at Carthage about the year 210, the son of a noted Senator of that city. He became proficient in the liberal arts, in oratory, and in eloquence, and taught rhetoric at Carthage. For a long time he lived an evil life. God used Cecilius, a holy Priest, as His instrument to bring about the conversion of Cyprian. Soon after his Baptism he sold his estate and distributed the money to the poor, and then led a holy, retired, penitential life. At the earnest request of the people, he was raised to the priesthood. Less than a year later, upon the death of Bishop Donatus of Carthage, the clergy and people demanded that Cyprian be chosen to fill the vacant See. He served as Bishop of Carthage from 249 to 258.

The Church enjoyed peace for about a year after he was made Bishop. Then Decius raised his bloody persecution against the Christians. The edict reached Carthage early in the year 250. No sooner was it made public than the idolators ran to the market place crying: "Cyprian to the lions. Cyprian to the wild beasts". Because of his remarkable conversion and zeal his name had become odious to the pagans.

When St. Cyprian was condemned to be put to death by the sword, he replied: "Blessed be God". He was martyred on September 14, 258, in the presence of many of his sorrowing flock, during the reign of Valerian.

✠

SEPTEMBER 17

THE IMPRESSION OF THE STIGMATA OF ST. FRANCIS

In 1224, on Mount Alvernia, St. Francis of Assisi received the Stigmata, or Impression on his body of the five Sacred Wounds of Our Lord Jesus Christ.

Regarding this miraculous event, St. Bonaventure, a contemporary of St. Francis, wrote:

"Two years before the truly faithful servant and minister of Christ, Francis, gave back his soul to Heaven, he retired apart into a high place, which is called Mount Alvernia, and began a forty-day fast in honor of the Archangel Michael. . . . One morning, about the feast of the Exaltation of the Holy Cross, as he was praying on the mountain-side, he saw what appeared to be a Seraph, with six shining and fiery wings, coming down from the highest heavens. It flew very swiftly through the air and approached the man of God, who then perceived that it was not only winged, but also crucified; for the hands and feet were stretched out and fastened to a cross; while the wings were arranged in a wondrous manner, two being raised above the head, two outstretched in flight, and the remaining two crossed over and veiling the whole body. As he gazed, Francis was much astonished, and his soul was filled with mingled joy and sorrow. The gracious aspect of him, who appeared in so wonderful and intimate a manner, rejoiced him exceedingly, while the sight of his cruel crucifixion pierced his heart with a sword of sorrowing compassion.

"He who appeared outwardly to Francis, taught him inwardly that, although weakness and suffering are by no means compatible with the immortal life of a seraph, yet this vision had been shown to him, that, as a friend of Christ, he might learn how his whole being was to be transformed into a living image of Christ Jesus crucified, not by martyrdom of the flesh, but by the burning ardor of his soul. After a mysterious and intimate colloquy, the vision disappeared, leaving the Saint's mind burning with seraphic ardor; and his flesh was impressed with an exact image of the Crucified, as though, after the melting power of that fire, it had next been stamped with the impress of a seal. For immediately the marks of nails began to appear in his hands and feet, those of the heads in the palms of his hands and the upper part of his feet, and their points visible on the other side. There was also a red scar on his right side, as if it had been wounded by a lance, and from which blood often flowed, staining his tunic."

✠

SEPTEMBER 18

ST. JOSEPH OF CUPERTINO

Joseph Desa was born at Cupertino, Italy, of poor, but virtuous parents. From early youth he showed signs of extraordinary fervor, and lived an austere, mortified life. At the age of seventeen he asked to be received amongst the Conventual Franciscans, but was refused because he had failed to pursue the necessary studies. He was accepted, however, as a lay-Brother by the Capuchins, but after eight months was dismissed, as he was not able to perform the required duties. Undaunted, he persisted in his resolution to embrace the religious state. Finally the Franciscans were moved to compassion and received him in their monastery at Grotella, near Cupertino.

After a most fervent novitiate Joseph made his vows and was received as a lay-Brother. He performed the lowly tasks assigned with perfect fidelity; redoubled his fasts and austerities; prayed constantly, and took only three hours sleep nightly. His humility, sweetness, love of mortification and penance gained him so much veneration that he was permitted to prepare for the priesthood. He was ordained in 1628, and was gifted by God with ecstatic prayer. He wrought numerous miracles during life and after his holy death, which occurred at Osimo, near Ancona, in 1672. He was canonized by Pope Clement XIII in 1767.

✠

SEPTEMBER 19

ST. JANUARIUS AND COMPANIONS

It was during the persecution of Diocletian, in 305, that St. Januarius, who was Bishop of Benevento, Italy, and other loyal Christians suffered martyrdom for the Faith. Upon learning that Sosius, Deacon of Misenum, Proculus, Deacon of Pozzuoli, and some prominent laymen had been imprisoned at Pozzuoli for professing their Faith, Januarius determined to go to see them in order to give them comfort and encouragement. The inquisitive keepers reported that an eminent person from Benevento had visited the Christian prisoners.

Timothy, who governed that district, ordered that Januarius, whom he found to be the visitor, should be arrested and brought before him at Nola. The Bishop's Deacon, Festus, and Desiderius, who were visiting the Bishop at the time, were also apprehended and shared in Januarius' sufferings. Soon afterwards, when Timothy went to Pozzuoli, these three confessors, loaded with irons, were obliged to walk before his chariot to that town. They were cast into the same prison where some other loyal Christians were being detained; they had been condemned by the Emperor to be thrown to the wild beasts and were awaiting execution of the sentence.

The day after St. Januarius and his companions arrived all were exposed in the amphitheater, but not one was harmed by the wild animals. The people, amazed, attributed their preservation to magic. The Martyrs were then condemned to be beheaded, and the sentence was executed near Pozzuoli.

About the year 400 the relics of St. Januarius were translated to Naples, which city honors him as its patron Saint. The people give him credit for delivering them from the plague in 1497, and for saving their city on several occasions when it was in danger of destruction from the eruption of Mount Vesuvius. Three times a year—on his Feast day September 19, December 16, and on the first Sunday in May—a sealed phial which contains the congealed blood of St. Januarius, when placed near the Martyr's head, liquifies and bubbles up. This miraculous event has occurred, with rare exceptions, ever since the translation of the Saint's body to Naples.

☩

SEPTEMBER 20

ST. EUSTACHIUS AND COMPANIONS

St. Eustachius, a nobleman, and his wife Theopista were known as Placidus and Tatiana before their conversion to Christianity. They had two sons, Agapius and Theopistus.

According to legend, Eustachius, while still a heathen served as a Roman general under Trajan. One day he saw a stag approaching with a crucifix between its horns, and at the same time he heard a voice telling him that he would suffer much for Christ's sake. He received Baptism, together with his wife and two sons. The vision is said to have occurred at Guadagnolo, between Tivoli and Palestrina, near Rome.

Loss of fortune caused the family to be separated for a while. Because Eustachius refused to sacrifice to the idols, Trajan was infuriated and ordered him and his family to be exposed to the lions. Not being harmed, they later suffered death in a heated bronze bull.

A church in honor of St. Eustachius was erected in Rome in ancient times, and his body rested therein until the 12th century, when it was translated to the Church of St. Denis in Paris. Some of the Martyr's bones were burnt by the Hugenots in 1567, but a portion of them still are venerated in the church of St. Eustachius in Paris.

✠

SEPTEMBER 21

ST. MATTHEW

St. Matthew, son of Alpheus and a native of Galilee, was employed as a publican, or tax-collector, for the Romans. As he sat one day in the customhouse by the lake at Capharnaum, Jesus passed by. The Savior said to him, "Follow Me"; and Matthew rose from his place and followed Him. Thus he was one of the Twelve chosen by Jesus to be an Apostle; he is also one of the four Evangelists. He wrote his Gospel, prior to the destruction of Jerusalem in 70 A.D., to prove to the converts from Judaism that Jesus was their Savior and King Who had been foretold by the Prophets.

The Jews considered the publicans as enemies of their country, as outcasts, and as notorius sinners; the Pharisees even refused to sit at table with a publican.

After his conversion, Matthew invited Jesus and His disciples and some of the publicans to dine at his home. When the Pharisees complained because the Master ate with publicans and sinners, Jesus said to them, "They that are in health need not the physician. I have not come to call the just, but sinners to penance".

St. Irenaeus says that St. Matthew preached the Gospel among the Hebrews; whilst St. Clement of Alexandria states that this mission lasted fifteen years. Other ancient writers claim that St. Matthew labored in Persia, Syria, Greece and Ethiopia. His shrine is at Salerno, Italy, whither his relics were translated in the 11th century.

✠

SEPTEMBER 22

ST. THOMAS OF VILLANOVA

St. Thomas was born at Castile, Spain, in 1488, of pious, charitable parents. At the age of sixteen he entered the University of Alcala, where, after receiving the master of arts and licentiate in theology, he filled the chair of arts, logic and philosophy.

In 1516, Thomas joined the Augustinians, and two years later was ordained to the priesthood. He held many offices of trust in his Order. He was an eloquent and zealous orator, and preached in the chief pulpits in Spain.

St. Thomas was called to the See of Valencia in 1544. Ten years later he received his nomination to the Archbishopric of Valencia. During his eleven years of episcopate rule he performed many noteworthy deeds. Among them were the founding of two colleges, one for young ecclesiastics, and the other for poor students; the rebuilding of the general hospital at Valencia, which had been destroyed by fire; the abolishment of underground prisons, and the distribution of all his earthly goods in order to help the poor.

St. Thomas wrote many valuable sermons on Ascetical and Mystical Theology. He died in 1555, and was canonized by Pope Alexander VII on November 1, 1658.

St. Thomas' title "of Villanova" was given because he was educated in that city.

May the prayers of the blessed Apostle and Evangelist Matthew aid us, O Lord. Through his intercession, may we obtain that which we cannot by our own possibility.

✠

SEPTEMBER 23

ST. THECLA

St. Thecla, a celebrated Saint who lived during the time of the Apostles, was converted at Iconium in Lycaonia by St. Paul when he preached there. At the age of eighteen she left her betrothed, and when her parents accused her of being a Christian, having first fortified herself with the sign of the Cross, she flung herself upon the burning pyre which had been prepared for her unless she renounced Christ. But the fire was extinguished by a sudden shower of rain. Later she went to Antioch, where she was cast to the wild beasts and bound to bulls driven in different directions, and then thrown into a pit full of serpents; but from all these she was set free by the grace of Jesus Christ.

Many were converted to Christ by St. Thecla's ardent faith and holy life. She once more returned to her native country and withdrew into solitude on a mountain. At length, renowned for many virtues and miracles, she passed to the Lord at the age of ninety and was buried at Seleucia.

✠

SEPTEMBER 24

OUR LADY OF RANSOM

In the 13th century when the terrible Saracen yoke oppressed the greater and more fertile part of Spain, and when many of the faithful were enslaved, at the risk of denying the Christian Faith and losing their eternal salvation, the most blessed Queen of Heaven graciously hastened to remedy these evils, and showed her exceeding

charity in ransoming them. For she herself appeared to
the holy Peter Nolasco, a man noted for his wealth and
piety, who, for some time had been striving to determine
means of helping the innumerable Christians living in
hardship as captives of the Moors. She told him it would
be very pleasing to her and to her only Son if a religious
Order were to be founded in her honor, whose members
should devote themselves to delivering captives from the
tyranny of the Turks. She likewise appeared to St. Raymund of Pennafort and King James of Aragon, making the
same request of them.

Consequently, on August 10, 1218, King James established by decree the royal, military and religious Order
of Our Lady of Ransom, and granted to its members the
privilege of bearing on their breasts his own arms. The
majority were knights, and while the clerics recited the
Divine Office in the commanderies, they guarded the coasts
and delivered the prisoners. It was not long before this
noble work spread everywhere. It produced heroes of sanctity and men of incomparable charity who collected alms
for the ransom of Christians. Many of them gave themselves
up as ransoms to deliver captives.

☩

SEPTEMBER 25

ST. FIRMIN

St. Firmin, Bishop of Amiens, was a native of Pam-
pelone in Navarre, Gaul. He was instructed in the Christian
Faith by Honestus, a disciple of St. Saturninus of Toulouse.
To enable him to preach the Gospel in the remoter parts
of Gaul, St. Firmin was consecrated Bishop by St. Honoratus, successor to St. Saturninus.

On his journey northward St. Firmin preached the
Faith in Agen, Anjou and Beauvais. When he reached

Amiens, he fixed his abode there and founded a church of faithful disciples. He received the crown of martyrdom in that city towards the end of the 3rd century.

✠

SEPTEMBER 26

ST. ISAAC JOGUES AND COMPANIONS

St. Isaac Jogues was born in 1607 at Orleans, France. He was the fifth child of a family of nine, and was extremely modest and prayerful—prime requisites for sanctity. Time was to prove that he was as great a Saint as the world has ever seen.

He entered the Jesuit novitiate in Rouen, and from there was sent to the college of La Fleche, where he made progress, without distinguishing himself. Convinced that he did not have a scholar's make-up, when the time came for him to receive his assignment, he asked to be sent as a missionary to Constantinople. However, when his spiritual director informed him, with prophetic insight, that his vocation was to labor and die in the New World, he acquiesced with joy. He was one of a group, which included Jean de Brebeuf, Charles Garnier, Gabriel Lalemant, Natalis Chabanel, Jean de Lalande, Anthony Daniel and Rene Goupil, that left France for North America.

After a short stay at Quebec and Three Rivers, Isaac Jogues was appointed to the Huron missions. He labored among the Indians, enduring many trials, sufferings and hardships, with very few conversions. It was most difficult to overcome their superstition, paganism, lack of trust in the White Man and interest in Christianity. After many years of work among the Hurons, Isaac Jogues was journeying with two companions between Montreal and Three Rivers when they were ambushed and captured by the Iroquois. His two companions, after great torture, were finally martyred. Isaac managed to escape, and eventually got back to France, his body and features so changed from all he had undergone, that he was not recognized when he arrived at the Jesuit College of Rennes.

Pope Clement VIII granted him permission to say Mass, which the mutilated state of his fingers would ordinarily have made impermissible. After a period of rest and care, St. Isaac Jogues returned to Canada and the Indians. He suffered martyrdom for the Faith near the present site of Auriesville, New York, on September 16, 1646. He and his companions were beatified by Pope Pius XI on June 21, 1925, and on June 29, 1930, they were canonized by the same Pope.

✠

SEPTEMBER 27

SS. COSMAS AND DAMIAN

Cosmas and Damian were brothers, born in Arabia. They became renowned as physicians in Syria, refusing to accept any remuneration for their services. Being devout Christians they healed not only the bodies of men, but also their souls. Their apostolic work soon reached the ears of Lysias, Governor of Cilicia, who ordered them brought before him to question them regarding their profession of faith and their manner of life. When they declared they were Christians and that the Christian Faith is necessary to salvation, they were subjected to various tortures and finally beheaded. This occurred during the persecution of Diocletian, about the year 303. Their bodies were later transported to Cyr, in Syria.

In the 5th century, Bishop Theodoret of that city mentions that the relics of these Saints were placed there in a church which bears their names. The relics were later brought to Rome, where Pope St. Felix erected a church in their honor.

Saints Cosmas and Damian have always been greatly venerated in the East and in the West.

✠

SEPTEMBER 28

ST. WENCESLAUS

Wenceslaus, Duke of Bohemia, was born of a Christian father, Wratislaus, and a pagan mother, Drahomira. They had another son, Boleslaus. The education of Wenceslaus, the elder son, was entrusted to his grandmother Ludmilla, a devout Christian, who lived at Prague. With the utmost care she endeavored to instill into his mind and heart a sincere devotion and love of God. On the other hand, Boleslaus was influenced by his cruel, pagan mother.

When the children were quite young their father died. Drahomira assumed the title of regent, seized the government, and gave vent to her rage against the Christians by closing the churches and forbidding Priests and others to teach the Christian religion.

Ludmilla encouraged Wenceslaus to assume control of the government. The young Duke obeyed, and the Bohemians showed their approval by dividing the country between him and his younger brother Boleslaus. Drahomira was enraged, and influenced Boleslaus in his hatred of Christianity. Wenceslaus strove to establish peace and justice in his dominions and to convert his subjects to Christianity. He ruled his kingdom by kindness rather than by authority. He had great devotion to Jesus in the Blessed Sacrament. Not content to pray in the churches during the day, he often rose at midnight to go and pray before the Blessed Sacrament. His mother never ceased to plot against him. She looked upon Ludmilla as the prime mover of all counsels in favor of the Christian religion, and plotted to take her life. The assassins found her prostrate in prayer in her domestic chapel, seized her, and strangled her with her own veil. She is honored in Bohemia as a martyr.

This crime grieved Wenceslaus. His piety was the occasion of his death. He had been treacherously invited to a banquet by his brother, at the instigation of their mother. Then Boleslaus, together with some wicked accomplices, killed him as he was praying in the church, aware of the death that awaited him. His blood is still to be seen sprinkled on the walls; and, by the vengeance of God, the earth swallowed up the inhuman mother, and the murderers perished miserably in various ways.

✠

SEPTEMBER 29

ST. MICHAEL THE ARCHANGEL

In the 10th chapter of Daniel (v. 13), St. Michael is called "one of the chief princes" who came to help him resist the King of the Persians. And in the 12th chapter of the Apocalypse (v. 10), we are given a vivid description of the battle in Heaven, during which the Archangel Michael and his Angels fought with the rebellious Angels over whom St. Michael triumphed, after which Satan and his Angels were cast into hell.

St. Michael is the leader of the Angelic Host. His name, Michael, means "Who is like to God?"—his battle cry in the encounter with the devil.

Whenever any work of great power is to be done, it is St. Michael who is chosen to be sent. He came to help the children of Israel; he prepared the Israelites for their return from Persian captivity; he led the brave Macchabees to victory, and he rescued the body of Moses from the hands of the devil.

St. Michael has always been invoked by the Church, both in the East and in the West, to "defend us in the battle" against the powers of darkness. In the 4th century a church was built near Constantinople and dedicated to him.

On May 8, 492, St. Michael appeared on Mount Gargano, in southern Italy, and the place became one of frequent pilgrimage. France honors St. Michael as patron of

Mariners at the famous shrine in Brittany, called Mont St. Michele.

During the plague in Rome in the 6th century, Pope Gregory the Great saw St. Michael in a vision sheathing his flaming sword to show that he would put an end to the scourge which was ravaging the city. In 608 a church was erected over Hadrian's mausoleum in thanksgiving to St. Michael for the help he gave.

✠

SEPTEMBER 30

ST. JEROME

St. Jerome, son of Eusebius, was born at Stridonium in Dalmatia in 329, during the reign of Emperor Constantine. He was baptized at an early age in Rome, in which city he was instructed in the liberal arts by Donatus and other learned men. Without a proper guide he neglected to lead a virtuous life, as he later confessed and bitterly lamented.

Desirous of further knowledge, Jerome decided to travel. In his first journeys he was led by the mercy of God into the paths of virtue and salvation. He first visited Gaul, where he met some learned, pious men, and he copied many sacred books with his own hand. He arrived at Trier shortly before the year 370, and it was in this city that the sentiments of piety which he had imbibed in his early youth were awakened, and his heart was entirely converted to God. He then proceeded to Greece, where he studied oratory and philosophy, and made friends with some of the greatest theologians. He studied under St. Gregory of Nazianzen at Constantinople, by whom he was taught sacred learning, and then he returned to Rome to answer God's call. After making a vow of celibacy, he went to Antioch; then fled to the wild Syrian desert, where he spent four

O God, You distribute the ministry of Angels and of men with ad-mirable order. Graciously grant that our earthly life may be protected by those who in Heaven continuously assist You and serve You.

years reading the Scriptures, contemplating heavenly beatitude, and constantly afflicting his body by abstinence,
weeping, and every kind of penance. His health impaired,
he left the desert and went to Antioch, where he received
Holy Orders from the hands of Paulinus, Patriarch of that
city, before the end of 377. He then returned to Rome to
settle the disputes that had arisen between certain Bishops,
and Pope Damasus engaged him to assist in writing his
ecclesiastical letters. After the Pontiff's death, envy and
calumny were hurled against St. Jerome. His reputation
was attacked most outrageously. After staying several years
in Rome, St. Jerome, yearning for solitude, returned to
the East in 385. He visited St. Epiphanus at Cyprus, and
then stopped at Antioch on his way to Palestine. The following spring he went to Egypt to improve himself in sacred
learning and in the perfect observances of the monastic
life, after which he returned to Palestine.

According to St. Augustine, St. Jerome had a remarkable knowledge not only of Latin and Greek, but also of
Hebrew and Chaldaic, and had read almost every author.
He translated the Old Testament from the Hebrew, and, at
the command of Pope Damasus, the New Testament from
the Greek. Besides this, he translated into Latin the writings of many learned men, and enriched Christian learning
from his own pen.

The Pelagians the year following the Council of Dios-
polis, in 416, sent bandits to Bethlehem to assault the holy
Monks and Nuns who lived under the direction of St. Jerome. The Saint escaped with great difficulty. He became
the target of hatred of all the enemies of the Church.
Having reached the age of ninety-one, and being renowned
for learning and holiness, St. Jerome passed to his heavenly
reward on September 30, 420, during the reign of Emperor
Honorius. His body was buried at Bethlehem, but was later
translated to the Basilica of St. Mary Major in Rome.

OCTOBER

ST. REMIGIUS

St. Remigius, the great apostle of France, was one of the shining lights of the Church of Gaul. Illustrious for his learning, eloquence, sanctity and miracles, at the age of twenty-two he became Bishop of Rheims. His episcopacy covered the years of Clovis, King of the Franks, whom he baptized. He led the Franks to the Faith of Christ the Lord by his teaching and miracles; raised a dead girl to life by his prayers; expounded many books of Holy Scripture; and governed the Church of Rheims in the most praiseworthy manner for more than seventy years. By his zealous endeavors he promoted the Catholic Faith in Burgundy, and completely crushed idolatry and the Arian heresy in the French dominions.

St. Remigius died in 533, during the ninety-fourth year of his age. The holiness of his life and death was proved by many miracles which later occurred. The holy Archbishop was buried at Rheims. In 852, and again in 1646, the Saint's body was found incorrupt.

✠

THE HOLY GUARDIAN ANGELS

In the Apocalypse we have St. John, its author, writing: "After I had heard and seen, I fell down to adore before the feet of the Angel who showed me these things; and he said to me: See thou do it not; for I am thy fellow-servant. . . . Adore God." Here, in this passage, one of the three Apostles who on Mt. Thabor witnessed the glory of Jesus in His transfiguration tells us that he was misled by the beauty and brilliancy of a heavenly spirit, but that he was corrected by the same spirit and told to adore God alone. Evidently St. John, who was about to offer supreme worship, mistook the Angel for the Son of God.

The confession by the beloved disciple of Our Lord must open our eyes to the worth of immortal souls, as also the beneficence of the Creator. For in that moment when God permitted us to make our entrance into the world He selected from the ranks of those whose glory deceived St. John, individual spirits, and gave them a charge and a command to watch over and protect our souls unto the day when, the present light fading, the brightness of the Beatific Vision will encircle us. Created, according to the Inspired Word, and made only a "little less than the Angels" we are entrusted to one of Heaven's hosts—our Guardian Angel.

A great fault—perhaps the greatest—of weak humanity is its failure to appreciate God's kindnesses. It would not be too much to expect that men on earth would vie with the blessed in Heaven and continuously sing the praises of the mercies of the Creator. Instead, we are confronted quite generally with forgetfulness, and very often with positive ingratitude.

Who will question that among the most precious gifts of God's mercy to men must be reckoned the Angel who, in the words of the Psalmist, has received "charge over us to keep us in our ways"? He, following the command of God, watches with tender care over the preservation of our bodies, our health and our life. He, with clearest knowledge that our immortal souls far surpass in worth our bodies, is continuously alert in safeguarding them. It is the Guardian Angel that suggests good thoughts to our minds, that warns us against dangers, that encourages and sustains us in times of temptation, that reproves our faults and gently leads us back to God if we should have lost Him by grievous sins. The Guardian Angel will stand by us in the hour of death. He will not leave us when our souls languish in Purgatory; there he will console us and, thence, finally, he will lead us into Heaven.

Oh, when shall ungrateful man recognize the gifts of God and thank Him! The month of October is dedicated by the Church to the Guardian Angels. Can we not, during this month, put forth an effort to show our appreciation of God's selection of a heavenly spirit to be our companion, guide and protector?

✠

OCTOBER 3

ST. THERESE OF THE CHILD JESUS

Therese Martin was born at Alencon, France, January 2, 1873. She was the ninth and youngest child, but as four of the children died in their infancy, she was the youngest of the five surviving, who were all girls. All five subsequently embraced the religious life, four of them, among whom was Therese, entered the Carmel of Lisieux; the other one, the Visitation Convent at Caen.

When Therese was about four and one-half years old her mother died, and her father left Alencon with his five children for Lisieux, in order that they might be near their mother's relatives. At the age of eight Therese was sent to the Benedictine Convent at Lisieux to be educated. Soon thereafter her sister Pauline, who had been a second mother to Therese, decided to enter the Carmelite Order. This turned the child's thoughts and aspirations towards the religious life, and she never wavered in her resolution to become a Carmelite. However, she had to pass through many trials.

The first was a serious illness, which terminated during the course of a novena to Our Lady of Victories. The statue of Our Lady in her room appeared to the child to advance towards her, and to smile graciously upon her.

When Therese was thirteen her eldest sister, Marie, followed Pauline's example and entered the Carmel of Lisieux. From that time until Therese entered Carmel two years later, Celine became her confidante. When she reached the age of fourteen and a half, Therese spoke to her father of her desire, and while he gave his consent, her uncle and the Superior of the convent opposed the entry of one so young. Therese then pleaded her cause with the Bishop of Bayeux. He encouraged her to go on the diocesan pilgrimage to Rome, and he promised to speak to the Superior of the convent in Lisieux. Nothing could shake the child's firm resolution to become a Spouse of Jesus.

She accompanied her father on the pilgrimage, and during the course of the interview given to the pilgrims by Pope Leo XIII, Therese fell at his knees and said to him: "Holy Father, I have a great favor to ask you. In honor of your jubilee, will you allow me to enter Carmel when I am fifteen?" The Vicar-General, surprised and displeased, said: "Holy Father, this is a child who desires to become a Carmelite, but the Superiors of the Carmel are looking into the matter". "Well, my child", replied His Holiness, "do whatever the Superiors decide." She clasped her hands, rested them on his knee, and made a final effort. "Holy Father, if only you say 'yes', everyone else would agree". He looked at her fixedly, and said clearly and emphatically: "Well, well! you will enter if it is God's Will".

Therese entered the Carmel of Lisieux on April 9, 1888; her investiture took place on January 10, 1889, and she was professed on September 8, 1890. She cried, in the fervor of her soul on that day, "My Jesus, grant me martyrdom, either of the heart or of the body, or rather give me both". God, Who, according to her own avowal, never refused her anything, granted her this request. Her life at Carmel was a continual martyrdom, all the more painful because so unsuspected.

She had a most tender love for Christ and the Church, and by her self-denial and self-sacrifice desired to assist Priests and missionaries, and to gain innumerable souls to Jesus Christ; all of which, when dying, she promised that she would obtain from God.

Therese's soul bloomed with the flowers of every virtue. When she read in the Sacred Scriptures, "Whosoever

O Lord, You have said: Unless you become as little children you shall not enter into the kingdom of Heaven. Grant that we may follow in humility and simplicity of heart the footsteps of the holy Virgin Theresa, so that we may arrive at the eternal reward.

is a little one, let him come unto Me" (Prov. 9:4), she determined to be a little one in spirit, and committed herself with childlike confidence to God forever, as to a most loving Father. She taught this path of spiritual childhood to the novices when but twenty-two years old, and she remained a "little one" to the end of her life. It is her mission to teach souls her Little Way to Heaven. Filled with apostolic zeal, she exemplified the path of evangelical simplicity to a world full of pride and vanity.

Her longing for sanctity redoubled itself under her trials. But Soeur Therese of the Child Jesus was not destined to feed for long the little flock committed to her charge. In April, 1896, a hemorrhage of the lungs conveyed to her the first intimation of her coming end. It was not until the beginning of July, 1897, that she was sent to the infirmary. Rapt in ecstasy, and frequently repeating the words, "My God, I love Thee", she went to meet her Spouse on September 30, 1897, at the age of twenty-four.

Two years before her death, Soeur Therese offered herself as a victim to the love of the merciful God, and when she was dying she promised that she would spend her Heaven in doing good upon earth, and would let fall a shower of roses. This promise she has fulfilled and continues to fulfill.

St. Therese was canonized by Pope Pius XI on May 17, 1925, and he appointed and declared her Patron of all the Missions.

✠

OCTOBER 4

ST. FRANCIS OF ASSISI

St. Francis, the Seraphic, "the poor man of Assisi", was born at Assisi, in 1182, of a rich merchant family. He was chosen by God to be a living manifestation to the world of Christ's life on earth, a life of poverty and suffering.

Because, even in earliest years, he distributed all his substance upon the poor, his father insisted that he renounce every right to an inheritance. This Francis did with great joy of spirit in the presence of the Bishop of Assisi. Thenceforth his life was one of poverty, of humility, of aiding the poor and afflicted. He was not content until he gave himself to the care of the lepers, consoling them in their sufferings.

One day, about the year 1206, Francis entered the neglected chapel of St. Peter Damian, and poured out his soul before the crucifix. Gazing with tearful eyes upon the cross, he heard a voice from the crucifix answering him: "Go, Francis, and restore My house which is falling". The Saint was filled with fear, dreading that he might be the victim of an illusion. But the same voice from the crucifix repeated, "Go, Francis, and repair My house which is falling into ruins". Then his fear redoubled and he asked himself from whence came this mysterious voice. A third time the crucifix answered, "Go, Francis, restore My house which is falling into ruins as you see."

Francis' soul was filled with ineffable joy, as he realized that it was God Who spoke to him from the crucifix. As he thought that Our Lord wished him to repair the church of St. Damian, he returned to Assisi and begged an alms from door to door to repair the church. When the work was completed he restored another church near Assisi, dedicated to St. Peter. He then commenced the restoration of St. Mary of the Angels, which belonged to the Benedictines, about one mile from the city.

While attending Mass in the restored chapel of Our Lady of the Angels (also known as *Portiuncula,* i.e., smallest portion), and which had become the object of his greatest affection and was destined to be the cradle of the Franciscan Order, Francis heard the words as read in the Gospel: "Do not possess gold nor silver, nor money in your purse, nor scrip for your journey, nor two coats, nor shoes, nor a staff". Francis was overjoyed, as he felt these words were addressed to himself. After the Mass he asked the

Priest to explain that passage of the Gospel. The explanation given, Francis cried out: "That is what I want, that is what I want, that is the object of all my ambition".

Now he clothed himself in a poorer and coarser garb, took off his shoes, laid aside his staff, gave away his money, and replaced his girdle with a rough cord. All of which caused him to say frequently: "I am married to Lady Poverty".

Disciples who soon were to go forth like the Apostles of old to evangelize the world flocked to him at his little chapel. The Franciscan Order spread rapidly throughout Christendom, as may be judged by the fact that in 1219 five thousand Friars attended its General Chapter.

In 1224, on the Feast of the Exaltation of the Holy Cross, as St. Francis was praying on Mount Alvernia, he received the Sacred Stigmata, that is, the Impression on his flesh of Our Lord's Five Most Sacred Wounds.

Two years later, on October 4, 1226, at the age of forty-four St. Francis died at Assisi; and on June 16, 1228, he was canonized by Pope Gregory IX.

It was St. Francis' deep love for the Christ Child that inspired him to build the first Christmas crib, which is the joy and inspiration of young and old in all Catholic churches.

St. Francis also directed St. Clare in the founding of the Poor Clares at St. Damian's in Assisi. The Sisters are known as the Second Order of St. Francis. In addition to these two Orders, St. Francis founded the Third Order, for persons living in the world and desirous of sharing the privileges and graces of the religious state.

✠

OCTOBER 5

ST. PLACIDUS AND COMPANIONS

St. Placidus was born at Rome in 515. Tertullus, his father, a man of high rank, placed him, at the age of seven,

O God, through the merits of blessed Francis, You enriched Your Church with a new family. Grant that, in imitation of him, we may despise worldly things and always rejoice in the participation of the heavenly gifts.

under the tutelage of St. Benedict at Subiaco. Daily the youth advanced in holy wisdom and in the perfect practice of all virtues. St. Benedict seeing the great progress which divine grace made in Placidus' tender heart loved him as one of the dearest of his spiritual children, and took him to Monte Cassino in 528. St. Placidus was then sent to Sicily to erect a church and monastery in honor of St. John the Baptist, near the harbor of Messina, where he lived a holy life with his Monks.

St. Gregory the Great mentioned in his Dialogues that St. Placidus was the youthful disciple of St. Benedict; that Saints Eutychius and Victorinus were brothers of St. Placidus and St. Flavia was their sister. One day when they came to visit Placidus, a certain cruel pagan pirate from Africa, named Manucha, landed in Sicily, and out of hatred of the Christian name, after sacking the monastery, and being unable to induce Placidus and his companions to deny Christ, ordered him and his brothers and sister to be cruelly put to death. Donatus, Firmatus the deacon, Faustus, and thirty other Monks were also martyred with them on October 5, about the year 539.

✠

OCTOBER 6

ST. BRUNO

St. Bruno, who founded the Carthusian Order, was born at Cologne, Germany, about 1030. From early youth he gave great promise of future sanctity. His pious parents placed him, when very young, under the tutorship of the clergy of St. Cunibert's church, where he gave extraordinary proofs of his piety. Bruno's parents then sent him to Paris, where he excelled in philosophy and theology, and was regarded as a great master and model of the schools. Because of his remarkable virtue he was appointed to a canonry in the Cathedral of Rheims.

Some years later St. Bruno, together with six close friends, went to see Bishop Hugo of Grenoble. On learning the cause of their visit, the Bishop understood that they had been signified by the seven stars he had seen falling at his feet in his dream the previous night, and he gave to them some wild mountains, called the Chartreuse, in his Diocese. Bruno and his companions retired to the solitude known as the Grande Chartreuse, thus laying the foundation of their Order, which still flourishes.

After St. Bruno led a hermit's life for several years, Pope Urban II, who had been his disciple, summoned him to Rome to be his Councillor. Bruno obeyed, but some years later he refused the Episcopal See of Reggio and obtained permission to return to his religious life. Loving solitude, he retired into the mountains of Calabria, where he assembled a community of Monks and resumed the life of the Grande Chartreuse. At length, full of virtues and merits, and renowned for holiness as well as for learning, Bruno fell asleep in the Lord in 1101. Five hundred years later he was canonized by Pope Gregory XV.

✠

OCTOBER 7

FEAST OF THE MOST HOLY ROSARY

His Holiness, Pope Leo XIII decreed that the month of October be called the month of the Most Holy Rosary, and it was he who added to the Litany of Loreto the invocation *Queen of the Most Holy Rosary*.

Tradition asserts that the Blessed Virgin Mary revealed the devotion of the Rosary to St. Dominic about the year 1208, while he was preaching among the irreligious Albigenses in southern France. He implored the holy Mother of God to enlighten him as to how he could labor more successfully for the conversion of those misguided souls for whom her Divine Son had laid down His life. One

night while he was kneeling in the chapel of Notre Dame
at Prouille, our Blessed Lady appeared to him holding a
Rosary in her hand. According to tradition, she instructed
him how to say it and bade him preach it among the
people as an antidote to heresy and sin. His efforts met
with marvelous success. Over a hundred thousand heretics
renounced their errors, and the conversion of a great many
notorious sinners testified to the power of this method
of prayer, with the result that it was adopted by all
Christendom.

Legend has attributed the signal defeat of the Albigensian heretics at the battle of Muret in 1213 to the
recitation of the Rosary by the Christian army under the
direction of St. Dominic. There are numerous other instances where the faith of those who have had recourse to
this devotion in times of great distress has been rewarded.
A striking example is that of the famous naval victory
gained by Don Juan of Austria over the Turkish fleet at
Lepanto on Sunday, October 7, 1571, on which day processions of the confraternities of the Holy Rosary were
taking place in Rome.

When the Mohammedans were threatening to overrun
Christian Europe, Pope Pius V, as early as 1569, had en-
joined the recitation of the Rosary on all Christendom
for the success of the Christian arms, and ordered all the
churches to conduct the Forty Hours Devotion, with public
processions and recitation of the Rosary.

Not only did Don Juan of Austria ascribe the triumph
of his fleet in the battle of Lepanto to the powerful intercession of the Queen of the Most Holy Rosary, but the
Venetian Senate wrote to the other States which had taken
part in the Crusade: "It was not generals nor battalions
nor arms that brought us victory; but it was Our Lady of
the Rosary".

The Feast of the Holy Rosary was instituted in thanksgiving for this famous naval victory. St. Pius V at first

ordered that the happy event should be commemorated on October 7, under the title of the *Commemoration of Our Lady of Victory*. But, at the request of the Dominican Order, Pope Gregory XIII, by decree of April 1, 1573, substituted for it the *Feast of Our Lady of the Rosary*.

✠

OCTOBER 8

ST. BRIDGET OF SWEDEN

St. Bridget was born in Sweden of noble and pious parents, in 1304. While she was yet in the womb, her mother was saved from shipwreck on her account. When Bridget was ten years old she heard a sermon on the Passion of Christ; the following night she saw Jesus on the Cross, covered with fresh blood, and speaking to her about His Passion. Thereafter whenever she meditated on the subject she was affected to such a degree, that she could never think of it without weeping.

Bridget was given in marriage to Prince Ulpho of Nericia, Sweden. By her word and example she encouraged her husband to works of piety. She devoted herself with maternal love to the education of her eight children, one of whom, Catherine, is honored as a Saint; and she most zealously cared for the poor and the sick.

By mutual consent, in order to sanctify their lives, they separated in later life; he becoming a Cistercian monk. He died shortly thereafter. Bridget, having heard the voice of Christ in a dream, founded the austere Order of St. Savior in the monastery of Wadstena under the Rule of the Savior, which was given her by Jesus Himself. At the command of God she went to Rome, where she kindled the love of God in many hearts. After making a pilgrimage to Jerusalem she returned to Rome, where she was attacked by fever and excruciating pains, which continued for a year.

On the day she had foretold, she passed to Heaven, in the year 1373, laden with merits. Three years later her body was translated to the monastery of Wadstena.

St. Bridget was canonized by Pope Boniface IX in 1391.

✠

OCTOBER 9

ST. LOUIS BERTRAND

St. Louis was born at Valencia, Spain, January 1, 1526, the eldest of nine children, all of whom were remarkable for their piety. Louis, a blood relative of St. Vincent Ferrer, like him, at the age of fifteen took the Habit of the Order of St. Dominic. He became an eminent doctor among the Dominican Friars, reformed the Order in Spain, was a renowned preacher and an apostle of the Moors in Spain.

His angelical modesty, the ardor of his love, the impression of which appeared in his countenance, and the tears he shed while offering up the Holy Sacrifice, inspired with tender devotion all who were present at his Mass. He was made Master of Novices in 1551. During the pestilence which raged in Valencia in 1557, St. Louis spared no pains in exhorting and assisting the sick, and in burying the dead.

When the pestilence ceased, permission was granted him to preach the Gospel to the Indians in America. He embarked at Seville in 1562, and landed in Golden Castile, South America. God conferred the gifts of tongues, of prophecy, and of miracles on this new apostle. He converted to Christ more than ten thousand souls, and baptized all the inhabitants of the city of Tubara and nearby places. He then preached with like fruit at Cipacoa and various other towns. The inhabitants of the mountains of St. Martha received him as an Angel sent from Heaven, and there he baptized about fifteen thousand persons. In the country of Monpaia, and in the island of St. Thomas, the Saint gained a new people to Christ. Heaven protected him more than once from the attempts made upon his life by poison, the sword, and other ways. He foretold many things that came to pass, and in the city of Carthagena raised a dead woman to life. He returned to Valencia in 1569.

St. Teresa consulted St. Louis, and received much comfort from his advice under her greatest difficulties.

The remaining twelve years of his life were spent in preaching the divine word in several dioceses in Spain. He foretold the day of his death almost a year before it occurred. The holy man gave up his soul to God, surrounded by the members of his Community, on October 9, 1581. Many miracles attested his favor with God, and he was canonized by Pope Clement X in 1671.

✠

OCTOBER 10

ST. FRANCIS BORGIA

St. Francis Borgia, fourth Duke of Gandia, was, on his father's side, a great-grandson of Alexander VI, and on his mother's side, the great-grandson of the Catholic King Ferdinand of Aragon. Francis lost his mother when he was ten years old. In 1521 a sedition amongst the populace imperiled the child's life and the position of the nobility. When the disturbance was suppressed, Francis was sent to Saragossa to continue his education at the Court of his uncle, the Archbishop. At the age of eighteen he was placed in the Court of Emperor Charles V, where he led a holy, austere life.

Francis married the virtuous Eleonora de Castro, by whom he had five children. While serving as Governor of Catalonia he was charged to convey the body of the Empress Isabella to her sepulchre at Granada. When the coffin was opened and he observed the horribly changed features of the former beautiful Queen, he vowed to cast aside as soon as possible the fleeting things of the world and to devote himself entirely to the service of the King of kings. On the death of his wife, he entered the Society of Jesus, in order to safely cut himself off from receiving any ecclesiastical dignities. He practiced great austerities, and spared no effort to conquer himself and to gain souls.

Francis was chosen by St. Ignatius as Commissary General for Spain, and soon afterwards, against his will, was elected Third General of the whole Society.

The Turks at that time were threatening Christendom, and Pope Pius V sent his nephew to gather Christian princes into a league for the defense of the Church. The holy Pope chose Francis to accompany his nephew. Although the health of Francis had been undermined by his austere life, he undertook the journey in the spirit of obedience, but died at Rome on October 10, 1572. In the Catholic Church he had been one of the most striking examples of the conversion of souls after the Renaissance, and for the Society of Jesus he had been the protector chosen by God to whom, after St. Ignatius, it owes most.

The remains of St. Francis Borgia are enshrined at Madrid. He was canonized by Pope Clement X in 1670.

✠

OCTOBER 11

THE MATERNITY OF THE BLESSED VIRGIN MARY

From all eternity God chose the most Blessed Virgin Mary, "a royal virgin of the race of David", to be the Mother of the Savior of mankind.

Pope St. Leo, in a sermon on the birth of the Savior, said:

"Jesus Christ our Lord enters these lower parts, coming down from the heavenly throne, and yet not quitting His Father's glory, begotten in a new order, by a new nativity . . . conceived by a Virgin, born of a Virgin, without the concupiscence of a paternal body, without injury to the maternal chastity; . . . by the power of God was it brought about, that a Virgin conceived, a Virgin brought forth, and a Virgin she remained".

In 1931, solemn rites were celebrated by Pope Pius XI at the completion of the 15th century after the Blessed Virgin Mary (from whom Jesus was born) had been acclaimed as the Mother of God by the Fathers, under the leadership of Pope Celestine, at the Council of Ephesus in opposition to the heresy of Nestorius. The Supreme Pontiff, Pius XI, wishing to perpetuate the memory of this most auspicious event, caused the triumphal arch and the transept in the Basilica of St. Mary Major on the Esquiline Hill to be tastefully restored. It had been decorated by his predecessor Sixtus III with mosaics of marvellous workmanship, which however, were falling to pieces with the decay of ages. Moreover, he narrated in an encyclical letter the true history of the ecumenical Council of Ephesus, expounding fully the ineffable prerogative of the divine Motherhood of the Blessed Virgin Mary, in such a way that the doctrine of this lofty mystery might sink deeper into the hearts of the faithful. In it he likewise sets forth Mary the Mother of God, blessed among all women, and the Family of Nazareth, as the most noble example above all others to be followed, as well as for the dignity and holiness of chaste wedlock, as for the holy education that should be given to youth. Finally, he ordered that a feast of the divine Motherhood of the Blessed Virgin Mary should be celebrated by the Universal Church every year.

☦

OCTOBER 12

ST. WILFRID OF NORTHUMBRIA

The famous words of the Apostle of Ireland were the motto of St. Wilfrid's entire life and labors: "As you are the children of Christ, so be you the children of Rome".

During a long and laborious episcopate, which lasted forty-four years, St. Wilfrid was often in conflict with the tyrannical Saxon Kings in defense of the rights of the Church, and was frequently cruelly misunderstood by his friends. When very young, Wilfrid's mother died, and his father remarried. His step-mother's harsh treatment caused Wilfrid to leave home when thirteen years of age and to enter the Court of Queen Eanfleda. He soon became dissatisfied with Court life and longed to become a religious. Renouncing all public and military service, he entered the monastery of Lindisfarne, and before long determined to journey to Rome. Arriving at Canterbury, he won the heart of King Ercombert by his piety, and was detained a year at his Court.

In 654 Wilfrid, in company with another young nobleman, reached Lyons, where he tarried a year with Archbishop Delphinus. Soon after his arrival in Rome he found a friend in Archbishop Boniface, who was secretary to Pope Martin. Wilfrid had an interview with the Pontiff, who gave him his blessing.

On revisiting Lyons he was welcomed most affectionately by Delphinus, with whom he stayed three years, receiving from him the Roman tonsure. His visit ended abruptly by a persecution which broke out, in which Archbishop Delphinus and seven other Bishops received the crown of martyrdom. As Delphinus was led away to death he forbade Wilfrid to follow him, but like St. Lawrence he cried out that father and son ought to die together. Wilfrid was stripped ready for death, and the martyr's palm seemed almost in his grasp, when one of the officers, hearing that he was a Saxon, forbade the execution. After recovering the body of Delphinus, Wilfrid gave it honorable burial and then started for home.

In 664 he was selected Bishop of York and went to Paris to receive the episcopal consecration. Impatient at Wilfrid's delay, St. Chad was given possession of the Diocese. St. Wilfrid then retired to his abbey of Ripon, where he remained until his restoration five years later. He entered with great zeal upon the labors of his large Diocese. So relentless were his enemies that his life was in danger. His possessions were confiscated and he was exiled.

At the age of seventy St. Wilfrid journeyed again to Rome to lay his cause before Pope John VI. After a full investigation Pope John decided in Wilfrid's favor, and sent letters to the kings of Northumbria and of Mercia, and an order to the Archbishop of Canterbury to summon a Synod, at which the exiled Bishop should be reinstated in his Diocese and his possessions.

The four remaining years of St. Wilfrid's life were spent chiefly at his beloved abbey of Ripon, which he had founded. But it was in a village near Northampton that he died, in the year 709.

☨

OCTOBER 13

ST. EDWARD

St. Edward, son of Ethelred the Unready by his second wife, Emma, daughter of Duke Richard I of Normandy, was born about the year 1003, during a most difficult period in English history. He was brought up in exile and educated in the palace of the Duke of Normandy, on account of the Danish occupation of England.

Upon the death of King Ethelred, Emma married King Canute, who reigned nineteen years. According to the terms of his marriage settlement with Emma, their son Harthacanute should have succeeded to the throne on the death of the King in 1035. But this prince was in Denmark, and his illegitimate brother Harold, supported by the Danish nobles and the entire population of Northern England, seized and held the kingdom.

In 1042, on the restoration of the Anglo-Saxon line, Edward was crowned King of England by Archbishop Edsy. The most influential nobles, headed by Earl Godwin, soon humbly urged the King to complete the happiness of the nation by taking to himself a royal consort. But Edward had made a vow of virginity in his early youth. After much prayerful deliberation he was inspired to the decision that if he could find a lady "like-minded with himself", armed with the same heroic virtue, and aiming at the same supernatural ideals, he would ask her to share his throne.

Two years after his accession to the throne, King Edward asked Edgitha, daughter of the powerful Earl Godwin, a Norman, to be his Queen and to unite herself with him in a purely spiritual companionship. Edgitha accepted the Saint's proposal, and on January 23, 1045, amidst the rejoicings of the people, the marriage was solemnized. They led truly virtuous, holy lives.

The laws framed by St. Edward were the fruit of his wisdom and endeared him to his people. The only foreign war in which he engaged, and which ended speedily and victoriously, was to restore Malcolm as King of Scotland.

St. Edward died at the age of sixty-three on January 5, 1066, having reigned twenty-three years, six months and twenty-seven days. He became a Saint in the midst of courtly life and in a degenerate age.

☫

OCTOBER 14

ST. CALLISTUS I

St. Callistus was a Roman by birth. He succeeded St. Zephyrinus in the Pontificate on August 2, 217, after having been his Archdeacon or representative. He governed the Church five years, one month, and twelve days, during most difficult times, and enacted many salutary measures. He instituted the four periods of the year called Ember days, on which fasting, according to apostolic tradition, should be observed by all; decreed that ordinations should be held in each of the Ember weeks; built the Church of Santa Maria Across the Tiber; enlarged the ancient cemetery on the Appian Way, in which many holy Priests and Martyrs were buried; whence it is called after him, the cemetery of St. Callistus.

He caused the body of the Blessed Calepodius, Priest and Martyr, which had been thrown into the Tiber, to be sought for, and, when found, to be honorably buried. After baptizing Palmatius, of consular rank, and Simplicius, of senatorial rank, together with Felix and Blanda, all of whom subsequently suffered martyrdom, he was cast into prison, where he restored health to Privatus, a soldier, and led him to embrace Christianity.

After a long starvation and frequent scourgings, St. Callistus was thrown headlong into a well, and thus suffered martyrdom under Emperor Alexander. He was buried in the catacombs of St. Calepodius, and his relics now repose in the Church of Santa Maria Across the Tiber.

☩

OCTOBER 15

ST. TERESA OF AVILA

St. Teresa was born in Avila, Spain, March 28, 1515. Don Alfonso, her father, was a man of solid piety, most charitable to the poor, very gentle and considerate with his servants. Beatriz, her mother, brought up her nine children in the fear and love of God, devout to Our Lady and the Saints, thus laying the foundation of the spiritual life of Teresa.

While reading the lives of the Saints, Teresa and one of her elder brothers thought that martyrdom was a very small price to pay for the vision of God. Therefore, when only seven years old Teresa and her brother planned to go to Africa, where they would be beheaded by the Moors. They left home, and when they reached the gates of the city they were met by one of their uncles, who took them home. Disappointed in their hopes of martyrdom, the two children resolved to become hermits in their father's garden.

Upon the death of her mother, when Teresa was fifteen years old, she went in her sorrow to the Chapel of Our Lady of Charity in the hospital of the city. There, before her image she implored the Blessed Virgin with tears to be to her a mother. Her prayer was heard, and Teresa relates that in all her trials she was always helped whenever she called upon that compassionate Mother.

After many trials Teresa resolved to be a Nun, but her father refused to grant permission, saying that she might do as she pleased after his death. Teresa saw the danger of delay, and made up her mind to execute her purpose no matter what the cost.

Whilst preparing to obey the call of God, Teresa persuaded one of her brothers to become a Friar. Early in the morning of November 2, 1533, they secretly left their father's house—he for the Dominican Monastery in Avila, she for the Carmelite Monastery of the Incarnation, where her friend Juana Suarez was a religious. Here she made her profession after many trials and sufferings. A severe illness, for which the physicians of Avila found no remedy, caused her father to bring Teresa home for special treatments. These proved futile and her condition worsened until she was at the point of death. She was paralyzed for nearly three years, and after praying to St. Joseph she partially recovered, but her health remained permanently impaired.

Returning to her monastic life, she became lax, but at last, in her thirty-first year, she surrendered herself wholly to God. In a vision St. Teresa saw the place destined for her in hell in the event she should be unfaithful to grace; ever afterwards she determined to seek a more perfect life and lived in the greatest distrust of self. She persevered in prayer, and God rewarded her abundantly with celestial visions and mystical prayer, her heart being pierced with Divine Love.

St. Teresa founded the convent of Discalced Carmelite Nuns of the Primitive Rule of St. Joseph at Avila on August 24, 1562, and six months later took up her residence there. With the assistance of Antonio de Heredia and

Lord, hear us, so that while we rejoice in the feast of blessed Teresa, Your Virgin, we may be nourished by the food of her heavenly doctrine and learn the affection of a pious devotion.

St. John of the Cross, she established her reform among the Friars. The greatness of her work may be determined from the fact that she founded fifteen monasteries of Friars and seventeen of consecrated women—the fruits of her sanctity and her legacy to the Church, of which she was always the humblest and most docile child.

St. Teresa died in the odor of sanctity on October 4, 1582. St. Teresa's body has remained incorrupt, surrounded with a fragrant liquid, and is honored with pious veneration. She was made illustrious by miracles both before and after her death; and in 1622, Pope Gregory XV enrolled her in the number of the Saints.

Pope Paul VI proclaimed St. Teresa a Doctor of the Church in 1970.

✠

OCTOBER 16

ST. HEDWIG

St. Hedwig, Duchess of Poland, was illustrious for her royal birth, but still more illustrious for the innocence of her life. She was a maternal aunt of St. Elizabeth, daughter of the King of Hungary. Her parents were Berthold and Agnes, of the Margraviate of Moravia. From childhood Hedwig was remarkable for self-control. At the age of twelve, her parents gave her in marriage to Henry, Duke of Poland. All her thoughts and actions were directed to please God and to sanctify her own soul and her household. After the birth of her sixth child, in order the more freely to serve God, Hedwig persuaded her husband to make a vow of chastity, which they made in the presence of the Bishop. After the death of the Duke thirty years later, she was inspired by God to take the Cistercian Habit at the monastery of Trebnitz, and lived in obedience to her daughter, Gertrude, who was then Abbess.

St. Hedwig was a model of the highest religious perfection, undertook menial offices, and waited upon the
poor. Her patience and strength of soul were admirable;
this was most conspicuous at the death of her son, Henry,
Duke of Silesia, when he was killed in a battle against the
Tartars in 1241.

St. Hedwig was noted for her miraculous power. She
died in 1243, and Pope Clement IV enrolled her among
the Saints. She is honored as Patroness of Silesia.

☩

OCTOBER 17

ST. MARGARET MARY ALACOQUE

St. Margaret Mary, the fifth of seven children, was
born on July 22, 1647, at Llautecour, a small hamlet in
the Burgundy valley of France. Her father was a judge,
and his brother a Priest, so the name Alacoque was one
of the best known and respected in the neighborhood.

When Margaret was four years old she was sent to
live for a time with her godmother, who resided three
miles distant, and who was wealthy and childless. The
change of scene developed in Margaret all the qualities
which afterwards made our Divine Lord choose her as
the humble recipient of His intimate revelations. At the
age of seven, Margaret made a vow of perpetual chastity.
For hours she would kneel, praying. "I was constantly
urged", she says, "to repeat these words, the sense of which
I did not understand": 'My God, I consecrate to You my
purity! My God, I make to You a vow of perpetual chastity'." While she did not know what the words *vow* and
chastity signified, she understood they meant the complete
gift of herself to God.

The following year, upon the death of her godmother,
Margaret returned to her father's home. A few months later
he died and left his temporal affairs in a most wretched

state. Margaret was then sent to a school of the Poor Clares at Charolles, where she was prepared to make her First Holy Communion, and where she was also Confirmed. She soon realized that the religious life was what God desired of her. A very serious illness curtailed her school life, and the child was taken home to her mother. No cure could be found for her malady until they offered her to the Blessed Virgin, promising that if she were cured she "should some day be one of her daughters". After four years of suffering Margaret's health was restored. The crosses she had to bear were heavy, but her love of prayer and of Jesus in the Blessed Sacrament consoled and strengthened her. She often spent the night in prayer, and practised many austerities. To sustain her in trials, Jesus began to appear to her. Frequently He presented Himself sensibly to her, either as crucified, as carrying the Cross, or as the *Ecce Homo,* thus increasing tenfold her thirst for suffering.

Madame Alacoque, desirous of settling her children in life, introduced them into "social life". Margaret, now seventeen, was much noticed and sought after. Scarcely had she beheld the world smiling upon her, when she began to adorn herself to please it and to amuse herself as much as possible for four years. But God, Who had great designs for Margaret, watched over her and preserved her from all sin.

"One day", she relates, "after Holy Communion He made me see that He was the most handsome, the richest, the most powerful, the most perfect and accomplished of lovers, and, since I had been promised to Him for so many years, how was it that I wanted to break everything off with Him, to take up with another: 'Oh! know that if you scorn me in this way, I shall abandon you forever. But if you are faithful to me, I shall not leave you, and I shall become your victory against all my enemies...."

Shedding abundant tears, Margaret renewed her vow of chastity, and resolved "rather to die than violate it".

She told her family of her resolution, and implored them to dismiss every aspirant for her hand.

On June 25, 1671, Margaret, then twenty-four years of age, entered the Visitation Convent of Paray-le-Monial. It was there that she received from Our Lord the mission to spread devotion to His Sacred Heart. During one of His visitations, Jesus said to her: "Behold this Heart which has so loved men that It has spared nothing, even to exhausting and consuming Itself, in order to testify Its love. In return I receive from the greater part of men only ingratitude, by their irreverence and sacrilege, and by the coldness and contempt they have for Me in this Sacrament of Love. . . ."

In the beginning St. Margaret Mary experienced many difficulties and considerable opposition, but with the assistance of Father de la Colombiere of the Society of Jesus, she was able to overcome them. It was he who was to be God's instrument for instituting the Feast of the Sacred Heart, and for spreading that devotion throughout the world.

St. Margaret Mary died on October 17, 1690, and was canonized by Pope Benedict XV.

✠

OCTOBER 18

ST. LUKE

St. Luke was born at Antioch, Syria. He was a physician and a Gentile, skilled in the Greek tongue. After his conversion to Christianity, he became a follower of St. Paul, who calls him his "fellow laborer", and "Luke, the beloved physician".

St. Luke is the inspired writer of the Third Gospel and also of the Acts of the Apostles. He was instructed in the Christian Faith not only by the Apostle Paul, who had never been with Jesus in the flesh, but also by the other

Apostles. Therefore, he wrote his Gospel from what he had heard; but he compiled the Acts of the Apostles from what he had himself seen. He is the evangelist, poet, artist and cantor of the Holy Infancy of the Savior of Mankind.

He accompanied St. Paul on his second and third missionary journeys, and when St. Paul was sent to Rome as a prisoner from Jerusalem in the year 61, St. Luke attended him and had the happiness of seeing him set at liberty in the year 63, the year in which he finished writing his Acts of the Apostles. He continued with St. Paul after his release, and the great Apostle, during his last imprisonment wrote that his other friends had all left him and that only Luke was with him.

After the martyrdom of St. Paul, St. Luke is said to have preached in Italy, Gaul, Dalmatia and Macedon. He is venerated as a Martyr, and as having suffered near Achaia, in Greece. His relics were distributed among many churches, and St. Gregory is said to have brought the head of St. Luke from Constantinople to Rome, and to have deposited it in the church of his monastery of St. Andrew. Some of his relics are also kept in the great Grecian monastery of Mount Athos. St. Luke was never married, and lived to be eighty-four years old. According to tradition, he was a skilled artist, and several pictures of Our Blessed Lady, venerated in Rome and elsewhere, are attributed to his brush.

✠

OCTOBER 19

ST. PETER OF ALCANTARA

St. Peter was born of noble parents at Alcantara, Spain, and from early youth gave promise of his future sanctity. At the age of sixteen he entered the Franciscan Order and became a model of every virtue. After his ordination to the priesthood he led numberless sinners to sincere repentance by his preaching. Desiring to restore his Order to its original strictness, he founded, with God's assistance and the approbation of the Holy See, a small, poor monastery near Pedroso. His austere manner of life was soon emulated in different provinces in Spain and the American Spanish Indies. In compliance with his request he was sent to the monastery of St. Onuphrius at Lapa, situated in a dreaded solitude, and at the same time was given the charge of Guardian of the house. During that retirement he composed his golden book "On Mental Prayer", which was esteemed highly by St. Teresa, St. Francis de Sales, Pope Gregory XV, and other masters of the spiritual life. In 1561 he was chosen Provincial of his reformed Order.

St. Peter's gift of prayer was admirable; his ecstasies in prayer were frequent. By perpetual vigils, fastings, disciplines, insufficient clothing, and every kind of austerity, he brought his body into subjection, having made a compact with it never to give it any rest in this world. He was endowed with the gifts of prophecy and discernment of spirits, as St. Teresa testifies. St. Peter rendered her great assistance and encouragement in the reform of the Carmelite Order.

While making the visitation of his monasteries, St. Peter fell ill. Realizing that his end was near, he asked to be carried to the monastery of Arenas. In his last moments he exhorted his brethren to perseverance and to the constant love of holy poverty. He died on October 18, 1562, at the age of sixty-three, and was canonized by Pope Clement IX in 1669.

✠

OCTOBER 20

ST. JOHN CANTIUS

St. John was born of pious parents at Kenty, a small town in the diocese of Cracow, Poland, from which he took his surname Cantius. His sweet, innocent, serious dis-

position gave promise of very great virtue. He studied
philosophy and theology at the University of Cracow. After
taking his degrees, he was appointed to the Chair of Theology at the university. He inflamed his hearers with the
desire of every kind of piety, no less by his deeds than
by his words.

For several years after he was ordained to the priesthood he had charge of the parish of Ilkusi, but fearing
the responsibility and the care of souls, he resigned his
post and, at the request of the University, resumed the
professor's Chair and taught there until his holy death at
the age of seventy-six.

St. John led a most austere, prayerful life, and from
time to time distributed to the poor all that he possessed.
At length, full of days and of merits, he prepared himself
long and diligently for death, which he felt was drawing
near. Fortified with the Last Sacraments, he passed to
Heaven on Christmas eve, 1473. He is devoutly honored as
one of the chief patrons of Poland and Lithuania. Illustrious
for his miracles, Pope Clement XIII added his name to the
calendar of the Saints on July 16, 1767.

✠

OCTOBER 21

ST. URSULA AND COMPANIONS

When the pagan Saxons fled from the south of England into Gaul, some settled in Armorica; others in the
Netherlands, near the mouth of the Rhine. St. Ursula and
her companions seem to have left Britain about the year
453, and to have met martyrdom in defense of their virginity from the army of the savage Huns, which at that
time was plundering the country and destroying everything
by fire and the sword.

The holy martyrs were buried at Cologne, where a large church was built over their tombs, which was very famous during the reign of St. Cunibert, who was Archbishop. Many miracles have taken place at their tombs, and these holy martyrs have been honored by the faithful for centuries.

St. Ursula, who was the leader and guide of so many holy souls, whom she encouraged in the practice of virtue and conducted to the glorious crown of martyrdom, is regarded as a model and patroness of those who undertake the training of youth. She is the patroness of the famous college of Sarbonne and of the Ursuline Sisters, who were founded by St. Angela de Merici to educate young girls.

✠

OCTOBER 22

ST. THEODORET

Theodoret, a zealous Priest of Antioch and Treasurer of the Church of that city, had been very active during the reign of Constantius in destroying idols and building churches and oratories over the relics of martyrs. He defied the edicts of Emperor Julian the Apostate against the Christians, and continued to minister publicly to the Faithful. Consequently, the Emperor commanded him to be apprehended, and had him most inhumanly tortured. The tyrant jeered him all the while, but the Martyr exhorted him to acknowledge the true God, and Jesus Christ His Son, by Whom all things were made. Julian then ordered that he should be tormented on the rack, and that lighted torches be applied to his bleeding body. The Saint, whilst enduring this terrible agony, lifted up his eyes to Heaven and prayed that God would glorify His Name throughout the ages. At these words the executioners fell on their faces to the ground and refused to apply their torches again when commanded to do so. They were ordered to be thrown into the water and drowned.

Theodoret was condemned to be beheaded; which martyrdom he suffered with joy in the year 362.

✠

OCTOBER 23

ST. IGNATIUS OF CONSTANTINOPLE

St. Ignatius was born at Constantinople about the year 799. He was the son of the Byzantine Emperor Michael I, who was driven from the throne by Leo the Armenian, the impious and barbarous General of the army. The family,— father, mother, two sons and two daughters—then embraced a monastic state. The younger son, who was fourteen years of age, changed his former name, Nicetas, into that of Ignatius. He underwent a most severe trial, being placed in a monastery which was governed by a tyrannical Iconoclast Abbot, from whom he had much to suffer. This caused Ignatius to continually practice patience and other Christian virtues. So conspicuous was the virtue of Ignatius that, upon the death of his persecutor, he was unanimously chosen Abbot. In 842 he was elected Patriarch of Constantinople.

His denunciation of the vices of the Court raised up many enemies against him. Chief among them was Bardas Caesar, uncle of the dissolute youth known as Emperor Michael the Drunkard.

Finally, Ignatius was driven into exile, and his See usurped by Photius, a clever but ambitious, unscrupulous man, who may be said to have originated the Greek Schism, which was consummated two centuries later by Michael Cerularius, and which cut off the East from communion with Rome.

Michael was murdered by his guards while he was drunk, in September 867. The following day Emperor Basil banished Photius and honorably restored St. Ignatius who had been in exile nine years. He was conducted with great pomp to the imperial city, and reinstated in the patriarchal chair on November 3, 867. He governed his Archdiocese until his death on October 23, 878, being nearly eighty years old.

✠

OCTOBER 24

ST. RAPHAEL, ARCHANGEL

What we know of St. Raphael is revealed in the Book of Tobias. He is "One of the Seven who stand before the Lord" (12:15), and is one of the three Archangels mentioned in Holy Scripture and honored by the Church. The other two are St. Gabriel and St. Michael.

St. Raphael, in the form of a beautiful youth, accompanied Tobias on his journey to Media to recover a sum of money lent by his father to Gabelus. Upon his return, Tobias said to his father: "Father what wages shall we give him? or what can be worthy of his benefits? He conducted me safe again, he received the money of Gabelus, he caused me to have my wife (Sara), and he chased from her the evil spirit, he gave joy to her parents, myself he delivered from being devoured by the fish, thee also he hath made to see the light of Heaven, and we are filled with all good things through him. What can we give him sufficient for these things?" Tobias and his father then called St. Raphael and urged him to accept half of all things they had brought.

St. Raphael said to them secretly: "Bless ye the God of Heaven, give glory to Him in the sight of all that live, because He has shown His mercy to you. . . ." Revealing that he was the Archangel Raphael and that he had offered all the good works of the elder Tobias to the Lord, he ad-

monished, not only a virtuous father and son, but all mankind, that: "Prayer is good with fasting and alms: more
than to lay up treasures of gold. Alms purgeth away sins,
and maketh to find mercy and life everlasting. They that
commit sin and iniquity are enemies to their own soul. The
Lord sent me to heal thee (the elder Tobias) and to deliver thy son's wife from the devil.... Fear not for when
I was with you, I was there by the will of God: bless ye
Him and sing praises to Him". (Chap. 12)

The Church recognizes St. Raphael as the help of the
sick and the Patron of travelers.

✠

OCTOBER 25

SS. CHRYSANTHUS AND DARIA

Chrysanthus and Daria were husband and wife, noble
by birth, and still more glorious by their Faith, which Daria
had received together with Baptism through her husband's
persuasion. At Rome they converted an immense multitude
to Christ, Daria instructing the women, and Chrysanthus
the men. On this account the prefect Celerinus arrested
them, and handed them over to the tribune Claudius, who
ordered his soldiers to bind Chrysanthus and put him to
the torture. But all his bonds were loosed, and the fetters
which were put upon him were broken. They then wrapped
him in the skin of an ox, and exposed him to the burning
sun; and next cast him, chained hand and foot, into a dark
dungeon; but his chains were broken and the prison filled
with a brilliant light. Meanwhile, Daria was forced to enter
a brothel, but she was protected by a lion, and remained
rapt in prayer, being defended from insult by divine power.
Finally, they were both led to a sand-pit on the Salarian
Way, where they were thrown into the pit and overwhelmed with stones; and thus they together won the
crown of martyrdom.

✠

OCTOBER 26

ST. EVARISTUS

St. Evaristus was born in Greece, and was Pope during the reign of Emperor Trajan. He succeeded St. Anacletus in the See of Rome, and governed the Church nine years and three months. He divided Rome into parishes and assigned a Priest to each; he ordained seven Deacons to attend the Bishop, thus originating the College of Cardinals. He suffered martyrdom in the year 112, and was buried near the tomb of St. Peter on the Vatican Hill.

✠

OCTOBER 27

ST. FRUMENTIUS

Frumentius, a Christian youth of the 4th century, while making a voyage with his uncle, Meropius, a philosopher of Tyre, was cast on the shore of Abyssinia. All on board the ship were massacred by the savage inhabitants except Frumentius and his younger brother, Edesius. The King took a fancy to them and special care was given to their education. Frumentius became his Treasurer and Secretary of State, and was entrusted with all the public writings and accounts. After the King's death Edesius, who was the King's cupbearer, returned to Tyre; Frumentius, desiring to spread the Christian Faith in that kingdom, remained. He went to Alexandria and asked the assistance of St. Athanasius, who ordained him Priest and consecrated him Bishop, and then sent him back to Abyssinia.

By his discourses and miracles, Frumentius converted King Aizan, his brother Sazan, and many other idolaters to the Faith. The Arian Emperor Constantius conceived an implacable jealousy against St. Frumentius, because he was linked in Faith and affection with St. Athanasius. The holy Bishop continued to feed and defend his flock until it pleased the Supreme Pastor to recompense his fidelity and labors. The Abyssinians honor him as the Apostle of the Axumites, which is the greater part of their country.

✠

OCTOBER 28

SS. SIMON AND JUDE

Simon was that Canaanite, who is also called the Zealot; while Thaddeus (who is also called Jude the brother of James, in the Gospel), was the writer of one of the Catholic Epistles. Simon went through Egypt preaching the Gospel, and Thaddeus did the same in Mesopotamia. They afterwards met together in Persia, where they begot countless children in Jesus Christ, and propagated the Faith in those far-spreading countries among barbarous peoples by their teaching and miracles. Finally, by a glorious martyrdom, they together rendered honor to the most holy Name of Jesus Christ.

✠

OCTOBER 29

ST. NARCISSUS

St. Narcissus was almost eighty years old when he was consecrated Bishop of Jerusalem, about the year 180. In 195, he and Theophilus, Bishop of Caesarea, presided in a Council of the Bishops of Palestine held at Caesarea, regarding the time for celebrating Easter. It was decreed that this Feast should be kept always on a Sunday and not with the Jewish Passover.

The historian Eusebius assures us that God wrought several miracles by this holy Bishop. One Holy Saturday the faithful were in great difficulty because no oil could

O God, through Your blessed Apostles Simon and Jude, You give us the knowledge of Your Name. Grant that we may celebrate their eternal glory by advancing in virtue, and that we may advance in virtue by celebrating such glory.

be found for the lamps in the church, necessary at the solemn celebration of the Feast. Narcissus ordered those who cared for the lamps to bring him some water. This being done, he said a devout prayer over the water and it was immediately converted into oil.

The veneration of the good people for this holy Bishop could not shelter him from the malice of the wicked. Three incorrigible sinners accused him of a detestable crime, confirming their calumny by dreadful oaths and imprecations. Notwithstanding their protestations, their accusation was not believed. Some time after divine vengeance struck the calumniators; one, with his entire family, perished when his house was destroyed by fire; the second became a victim of leprosy; while the third, terrified at the fate of his two companions, confessed the conspiracy and slander, and by the abundance of tears he shed for his sins, lost his sight before his death.

Narcissus, on account of the bold calumny, made it an excuse for leaving Jerusalem to live a life of solitude. After spending several years undiscovered in his retreat, he returned to his parish church. The entire congregation welcomed their holy pastor and implored him to reassume the administration of the diocese. He acquiesced; but later, on account of his extreme age, made St. Alexander his coadjutor. St. Narcissus continued to serve his flock, and even other churches, by his assiduous prayers and his earnest exhortations to unity and concord. He lived to be about one hundred and sixteen years old.

☩

OCTOBER 30

ST. MARCELLUS

During the pompous birthday celebration in honor of Emperor Maximian Herculeus in the year 298, sacrifices to the Roman gods constituted part of the solemnity. A centurion by the name of Marcellus, in the legion of Trajan, refused to participate in the pagan rites, declaring that he was a soldier of Jesus Christ, the Son of God. The Prefect of the legion, Anastasius Fortunatus, ordered Marcellus to be imprisoned. After the festival Marcellus was brought before the Prefect. As Marcellus renewed his act of faith in Christianity, his case was laid before Emperor Maximian and Constantine Caesar, who sent the prisoner under a strong guard to Aurelian Agricolaus, vicar to the Prefect of the praetorium, at that time in Tangier, Africa. The vicar passed sentence of death upon Marcellus for desertion and impiety, as he termed his action.

St. Marcellus was forthwith led to execution and beheaded, on October 30th. His relics were later translated to Leon in Spain, where they are kept in a beautiful shrine in the chief parish church in that city, of which he is the titular Saint.

✠

OCTOBER 31

ST. ALPHONSUS RODRIGUEZ

St. Alphonsus Rodriguez was born at Segovia, Spain, July 25, 1532. His father was a wool merchant who had been reduced to poverty when Alfonso was still young.

At the age of twenty-six Alfonso married Mary Suarez; five years later he became a widower with one surviving child, two others having died previously. He now began a life of prayer and mortification, and on the death of his third child his thoughts turned to a life in some religious Order. Previous associations had brought him into contact with Blessed Peter Faber and some of the Jesuits who first came to Spain, but as he was without education it was apparently impossible for him to carry out his desire to enter the Society of Jesus. At the age of thirty-nine he attempted to make up this deficiency by following the course at the College of Barcelona, but without success. Besides,

his austerities had undermined his health. After considerable delay he was finally admitted into the Society on
January 31, 1571 as a lay-Brother.

It is not certain whether he began his term of proba-
tion at Valencia or at Gandia, but after six months he was
sent to the recently-founded college at Majorca, where he
remained for forty-six years filling the humble position of
porter. He exercised a marvellous influence on the sanctification not only of the members of the household, but upon
great numbers of people who came to the porter's lodge
for advice and direction. St. Peter Claver lived with him
for some time at Majorca, and followed his advice in asking
for the missions of South America.

After leading a long and holy, austere life, St. Alphonsus Rodriguez died at Majorca, October 31, 1617. He was
declared Venerable in 1626, and in 1633 was chosen by the
Council General of Majorca as one of the special patrons
of the city and island. He was canonized by Pope Leo XIII
on September 6, 1887.

✠

FEAST OF
OUR LORD JESUS CHRIST, KING

Jesus, our King, is often represented as the Man of
Sorrows, the "Reproach of Men and the Outcast of the
People". And yet, no less an authority than the Apostle of
the Gentiles tells us that, precisely because of His shame
and His sufferings, Jesus became the King of eternal
glory, to Whom the Father gave all power in Heaven and
on earth, and in whose Name all knees must bow: "To this
end Christ died and rose again; that He might be Lord
both of the dead and of the living". (Rom. 14:9.)

Shall we not consider it rather more than a coincidence
that our Savior allowed His Kingship to be proclaimed, only
at times when He was subjected to poverty, or to insult

and sufferings? After the miracle of the loaves and fishes, when five thousand men's hunger had been appeased and their minds were illumined to recognize that "this is of a truth the prophet, that is to come into the world", Jesus did not allow Himself to be made King. "Jesus therefore, when He knew that they would come to take Him by force, and make Him king, fled again into the mountain Himself alone." (St. John 6:15.) "My kingdom is not of this world." (St. John 18:36.) But, when He lay, in greatest poverty, on straw in a stable, with swaddling clothes for covering and the breath of animals dispelling the chill, He was willing that the Wise Men announce His Kingship with their question: "Where is He that is born king of the Jews"? (St. Matt. 11:12.) Nor was He averse to the offer of gold in token that He was a King. The prophet Zacharias foretold;"Behold Thy King will come to thee, the Just and Savior: He is poor, and riding upon an ass, and upon a colt the foal of an ass". When, now that time arrived, lest it appear that the Savior's triumphal entry into Jerusalem liken too much the entry of a worldly king into his royal city, Jesus would have His disciple St. Matthew note; "Now all this was done that it might be fulfilled which was spoken by the prophet":—and the prophet had said; "He is poor".

Yet, not only nor principally in poverty, but in insult and suffering, did Jesus lay claim to the title under which we Catholics give homage to Him. Behold Him in the court of the palace, naked except for the scarlet cloak thrown about His shoulders, with torn and quivering flesh, with crown of thorns pressed down upon His sacred brow, with blood and spittle blinding Him;—ah! then He would allow men to cry out: "Hail, king of the Jews". (St. Matt. 27:29.) Behold Him, the Ecce Homo, in the hall of Pilate, with the multitude without reviling and thirsting for blood, and the Roman governor asks: "Art thou a king then?", and He Himself declares His Kingship: "Thou sayest that I am a King. For this was I born, and for this came I into the world; that I should give testimony to the truth".

(St. John 18:37.) Behold Him, Whose "hands and feet have been dug", and "all of Whose bones have been numbered" (Ps. 21:17), hanging on the gibbet of infamy; and they who revile and mock, in spite of their demand to have it otherwise, are obliged to read the title of His Kingship in three languages, because He wished it thus, that all the world might see and know: "Jesus of Nazareth, the King of the Jews".

Truly, in poverty and insult and sufferings Jesus would be known as mankind's King. Now He reigns in glory, at the right hand of the Heavenly Father, and shall forevermore. That day will dawn when they who have led just lives on earth, will partake of the glory of their King in heaven. However, as regards the present hour in a vale of tears, all Christians must never forget that by bearing poverty and insult and suffering they become like to Jesus the King. To the Christian who does not forget this truth, the King has made His promises:

"Blessed are the poor in spirit: for theirs is the kingdom of heaven.

"Blessed are ye when they shall revile you, and persecute you, and speak all that is evil against you, untruly, for My sake: be glad and rejoice, for your reward is very great in heaven". (St. Matt. 5:3, 11, 12.)

NOVEMBER

FEAST OF ALL SAINTS

The Feast of All Saints is divinely described in St. John's Apocalypse (Chap. 7:9-17):

"I saw a great multitude, which no man could number, of all nations and tribes and peoples and tongues, standing before the throne and in sight of the Lamb, clothed with white robes, and palms in their hands. And they cried with a loud voice, saying: Salvation to our God, Who sitteth upon the throne, and to the Lamb. And all the angels stood round about the throne and the ancients and the four living creatures. And they fell down before the throne upon their faces and adored God, saying: Amen. Benediction and glory and wisdom and thanksgiving, honor and power and strength, to our God, for ever and ever. Amen.

"And one of the ancients answered and said to me: These that are clothed in white robes, who are they? And whence came they? And I said to him: My Lord, thou knowest. And he said to me: These are they who are come out of great tribulation and have washed their robes and have made them white in the blood of the Lamb. Therefore, they are before the throne of God: and they serve Him day and night in His temple. And He that sitteth on the throne shall dwell over them. They shall no more hunger nor thirst: neither shall the sun fall on them, nor any heat. For the Lamb, which is in the midst of the throne, shall rule them and shall lead them to the fountains of the waters of life: and God shall wipe all tears from their eyes."

☩

NOVEMBER 2

ALL SOULS' DAY

Holy Scripture warns: "It is better to go to the house of mourning, than to the house of feasting: for in that we

were put in mind of the end of all, and living thinketh what
is to come". (Eccl. 7:3.)

Recognizing this important truth, the Church invites
her children through the month of November to center
their thoughts on the faithful departed: for devoted and
pious meditation on those in "the house of mourning", must
have a favorable reaction on all except the most indifferent
Christian. Such meditation, in the first place, affects the
three cardinal virtues—faith, hope and charity—without
which there is no chance for salvation. It urges, also, a
change in life, when life is not what it should be, and a
patient continuance of the ascent up the steep and rocky
path, when the path appears as long and wearisome and
difficult.

What a monumental error the so-called Reformers
made in rejecting the article of Faith on the "Communion
of Saints"! Our belief that the triumphant, the suffering and
the militant members of the Church are united by closest
bonds in one great society is, as every Catholic knows, a
belief most consoling and encouraging. There is no believer
in this dogma who is not encouraged by the remembrance
that we have strong friends before the throne of God in
Heaven, and will have grateful friends, as soon as they who
are now in Purgatory enjoy the Beatific Vision. There is no
one, deeply wounded by the loss of parents, brothers, sisters, friends, who does not find comfort in the knowledge
that he may continue to manifest love and kindness to the
dear departed.

November speaks plainly, strengthening our faith in
the communion of Saints. In the preface of the Requiem
Mass the Church prays that "they who are grieved by the
certainty of death may be consoled in the promise of future
immortality". Death is a punishment for sin; as such, it
must continue, necessarily, to bring sorrow. It brings sorrow
both to those who leave and to those who remain. However,
not all is darkness; for we cherish the hope that we shall

not be given over to eternal corruption. We are consoled by the knowledge of resurrection and reunion. And this cheering hope, founded on the solemn promise of the Conqueror of death and the grave, our Lord and Savior Jesus Christ, is nourished by thoughts of the faithful departed.

There remains charity. On the day of judgment the Judge will say to those at His right side: "I was in prison and you visited me". Now, it is not given to everyone to visit those who languish in the penal institutions of the individual States. And, nevertheless, all Catholics can make themselves worthy of those words of praise from the lips of Jesus. The Poor Souls are in prison, and we may visit them whenever we wish and as frequently as we wish. We shall not be barred from offering them consolation or from giving aid in their escape from the fetters which hold them bound. Here, then, is charity which reaches beyond life, beyond the grave; and this charity is encouraged by the Church when she directs that the faithful spend the entire month of November in more-than-usual diligence on behalf of the suffering souls. It is expected that Catholics will recite many indulgenced prayers, that they will apply the merits of Holy Communion received frequently, and have offered up the august Sacrifice of the Mass for the departed.

Finally, November with its devotion to the Poor Souls reminds us of the great truth that "today was their day and tomorrow will be ours". Through the portals through which they have gone, we must pass; the account which they have made, shall be asked of us; and in all likelihood their present lot will be our future portion. Salutary remembrance! Only the unbeliever will continue in his evil ways. They who love their immortal souls will return to God and be willing to carry their crosses in patient reparation for life's trangressions.

November and the Poor Souls teach us to despise earthly pleasures and vanities and to labor for the eternal mansions of peace and happiness.

✠

NOVEMBER 3

ST. HUBERT

St. Hubert, the eldest son of Bertrand, Duke of Aquitaine, and grandson of Charibert, King of Toulouse, was born about 656.

As a youth Hubert went to the Court of Neustria. His charming manners won universal esteem, and he was given a prominent position among the courtiers, which led to the dignity of "Count of the Palace". He was a worldling and a lover of pleasure, his chief passion being the chase. After marrying the daughter of the Count of Louvain, he gave himself up entirely to the pomp and vanities of the world.

One Good Friday morning, when the faithful were crowding the churches, Hubert went to the chase. While pursuing a beautiful stag, the animal turned, and, according to the legend, he was astonished to see a crucifix between the antlers, while he heard a voice saying: "Hubert, unless you turn to the Lord, and lead a holy life, you will go down into hell". Hubert dismounted, prostrated himself, and said: "Lord, what would You have me do?" He received the answer, "Go and seek Lambert, and he will instruct you".

Immediately he set out for Maestricht, of which place St. Lambert was Bishop. Hubert was received kindly, and St. Lambert became his spiritual director. Shortly afterwards Hubert's wife died. He then renounced all his honors and military rank, and gave up his birthright to the Duchy of Aquitaine to his younger brother, whom he made guardian of his infant son, Floribert.

After distributing his personal wealth among the poor, Hubert entered upon his studies for the priesthood, and was soon ordained. He became one of St. Lambert's chief associates in the administration of his Diocese. Upon the advice of St. Lambert, Hubert made a pilgrimage to Rome. During his absence, St. Lambert was assassinated by the followers of Pepin. At the same hour this was revealed to the Pope in a vision, with the command to appoint Hubert to the bishopric. With incredible zeal he penetrated into the most remote and barbarous places of Ardenne, and extirpated the remnants of idolatry. People flocked from distant places to hear him preach the word of God, as he spoke with such great unction and sweetness.

He translated St. Lambert's relics and See to Liege in 727. Hence St. Lambert is honored at Liege as principal patron, and St. Hubert as founder of the city and church, and its first Bishop. After a short illness St. Hubert died on May 30, 727. In 835 his remains were translated to the Abbey called after him in the Ardennes.

St. Hubert is venerated as Patron Saint of hunters.

✠

NOVEMBER 4

ST. CHARLES BORROMEO

If ever the gates of hell could have prevailed it was in the 16th century. It was during this turbulent period when the enemies of the Church were striving to destroy her that St. Charles Borromeo was born. In October, 1538, at Arona, on the shores of Lake Maggiore, Charles first saw the light of day. His ancestors had been eminent in Church and State. His father, Count Gilbert Borromeo, possessed great piety and rare diplomatic ability. It was from him that Charles learned his love of prayer and tender solicitude for the poor. The mother of St. Charles, Margaret de Medici, sister of Cardinal de Medici, afterwards Pope Pius IV, was a worthy wife of the Count, both by nobility of family and the practice of virtue.

From early youth Charles showed an unusual gravity and love of solitude; his recreation was spent in building altars to Our Lady and in singing psalms. His father, convinced of the boy's vocation, permitted him to receive the tonsure and to wear the cassock when quite young, as was the custom in those days. Determined that he should receive a fitting education, Charles was sent to Milan to pursue his studies. One of his masters remarked, "You do not know this young man; he will one day be the reformer of the Church and will do wonderful things". It was while at Milan that the death of Charles' mother occurred, which event increased the already seriousness of the youth. From Milan Charles went to Pavia to complete his studies. At the age of twenty-two he took the Doctor's degree. During these years of study his father died and the care of the family devolved upon his young shoulders.

The death of Pope Paul IV and the election of Cardinal de Medici, in 1559, was the dawn of a glorious future for the two young nephews of the new Pontiff, Pius IV. Recognizing and appreciating the extraordinary talents and sanctity of Charles, he desired to employ him in the service of the Church. Charles was at once created a Cardinal-Deacon and entrusted with many high offices at the Vatican, besides being made Administrator of the See of Milan. His rare intellectual qualities soon determined the Pope to make him his Secretary of State.

The death of his brother, Count Frederick, in 1562, filled his mind more than ever with a sense of the hollowness of earthly glory, and made him determined to adopt a stricter rule of life. He chose a Jesuit Father for his confessor, who helped him greatly. Soon after he was made Cardinal-Priest he was consecrated Bishop. He lived a life of penance and prayer, faithfully visiting his Diocese and scrupulously employing his revenues for the good of the Church and of the poor. During a terrible famine in Milan, the Saint exerted himself to the utmost to keep his poor from starvation. For three months he fed over three thousand people at his own expense, and having rendered himself penniless collected alms from all quarters. "Charity", he said, "should know no bounds, neither therefore must almsgiving." His devotedness to his flock during the Great Plague of 1576 caused him to be revered by the Milanese.

Much of the success of the Council of Trent is due to his indefatigable labors in the cause of reform. Many were the hospitals, houses of mercy, homes of refuge, and other similar institutions established by the Cardinal, and, in many cases, maintained at his own expense.

On November 4, 1584, surrounded by his confessor and many Priests, whose weeping rendered their pious utterances unintelligible, St. Charles gave them his blessing, and in the greatest peace breathed out his soul into the hands of God. His body was enshrined under the High Altar of the Cathedral, and the canonization took place in 1610.

✠

NOVEMBER 5

ST. BERTILLE

St. Bertille was born of an illustrious family near Soissons, during the reign of Dagobert I. From her earliest years she preferred the love of God to that of creatures, and shunned their company whenever possible. As she grew older she relished daily more and more the consolation of conversing with God. Despising the world, she earnestly desired to renounce it, but feared to make known her inclinations to her parents.

St. Owen, whom Bertille consulted, encouraged her to pray for guidance. When her parents were informed of their daughter's desire, they willingly accompanied her to the monastery of Jouarre, in Brie, four leagues from Meaux. St. Thelchilde, who was the first Abbess of Jouarre, received Bertille with great joy and trained her in the way of perfection. In all her employments she acquitted herself with such great charity and edification that she was chosen Prioress, to assist the Abbess.

When St. Bathilde, wife of Clovis II, refounded the Abbey of Chelles, which St. Clotilde had instituted near Paris, she requested St. Thelchilde to furnish this new community with some of the most experienced and virtuous Nuns of Jouarre who would be able to train the novices in the rule of monastic perfection. St. Bertille was sent at the head of this holy group, and was appointed the first Abbess of Chelles, about 646. Her reputation for sanctity and prudence, and the excellent discipline which she established, drew several foreign Queens to this Abbey. Among others Bede mentions Hereswith, Queen of the East Angles, and Queen Bathilde, who retired there in 665 when her son Clotaire III reached his majority.

St. Bertille governed this renowned monastery for forty-six years. In her old age her fervor increased, and she strove only to increase her penances and devotions. In these holy dispositions St. Bertille closed her penitential life in 692.

✠

NOVEMBER 6

ST. LEONARD

St. Leonard, or Lienard, was a French nobleman in the Court of Clovis I. After he was converted to Christianity by St. Remigius, he left the Court to become a disciple of St. Remigius. He acquired the very spirit of his master and was animated with the same simplicity, disinterestedness, modesty, zeal and charity. Finding it very difficult to resist the King's importunities to return to Court, and desiring to give himself up entirely to a life of penance and prayer, Leonard retired privately to the monastery of Micy (called afterwards St. Mesmin's), near Orleans. Under the direction of St. Mesmin, he took the religious habit and fervently observed the regular discipline. Later, aspiring after a stricter solitude, St. Leonard, with the permission of St. Mesmin, left Micy and chose for his retirement a forest four leagues from Limoges. Here he built himself a cell, lived on wild herbs and fruits, and for some time had no other witness of his penance and virtues but Almighty God.

Since his zeal and devotion sometimes carried him to neighboring churches, his reputation for sanctity and miracles spread far and wide. Before he retired to Micy he was most remarkable for his charity towards captives and prisoners; he now resumed that work. Gradually others desired to imitate his manner of life and joined him in his solitude. The King bestowed on them a considerable part of the forest where they dwelt. Frequently St. Leonard made excursions to preach and instruct the people in the surrounding country. When he had filled up the measure of his good works, his labors were crowned with a happy death, about the year 559. Many churches in France and England bear his name.

☩

NOVEMBER 7

ST. WILLIBRORD

St. Willibrord was born in Northumbria in 658. He was educated at the Abbey of Ripon near York, as a disciple of St. Wilfrid, and then entered the Benedictine Order. At the age of twenty he went to Ireland, where he spent twelve years under St. Egbert, from whom Willibrord and eleven companions received the mission to Frisia, at the request of Pepin. They went to Utrecht but did not remain there, going instead to the Court of Pepin.

Willibrord visited Rome in 692 and received Apostolic authorization for his missionary labors. At the request of Pepin, he went a second time to Rome and was consecrated Bishop of the Frisians on November 21, 695, by Pope Sergius I and given the name of Clement. He founded a monastery at Utrecht, and built a church in that city in honor of the Holy Redeemer, which he made his Cathedral. In 698 he established an abbey at the Villa Echternach on the Sure, and frequently spent some time there for the sanctification of his soul.

As Radbod gained possession of Frisia in 716, Willibrord was obliged to leave. Radbod destroyed most of the churches, replacing them with temples and shrines to the idols, and killed many of the missionaries.

Willibrord and his companions made many trips to the north of Brabant in Thuringia and Geldria, but they met with no success in Denmark and Helgoland. After the death of Radbod in 719, Willibrord returned to Frisia. With the assistance of St. Boniface, he repaired the damage that had been done to the churches. Numberless conversions were the result of their labors.

St. Willibrord died at Echternach, Luxemburg, on November 7, 739, and was buried in the oratory of the Abbey there. Almost immediately he was honored as a saint. Echternach became a place of pilgrimage, and Alcuin mentions miracles wrought there. St. Willibrord's relics were translated to a new Basilica in 1906.

✠

NOVEMBER 8

ST. GODFREY

St. Godfrey was born of noble and pious parents, near Soissons. When his father became a widower he consecrated himself to God in the monastic habit. At the age of five Godfrey was placed in the monastery of St. Quentin, under the care of the holy Abbot Godfrey, who was his godfather.

The saint in his youth spent much of his time, day and night, in prayer. At the age of twenty-five he was ordained a priest, and soon afterwards was chosen Abbot of Nogent, in Champagne. In 1103, much against his will, he was consecrated Bishop of Amiens. He was remarkable for his meekness and patience, and for his great charity towards the poor.

While on his way to Rheims to confer with his Metropolitan regarding certain important matters, St. Godfrey was taken ill. He received the Last Sacraments and joyfully departed this life on November 8, 1118, in the Abbey of St. Crispin at Soissons, where he was interred.

✠

NOVEMBER 9

ST. THEODORE

Theodore was a Christian soldier in the Roman legion at Amasea. When the edict against the Christians was issued by the Emperors, he was brought before the Court at Amasea and commanded to offer sacrifice to the gods. Theodore refused, professing his belief in the Divinity of Jesus Christ. The judges, pretending pity for one so young, gave him time to reconsider. This he employed in destroying the Temple of Cybele by fire. Theodore was arrested again, and after being cruelly tortured was burned to death for the Faith, in the year 306.

✠

NOVEMBER 10

ST. ANDREW AVELLINO

Andrew Avellino, a native of Sicily, was born in 1521. He was baptized Lancelotto, but out of love for the cross he changed his name to Andrew when he entered the Order of Theatines. From early youth he had a great love for chastity. He pursued his studies by taking a course in the humanities and in philosophy at Venice; later he studied canon and civil law at Naples, and was ordained a priest at the age of twenty-six.

While holding the office of lawyer at the Ecclesiastical Court of Naples, a lie escaped his lips one day as he pleaded the cause of a friend. Shortly afterwards his eyes fell upon the following passage in the Bible: "The mouth that belieth killeth the soul" (Wisdom 1:11). Feeling deep remorse, he renounced his profession as ecclesiastical lawyer and spent some time in holy meditation and other spiritual exercises. He was then commissioned by the Archbishop of Naples to reform a convent in that city, which had become a source of great scandal because of its laxity in discipline. After many and great difficulties he succeeded in bringing about the necessary reform. Yet, in accomplishing this, one night, after being assaulted and severely wounded, he was brought to the monastery of the Theatines to recuperate. He now decided to enter this Society. Consequently, on the vigil of the Assumption he was invested, being then thirty-five years old. Later he was made Master of Novices, which office he held ten years. He was then elected Superior, and his deep humility and sincere piety induced the General of the Society to entrust him with the foundation of new Theatine houses at Milan, Piacenza, and in other dioceses of Italy. By his prudent direction of souls and his eloquent preaching he succeeded in converting many sinners and heretics.

St. Charles Borromeo was a close friend of St. Andrew and sought his advice in most important Church affairs. St. Andrew wrote many volumes of ascetical works. He died on November 10, 1608 and was canonized by Pope Clement XI. He is venerated as Patron Saint in Naples and Sicily, and is invoked especially against a sudden death.

✠

NOVEMBER 11

ST. MARTIN OF TOURS

St. Martin was born in 316 in Pannonia, Lower Hungary, and soon afterwards his parents moved to Pavia, Italy, where the child was educated. From his earliest years Martin seemed drawn to God and to have no relish for anything but for His service, though his parents were idolaters.

It was in Pavia, and when only ten years old, that he found his way to a Christian church and asked to receive instruction in preparation for Baptism. When his father, an officer in the army, discovered that he was receiving Christian instruction, he determined to take the boy away; he insisted upon sending him into the army, at the early age of fifteen, accompanied by a single servant. In his wandering life, Martin was exposed to many dangers, but always remembered the instructions received from his Christian teachers, and practiced them as best he could.

It was this Christian seed in his heart which suddenly sprang forth and blossomed under the imploring look of a beggar at the gate of Amiens. It was during the intensely cold winter of 335, when many persons perished in Northern France for want of proper clothing and exposure, that one day as a regiment of soldiers were marching through the gate of the city of Amiens, a poor man, clothed in rags and shivering with cold, held out his thin hand for charity. Officers and well-clad soldiers passed him without dropping a coin or inquiring about his needs. At length Martin, now a young officer and scarcely eighteen years of age, rode through the gate. A flush passed over his face as this suffering fellow-creature met his eye. Without a word, the young officer drew his sword from its scabbard and cut his military cloak in two; and while one-half still hung from his own shoulders, the other had been thrown over those of the shivering beggar. Leaning towards the beggar, he said: "It is all I have to give, for I have no money"; and then spurred on with his regiment.

That night the young officer dreamed that Jesus Christ appeared to him wearing on His shoulders the half of his cloak which had been given to the beggar, and He said to Martin: "Look at this cloak, and see if you recognize it".

Then the shining Visitor turned from the young officer to the troop of Angels who accompanied Him, saying: "Martin, though only a catechumen, has clothed Me with this garment".

Martin lost no time in securing the grace of Baptism. From this time his noble soul was given up entirely to the love of God, and his one desire was to give his mind and body to the service of Jesus Christ. After five years' service in the army, he revisited his native Hungary and brought about the conversion to Christianity of his own mother. This pious errand accomplished, he returned to Poitiers, and at his request, St. Hilary, the Bishop, gave him a piece of land two leagues from the city. On this land St. Martin built a monastery, which some think was the first monastery in Gaul (France), to which not only Christians, but those desiring to become Christians, were welcomed. Among the latter was a young man preparing for Baptism. Soon after his arrival, Martin was called from the monastery. On returning he was grief-stricken to find that the young man had died suddenly without Baptism and was being prepared for burial. Like another Elias, after asking the Monks to leave the room, he stretched himself on the dead youth, and after praying fervently he felt the body growing warm under his touch. Restored to life, Baptism was immediately administered, and he lived many years after to be a standing witness to the mercy of God, and to the efficacy of St. Martin's holy prayers.

In 371 St. Martin was chosen Bishop of Tours. Though henceforth engaged in spreading the Gospel by his zealous labors and by his virtuous life, as well as by the exercise of his gifts of prophecy and miracle working, he strove to the end of his life to observe monastic discipline by retiring at intervals to the nearby Abbey of Marmoutier.

St. Martin died November 11, 397, in a small town on the very borders of his Diocese, but the city of Tours claimed his precious relics. Many churches and towns throughout Western Europe have been placed under his patronage.

✠

NOVEMBER 12

ST. MARTIN I

St. Martin I was elected Pope at Rome on July 21, 649, to succeed Theodore I. He is one of the noblest personages in the long line of Roman Pontiffs. He governed the Church during the time the leaders of the Monothelite heresy, supported by the Emperor, were making strenuous efforts to spread their heretical doctrine in the East and the West.

Martin convoked at Rome a Council, where the Monothelites were condemned. As a consequence, he was treacherously seized by order of the heretics Heraclius and Constans. Desiring to avoid the shedding of human blood, St. Martin forbade resistance and declared himself willing to be brought before the Emperor. The holy prisoner, accompanied by only a few attendants, and suffering greatly from bodily ailments and privations, arrived at Constantinople on September 17, 653 or 654, after being kept on the island of Naxos for a year. Messengers were dispatched to the imperial city to announce the arrival of the prisoner, who was branded as a heretic and a rebel, an enemy of God and of the State. For three months he was confined in a dungeon. After enduring much suffering and humiliation, the venerable Pontiff was exiled to Cherson in 655, while a terrible famine raged in that region. From his sad exile he meekly complained to his friends of the neglect and indifference of those with whom he had been in contact; they were afraid to render him the slightest assistance.

The prolonged sufferings of St. Martin were brought to an end in 655. He was buried in the church of Our Lady near Cherson. Many miracles were wrought by him in life and after death. His body was translated to Rome, where it reposes in the Church of Saints Sylvester and Martin on the Esquiline Hill.

✠

NOVEMBER 13

ST. STANISLAS KOSTKA

St. Stanislas was born at Rostkovo, Poland, in October, 1550. His father, John Kostka, was a Senator in the Kingdom of Poland and Lord of Zabraczym; his mother was the sister and niece of the Dukes Palatine of Masovia and the aunt of Felix Kryski, Chancellor of Poland. Their marriage was blessed with seven children, Stanislas being the second. His older brother, Paul, lived to see him beatified in 1605.

The two brothers were educated at home; then they were sent to the Jesuit college in Vienna, where they remained three years. St. Stanislas was conspicuous not only for his amiable and cheerful disposition, but for his religious fervor and angelic piety. While at the college, among other practices of devotion Stanislas joined the Congregation of St. Barbara. He confided to his tutor, and later to a Jesuit in Rome, that it was St. Barbara who brought two Angels to him during a serious illness in order to give him the Sacred Host in Holy Communion. Paul was displeased with the piety of his younger brother, and he often treated him with violence.

Burning with love of God and Our Lady, Stanislas desired to enter the Society of Jesus. They hesitated to receive him in Vienna, fearing the trouble his father might cause the Society. Stanislas decided to apply to the General of the Society in Rome. Without guide or resources, when the first opportunity presented itself, Stanislas left Vienna and walked the way to Rome, five hundred leagues distant. He stayed for a month at Dillingen with St. Peter Canisius, and on October 25, 1567, arrived in Rome. As he was greatly exhausted from the journey, St. Francis Borgia, then General of the Order, would not permit him to enter the novitiate of St. Andrew until several days later. The remaining ten months of his life Stanislas was a model and mirror of religious perfection. Many supernatural favors were bestowed upon the innocent youth by Almighty God. In his 18th year of life he implored the Blessed Virgin to call him to the "skies", there to celebrate with her the anniversary of her glorious Assumption. His confidence in her was rewarded. On August 15, 1568, while praying to God, the Saints, and the Blessed Virgin Mary his beautiful soul passed to its Creator. He was canonized on December 31, 1726. St. Stanislas is one of the favorite Saints of Poland.

✠

NOVEMBER 14

ST. JOSAPHAT

Josaphat, a native of Wlademir, Lithuania, belonged to a noble family. His father devoted himself to commercial pursuits and held the office of Town-Councillor. Both parents strove to implant the seed of piety in the heart of their child, who gave evidence of unusual talent. Due to their straitened circumstances, he was apprenticed to a merchant at Vilna, and in that corrupt city he advanced in learning and virtue.

At the age of twenty-four he entered the Basilian monastery of the Trinity at Vilna, and in 1609 was ordained to the priesthood. He subsequently became Superior in several monasteries, and was reluctantly consecrated Bishop of Vitebsk on November 12, 1617, with right of succession to the archbishopric of Polotsk. He became Archbishop in 1618.

The apostolic zeal of the young Archbishop excited against him the hatred of the schismatics. He was attacked by them at Vitebsk on November 12, 1623; an ax stroke and a bullet brought Josaphat his martyr's crown. He is noted for his indefatigable efforts in uniting the schismatic Greek Church with the Roman Church.

After numerous conversions and miracles had occurred, a commission was appointed by Pope Urban VIII in 1628 to inquire into the cause of Josaphat. Five years after his death his body was still incorrupt. He was canonized by Pope Pius IX in 1867.

☩

NOVEMBER 15

ST. ALBERT THE GREAT

St. Albert the Great (Albertus Magnus) was born in Swabia about 1206, and as a child had a very special love for the Blessed Virgin. He pursued his studies at Padua, and in 1223 he entered the Order of St. Dominic. After completing his studies he taught theology at Hildesheim, Freiburg, Ratisbon, Strassburg and Cologne. In 1245 he was ordered to go to Paris, where he received the Doctor's degree in the university.

While teaching in Paris and Cologne, amongst his hearers was St. Thomas Aquinas, whose genius he recognized and whose future greatness he foretold.

In 1254 Albert was elected Provincial of his Order in Germany, but resigned the office in 1257 so as to be able to devote himself to study and to teaching. In 1260 he was appointed Bishop of Ratisbon, and governed the Diocese two years; then voluntarily resumed the duties of a professor in the Stadium at Cologne.

Pope Gregory X called him to attend the Council of Lyons in 1274, and he took an active part in the deliberations. The announcement of the death of St. Thomas Aquinas at Fossa Nuova on his way to the Council, was a heavy blow to Albert, and he declared that "The Light of the Church" had been extinguished.

Some time after 1278, St. Albert suffered a lapse of memory; his strong mind gradually became clouded; while his body, weakened by vigils, austerities and many labors, sank under the weight of years. He died at Cologne November 15, 1280. He is called "the Great", and "Doctor Universalis" (Universal Doctor), in recognition of his extraordinary genius and extensive knowledge. Under God, we owe to St. Albert the "Summa Theologica" of St. Thomas. Two editions of St. Albert's works were published at Lyons in 1651, in twenty-one folio volumes; the other at Paris, 1890-1899, in thirty-eight quarto volumes.

✠

NOVEMBER 16

ST. GERTRUDE

St. Gertrude, born at Eisleben, Germany, in 1263, was a sister to St. Mechtildes. When five years old Gertrude was offered to God in the Benedictine convent of Rodalsdorf. Twenty-five years later she was chosen Abbess, and the following year was obliged to assume the government of the monastery of Heldelfs, to which she removed with her Nuns.

St. Gertrude studied Latin in her youth, as was the custom for Nuns to do. She was also versed in sacred literature and wrote and composed in Latin very proficiently. She considered Divine contemplation and devout prayer her principal duty. While meditating on the Passion of Christ, which was her favorite devotion, frequently she was unable to withhold the torrents of tears which flowed from her eyes. She spoke of Christ and of the mysteries of His life with so much unction, and in such transports of holy love, as to inspire all who heard her. Ecstasies and raptures of Divine love as well as gifts of Divine union in prayer. were familiar to her. Her profound humility and perfect meekness laid the foundation of the great virtues and graces bestowed upon her by her Divine Spouse.

Watching, fasting, abstinence, perfect obedience, and the constant denial of her own will were the means by which she subjected her flesh, and subjected or subdued whatever could oppose the Will of God in her affections. Possessed with the greatest natural talents and the most extraordinary gifts of Divine grace, her mind was filled with the deepest sentiments of her nothingness, baseness and imperfections, and it was her sincere desire that others should have the same contempt of her which she had of herself. Though she was the Superior and Mother of the Community, she acted towards all as if she were the lowest servant.

Jesus chose St. Gertrude to be the herald of devotion to His Sacred Heart four centuries before He revealed to St. Margaret Mary His desire that It be given public veneration.

We have a living portraiture of St. Gertrude's pure and holy soul in her short book, "Of Divine Insinuations, or Communications and Sentiments of Love". It is perhaps the most useful work, next to the writings of St. Teresa, with which any female Saint ever enriched the Church for nourishing piety in a contemplative state.

In her seventy-second year, after having been Abbess for forty years, St. Gertrude was called to the embrace of her heavenly Spouse in 1334. Miracles attested how precious her death was in the sight of God. The Catholic Church has distinguished her from all others of her sex by adding to her name the honorable title, "the Great".

☩

NOVEMBER 17

ST. GREGORY THAUMATURGUS

St. Gregory (the miracle-worker) was born a pagan at Neo-Caesarea in Pontus, about the year 200. It was while visiting in Caesarea in Palestine that he and his brother met and conversed with the celebrated scholar Origen, head of the catechetical school of Alexandria, who resided there. Soon both youths forgot about Beirut and Roman law, and were gradually won over to Christianity. In 238 or 239 the two brothers returned to Pontus. Before leaving Palestine Gregory delivered in the presence of Origen a public farewell oration in which he thanked the illustrious master he was leaving. This oration contains much useful information concerning the youth of Gregory and his master's method of teaching.

Gregory was forty years old when consecrated Bishop, and he ruled his Diocese for many years. There were only seventeen Christians in Caesarea when he began his apostolic work, and at his death there remained but seventeen pagans in the town. He was famous for his sanctity and his doctrine, and became still more so by the prodigies and miracles which God multiplied through the years, that he was surnamed *Thaumaturgus* or worker of miracles.

Putting into practice what Our Lord said to His disciples: "Have the faith of God. Amen, I say to you whosoever shall say to this mountain, Be thou removed and be cast into the sea; and shall not stagger in his heart, but believe that whatsoever he saith shall be done, it shall be done unto him" (Mark 11:22, 23), one day Gregory commanded a mountain to draw back so as to leave sufficient room for the erection of a church, and the command was obeyed.

St. Gregory died about the year 270.

✠

NOVEMBER 18

ST. ODO OF CLUNY

St. Odo was born at Tours in 879. After spending several years at the Court of William, Duke of Aquitaine, he entered the Abbey of St. Martin at Tours. About 909 he received the Benedictine Habit at Baume, and in 924 became Abbot of the renowned abbey of Cluny, which was then being erected. Many distant monasteries received his regulations and subjected themselves to his jurisdiction, so that the abbey of Cluny became most numerous and flourishing. St. Odo founded the monastery of Our Lady on the Aventine and reformed several convents, including Subiaco and Monte Cassino. St. Odo was entrusted by

Popes and princes with several important political missions, all of which he handled successfully. It was while he was on one of these missions of mercy that he was taken ill at Rouen, and at his urgent request was carried back to Tours, where he died at the feet of "his own St. Martin", on November 18, 942. He was buried in the church of St. Julian, but the Huguenots burned the greatest part of his remains.

DEDICATION OF THE BASILICAS OF SAINTS PETER AND PAUL

The Basilica of St. Peter on the Vatican Hill and that of St. Paul Outside-the-Walls, were erected by Constantine on the site of the martyrdom of these two Apostles. They were consecrated by St. Sylvester on November 18.

The Basilica of St. Peter is on the site of the circus of Nero, and beneath its High Altar lie the sacred remains of the Chief of the Apostles, making the church with St. John Lateran the center of the whole Christian world.

The Basilica of St. Paul Outside-the-Walls was also built in the 4th century over the tomb of the Apostle of the Gentiles. It was almost completely destroyed by fire in 1823, but was rebuilt on a grander scale by Popes Gregory XVI and Pius IX, and consecrated by the latter on December 10, 1854.

☩

NOVEMBER 19

ST. ELIZABETH OF HUNGARY

Elizabeth, daughter of Andrew II, King of Hungary, was born in 1207. When only four years old she was sent to the Court of Hermann, Landgrave of Thuringia, to be betrothed to his son, Ludwig. She was brought up at the

Thuringian Court, in accordance with the customs of those times, and educated in company with her future husband, so that from their childhood they loved each other as most dear companions.

From her earliest years Elizabeth possessed, by the grace of God, a marvelous spirit of prayer, great simplicity and profound charity. She hated rich garments, and avoided taking part in the pomps and ceremonies of the Court. Her great love was to visit the poor and the sorrowful, to minister to their needs, to relieve their sufferings. In the meantime she had to contend with future relatives who had little, if any, sympathy with her life filled with works of charity.

Elizabeth and Ludwig were married in 1220. Hardly more than a child in years, Elizabeth entered upon the full duties and responsibilities of womanhood. Thanks to the influence of her example and that of her husband, the Thuringian Court became famous throughout Germany for the valor and honor of its knights and the purity and holiness of its ladies.

But it was not by her individual good works alone that Elizabeth came to be known and loved throughout the whole extent of her husband's dominion and beyond it. She and he were untiring in their efforts to help the weak and the oppressed. To Ludwig is due the foundation of the famous Benedictine Abbey of Rheinhartsbrunn, while Elizabeth rejoiced to welcome the first Franciscan Friars to Eisenach, and placed herself under their direction. With her husband's permission, she multiplied her works of mercy, for her love of the poor was boundless. Even in her dress she endeavored to be like them.

One day as she was carrying under her mantle some provisions for the poor, she met her husband returning from the chase.

"What have you there, sweet lady?" asked Ludwig.

Elizabeth opened her cloak, and behold! the heavy burden was no longer there—only some beautiful fragrant roses, although it was not the season for them. The briar roses that grow on the steep hillside above Eisenach are still called "Elisabethblumen", "Elizabeth's flowers".

Eight years had passed since their marriage—years of extreme happiness and increased saintliness. Elizabeth had become the mother of one son and two daughters and was expecting another child; the time of trial was at hand.

While on his way with a new Crusade to the Holy Land, with the Emperor Frederick Barbarossa, Ludwig fell a victim to fever which broke out amongst the imperial troops before they embarked from Brindisi. He died at Otranto, with the calm resignation of the true Christian knight he had always been.

Elizabeth, with her children, was stripped of everything by her brother-in-law, who was bent on usurping the inheritance which rightly belonged to Elizabeth's son, Hermann. Elizabeth was driven from her palace and after wandering through the streets with her little children, a prey to hunger and cold, was finally befriended. She welcomed all her sufferings.

She gave her little son Hermann to be educated as a worthy son of his father, and in due time to enter upon his inheritance. Her eldest daughter was betrothed, as she had been, to the Duke of Hesse-Cassel, and confided to the care of her future husband's mother. The two youngest she placed in the care of her aunt the Abbess. Then on Good Friday, 1230, Elizabeth made the supreme sacrifice. Kneeling before the Crucifix, she laid aside her widow's sombre robes and assumed the coarse brown Habit of St. Francis, dedicating herself finally to serve God in absolute poverty and humility. She busied herself to the day of her death in works of charity and piety.

In 1232, God revealed to her the time of her death, which came just before dawn on November 19, 1232. Her relics are enshrined at Marburg, the place of her decease, in Thuringia. Four years after her death she was canonized by Pope Gregory IX.

✠

NOVEMBER 20

ST. FELIX OF VALOIS

St. Felix, of the Royal House of Valois in France, was born in 1127. After having led a most austere life as a hermit in a dense forest in the Diocese of Meaux, he was joined by St. John of Matha. Together they founded the Order of the Most Holy Trinity (Trinitarian Order) for the ransom of the Christian captives held in slavery by the Moors of Spain and North Africa. The new Institute was approved by Pope Innocent III. Within forty years the Order possessed six hundred monasteries in nearly every country of the world.

Shortly before his death on November 4, 1212, at his old hermitage Cerfroid, St. Felix was favored with a vision of Our Lady wearing the Trinitarian Habit. Though the Bull of his canonization is no longer in existence, it has been the constant tradition of the Order that St. Felix was canonized by Pope Urban IV in 1262. In 1666 Alexander VII declared him a Saint.

✠

NOVEMBER 21

THE PRESENTATION OF THE BLESSED VIRGIN MARY

It is an ancient tradition that Mary was vowed to God by her parents, and that at the age of three was brought by them to the Temple, there to be educated; that she lived in the precincts of the Temple with other young Jewish girls and the holy women who cared for them.

During the years of Mary's service in the Temple, her pure soul was adorned with the most precious graces, an object of amazement and praise to the Angels, and of the highest complacence to the Most Holy Trinity.

✠

NOVEMBER 22

ST. CECILIA

St. Cecilia was born of a noble Roman family about the year 214. She was brought up from infancy in the precepts of the Christian Faith and vowed her virginity to God, and, in the spirit of this promise, shunned the pleasures and vanities of the world. She excelled in music, and this charming gift she consecrated to God by composing hymns in His honor.

Against her will, she was given in marriage to Valerian. On the first night of the nuptials she told him of the solemn promise she had made to preserve her virginity, and of the Angel who was ever at her side to protect her, and asked Valerian not to do anything that might kindle God's wrath against him. Valerian, moved by her words, did not dare touch her, and even said that he would believe in Christianity if he could see the Angel. When Cecilia said that would be impossible unless he received Baptism, he, burning with a desire to see the Angel, replied that he was willing to be baptized.

Following the virgin's advice, Valerian went to Pope Urban, who, on account of the persecution, was hiding among the tombs of the Martyrs on the Appian Way, and by him was baptized. When he returned to Cecilia he found her at prayer, and beside her an Angel shining with a divine splendor. As soon as he recovered from his fear, he summoned his brother Tiburtius, whom Cecilia also instructed in the Faith of Christ. After being baptized by Pope Urban he was also privileged to see the Angel. Both brothers shortly afterwards courageously suffered martyrdom, under the prefect Almachius. The prefect then com-

O God, You gladden us with the annual memorial of blessed Cecilia, Your Virgin and Martyr. Grant that we may imitate her holy life.

manded Cecilia to be arrested. When he learned that she had distributed among the poor the property of Tiburtius and Valerian he was so enraged that he commanded her to be put to death by the heat of the bath in her own house. After spending a day and a night there she remained unhurt by the fire; therefore, an executioner was sent, who, unable with three strokes of an ax to cut off her head, left her half-dead. Three days later, on November 22, 230, during the reign of Emperor Alexander, Cecilia took her flight to Heaven, adorned with the double palm of virginity and martyrdom. Pope Urban interred her body in the cemetery of Callixtus, and on the ground formerly occupied by the house in which St. Cecilia was born a church was consecrated in her name. Pope Paschal I brought her body, together with those of Popes Urban and Lucius, and of Tiburtius, Valerian and Maximus, and laid them all in this church of St. Cecilia in Rome.

✠

NOVEMBER 23

ST. CLEMENT I

St. Clement was a Roman by birth, and we learn from his Epistle to the Corinthians that he was of Jewish extraction. He was the fourth successor of St. Peter, and according to Tertullian, writing in 199, the Roman Church claimed that Clement was ordained Bishop by St. Peter.

A schism having arisen in the Church of Corinth, St. Clement wrote to the Corinthians in the name of the Church of Rome appealing for the restoration of peace and unity. In a second Epistle, he exhorted them to despise the vanities of the world for the sake of eternity.

From earliest times it has been the belief that St. Clement suffered martyrdom. The Church of St. Clement in Rome lies in the valley between the Esquiline and Coelian Hills, on the direct road from the Coliseum to the Lateran.

St. Clement governed the Church nine years, eleven months and twenty days. He died in the year 100.

ST. FELICITAS

St. Felicitas was the widowed mother of the seven brothers who met martyrdom for the Faith during the reign of Marcus Aurelius, about 165 A.D. She strengthened the hearts of her sons in the love of their heavenly country by her exhortations; and she gave them birth in spirit, just as she had brought them into the world according to the flesh, that her teaching might bear to God the children whom her body had borne in the world. She was the first to come to tribulation, but the eighth to attain the reward.

✠

NOVEMBER 24

ST. JOHN OF THE CROSS

St. John was born near Avila, Spain, in 1542. At the age of twenty-two he entered the Carmelite Order and took the name of John of the Cross. He was ordained Priest in 1567, and led a most holy, austere, prayerful life. Inflamed with a desire to live a retired life, he considered entering the Carthusian Order. Instead, he was led by St. Teresa to found the Order of Bare-Footed Carmelites, whose Institute was approved by Pope Pius V, and confirmed by Gregory XIII in 1580. John was soon joined by some others, all of whom renewed their profession in Advent, 1568. Their sanctity spread throughout the village of Durville and soon over all of Spain.

St. John's intense love of the cross appeared in all his actions, and it was by meditating continually on the sufferings of Christ that it increased daily in his soul. He not only passed through many spiritual and interior trials, but underwent much persecution and even imprisonment for nine months at Toledo.

St. Teresa, when made Prioress of the convent at Avila where she had made her profession, appointed St. John spiritual director of the house in 1576. He gave her his powerful help in reforming the Order.

Once St. John heard Christ say to him: "John, what recompense dost thou ask of thy labors?" He answered, "Lord, I ask no other recompense than to suffer and be contemned for Thy love". The love of God so powerfully possessed his soul, and its fire was so violent, that his words were sufficient to kindle a flame in others. His wonderful works on Mystical Theology, "The Ascent of Mount Carmel", "The Dark Night", "The Spiritual Canticle", "The Living Flame", make him the master and guide of all who are favored with the gift of supernatural prayer. He lays down in his works two fundamental rules of perfection: (1) that a person endeavor to perform all his actions in union with those of Jesus Christ, desiring to imitate Him and to put on His spirit; (2) to mortify his senses in all things, denying them whatever does not seem most to contribute to the glory of God.

St. John often begged God not to let him pass a day without suffering and to permit him to die where he would be unknown to all. God answered his prayer, for the reform of Carmel caused him great suffering, and even banishment. For three months prior to his death, he endured excruciating pains and fever from an ulcerated leg. He calmly breathed forth his soul on December 14, 1591, as he pressed the crucifix on his breast and said, "Lord, into Thy hands I commend my soul".

St. John was canonized by Pope Benedict XIII in 1726, and was proclaimed a Doctor of the Church by Pope Pius XI on November 24, 1926.

☩

NOVEMBER 25

ST. CATHERINE OF ALEXANDRIA

St. Catherine glorified God by an illustrious confession of the Faith of Christ at Alexandria, Egypt, under Maximinus II. She was, in truth, the very flower of the Alexandrian nobility. At the age of eighteen she was a prodigy of learning, for she had been educated at the feet of the successors of Pantaenus of Alexandria and of his disciple, St. Clement.

When Emperor Maximinus began his persecution of the Christians, Catherine did not fear to throw her rank, her learning, and her eloquence on the side of the oppressed Church. Contemning the overtures of the tyrant Maximinus, after much persecution she was sent into exile. According to tradition, when she returned she was put to death, in 310, by means of an engine fitted with a spiked wheel, after vain attempts by means of torture to force her to heathenism. The Christians, hearing of Catherine's glorious confession, reverently interred her body among them. Tradition continues to recount how in the 8th century it was conveyed by Angels to the top of Mt. Sinai, where it continues to be the object of great veneration.

St. Catherine is recognized as the Patron Saint of Christian philosophers. In Christian art she is depicted as being borne through the air by the Angels, one bearing her palm, another the sword by which her spirit was released from the bondage of earth. In all other pictures, St. Catherine of Alexandria is known by the broken wheel at her side.

☥

NOVEMBER 26

ST. SYLVESTER

St. Sylvester was born of noble parents at Osimo, about fourteen miles from Loretto, Italy, in 1177. After studying law and theology at Bologna and Padua, the Canons of the Cathedral at Osimo shared their dignity with him. His zeal in reproving those leading depraved lives caused him to have many enemies; while his Bishop, whom he warned of neglecting certain duties, accused him of being his persecutor. These trials served to purify the heart of Sylvester, and prepared him for the grace of the pure love of God.

One day he was present at the funeral of a man whom he had admired for his beauty and rare accomplishments. Struck by the hideous appearance of the man's body in death, he exclaimed, "I am today what he was, and one day I shall be what he is". Sylvester, who was then forty years old, immediately gave up everything and retired into a desert thirty miles from the city, where he devoted himself to penance and prayer. "Later, he built at Monte Fano", says the Roman Breviary, "a church in honor of the very holy Father Benedict who advised him in a vision to found a religious Order whose Rule and Habit he described to him. It was the Order of the Sylvestrines."

Sylvester lived to found twenty-five monasteries in Italy, and leaving his disciples heirs of his double spirit of penance and prayer, he surrendered his soul to God on November 26, 1267, at the age of ninety years. God was pleased to work several miracles at his tomb, and his name is inserted in the Roman Martyrology.

☩

NOVEMBER 27

ST. MAXIMUS

St. Maximus was born in Provence of truly Christian parents, who brought him up in the love and practice of virtue. As his mind and heart were engrossed with heavenly things, he made a resolution to observe perpetual chastity. After distributing his fortune among the poor, he retired to the monastery of Lerins, where he was kindly received by St. Honoratus. When Honoratus was made Archbishop of Arles, in 426, Maximus was chosen the second Abbot of Lerins, which office he held for seven years. The gift of miracles with which he was favored, and the great reputation of his sanctity drew large crowds to the monastery from many parts of the continent. Since the visitors prevented him from leading a secluded life, he felt obliged to spend some days in a forest on the island.

About the year 433 the See of Ries in Provence became vacant. Maximus fled to the coast of Italy to shun the dignity, but was pursued and brought back and compelled to fill the vacancy. He retained the same love of poverty, the same spirit of penance and prayer, the same indifference to the world, and the same humility for which he had been so conspicuous in the cloister. His new office required him to be the physician, pastor and teacher of a great many people, whom he strove to help to gain eternal life.

St. Maximus assisted at the Council of Ries in 439, of Orange in 441, and of Arles in 454. He died on the 27th of November before the year 462. His body rests in the Cathedral at Ries, which bears the names of the Blessed Virgin and St. Maximus.

✠

NOVEMBER 28

ST. CATHERINE LABOURE

When France seemed doomed to perish in the blood of her children and religion was threatened with destruction, the Blessed Virgin appeared to Catherine Zoe Laboure.

Zoe Laboure was born on May 2, 1806, and when she was nine years old her mother died; the child then found all her consolation in the Maternal Heart of Mary. The days passed, and when she received her First Holy Communion, she offered her virginal heart to Jesus. When she reached the age of twenty-four she entered the Novitiate of the Daughters of Charity on the Rue du Bac in Paris. One day she pleaded with her Guardian Angel to "Tell the Mother of God I wish to see her". Her life-story tells us that it was about 11 p.m. on July 18, 1830, that Novice Catherine (which name she took in religion) heard someone call her by name. She drew aside the curtain of her bed and saw a beautiful child standing close by. The vision said: "Come to the chapel, the Holy Virgin is waiting for you". Quickly donning her religious dress, the Novice followed the child. Rays of light that issued from the angelic visitor lighted

the way through the dark corridors. Upon reaching the
chapel, the doors swinging open of themselves, the two
entered. The chapel was filled with a brightness like that
of the sun.

Catherine knelt at the altar rail and prayed. At midnight her celestial guide said to her: "Behold the Mother
of God". Instantly she heard the rustling of a silken garment and a beautiful Lady appeared, seating herself on a
large chair at the Gospel side of the altar. Filled with awe,
Catherine knelt at the feet of the Blessed Mother and
placed her hands on the knees of the "apparition". "At that
moment", she told her Superior later, "I felt the greatest
happiness of my life." The second apparition occurred
November 27th, and the third early in December.

On the second occasion, St. Catherine records that the
Blessed Virgin appeared as if standing on a globe holding
a globe in her hands; and as if from rings set with precious stones dazzling rays of light were emitted from her
fingers. These, she stated, were symbols of the graces which
would be bestowed on all who ask for them. Then an
oval frame formed around the Blessed Virgin and Catherine
read in letters of gold: *O Mary, conceived without sin,
pray for us who have recourse to thee.* The vision reversed
and she beheld the letter "M" surmounted by a cross, at
the foot of the cross a bar, and below all the Heart of
Jesus crowned with thorns, and the Heart of Mary pierced
with a sword. A voice said to her: "Have a medal made
according to this model. Persons who wear it when it is
blessed will receive great graces, especially if they wear
it suspended about their necks". This medal is now universally known as "The Miraculous Medal".

During the first apparition, the Holy Virgin said to
Catherine: "When you have sorrows or troubles bring
them to the altar and lay them in the Heart of Jesus;
there you will receive all the consolation and strength you
need". Mary also foretold that Catherine would have many
difficulties to undergo; but she encouraged her to have
confidence, and then promised: "You will always have the

graces necessary to withstand your trials. . . . I myself will be with you to bring you the graces you need". . . ."Grace is shed most abundantly on those who ask for it in prayer; but, alas, where are those who pray!"

St. Catherine died December 31, 1876, and was canonized by Pope Pius XII on July 27, 1947.

✠

NOVEMBER 29

ST. SATURNINUS

About the year 250, during the reign of Decius and Gratus, Pope Fabian commissioned Saturninus to preach the Faith in Gaul. The Saint fixed his See at Toulouse, and thus became the first Christian Bishop of that city. Like to the earliest days of the Church, he brought about the conversion of many from paganism.

In order to reach the church he established it was necessary for him to walk by the capitol, where there was a pagan temple. According to the Acts of St. Saturninus, the pagan priests ascribed to the Saint's frequent journeys before the temple the silence of their oracles. Therefore, one day as he approached they seized him. Refusing to sacrifice to the idols, Saturninus was condemned to be tied by his feet to a bull, which dragged him through the town until the rope broke. His mangled body was taken and buried by two Christian women in order to prevent further profanation by the pagans.

Saints Hilary and Exuperius, his successors, gave the Martyr an honorable burial. The church which was erected where the bull stopped still exists, and is called the church of the *Taur* (the bull).

At an early date the Martyr's body was translated to the Church of St. Sernin (or Saturninus), which is one of the most ancient and beautiful of Southern France.

☩

NOVEMBER 30

ST. ANDREW

St. Andrew was one of the twelve Apostles chosen by Jesus. He was brother of Simon Peter, born in Bethsaida of Galilee, both of whom were fishermen. From St. John's Gospel we learn that Andrew was a disciple of St. John the Baptist, whose testimony led him and St. John, the beloved disciple, to follow the Savior. Andrew immediately recognized Jesus as the Messiah, and hastened to introduce to Him his brother Peter, who eventually was to be the rock upon which Jesus would found His Church.

On the occasion of the miraculous feeding of the five thousand, it was Andrew who pointed out the boy who had "five barley loaves and two fishes". A few days before the death of Jesus, certain Greeks asked Philip that they might see Him. Philip referred the matter to Andrew, as to one of greater authority, and then both told the Master.

Andrew was present at the Last Supper; saw the Risen Savior; witnessed the Ascension; shared in the graces and gifts of the first Pentecost, and endeavored to establish the Faith in Palestine amidst threats and persecution.

St. Andrew was crucified for the Faith at Patras in Greece, by order of the Roman Governor, during the reign of Nero, on November 30 in the year 60. He was bound, not nailed, to the cross, in order to prolong his sufferings. Outstanding in his martyrdom is the greeting wherewith he welcomed the cross on which he was to die: "Hail, precious cross, receive the disciple of Him Who hung upon thee, my Master Jesus".

DECEMBER

ST. ELIGIUS

St. Eligius, though born at Catelat near Limogues, about the year 588, was not of French, but of Roman-Gaulish extraction. His virtuous parents brought him up in the fear of God. As the child was industrious, they placed him with a renowned goldsmith, and he became very skillful in his profession. The tombs of St. Martin of Tours, and of St. Dionysius near Paris, were sumptuously and uniquely adorned by him. The shrines of St. Germanus, St. Genevieve, and other Saints were made by St. Eligius. While engaged at his work he had some good book before him, on which he frequently cast his eyes in order to kindle a fresh flame of devotion in his affections.

King Clotaire died in 628. His son and successor, Dagobert, entertained such a high opinion of St. Eligius' virtue and wisdom that he frequently consulted him regarding public affairs, and followed his directions for his own personal conduct.

Through the generosity of King Dagobert, Eligius was able to build the Abbey of Solignac, near Limogues. Soon one hundred and fifty persons inhabited the abbey, working at several trades. A house in Paris, which Dagobert also gave to our Saint, he converted into a convent and placed three hundred religious women in it under the direction of St. Aurea.

St. Eligius, while a layman, was instrumental in having procured a Council held at Orleans against certain heretics, drove a number of impious persons out of Paris, and, with St. Owen, employed his efforts to effectually root out simony. The Bishops were greatly edified by the sanctity of these two zealous men and resolved to raise them to the episcopacy. After two years' preparation both were consecrated at Rouen, about 640. St. Eligius was chosen Bishop of Upper Picardy, while St. Owen, of Rouen. A

great part of Flanders was chiefly indebted to St. Eligius
for the happiness of receiving the light of the Gospel. He
preached in the territories of Antwerp, Ghent and Cour-
tray. Every year at Easter he baptized great numbers of
adults and youths, whom he had instructed during the
preceding twelve months. Many blind, lame and sick persons were restored to health by the prayers of St. Eligius.

Among other prophecies, he foretold the division of
the French monarchy among the three sons of Clovis II,
and its reunion under Theodoric, the youngest of them.

St. Eligius having governed his flock fourteen years
and a half, was favored with a foresight of his death, and
a short time before he was seized with his last sickness,
foretold it to his disciples. On the sixth day after he fell
ill of a fever, as he fervently commended his soul into the
hands of his Redeemer, he happily expired on December 1,
665 or 669. St. Owen relates many miracles which followed
his death. The greatest part of his remains are kept at
Noyon.

✠

DECEMBER 2

ST. BIBIANA

St. Bibiana was a native of Rome, daughter of Flavian,
a Roman knight, and his wife Daphrosa, who were zealous
Christians.

Ammianus Marcellinus, a pagan historian of that age,
and an officer in the Court of Julian the Apostate, informs
us that this Emperor made Apronianus Governor of Rome
in 363. He had the misfortune to lose an eye while on his
way to that city. He blamed the magicians for the accident, and resolved to punish and exterminate them; the
Christians were likewise accused on account of the many
wonderful miracles which were wrought in the early days
of the Church.

Bibiana, her sister Demetria, and her parents all laid
down their lives for Christ. St. Bibiana herself was scourged

to death in 363. Her fame has been widespread from early ages. She is Patron Saint of churches in Spain, Germany, and the United States. About one hundred years after her death her church in Rome was dedicated by Pope St. Simplicius. It was repaired by Honorius III, and sumptuously rebuilt by Urban VIII in 1628, who placed in it the relics of Saints Bibiana, Demetria and Daphrosa, which were discovered in what has been sometimes called St. Bibiana's cemetery.

✠

DECEMBER 3

ST. FRANCIS XAVIER

In every age God has raised up men, filled with His Holy Spirit, whose mission has been to spend their lives in working for souls. Therefore it is not surprising that the 16th century, the era of countless heresies, should have been the time chosen for raising up the great St. Francis Xavier, who, zealous for the glory of God and the good of souls, became the *Apostle of the Indies*.

Francis was born at the castle of Xavier on April 7, 1506, near Pampeluna, Spain, of noble parentage. Desirous of a literary career, he was sent to the University of Paris to complete his course of Humanities. Upon receiving the degree of Master of Arts, he began to teach, with great acclamation. A brilliant career now lay open to him.

Among Xavier's companions at the University were Peter Faber, a Savoyard of lowly parentage, and Ignatius of Loyola, who a few years before had dedicated himself to God's service. Ignatius soon discerned that both these young men possessed the qualities which fitted them admirably for the work he had in view. Faber, from his earliest years, was devoted to God, so that Ignatius had little difficulty with him, but Xavier did not prove so easy a subject.

Having ingratiated himself with Xavier, Ignatius determined to gain him to God. No better weapon could he have used than the words of Our Lord Himself: "What doth it profit a man if he gain the whole world, and suffer the loss of his own soul?" These words Ignatius frequently whispered into the ears of Xavier. Grace finally triumphed. By this time Ignatius had won over four other members of the University. They bound themselves by the vows of voluntary poverty, perpetual chastity, and to go to the Holy Land to work for the salvation of souls. In the event of their not being able to go to the Holy Land, it was agreed that after waiting a year in Venice they should then proceed to Rome and place themselves at the disposal of the Sovereign Pontiff. It was not God's Will that they go to the Holy Land.

God tried Xavier with a serious illness. Before he had recovered he went to Bologna. Here, his untiring zeal found considerable work in the hospital, until he was attacked with an intermittent fever, which did not leave him for months. When he was summoned to Rome by St. Ignatius he was almost at death's door. After his health improved he spent some time in works of charity in that city. Frequently he was favored with visions foreshadowing his future life and labors. He spoke of nothing but the blindness of paganism and the happiness of those who were allowed to give their life for the Faith. Eagerly he longed for a Mission in the East.

After taking counsel with God, Ignatius chose Francis Xavier to go on the India Mission. The joy of Francis was unbounded; the desire of his heart was now to be realized. God was to show him "what great things he had to suffer for His Name". With but one day to bid farewell to his friends and to receive the blessing of His Holiness Paul III, Xavier left Rome on March 16th for Lisbon, which was not reached until the end of June. Here he met Father Rodriguez, whom he cured completely from an illness by a single embrace.

On April 7, 1541, Xavier boarded a sailing vessel bound for India. Five months later, after many hardships and illnesses, they reached Mozambique, on the east coast of Africa. They embarked again on March 16, 1542, and on

May 6th, thirteen months after their departure from Lisbon, reached Goa. Everywhere idolatry, immorality, and wickedness prevailed.

For ten years Xavier labored incessantly to bring the Gospel to India, Malaya and Japan. Instead of being encouraged and helped by his associates, his efforts were thwarted by their jealousy, covetousness and carelessness. Neither their opposition nor the innumerable difficulties he encountered could make him diminish his labor for souls.

Xavier longed to bring the Faith to the Chinese, but the governor of Malaya opposed this intended voyage. Xavier was resolved to risk his life, and embarked for Sancian, hoping from there to gain an entrance into China. Shortly after his arrival he was struck by a fever. God tried His faithful servant to the last, treating him as He had treated Moses, dying in sight of the Land of Promise.

On Friday, December 2, 1552, with his eyes lovingly fixed upon his Crucifix, while tears of heavenly joy poured from his eyes, St. Francis Xavier breathed his last, repeating the words: "In Thee, O Lord, have I hoped, let me not be confounded forever".

Many miracles were performed before and after the Saint's death. He was canonized by Pope Gregory XV in 1622. His body, after four hundred years, lies incorrupt in Goa.

☩

DECEMBER 4

ST. BARBARA

Heliopolis, or the City of the Sun, in Egypt, was celebrated for its learned men and women. Dioscorus was no exception to the rule of learning, and took pains to have his daughter Barbara well taught from her earliest years. Indeed, when he saw the beauty of this child first budding forth, he could think of no one whom he thought worthy of her. As all the young men of noble families were as wicked as they were learned and polished, he was not displeased when he found that Barbara loved study more than she loved society. Because of his jealousy, he secluded her in a lonely tower built for that purpose. As she would watch the burning sun setting behind the three mighty pyramids that stood in a cluster beyond the Nile, she would say, "The One Who created the sun must be greater than the sun itself! Why, then, do we worship the sun, instead of Him Who created it?" And from this time she directed her worship towards the Creator of all things, holding in contempt the idols of wood and stone which were adored by her countrymen.

Through a trusted servant, Barbara communicated with Origen, who had become renowned for his Christian teachings in Alexandria. She contrived to receive instruction and Baptism. When her father discovered her conversion, he was so filled with rage that he denounced her before the civil tribunal. Barbara suffered horrible tortures, after which the pro-consul ordered that she be beheaded. The Virgin-Martyr lifted up her soul to her Divine Spouse praying thus: "Lord Jesus, Whom all things obey, grant that all those who invoke Thy Holy Name in memory of me, may find their sins forgotten on the Day of Judgment!" And these words had no sooner fallen from her lips than the sword severed her head from her body.

St. Barbara is still invoked in behalf of the dying. St. Stanislas Kostka implored her aid under circumstances which deprived him of human assistance, and the holy youth was allowed to receive the Bread of Life at the hand of an Angel.

✠

DECEMBER 5

ST. SABBAS

St. Sabbas, a Cappadocian by birth, became one of the most renowned Palestinian Monks. He was remarkable for his austerity of life and for the perfect way in which he observed his monastic Rule. Many persons placed themselves under his direction, and he founded a number of monasteries. At the age of seventy he journeyed to Constantinople and rendered valuable service to the Eastern Church, which was much troubled by the Eutychian heretics.

He also went to Caesarea, Scythopolis and other places to preach the Catholic Faith, and brought back many Monks and seculars into its fold. The prayers of the Saint obtained supplies for his seven monasteries in their extreme necessity during a drought which had continued for five years, producing a famine in Palestine.

In his 91st year, at the request of Patriarch Peter of Jerusalem, St. Sabbas undertook a second journey to Constantinople to aid the Christians of Palestine who had been calumniated at court. He was received with great honor by Emperor Justinian, who granted him all his requests and offered to settle annual revenues for the maintenance of all his monasteries. The holy Abbot thanked the Emperor, but said that as long as the Monks should serve God they stood not in need of such revenues. However, he begged a remission of all taxes in favor of the people of Palestine for a certain period on account of what they had suffered by the plundering of the Samaritans; that he would build a hotel at Jerusalem for pilgrims, and a fortress for the protection of the hermits and Monks against the inroads of barbarians; that he would adorn the recently built church of Our Lady, and afford protection to Catholics. All of which things were granted.

St. Sabbas died at the age of ninety-four, in the year 532.

☧

DECEMBER 6

ST. NICHOLAS

In the last half of the 3rd century there was born at Patara, in the province of Lycia in Asia Minor, a son to a noble Christian. The child had been asked of God with many prayers, and was named Nicholas. As he grew in body and mind, he kept all the innocence of his first years. At an early age he was taken to the monastery of Sion, there to be perfected in the science of sanctity. Nicholas was still quite young when his parents died of the plague, leaving him the sole heir of their vast possessions. He became a Monk in the monastery of Sion near Myra, and later was made Abbot by its Founder.

When the metropolitan church at Myra became vacant, the holy Abbot Nicholas was chosen Archbishop, and in that exalted position became famous by his extraordinary piety, zeal, charity, and unnumbered miracles. It is related that while Nicholas was the Bishop of Myra, a terrible famine afflicted the country. Full of compassion for his people, the Bishop not only obtained a miraculous supply of bread for the multitude in his episcopal See-city, but visited every part of his vast diocese in order to acquaint himself with the condition of all his people. On one of these visitations he stayed in the house of a man into whom Satan seemed to have entered; for, when meat failed for his table, he supplied it with the flesh of little children whom he stole and murdered in order to serve as meat to the travelers who were his guests. It was this horrible repast, disguised with his best skill, that this wicked man dared to set before the Bishop and his companions. No sooner had the man of God set his eyes upon the sumptous table and upon the meat prepared for him, than he understood the horrible fraud. He charged the host with his abominable crime, and the man, trembling, confessed his sin. Then St. Nicholas led the way to the place where the remains of other victims had been hidden. To the horror of all, they found them salted down in a tub. Clothed with the majesty of a Bishop of God, and endowed with the power which the Almighty One gives to His Saints, no sooner had St. Nicholas made over them the sign of the cross, than the three little children were restored to life, and then given back to their mother. St. Nicholas has come to be regarded as the Patron Saint for children.

It is claimed that he suffered imprisonment for the Faith and that he died in 342. Several hundred years later his holy relics were translated to Bari, Italy.

The familiar "Santa Claus" is a corrupt form of St. Nicholas' name.

☦

DECEMBER 7

ST. AMBROSE

St. Ambrose is one of the four great Fathers and Doctors of the Western Church. His father was Prefect of Gaul and also of part of Germany and Italy. He and his wife were Romans and Christians, and their three children were raised in Christian surroundings. After the death of the Prefect, his devoted wife returned to Rome with her three children. One day little Ambrose seeing his mother and sister kiss the hand of a Bishop, held out his own hand to them to kiss, saying: "I shall one day be a Bishop". And yet it was not for a Priest that he was educated, but for public affairs and to follow the career of his father. While quite young he won the favor of Symmachus, prince of the Roman Senate, and of Probus, whom Emperor Valentinian had made the chief Prefect of the Roman empire. Ambrose had scarcely reached man's estate when he was made Prefect of Liguria, that is, Governor of Northern Italy.

Soon after the new Governor arrived in Milan the whole city was stirred by the death of the Bishop who had governed the Church there for twenty years. The Diocese was torn asunder by rival factions, necessitating the intervention of the Prefect to ensure an orderly election of a successor. Ambrose went to the scene of disorder and took his place among the orators. As soon as he spoke, the crowd was stilled. He encouraged the people to hold a peaceable election. While he was speaking, and every eye was upon him, a child's voice was heard calling out, "Ambrose for Bishop!" The multitude, moved by the grace of God, took up the cry and demanded: "Ambrose for Bish-

op!" Later, the Emperor Valentinian III also endorsed
Ambrose. All of his objections were overruled. Convinced
that the election was the Will of God, he promptly received
the Sacraments, was ordained Priest, and consecrated Bishop
on December 7, 374. He then distributed his wealth to
the poor; to the Church in Milan he gave his estates,
reserving only an annuity for his sister Marcellina.

Arianism was rampant in his Diocese. The Bishop
experienced many fierce, bitter struggles in his efforts to
eradicate the heresy. A glory seemed to crown the city of
Milan as well as the head of Ambrose. He built churches
and enriched them with relics; he preached, instructed,
and won all hearts by his wonderful eloquence; his Priests
ripened into Saints in the sunshine of his zeal; his sermons
on the excellence of the religious state inspired many virgins to become spouses of Jesus Christ; while the poor,
the imprisoned, widows, orphans and the unfortunate, won
his time and attention. The entire city of Milan, nobles
and people, filled the ranks of processions in honor of
God and of His Saints.

It was during this time of holy prosperity that the
famed pagan philosopher Augustine came to Milan. Soon
he was seen amongst the crowd who came to listen to the
great Archbishop. Day by day Augustine listened; faithfully his mother, Monica, prayed for his conversion. Before
this two-fold force of prayer and preaching, all the blindness of unbelief vanished until, on Holy Saturday in the
year 387, St. Ambrose baptized Augustine, the philosopher
and poet of Carthage.

The pen of St. Ambrose was as eloquent as his tongue;
his writings are voluminous, and those regarding religious
doctrine still are constantly quoted and appealed to as
proof of Christian teaching. His courage in reproving and
excluding from church services even Emperor Theodosius
the Great, who was guilty of the cruel massacre of seven
thousand persons of Thessalonica, is one of the most
remarkable examples of Christian heroism recorded in
history.

St. Ambrose died April 4, 397, being about fifty-seven years old, and having been Bishop twenty-two years and four months. He was buried by the side of the Martyrs SS. Gervase and Protase, whose relics he had enshrined at Milan.

✠

DECEMBER 8

FEAST OF THE
IMMACULATE CONCEPTION

The definition promulgated by Pope Pius IX, of saintly memory, expresses the Catholic belief in the Immaculate Conception of the Blessed Virgin Mary in most concise and clear language: "We define the doctrine, which holds that the Most Blessed Virgin Mary, in the first instant of her Conception, was preserved free from all stain of original sin by the singular grace and privilege of Almighty God, and through the merits of Jesus Christ the Savior of the human race, to be a doctrine revealed by God, and therefore, to be firmly and continually held by all the faithful".

In approaching the dogma of the Catholic Faith, three truths must steadily be borne in mind. First, the soul of the individual man is not pre-existent, but is created by God in the moment of conception. Second, it was God's intention, if Adam and Eve did not sin, that every soul be created in a state of friendship with the Creator. In other words, the Creator intended to endow each soul, as He created it, with sanctifying grace. Third, whatever part the body may have in any sin, sin itself inheres in the soul; and in the last analysis mortal sin is the deprivation of sanctifying grace.

Beyond these three truths, it is necessary to know the story of our first parents, as told in the second and third chapters of Genesis. God formed the bodies of Adam and Eve, and into these bodies He breathed grace-enriched souls. Disobeying God's commandment, Adam and Eve ate of the fruit whereof God forbade them to eat. That physical act was soon over; what it produced in their souls, and what effect it was to have on other souls, when created, continued. The act of disobedience took from Adam and Eve God's greatest gift to them, namely, sanctifying grace. They were now in the state of mortal sin. It took from the children that would be born to them the privilege that their souls would come forth from God possessed of grace; which deprivation of grace in each newly-created soul is known by the name of Original Sin.

The soul of the Blessed Virgin Mary had to be created by an act of God in the moment of the conception of her body. As a daughter of Adam and Eve, Mary's soul, in the natural order of things, would go forth from God deprived of grace. But through the merits of Jesus Christ, and in view of the fact that this soul was the soul of the future mother of the Savior of Mankind, that soul was endowed with grace; it was created in the same state in which the souls of Adam and Eve were created.

Could God do this? What he did for our first parents, He could do for Her who was to be the mother of His Eternal Son. Did He do this? Catholics believe that He did—and, prescinding from the proofs which sound reason dictates, their belief is taken out of the realm of doubt and speculation by the word of Holy Scripture, by the teachings of the Fathers of the Church, and by the infallible voice of Christ's Vicar on earth.

✠

DECEMBER 9

ST. PETER FOURIER

Peter Fourier was born November 30, 1565, at Mirecourt, an ancient town of Lorraine. From early youth he gave signs of a vocation to the priesthood, and when fifteen years old was sent to the University of Pont-a-Mousson, then under the direction of the Jesuits. He was remarkable for his piety and literary accomplishments.

At the age of twenty he received the Habit of the
Canons Regular of St. Augustine; in 1587 he made his sol-
emn profession, and on February 25, 1589, was ordained
Priest at Treves. He became so proficient in patristic theol-
ogy that in later years he would often quote by heart long
extracts from St. Basil, St. Chrysostom, St. Augustine and
St. Gregory. His knowledge of the Angelic Doctor was so
profound that his companions would say that should the
Summa of St. Thomas be destroyed it could be restored by
Peter Fourier.

For thirty years he served as pastor at Mattaincourt.
Many vices and the germs of Protestantism had crept into
the parish through the frequent intercourse of the people
with Switzerland, and it had acquired the name of "Little
Geneva". But soon after Father Fourier assumed charge a
change took place and a moral revolution was accomplished.
By his instructions, patience, example, and continual prayer
the holy Priest rooted out every disorder, and religion was
restored.

He was generous with those in need, but he, himself,
led a temperate, poor and mortified life to the extreme. In
order to train the young in virtue and to educate them,
Peter Fourier founded the first Congregation devoted to
the free education of poor girls. Approved by the Holy See,
the Daughters of Our Lady soon spread from Lorraine
through France and Germany. In 1657 they opened a school
in Montreal, Canada.

In 1621 the Bishop of Toul obtained from Rome a brief
naming Peter Fourier Visitor-General of the abbeys of his
Order, to bring about a needed reform of the Canons
Regular. In the midst of his labors for Christian education
and the reform of his Order, Fourier, in 1625, received from
his Bishop a commission to undertake another most difficult
work. It was to combat Protestantism which had invaded
the Principality of Salm near Nancy. The holy missionary
began by preaching in the streets of Badonviller, being
often insulted and even beaten, but always remaining calm
and benevolent. Then, accompanied by two Jesuits, he

preached in all the neighboring villages, and with so great success that six months after his arrival he had the consolation to see the Protestant place of worship dedicated to God in honor of the Blessed Virgin. In addition to these evangelical labors among the Protestants, the holy Priest was also employed by his Bishop in visiting the Diocese and giving missions throughout the country. In this work, too, he was most successful.

Peter Fourier's well-known attachment to the House of Lorraine raised a powerful enemy against him in the person of Cardinal Richelieu, who drove him into exile. In May, 1638, at the age of seventy-two, after bidding adieu to his country and to his beloved Mattaincourt, accompanied by some of his Nuns from Mirecourt, and by one of his Canons, he entered Gray. A benefactor gave them a house, which was turned into a Convent of Canonesses. Fourier reserved for himself a small room, and there spent the remaining years of his mortal life. A free school for poor children was soon opened, and Fourier in his old age taught "the most stupid and troublesome of the scholars with admirable patience".

On December 9, 1640, after blessing the religious and the whole congregation, the Saint raised his hands three times, made the sign of the cross over his body, invoked the sweet names of Jesus and Mary, and with his eyes fixed on heaven, calmly slept in the Lord. Pope Leo XIII on Ascension Day, 1897, solemnly added Peter Fourier to the catalogue of the Saints.

✠

DECEMBER 10

ST. MELCHIADES

St. Melchiades succeeded St. Eusebius in the chair of St. Peter, in 311. The following year he witnessed the triumph of the Cross through the defeat of Maxentius and the entry into Rome of the Emperor Constantine (now converted to Christianity), after the victory at the Milvian

Bridge, October 27, 312. That same year Constantine issued edicts which granted freedom of worship and permission to build churches. He obliged all soldiers to pray on Sundays to the one, true God, and abolished all pagan festivals. Later the Emperor presented the Roman Church with the Lateran Palace, which then became the residence of the Pope, and consequently also the seat of the central administration of the Church.

The Pope rejoiced exceedingly at the prosperity of the Church, and by his zealous efforts extended its territory. However, he was afflicted to see it torn by internal division on account of the Donatist schism which raged in Africa.

St. Melchiades presided over the Council of Bishops from Italy and Gaul, which decided in favor of Cecilian, Bishop of Carthage, against Donatus. This decision did not prevent the later development of the Donatist heresy or schism in Africa after the Pope's death in 314.

St. Augustine describes St. Melchiades as "an excellent man, a true son of peace, and a true father of Christians". He is honored as a martyr because of the sufferings he endured in early life during the persecution of Diocletian. St. Melchiades died January 10, 314, having reigned two years, six months and eight days, and was buried on the Appian road, in the cemetery of St. Calixtus.

✠

DECEMBER 11

ST. DAMASUS

Upon the death of Pope Liberius on December 24, 366, Damasus, who was then sixty years old and had attended Liberius when in exile, was chosen Bishop of Rome, and consecrated in the Basilica of St. Laurence. St. Jerome calls him "An incomparable man, the Virgin Doctor of the Virgin Church".

Damasus had to struggle against Ursinus, an anti-Pope, whose rebellion was finally crushed, not without bloodshed, by Emperor Valentinian. It appears from the writings of Pope Damasus that he had made a vow to God in honor of certain martyrs, to ask their intercession for the conversion of those Priests who continued obstinate in the schism; and that when these clergymen were converted to the unity of the Church, in gratitude, they adorned at their own expense the tombs of these martyrs.

Arianism reigned in the East under the protection of Bishop Valens; in the West it was confined to Milan and Pannonia. In order to extirpate it in that part of the world, Pope Damasus, in a Council at Rome in 368, condemned Urascius and Valens, famous Arian Bishops in Pannonia; and in Councils in 370 and 374, Auxentius of Milan and Apollinarius.

The ancient Fathers particularly commend St. Damasus for his constancy in maintaining the purity of our holy Faith, for his humility and holiness of life, his compassion for the poor, his piety in adorning holy places, especially the tombs of the martyrs, and for his singular learning. He was the great patron of St. Jerome, who under his direction re-translated into Latin or revised Holy Scripture. He also had a considerable share in developing the Roman Liturgy, chiefly by introducing certain elements borrowed from the Eastern rites.

Having reigned eighteen years and two months, St. Damasus died on December 10, 384.

✠

DECEMBER 12

FEAST OF OUR LADY
OF GUADALUPE

In December, 1531, the Blessed Virgin appeared to Juan Diego four times on the hill Tepeyac, about three miles from Mexico City, Mexico, and in this apparition she is known as *Our Lady of Guadalupe*.

Juan was hurrying down Tepeyac hill on Saturday, December 8th, to assist at Mass of the Most Blessed Virgin at Tlatelolco, a Franciscan mission. The Blessed Mother of God appeared to Juan and sent the poor but pious Indian to Bishop Fray Juan de Zumarraga with the request that a church be built where she then stood. At the same place, that evening and the following day, Sunday, she appeared in order to receive the Bishop's answer.

From the original history attributed to a learned Indian, Antonio Valeriano, and who was contemporaneous with the favored Indian, we draw the following account:

"When he reached the top of the hillock called Tepeyac, dawn was breaking; and thence he heard strains of music coming. It sounded like the song of rare and wonderful birds. For an instant the singing ceased, and then it seemed as if the mountains echoed with response. The song, very sweet and delicate, resembled that of most beautiful birds.

"Juan Diego stopped to look about him and said to himself: 'How can I be worthy of what I am hearing? Am I dreaming? Have I ceased to sleep? Where am I? Am I in the terrestrial Paradise, of which our elders told us? Am I already in Heaven?'

"He gazed about, looking toward the east, beyond the hillock, whence came the celestial song; and when suddenly this ceased and there was silence, this was followed by the sound of a voice which called to him, saying, 'Juanito, Juan Dieguito'.° Then he ventured to pursue the sound. . . . When he reached the summit, he saw a Lady of marvelous beauty, who was standing there serenely, and who motioned to him that he should approach. Once arrived within the radius of her presence he greatly marveled at this, for there was something supernatural about it. Her garments were shining like the sun. The cliff on

---

"*Juanito*" and "*Juan Dieguito*" are affectionate diminutives of Juan Diego, such as any fond mother would use when speaking to a child.

which she stood glittered with glory, like an anklet of precious stones, and illumined the earth like a rainbow. . . .

"He bowed before her and hearkened to her words, . . . 'Juanito, the least of my sons, where art thou going?' He replied, 'My Lady and my Child, I must needs go to the church at Tlatelolco, to study divine mysteries, which are taught by our Priests, the emissaries of Our Lord and Savior'. Immediately she resumed her discourse and revealed her sublime will.

" 'Know and take heed, thou, the least of my sons, that I am Holy Mary, Ever Virgin Mother of the True God for Whom we live, the Creator of the world, Maker of Heaven and Earth. I urgently desire that a temple should be built to me here, to bear witness to my love, my compassion, my succor and protection. For I am a merciful Mother to thee and to all thy people on this earth who love me and trust me and invoke my help. I listen to their lamentations and solace all their sorrows and their suffering. Therefore, to realize all that my clemency claims, go to the palace of the Bishop in Mexico, and say that I sent thee to make manifest to him my great desire; namely, that here in the valley a temple should be built to me. Tell him word for word all that thou hast seen and heard and admired. Be assured that I shall be grateful and that I will reward thee, for I will make thy life happy and cause thee to become worthy of the trouble thou hast taken and the labor thou performest to do that which I enjoin thee. Now thou hast heard all my bidding, least of my sons, go and do thy utmost'.

"At this point he bowed before her and said: 'Lady, I go to do your bidding. As your humble servant, I take my leave of you'. Then he went on to accomplish her will, taking the causeway that leads directly to Mexico City."

Bishop Zumarraga, however, did not immediately believe Our Lady's messenger. After cross-questioning him, he had him watched, and finally told him to ask a sign of the Lady who said she was the Mother of the true God, leaving the sign to the "apparition".

All day Monday Juan was occupied in caring for his uncle, Bernardino, who appeared to be dying of fever. At daybreak on Tuesday, December 12th, the grieved nephew was running to St. James convent for a Priest. In order to avoid the apparition, he went by another way. However, the Blessed Virgin crossed down to meet him and said: "What road is this thou takest, son?" A tender dialogue followed. She reassured Juan about his uncle, whom at that instant she had cured, appearing to him also and calling herself *Holy Mary of Guadalupe;* she now bade Juan to go again to the Bishop. Immediately Juan asked for a sign. She told him to go up to the rocks and gather roses. Although it was neither the time of the year nor the place for roses, Juan went and found them. After gathering a number and placing them in his *tilma*—a long cloak worn by Mexican Indians—he came back. Our Lady rearranged the roses, and told him to keep them untouched and unseen until he reached the Bishop. Upon his arrival, Juan offered to the Bishop "the sign". Unfolding his cloak the roses fell out. Juan was startled to see the Bishop and his attendants fall down upon their knees before him: for the life-size figure of the Virgin Mother, just as he had described her was imprinted in glowing colors on the poor *tilma*. The picture was venerated and guarded in the Bishop's chapel. Shortly afterwards, it was carried in procession to the preparatory shrine, and it now reposes in the Basilica which was erected, in 1709, to replace the previous shrines. This famous shrine has ever since been a place of pilgrimage, and many miracles have occurred there.

☩

DECEMBER 13

ST. LUCY

St. Lucy was born in Syracuse, Sicily, of wealthy, honorable Christian parents. However, at the age of fourteen she was betrothed by them to a young pagan nobleman.

Lucy endeavored in every way to prevent the marriage, as she had already given her heart to God. Finally, her mother was stricken with a grievous disease, under which she languished for four years, and no physician was found able to help her. Lucy urged her mother to visit the tomb of St. Agatha (in Catania, Sicily,) who, in 251, suffered a most cruel martyrdom for her Divine Spouse. Lucy accompanied her mother to the tomb. Through her prayers and those of St. Agatha, she obtained the cure of her mother. Lucy then told her of the promise she had made to God, and begged to be allowed to fulfill it and to sell all her possessions in order to give them in alms to the poor. Eutychia, her mother, in gratitude for her cure, consented.

When the young nobleman to whom Lucy had been betrothed, heard of this, he was greatly enraged and went immediately to Pascasius, the Governor, and denounced her as a Christian.

Pascasius ordered Lucy to be brought before him, and commanded her to sacrifice to the gods. When she refused, he ordered her to be taken to a place of shame and treated with indignity. When the wicked men attempted to seize her and drag her away by force, the maiden suddenly became, by the power of God, immovable. The more they tried to move her, the more firmly she stood before them. In his rage, Pascasius ordered a fire kindled around her. Seeing that she was unharmed, one of the servants thrust a sword through her throat, and of this wound God was pleased to let her die.

It is not related in her Acts how or when she suffered the loss of her eyes, but most careful historians mention this as one of her grievous torments. St. Lucy is invoked by those who wish to preserve the precious gift of sight.

After her death the Christians took her body and buried it at the very place where she had suffered with such constancy, and a church was erected there afterwards bearing her name.

St. Lucy suffered martyrdom on December 13, 304, the same year in which St. Agnes gave up her young life for

Christ. These Virgin-Martyrs have come down together through the ages, in the Litany of the Saints, where with St. Cecilia, St. Catherine and St. Agatha, they shine as the five wise virgins who took the oil of divine love in their lamps and went joyfully forth to meet their celestial Bride groom.

✠

DECEMBER 14

SS. NICASIUS, EUTROPIA AND OTHERS

In the 5th century an army of barbarians from Germany ravaged part of Gaul and plundered the city of Rheims. Nicasius, who was Bishop of Rheims, foretold this calamity to his flock. When the enemy appeared at the gates and in the streets, the holy Bishop, forgetting himself, went from door to door encouraging his spiritual children to patience and constancy. In attempting to save the lives of some of his flock he exposed himself to the swords of the infidels. After enduring countless insults and indignities he suffered death at the hands of the barbarian invaders. His deacon and his lector were massacred by his side.

His sister Eutropia, a virtuous virgin, seeing herself spared in order to be reserved for wicked purposes, boldly told the infidels that she would rather sacrifice her life than her Faith or her integrity and virtue. Whereupon she was put to death with their swords.

St. Nicasius and St. Eutropia were buried in the churchyard of St. Agricola. Their tombs became famous on account of the many miracles which occurred there. In 893 Archbishop Fulco translated the body of St. Nicasius into the Cathedral which the martyr himself had built and dedicated in honor of the Blessed Virgin Mary. His head is kept in the abbey of St. Vedastus at Arras.

✠

ST. MAXIMIN

St. Maximin (Mesmin), a native of Verdun, was the first Abbot of the famous monastery of Micy, which was founded near Orleans by his uncle, King Clovis.

St. Maximin's sanctity and miracles attracted many disciples, several of whom, like St. Avitus, St. Calais and St. Urban, were afterwards enrolled in the calendar of Saints. During a dreadful famine St. Maximin fed almost all the inhabitants of Orleans with wheat from his monastery, which appeared to be miraculously multiplied; he also drove a huge serpent out of the place where he was afterwards buried.

St. Maximin governed his monastery for ten years, and died in the odor of sanctity about the year 520.

✠

ST. EUSEBIUS OF VERCELLI

St. Eusebius was born in Sardinia in 283. He lived in Rome for some time, and then went to Vercellae (the present Vercelli). In 340 he was unanimously elected Bishop of that city by the clergy and the people, and received episcopal consecration at the hands of Pope Julius I on December 15 of the same year. According to St. Ambrose, Eusebius was the first Bishop of the West who united monastic with clerical life. For this reason the Canons Regular of St. Augustine honor him with St. Augustine as their founder.

Eusebius was a great and zealous champion of the Catholic Faith against the Arians. Through their intrigues he was banished to Syria, where he suffered many hardships. On the accession of the Emperor Julian, the exiled

Bishop was permitted, in 362, to return to his See. Eusebius, however, remained in the Orient for some time helping to restore peace to the Church. He went to Alexandria to consult with St. Athanasius about convoking the synod which, in 362, was held there under their joint presidency. He returned to Vercellae in 363, and in the words of St. Jerome, "Italy put off her mourning". Thenceforth until his death, in 370, he assisted St. Hilary of Poitiers in extirpating Arianism in the Western Church. St. Eusebius is honored as a martyr by the Church.

☩

DECEMBER 17

ST. OLYMPIAS

St. Olympias was a wealthy lady of illustrious descent, born about 368. She was left an orphan and was placed in the care of Procopius, who seems to have been her uncle. It was her greatest happiness to have been brought up under the care of Theodosia, a most virtuous and prudent woman, whom St. Gregory Nazianzen called a perfect pattern of piety.

When very young, Olympias married Nebridius, treasurer of Emperor Theodosius the Great, but he died after only three weeks of married life. Olympias thenceforth declined all offers of marriage, and embraced a life of penance and prayer. Her revenues were used to aid destitute churches and the poor; her charities were boundless.

God permitted the devil to assail her by many trials. She also suffered frequently from severe sicknesses, as well as from slanders, insults and injuries. She bore all with meekness, humility and patience.

Nectarius, Archbishop of Constantinople, appointed her Deaconess of the Church of Constantinople. St. John Chrysostom succeeded him, and he, too, had great respect for the sanctity of Olympias. When he was banished on June 20, 404, she was one of the last persons whom he took leave of. After his departure she suffered much in the per-

secution in which all of his friends were involved. Several
Greek Fathers spoke in her praise.

St. Olympias died after 408, as she was still living
when Palladius wrote his Dialogue that year on the Life
of St. Chrysostom.

✠

DECEMBER 18

SS. RUFUS AND ZOSIMUS

It was during the reign of Trajan, about the year 116,
that Saints Rufus and Zosimus suffered martyrdom for the
Faith. Whether it was at Antioch or Philippi, where it seems
they preached, or some other city of the East that was the
theatre of their triumph, is uncertain. St. Polycarp, writing
to the Philippians, said: "Wherefore I exhort all of you that
ye obey the word of righteousness, and exercise all patience,
which ye have seen set forth before your eyes, not only in
the blessed Ignatius, and Zosimus, and Rufus, but in others
that have been among you; and in Paul himself, and the
rest of the Apostles".

✠

DECEMBER 19

ST. FAUSTA

St. Fausta was renowned for her nobility of birth and
for her holiness. She was the mother of St. Anastasia, and
died in Rome towards the end of the third century.

✠

DECEMBER 20

ST. DOMINIC OF SILOS

Dominic was born in Cantabria, in the northwestern
part of Spain. His parents were poor, and as a child Dominic
tended their sheep. As he was very pious and eager to

learn, he studied for the priesthood and embraced a hermit's life, following the Rule of St. Benedict. He was elected Prior of St. Milan in Aragon. Refusing to surrender certain goods of the monastery to the King of Navarre, he was banished from the country. The King of Castile welcomed him and appointed him Abbot of St. Sebastian's at Silos, which monastery he thoroughly reformed.

On account of the many miracles St. Dominic wrought, his fame spread far and wide. After his holy death in 1073, he miraculously delivered more than three hundred prisoners taken by the Moors. His shrine is still decorated with many chains as "ex votos".

The Countess Guzman recommended herself to his intercession, and in answer to his prayers gave birth, in 1170, to the great St. Dominic, founder of the Order of Friars Preachers. To the end of the Spanish Monarchy, the Abbot of Silo continued to bring to each succeeding Queen of Spain, when in labor, the staff of St. Dominic, which remained by her bedside until the birth had taken place.

✠

DECEMBER 21

ST. THOMAS

St. Thomas was one of the chosen Twelve, otherwise called Didymus (twin). His name occurs in all of the Gospels, but in St. John's Gospel he plays a prominent part. When Jesus announced His intention of returning to Judea to visit Lazarus, it was Thomas who said to his fellow disciples, "Let us also go, that we may die with Him". (John 11:16.) It was St. Thomas who raised an objection during the Master's discourse before the Last Supper: "Thomas saith to Him: Lord, we know not whither Thou goest; and how can we know the way?" (John 15:5.)

St. Thomas is especially remembered for his incredulity when the other Apostles told him of Christ's appearance to them after His Resurrection: "Except I shall see in His hands the print of the nails, and put my finger into His side, I will not believe". (John 20:25.) Eight days later when he was invited by the Savior to inspect for himself the marks of the Five Wounds in the Body of Jesus, it is the opinion of the Fathers of the Church that St. Thomas rendered invaluable service to Christianity. Kneeling, he cried, "My Lord and my God". Jesus kindly rebuked him, saying: "Because thou hast seen Me, Thomas, thou hast believed: blessed are they that have not seen, and have believed". (John 20:29.)

After the Ascension, St. Thomas went forth into the world to preach the Gospel of Christ Jesus to the Parthians, Medes, Persians, and the inhabitants of other provinces of Persia, close to the Caspian sea. Finally, he entered India, where he instructed the people in the Christian religion. In the end, his life and teaching and the greatness of his numerous miracles, which won the hearts of the people, caused violent anger amongst the priests of the idols. In consequence, St. Thomas was condemned to death and pierced with arrows, thus meriting the crown of the apostolate and of martyrdom at Calamina.

☩

DECEMBER 22

ST. FRANCES XAVIER CABRINI

Frances Xavier Cabrini was born in Lodi, Italy, in 1850, and died at Chicago, Illinois, December 22, 1917.

In 1880 she was summoned by the Bishop of Lodi, who had long been aware of her desire to be a religious, and in particular a missionary. His words spoken that memorable November ring down the years and are deeply embedded in the heart of every member of the community:

"You wish to become a missionary. I do not know of any such institute for women. Found one yourself".

O Lord Jesus Christ, You kindled blessed Frances Xavier Cabrini, with the flame of Your Most Sacred Heart, and led her across the wide world to win souls to You. Through her, You raised up in Your Church a new family of Virgins. Through her intercession, may we too be clothed with the virtues of Your Sacred Heart and merit to arrive at the haven of eternal beatitude.

Filled with confidential humility and daring courage, she replied: "I will look for a house". That house was found at Codogno, Italy. New houses succeeded one another by the Missionary Sisters of the Sacred Heart of Jesus, which Order Mother Cabrini founded. Within the short space of seven years Mother Cabrini had accomplished a desired objective—establishment in Rome and Papal approval of the Institute. From Rome the Institute spread rapidly.

Pope Leo XIII urged Mother Cabrini to send her Sisters to America to aid the Italian emigrants, when he said: "Not to the East, but to the West. Go to the United States where you will find a large field of labor". Obediently surrendering her own plans to go to China, Mother Cabrini set sail for America, and arrived on March 31, 1889.

The Cross of Christ greeted her. She had come with the understanding that her Sisters were to conduct an orphanage for Italian children. All things were supposedly ready, but nothing was ready. A letter had been sent her by Archbishop Michael Corrigan of New York. Evidently she had left before the letter arrived. The Archbishop advised her to return to Italy, but he did not know Mother Cabrini. "No, Your Excellency", she replied. "I have come here by the order of the Holy See and here I have to remain."

And remain she did. The whole United States was visited by her, and she left in her wake establishments in New York, Brooklyn, Scranton, New Jersey, Philadelphia, New Orleans, Chicago, Denver, Seattle, and California. From the United States she worked down to Central and South America.

Within her lifetime she had founded sixty-seven houses, including orphanages, hospitals, and schools. She trusted blindly in the Heart of Jesus, and that trust was not misplaced.

St. Frances Xavier Cabrini's remains are venerated in the chapel of the Mother Cabrini High School, New York City. She was canonized by Pope Pius XII on July 7, 1946.

✠

DECEMBER 23

ST. SERVULUS

Servulus, who had been paralyzed from birth, spent a number of years in prayer on the porch of the church of St. Clement in Rome, living on the alms of those who passed by. His sufferings and humiliations were excellent means which he used to sanctify his soul by practicing patience, meekness, resignation and penance.

Perceiving that his end was drawing near, he requested those near him to sing sacred hymns and psalms. Joining his voice with theirs he suddenly cried out: "Silence; do you not hear the sweet melody and praises which resound in the heavens!" Shortly after Servulus had spoken these words he expired, and his soul was carried by Angels into everlasting bliss. According to the Roman Martyrology, his body was interred in St. Clement's Church and honored with miracles.

✠

DECEMBER 24

ST. GREGORY OF SPOLETO

This Martyr was a holy Priest at Spoleto, whose time was spent night and day in prayer and fasting, and in teaching others the holy law of God.

The Emperor Maximian Herculeus sent Flaccus, one of his Generals, to Spoleto in 304 with orders to punish all Christians. He was informed that Gregory was a Christian who held in contempt the gods and the emperors. Soldiers were sent immediately to bring him bound before the tribunal. When Gregory appeared, Flaccus sternly asked: "Are you Gregory of Spoleto?" "I am", he responded. Flaccus then asked, "Are you the enemy of the gods and the contemner of the emperors?" St. Gregory calmly answered, "From my youth I have always served the God Who framed me out of the earth". Flaccus then inquired, "Who is your God?" "He Who made man to His own image and likeness, Who is all-powerful and immortal, and Who will render to all men according to their works", replied the Martyr.

Flaccus, in anger, said: "Do not use many words, but do what I command you".

"I know not what your command implies", answered Gregory, "but I do what I am bound to do."

Flaccus demanded earnestly, "If you desire to save yourself, go to the wonderful temple and sacrifice to the great gods, and you shall be our friend and shall receive many favors from our most invincible emperors".

St. Gregory, courageously, replied: "I desire not such a friendship, nor do I sacrifice to idols, but to my God, Jesus Christ".

The judge, infuriated, commanded that Gregory be struck on the face, beaten with clubs, and tortured on the rack; then ordered that he be beheaded.

St. Gregory's relics lie in a church which bears his name at Spoleto. Baronius testifies that a wonderful miracle was wrought by their touch in 1037.

✠

DECEMBER 25

FEAST OF THE NATIVITY OF CHRIST

From early ages the Church set apart December 25th for the solemn celebration of the Nativity of Our Lord and Savior Jesus Christ. In the East the Feast is kept on January 6th. For that reason both festivals have been continued—December 25th as the Nativity, and January 6th as the Epiphany, or manifestation of Jesus to the Gentiles.

St. Thomas of Villanova, preaching on the birth of the Savior, declares: "At the crib one finds a summary of the divine teachings".

For, there, "at the crib", in the choice of an immaculate Virgin for His Mother, and of a chaste St. Joseph for His foster-father, Jesus teaches love of purity.

There, in the descent from Heaven in order to fulfill the Will of His Eternal Father, Jesus is the model of obedience.

There, accepting a stable in lieu of His heavenly home, a manger in lieu of the royal bed He might have chosen in Herod's palace, poor swaddling clothes in lieu of downy, soft coverlets, the breath of an ox and ass in lieu of radiant warmth in the homes of the great and rich, Jesus, Whose creative power had not ceased with the assumption of mortal flesh, inculcates humility.

There, too, the arrival in the obscure darkness of a hillside cavern, at midnight, in the cold winter; the arrival at a time when His parents were distant from their humble dwelling and from their friends, making it impossible that the most meagre home comforts of even the poorest people be extended to Him—this arrival characterizes Jesus as the exemplar of mortification.

All of which St. Paul, the Apostle of the Gentiles, reduces into one famous sentence:

"The grace of God our Savior hath appeared to all men, instructing us, that, denying ungodliness and worldly desires, we should live soberly and justly and godly in this world, looking for the blessed hope and coming of the glory of the great God and our Savior Jesus Christ: Who gave Himself for us, that He might redeem us from all iniquity and might cleanse to Himself a people acceptable, a pursuer of good works". (Letter to Titus.)

✠

DECEMBER 26

ST. STEPHEN

There is no doubt that St. Stephen was one of the seventy-two disciples of Christ; for, immediately after the **descent of the Holy Spirit, we find him perfectly instructed** in the Christian teachings. After the Ascension seven Deacons were chosen, and the first one named was "Stephen, a **man full of faith and of the Holy Spirit". His ministry was** very fruitful, for he was "full of grace and fortitude", and "did great wonders and signs among the people".

When the Jews found they could not withstand his arguments, they bribed witnesses, as in the case of Jesus Himself, to charge him with blasphemy against Moses and against God. Upon this false charge he was dragged before the Sanhedrin, the highest Jewish court, and, after the accusation had been read, Caiphas, the High Priest, ordered him to make his defense.

St. Stephen showed great courage and constancy, and with fiery eloquence reminded them of the prophecies, beginning with the books of Moses, concerning the Messiah, and how the sacrifices of the Temple were a figure, well understood by the Jewish doctors of the law, of a better and more perfect Sacrifice, which he showed to have been completed in the Sacrifice of Jesus on the Cross.

Seeing their unbelief depicted on their countenances, St. Stephen then accused them in burning words of having rejected and slain those Prophets "who foretold the Just One; of Whom", he said, "you are now the betrayers and murderers". They were inflamed with anger, and gnashed their teeth against him. But St. Stephen was not frightened. **"Filled with the Holy Spirit and looking up to heaven, he** cried out, 'Behold, I see the heavens opened and the Son of Man standing at the right hand of God' ". No longer able to contain themselves for fury and revenge, "Crying out with

O Lord, grant that we may imitate Stephen whom we venerate, so that we may learn to love our enemies; for we celebrate the feast of him who knew how to pray even for his persecutors to Your Son our Lord Jesus Christ.

a loud voice, and stopping their ears, with one accord they ran violently upon him. And casting him forth without the city they stoned him". "Falling on his knees he cried with a loud voice saying: Lord, lay not this sin to their charge. And when he had said this he fell asleep in the Lord." (Acts of the Apostles: chapters 6 and 7.)

Such was the death of the first Martyr, "the Protomartyr", as St. Stephen is called.

✠

DECEMBER 27

ST. JOHN

St. John, the Evangelist, who is styled in the Gospel "the beloved disciple", was a Galilean, son of Zebedee and Salome, and brother to St. James the Greater, both of whom were fishermen. The two were called by Jesus to be disciples as they were mending their nets by the Sea of Galilee.

Jesus showed St. John particular instances of kindness and affection above all the rest. He had the happiness to be present with Peter and James at the Transfiguration of Christ, and was permitted to witness His agony in the Garden. He was allowed to rest on Our Savior's bosom at the Last Supper, and to him Jesus confided the care of His holy Mother as He hung dying on the Cross.

St. John was the only one of the Apostles who did not forsake the Savior in the hour of His Passion and Death.

It seems that St. John remained for a long time in Jerusalem, but that his later years were spent at Ephesus, whence he founded many churches in Asia Minor. St. John wrote his Gospel after the other Evangelists, about sixty-three years after the Ascension of Christ; also three Epistles, and the wonderful and mysterious Book of the Apocalypse or Revelation. He was brought to Rome and, according to tradition, was cast into a caldron of boiling oil by order of Emperor Domitian. Like the Three Youths in the fiery furnace of Babylon, he was miraculously preserved unhurt.

He was later exiled to the Island of Patmos, where he wrote the Apocalypse, but afterwards returned to Ephesus.

In his extreme old age he continued to visit the churches of Asia, and St. Jerome relates that when age and weakness grew upon him so that he was no longer able to preach to the people, he would be carried to the assembly of the faithful by his disciples, with great difficulty; and every time said to his flock only these words: "My dear children, love one another".

St. John died in peace at Ephesus in the third year of Trajan (as seems to be gathered from Eusebius' history of the Saint) that is, the hundreth of the Christian era, or the sixty-sixth from the crucifixion of Christ, St. John then being about ninety-four years old, according to St. Epiphanus.

✠

DECEMBER 28

HOLY INNOCENTS

The Feast of the Holy Innocents dates back to about the 5th century. Herod believed the words of the Magi and those of the High Priest whom he consulted, and saw a rival in the Infant of Bethlehem. Deceitfully he told the Magi to advise him when they found the Child, in order that he, too, might come and adore Him. God, however, informed the Magi, in a dream, to return by another way to their own country.

Herod, finding that he had been deluded by the Magi, was filled with rage, and determined to kill the new-born "King of the Jews". To execute his plan, he formed the bloody resolution of murdering all the male children in Bethlehem and the neighboring territory who were two years old and younger.

The massacre of these infants manifests the royal character of Jesus. "The innocents by dying confess" the advent of the Savior King. How great a happiness was such a death to these glorious martyrs!

God so directed events that the tyrant Herod did not give the final orders for the slaughter of the children until the Blessed Virgin and her Child had safely complied with the requirements of the law in the Temple of Jerusalem, and St. Joseph was warned by an angel who appeared to him in sleep, saying: "Arise, and take the Child and His Mother, and fly into Egypt: and be there until I shall tell thee. For it will come to pass that Herod will seek the Child to destroy Him". (Matt. 2:13.) Thus in vain did Herod attempt to frustrate the designs of God.

✠

DECEMBER 29

ST. THOMAS OF CANTERBURY

St. Thomas, son of Gilbert Becket, was born in London on December 21, 1118, the feast-day of the Apostle, whose name was given to him at his baptism on that same day. He became Archdeacon of Canterbury, then Lord High Chancellor of England, under King Henry II, when thirty-eight years of age.

On Trinity Sunday, 1160, St. Thomas was consecrated Bishop of Winchester upon the insistence of the King. After the ceremony, the aged prelate said to his young primate: "Dearest brother, I give you now the choice—you must lose the favor either of your earthly or of your heavenly King". Upon his knees and with uplifted hands, St. Thomas replied: "By God's help and strength I make my choice; and never for the love or favor of any earthly king will I forfeit the grace of the Kingdom of Heaven".

As Archbishop of Canterbury, he became by that very fact Abbot of Christ Church. Though not a Monk, he made himself like unto one by his life. He resisted the royal customs which violated the liberties of the Church and the laws of the realm.

The news of St. Thomas' change of life displeased the King, who saw clearly that the Archbishop's words were

coming true, and that St. Thomas was sure to prefer his
duty to the royal pleasure. A further proof was his resignation as Chancellor, whereupon the King angrily ordered
him to resign the Archdeaconry of Canterbury.

After six years of contention, partly spent in exile,
St. Thomas, though fully aware that martyrdom awaited
him, returned to his Archiepiscopal See.

On the 29th of December, 1170, at the beginning of
Vespers, four knights broke into the Cathedral, crying:
"Where is the Archbishop? Where is the traitor?" The
Monks fled, but St. Thomas, who might easily have es-
caped, advanced saying: "Here I am, then, no traitor, but
the Archbishop. What seek you?" "Your life", they cried.
"For the Name of Jesus, and the defense of the Church, I
am ready to die", was the reply; and bowing his head, the
invincible Martyr was hacked and hewn before the altar of
St. Benedict until his soul went to God. Six months later
Henry II submitted to be publicly scourged at the Saint's
shrine, and restored to the Church her full rights.

☩

DECEMBER 30

ST. SABINUS AND COMPANIONS

In the year 303 the cruel edicts of Diocletian and
Maximian against the Christians, were published. St. Sabinus, Bishop of Assisi, and several of his clergy were arrested.
When the Governor of Umbria reached that city Sabinus
courageously confessed his Faith; whereupon the Governor
ordered that the hands of Sabinus be cut off; and his two
Deacons, Marcellus and Exuperantius, to be scourged,
beaten with clubs, and torn with iron nails, under which
torments they both expired.

It is claimed that Sabinus restored sight to a blind boy,
and cured a weakness in the eyes of Venustianus himself,
who was thereupon converted, and afterwards beheaded

for the Faith. Lucius, his successor, commanded Sabinus to be beaten to death with clubs. He was buried about a mile from the city of Spoleto.

✠

DECEMBER 31

ST. SYLVESTER I

St. Sylvester, a native Roman, was chosen by God to govern His holy Church during the first years of Her temporal prosperity and triumph over Her persecuting enemies. Pope Melchiades died in January, 314, and St. Sylvester was chosen as his successor. He governed the Church for more than twenty-one years, ably organizing the discipline of the Roman Church, and taking part in the negotiations concerning Arianism and the Council of Nicaea. He also sent Legates to the first Ecumenical Council.

During his Pontificate were built the great churches founded at Rome by Constantine—the Basilica and baptistery of the Lateran, the Basilica of the Sessorian palace (Santa Croce), the Church of St. Peter in the Vatican, and several cemeterial churches over the graves of martyrs. No doubt St. Sylvester helped towards the construction of these churches. He also established the Roman school of singing. On the Via Salaria he built a cemeterial church over the Catacomb of St. Priscilla, and it was in this church that he was buried when he died on December 31, 335.

SAINTS

Autobiography of St. John Neumann, C.SS.R.

Translation, Introduction, Commentary and Epilogue by Alfred C. Rush, CSSR

"This autobiography is important for the insight it gives us into the character of Bishop Neumann, of Philadelphia, into Neumann as a person...how he faced life, how he coped with difficulties, disappointments and setbacks....

"The life of John Neumann remains a challenge to all of us...to manifest to all the world our loyalty to Jesus Christ and His Church." —John Cardinal Krol
118 pages

— ST0010

Breviary Lives of the Saints

Rev. Frederick J. Murphy, MA, STL

Two volumes (I: September to January; II: February to May). Latin selections with commentary and a vocabulary. Each of these two volumes will satisfy a semester language requirement in Latin and at the same time be a vehicle for classroom learning and appreciation of the history and tradition of the Church.

Vol. I: September to January;
   328 pages; available in paper only
      — ST0020
Vol. II: February to May; 310 pages;
   available in cloth only
   ST0030

A translation for student use.
(Vol. I-II)   — ST0031

Doctor Luke, Beloved Physician

Msgr. Leo Gregory Fink

A vibrant presentation of the Christ-like personality of the great physician of early Christian times. 216 pages

— ST0040

Every Man My Brother

Francis Sweeney, SJ

The colorful life of Bernardine Realino, who dramatically abandoned a career of law and politics in Renaissance Italy to become a Jesuit, a minister of God's mercy and a saint. 178 pages

— ST0049

Every Man's Challenge

Daughters of St. Paul

The warm and dynamic personalities of 38 saints are captured in brief inspiring profiles. Their lives confirm Christ's message: sanctity is "everyman's challenge."
345 pages

— ST0050

Families That Followed the Lord

Martin P. Harney, SJ

This book contains the lives of over one hundred fifty brother and sister saints of various nationalities, places, and times. This account of fraternal and religious loyalty, which blends the best of what is human and divine, cannot fail to touch and inspire the reader of today.
145 pages

— ST0060

Hands for Others

Sister Louis Passero, FMA

Mary Mazzarello, a peasant woman of our times, though handicapped by poverty and little learning, founds a religious congregation, the Salesians, dedicated to teaching, nursing and social works of the Church. A compelling biography of a woman of great hope. 80 pages

ST0070

Heavenly Friends, A Saint for Each Day

Rosalie Marie Levy

A superb book, epitomizing the lives of more than 400 famous saints. 486 pages

deluxe   cloth or plastic
— ST0080

In Garments All Red

Godfrey Poage, CP

The life of St. Maria Goretti, a shining example of teenage heroism: This young Italian girl from a peasant family preferred death rather than sin against purity. 119 pages

— ST0090

Joseph, the Just Man

Rosalie Marie Levy

A complete biography, supplemented with accounts of favors granted and selections of special prayers. 285 pages

— ST0100

Joseph: The Man Closest to Jesus

Francis L. Filas, SJ

Never before has all this wealth of intensely interesting and little-known facts about St. Joseph been compiled into a single book. This can truly be called a "little Summa" of St. Joseph, as the only survey existing in any language of the complete life, theology, and devotional history of St. Joseph. 682 pages

— ST0110

The Legacy of St. Patrick

Martin P. Harney, SJ

The legacy of St. Patrick, which he would bequeath to his brethren and their descendants, was his own holy idealism. It can be found in his two writings, the Confession of St. Patrick and the Letters to the Soldiers of Coroticus.

A thoughtful perusal of the Confession and of the Letter will reward the reader with a true and an intimate knowledge of St. Patrick. 148 pages

— ST0120

The Little Bishop
Episodes in the Life of St. John Neumann, CSSR

Paschal Turbet, CSSR

Human but faith-filled incidents from the life of St. John Neumann—priest, missionary, bishop—the man of prayer and action who toiled for the Church and all God's people in the strife-torn years of 19th century America. 148 pages

— ST0130

Magnificent Witnesses

Martin P. Harney, SJ

Simple, heart-warming, soul-stirring sketches of the English and Welsh martyrs, canonized by Pope Paul VI on October 25, 1970. The martyrs included 13 secular priests, 20 religious (of 5 orders), 4 laymen and 3 laywomen. All gave their lives for the fundamental doctrine of the Primacy of the Pope. 80 pages

— ST0140

The Man in Chains, St. Paul

Rosalie Marie Levy
An intriguing life of one of the world's greatest heroes and saints—the Apostle Paul. 225 pages

— ST0150

Moments of Decision

Daughters of St. Paul
Profiles of 28 saints from many backgrounds and states in life. Portrayed with warmth and vitality, their lives teach us to use our "moments of decision" for Christ and His people. 315 pages

— ST0170

Mother Cabrini

Daughters of St. Paul
Animated story of the labors of the first American-citizen saint, whose greatest happiness lay in caring for the orphans, the sick and the destitute, and saving souls in a new land. 223 pages

— ST0180

Mother Seton—wife, mother, educator, foundress, saint

Daughters of St. Paul
This fast-paced life of "an authentic daughter of America" (Pope John's term) is completed by selections from Mother Seton's own writings—Spiritual Gems—that permit us to glimpse the deep spirituality of the first American-born saint. 140 pages

— ST0160

Saint and Thought for Everyday

Profiles by Daughters of St. Paul
Thoughts by Rev. James Alberione, SSP, STD
Brief sketches of lives of the saints for all year are presented according to the new calendar of saints.

Challenging daily thoughts by the renowned author Fr. James Alberione are arranged so as to assist us in our growth to full stature in Christ. 311 pages

— ST0190

Saint of the Impossible

Daughters of St. Paul
Fast-paced chapters tell of St. Rita's childhood and youth, of her will to succeed in her stormy marriage, of the transformation worked in her husband by her prayer and suffering for him, of her two sons, their death and her widowed loneliness. Even St. Rita's desire for religious life was thwarted at first, but the belief in God's unfailing care never left her...and she succeeded. 104 pages

— ST0290

Saints for the Modern Woman

Rev. Luke Farley
This book brings to the fore the modern woman's very real call to holiness by introducing her to some of her feminine predecessors in sanctity—women like herself from every century and walk of life. 264 pages

— ST0360

Saint Anthony of Padua The Life of the Wonder-Worker

Isidore O'Brien, OFM
Flaming charity, unflagging zeal, unique power as preacher and teacher of the Faith—these qualities combine to make St. Anthony a powerful wonder-worker and intercessor on our behalf. 174 pages

— ST0200

St. Bernard of Clairvaux

Msgr. Leon Cristiani

Bernard influenced the 12th century as no other monk did. But our interest is especially focused on what went on inside of him, within his soul, in his cloistered and hidden life, his life of prayer and penance, his life of union with God, in a word, in his religious and mystical life.

172 pages

— ST0210

St. Catherine of Siena

Igino Giordani

The 14th century was one of the most turbulent in the history of Christianity. A semi-literate Italian woman dominated that century with her prodigious temporal activity. Readers are deeply led into the recesses of Catherine's mysticism— an outstanding life of a recently proclaimed Doctor of the Church.

258 pages

— ST0220

St. Francis de Sales and His Friends

Maurice Henry-Couannier

In selecting the most significant features of his life the author has discovered that St. Fráncis is probably best understood through his friends and friendships and against the background of the people he knew and loved, for in a very special way he deserves to be called the Saint of Friendship.

414 pages

— ST0230

St. Francis of Assisi

Msgr. Leon Cristiani

Msgr. Leon Cristiani's life of St. Francis offers the reader facts, authentic traditions, revered texts and a hope to foster in the reader a deep love and admiration for the saint whose fruitful life he tells. 164 pages

— ST0240

St. Gemma, the Passion Flower

Msgr. Joseph Bardi

An extraordinary story of a young woman whose intense love for Jesus Christ became incarnate through an exceptional gift of God—the stigmata, the very wounds of Christ. 182 pages

— ST0250

St. Joan of Arc, Virgin— Soldier

Msgr. Leon Cristiani

The author scrupulously strives to present the simple, naked, historical truth about the life and times of Joan of Arc. He also outlines the supernatural in Joan's life in all its clarity.

160 pages

— ST0260

St. Margaret Mary Alacoque

Msgr. Leon Cristiani

An unforgettable biography of the great apostle and missionary of the Sacred Heart. Drawing from her own writings, we relive the drama of the "great revelations" which were to cause repercussions throughout the Christian world. 156 pages

— ST0270

St. Martin de Porres

Richard Cardinal Cushing

For forty-five years St. Martin dedicated himself almost entirely to the performance of spiritual and corporal works of mercy. "A thumb-nail sketch in which the 'digitus Dei' clearly appears in the life and work of St. Martin."

"Central California Register"
80 pages
— ST0280

St. Patrick and the Irish

Richard Cardinal Cushing

An absorbing biography of a great conqueror for Christ and his saintly followers, including Columbanus, Bridget and Brendan. 144 pages
— ST0300

St. Paul, Apostle and Martyr

Igino Giordani

By a happy choice the author has built his simple, direct and scholarly picture upon this word: Apostle—an excellent account of the infant Church—enhanced also by a pictorial biography of Paul done in famous art masters and two sections of stimulating photos. 38 full-color illustrations and 33 in black and white. 392 pages
— ST0310

St. Pius X, Pope

Most Rev. Jan Olav Smit

Journey through the boyhood, priesthood, papacy and sainthood of this remarkable man— warm, lovable, humorous— capable of leading the people of God with extraordinary wisdom— the influence of which we still feel in the Church today. 184 pages
— ST0320

St. Teresa of Avila

Giorgio Papasogli

It took the author a year's visit to Spain, exhaustive research and an intensive study of all the existing material before he was ready to write. The result was an entirely new biography of one of the most written-about women in the world. 410 pages
— ST0330

St. Theresa, the Little Flower

Sister Gesualda of the Holy Spirit

The story of this young Carmelite nun has won worldwide fame. Read her simple way of love and perfection—her efficacious key to sanctity. Thousands of souls have received favors through the intercession of this "Patroness of the Missiohs" who promised to shower petals of roses on everyone. 270 pages
— ST0340

St. Vincent de Paul

Msgr. Leon Cristiani

Known as the "saint of charity," and founder of several religious congregations, Vincent de Paul is portrayed in these pages as the father of the poor. All will feel inclined to pray to this great saint and to imitate him who burned with the love of Christ and his neighbor. 170 pages
— ST0350

Son of the Passion

Godfrey Poage, CP

A popular teenage boy, Gabriel Possenti entered the Passionist Order and achieved sainthood ... not by doing extraordinary things —but by doing ordinary things extraordinarily well! 120 pages
— ST0370

The Story of Monica and Her Son Augustine

Msgr. Leon Cristiani

The stirring story of a woman's faith and steadfastness in prayer that won the conversion of her wayward son. 176 pages
— ST0380

Three Ways of Love

Frances Parkinson Keyes

The world-famous author here captures the romance, the

tragedy and the history of three great women: St. Agnes, whose name has become synonymous with courage; St. Frances of Rome, a mother and the protectress of the poor and sick; and St. Catherine of Siena, the famous ambassadress and stateswoman. 304 pages

ST0390

The Village Priest Who Fought God's Battles
St. John Mary Vianney
Msgr. Leon Cristiani

The lovable Cure of Ars, patron of all diocesan priests, is widely known for his battles with the devil and his victory over the power of evil. Here he comes alive in his ministry of prayer, penance and apostolic zeal. But first we meet the man who fought his own spiritual battles—a great source of inspiration and courage in our own war against evil. 172 pages

ST0400

PROFILES IN GREATNESS
stories of great men and women of God
on cassette

What was so special about the saints?

To answer that question first-hand we invite you to spend a quarter of an hour in the company of some of history's most extraordinarily ordinary people. People who took the Gospel message to heart. Real people who met the challenge of life squarely.

Profiles in Greatness *portrays their moments of decision in a realistic, factual and fascinating way.*

1. St. Bernard

A great master of the spirit blends a deep prayer life with intense activity.

St. Henry Morse

A hunted priest works ceaselessly among the plague victims of London until his martyrdom. CS0010

2. St. Jane Frances de Chantal

A young widow struggles to accept her husband's death and to discover God's will for her.

Bartholomew de la Casas

A champion of the exploited Indians of the New World demands humane treatment for them. CS0050

3. St. Elizabeth Seton

An indomitable young woman of old New York surmounts every obstacle to live her new faith totally.

St. Edmund Campion

This daring priest, one of the most hunted men in English history, serves his God and his people to the end. CS0030

4. St. John Fisher

Neither imprisonment nor threat of death shake his firm fidelity and amazing calm.

St. Stanislaus

Persecuted by an irreligious brother, a young Polish noble battles for his purity and his vocation. CS0060

5. St. Dominic

This great preacher and his followers bring truth to a world torn by error and immorality.

St. Peregrine

A village hoodlum strikes a priest and then is won over to follow him in his priesthood and holiness. CS0020

6. St. Francis Xavier

His incredible missionary activity witnesses to the power of love at work in the human spirit.

St. Benedict Joseph Labre

The one looked upon as "a good-for-nothing beggard" is revealed as a great mystic. CS0040

7. St. Peter Claver

Below the decks of African slave ships, a priest finds Christ crucified in the person of the downtrodden.

St. Maria Goretti

A young farm girl's tremendous choice involves death rather than sin. CS0090

8. St. Philip Neri

The cheerful "fool for Christ" helps countless people to trust in God's mercy.

Blessed Anne Marie Javouhey

Not even the French Revolution could stop this courageous woman with her daring schemes for Christ. CS0100

9. St. Catherine of Siena

Diplomat, peacemaker, counselor to kings and Popes, she is first of all a bride of Jesus Christ.

Blessed Luchesio and Bona

A prosperous businessman and his wife give up their wealth to become followers of St. Francis. CS0070

10. St. Rita

Love and fidelity lead a wife and mother to great heights of holiness.

St. Camillus

A brawling gambler, disgusted with life, finds peace in caring for the sick. CS0065

11. St. Martin de Porres

The friend of his fellow blacks and of all God's people.

St. Zita

Selfless dedication, despite slander and calumny, wins her the trust of her employers and the favor of God. CS0080

12. St. Pius V

A great Pope champions renewal, befriends the poor, and spreads devotion to the rosary.

St. Benedict the Moor

A freed Negro slave serves his fellow man as a Franciscan lay brother. CS0110

SPECIAL OFFER—All 12 cassettes
CS0111

(To order see addresses on following page.)

Daughters of St. Paul

MASSACHUSETTS

50 St. Paul's Ave., Jamaica Plain, Boston, MA 02130; **617-522-8911.**

172 Tremont Street, Boston, MA 02111; **617-426-5464; 617-426-4230.**

NEW YORK

78 Fort Place, Staten Island, NY 10301; **718-447-5071; 718-447-5086.**

59 East 43rd Street, New York, NY 10017; **212-986-7580.**

625 East 187th Street, Bronx, NY 10458; **212-584-0440.**

525 Main Street, Buffalo, NY 14203; **716-847-6044.**

NEW JERSEY

Hudson Mall—Route 440 and Communipaw Ave.,
Jersey City, NJ 07304; **201-433-7740.**

CONNECTICUT

202 Fairfield Ave., Bridgeport, CT 06604; **203-335-9913.**

OHIO

2105 Ontario Street (at Prospect Ave.), Cleveland, OH 44115;
216-621-9427.

616 Walnut Street, Cincinnati, OH 45202; **513-421-5733; 513-721-5059.**

PENNSYLVANIA

1719 Chestnut Street, Philadelphia, PA 19103; **215-568-2638.**

VIRGINIA

1025 King Street, Alexandria, VA 22314; **703-683-1741; 703-549-3806.**

SOUTH CAROLINA

243 King Street, Charleston, SC 29401; **803-577-0175.**

FLORIDA

2700 Biscayne Blvd., Miami, FL 33137; **305-573-1618; 305-573-1624.**

LOUISIANA

4403 Veterans Memorial Blvd., Metairie, LA 70006; **504-887-7631;
504-887-0113.**

423 Main Street, Baton Rouge, LA 70802; **504-343-4057; 504-381-9485.**

MISSOURI

1001 Pine Street (at North 10th), St. Louis, MO 63101; **314-621-0346;
314-231-1034.**

ILLINOIS

172 North Michigan Ave., Chicago, IL 60601; **312-346-4228; 312-346-3240.**

TEXAS

114 Main Plaza, San Antonio, TX 78205; **512-224-8101; 512-224-0938.**

CALIFORNIA

1570 Fifth Ave., San Diego, CA 92101; **619-232-1442.**

46 Geary Street, San Francisco, CA 94108; **415-781-5180.**

WASHINGTON

2301 Second Ave., Seattle, WA 98121; **206-441-3300; 206-441-3210.**

HAWAII

1143 Bishop Street, Honolulu, HI 96813; **808-521-2731.**

ALASKA

750 West 5th Ave., Anchorage, AK 99501; **907-272-8183.**

CANADA

3022 Dufferin Street, Toronto 395, Ontario, Canada.